PENGUIN BOOKS
THE SECRETS OF RUE ST ROCH

'An extraordinary story, lost for almost eighty years' *The Times*

'An engrossing spy story . . . a large cast of brave, resourceful and frankly eccentric characters . . . Not the least of Morgan's achievements is to have triumphantly restored one small but important part of history to the record' Nigel Jones, *Literary Review*

'Possibly the most complete surviving record of an Allied espionage operation from the Great War' *Scotsman*

'A well-written, moving account . . . there is much else that makes this book thought-provoking: Morgan's accounts of the military background to events, which are deftly handled and seamlessly woven into the story; her evocations of life under occupation, and in Germany itself later on; her interest in other aspects of her story – the role of pigeons in intelligence, the technicalities of early ballooning, the misdeeds of an officer called Cameron' Alan Judd, *Daily Telegraph*

'I raise a special paean of praise to Janet Morgan for matching this intelligence so closely with the concurrent events of World War One' Sir Colin McColl, Head of MI6 1988–9

ABOUT THE AUTHOR

Since 1995, when Captain Bruce's files were rediscovered, Janet Morgan has spent most of her spare time searching the Continent for his agents' descendants, deciphering coded letters and secret reports, examining maps, timetables, moonlight diagrams and methods of escaping from prison camps, and learning about railways, espionage, pigeons and ballooning. The greater part of her working life, meanwhile, is spent as a director of various public companies in the telecommunications, transport, construction, financial and energy industries. She lives in Scotland and, like Madame Rischard, is a housewife. Her other books include the four-volume edition of the Crossman Diaries and the authorized biographies of Agatha Christie and Edwina Mountbatten; *The Secrets of Rue St Roch* is a jigsaw puzzle on an even bigger scale.

No. 41 Rue St Roch

JANET MORGAN

The Secrets of Rue St Roch

Hope and Heroism
Behind Enemy Lines
in the First World War

with a Preface
by Sir Colin McColl

PENGUIN BOOKS

PENGUIN BOOKS

Published by the Penguin Group
Penguin Books Ltd, 80 Strand, London WC2R ORL, England
Penguin Group (USA), Inc., 375 Hudson Street, New York, New York 10014, USA
Penguin Group (Canada), 90 Eglinton Avenue East, Suite 700,
Toronto, Ontario, Canada M4P 2Y3
(a division of Pearson Penguin Canada Inc.)
Penguin Ireland, 25 St Stephen's Green, Dublin 2, Ireland
(a division of Penguin Books Ltd)
Penguin Group (Australia), 250 Camberwell Road,
Camberwell, Victoria 3124, Australia (a division of Pearson Australia Group Pty Ltd)
Penguin Books India Pvt Ltd, 11 Community Centre,
Panchsheel Park, New Delhi – 110 017, India
Penguin Group (NZ), cnr Airborne and Rosedale Roads, Albany,
Auckland 1310, New Zealand (a division of Pearson New Zealand Ltd)
Penguin Books (South Africa) (Pty) Ltd, 24 Sturdee Avenue,
Rosebank, Johannesburg 2196, South Africa

Penguin Books Ltd, Registered Offices: 80 Strand, London WC2R ORL, England

www.penguin.com

Published by Allen Lane 2004
Published in Penguin Books 2005
1

Copyright © Janet Morgan, 2004

Typeset by Palimpsest Book Production Limited, Polmont, Stirlingshire
Printed in England by Clays Ltd, St Ives plc

This book is for Robert

Contents

List of Maps

List of Illustrations

INTEGRATED ILLUSTRATIONS

PLATES

Principal Characters

Sous-Lieutenant Albert-Ernest Baschwitz Meau	Belgian volunteer soldier, escaper, agent and balloonist
Captain George Bruce	Chief of the Paris Office
Captain Brunt	Meteorologist, attached to the Royal Flying Corps
Lieutenant Sidney Buckley	Aviator, organizer of the escaping scheme
Father Cambron	French priest, exiled to Switzerland, subscriber to *Der Landwirt*
Major Cecil Cameron	Bruce's immediate chief, based at Folkestone
Captain Lewis Campbell	Former agent in Switzerland, now in the Paris Office
Brigadier-General Sir John Charteris	Head of Intelligence Staff at GHQ in France from 1915–17
'Interpreter' Jean Chocqueel	French notary, assigned to the Paris Office
Brigadier-General Cox	Charteris's successor as Head of Intelligence Staff at GHQ
Captain Sir Mansfield Cumming ('C')	Head of the Secret Service Bureau, later MI1 (c)
Miss Dorothy Done	English member of the Secretariat in the Paris Office

Mademoiselle Andrée Dorgebray	French member of the Secretariat
Major Reginald Drake	Head of Intelligence (b), based at GHQ in France
Madame Fresez-Settegast	Forwarder of coded letters from Switzerland; Madame Rischard's aunt by marriage
Lieutenant Julian Fuller	I(b)'s man at Evian on the French/Swiss border
Joseph Hansen	Schoolmaster and journalist-agent
Captain J. L. Hardy	Notable escaper, Baschwitz-Meau's escaping colleague
Lieutenant Hazeldine	Of I(b), organizer of the 'Suicide Club' and of Agent Balloonists at Bruay
Pierre Huss	Luxembourg chemist and agent
Charles Jubert	Luxembourg civil servant, based in Ministry of Foreign Affairs and afterwards Office for Refugees and Repatriates in Paris. Bicyclist
Major Walter Kirke	First head of I(b), 1914–17, Drake's predecessor
Colonel George Macdonogh	First Chief of the Intelligence Staff at GHQ from 1914 to 1915, when he became Director of Military Intelligence in London
Armand Mollard	French Minister in Luxembourg, Jubert's chief at the Ministry of Foreign Affairs in Paris
Lieutenant Monthaye	Belgian soldier, trainer of agents for the Paris Office

Commander William 'Pink Tights' Pollock	Head of Naval Ballooning School, Hurlingham
Dr Camille Rischard	Luxembourg doctor, reluctant agent
Madame Lise Rischard	Network Chief in Luxembourg
Principal Assistant Station Master Jean Rockenbrod	Railwayman and agent, together with Principal Assistant Station Master Joseph Offenheim, Assistant Station Masters Auguste Diderich, Ernest Kraus, Jean Kneip, *Chef-Manoeuvre* Edouard Bram
Mathias Schmit	Mathematics teacher, agent, cousin of Edouard Bram
Jeanne Schroell	Acting publisher of *Der Landwirt*
Paul Schroell	Journalist, publisher and musician, exiled to Paris
Lieutenant Tangye	Cameron's, then Bruce's, man at the Paris Office
Commandant Tessmar	German officer in charge of occupied Luxembourg
Major Ernest 'Peg Leg' Wallinger	I(b)'s head of secret work in Belgium, Cameron's rival
Colonel Jean Wallner	Head of Paris branch of the French Secret Service, the *Deuxième Bureau*
Lieutenant-Commander Williams	'Fixer' in the Admiralty's Heavier Than Air Supply Department in London
Lieutenant S. H. C. Woolrych	Bruce's predecessor as Chief of the Paris Office, 1916–17

Plus Generals, Escapers, Agents, Railwaymen, Aviators, Meteorologists and other experts

Preface

This book is about the creation and maintenance of a highly successful intelligence-gathering network. Because they involve a lot of people, such secret networks present formidable problems of efficiency and security; of efficiency because – as all of us know who have played Chinese Whispers – information can be distorted as it passes down the line, and of security because Agent A recruits Agent B who recruits Agent C and as the network grows so does the danger that someone – and these people are often inexperienced – will make a mistake which can be picked up and exploited, lethally, by the opposition.

Networks paid a heavy price for such mistakes in World War II, and in the Cold War counter-intelligence on both sides became so powerful and effective that networks were largely abandoned as being inherently insecure.

But in intelligence work, just as there is little that is entirely new, so there is little that becomes entirely obsolete, and the fact that networks were shelved in the Cold War does not mean that they could not be again of value in a rapidly changing world. So Janet Morgan does us a service in demonstrating, on the basis of a richly detailed archive, that intelligence networks have one major advantage. This is their ability to provide a wide spread of intelligence collection and to do so at a remarkably low cost in terms both of money and of officers in the field. The team in the Rue St Roch, which clearly ran many other operations than the Luxembourg project, was never more than nine in number and the operation itself cost just Ff20,000, the equivalent today of £18,000.

The book highlights some important truths which will be familiar to those who have worked in this field: the vital need for trust between the players and, as part and parcel of this, the constant need for the human touch in addressing people's problems and anxieties; the difficulty of sustaining this trust at long range over a severely restricted channel of communication; passionate attention to detail – wonderfully reflected in this book by a writer who is not only passionate about detail herself but finds in it a constant source of delight and humour; and, perhaps most important of all, the ability to recognize golden opportunities and to grab them as they come – they don't come twice. In this operation there were two such opportunities: the discovery of Madame Rischard, who had superlative access to the target in question coupled with great ability and a natural authority among her own people, and of Baschwitz Meau who was one in a million in terms of experience, plausibility, courage, languages and motivation. Bruce earns high marks throughout the story but he deserves the highest mark of all for the determination with which he overcame all obstacles (and they were fearsome) to bring these two stars into play.

The mechanics of intelligence work are in themselves fascinating, as they certainly are in this story; but in some accounts of intelligence work there is a tendency for the fascination of the mechanics to eclipse the wider issues to which the intelligence work is directed. I therefore raise a special paeon of praise to Janet Morgan for matching this intelligence story so closely with the concurrent events of World War I. It is difficult as a reader to separate one's excitement and anticipation over the Luxembourg operation from the nailbiting roller-coaster of attacks and retreats, near-defeats and near-victories in that astonishing year of 1918. The two stories march together and in both we won. But, given the attention shown to the Luxembourg families by the Germans in 1940, it looks as if in Luxembourg as on the Western Front it may have been a close-run thing.

Colin McColl
Head of MI6, 1988–94

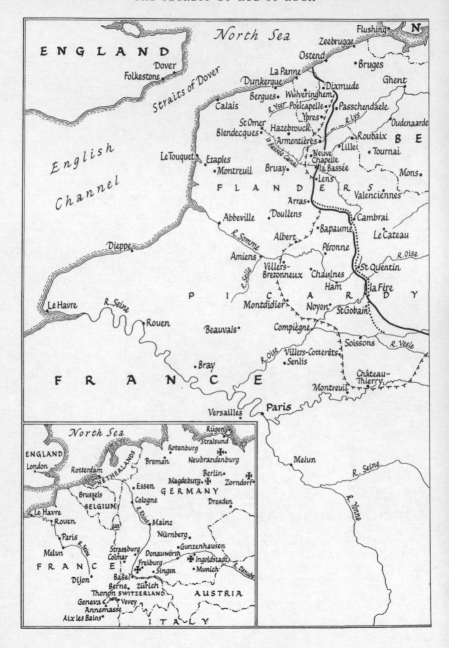

THE WESTERN FRONT 1917–18
.... The Hindenburg Line
———— Front line, Spring 1917
⊤⊤⊤⊤ July 1918, after German offensive
✠ German prisoner-of-war camps

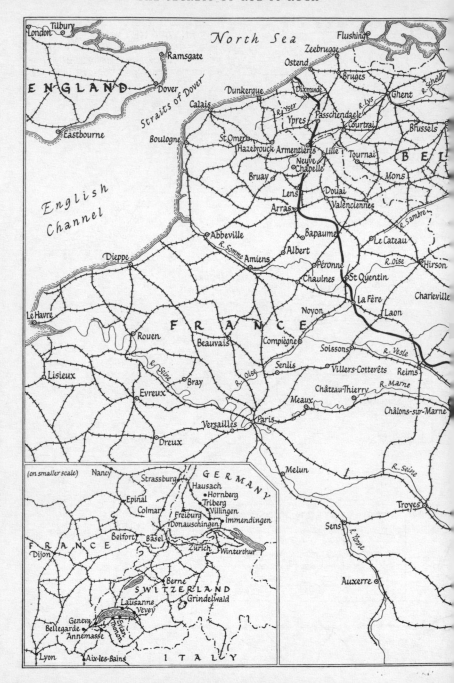

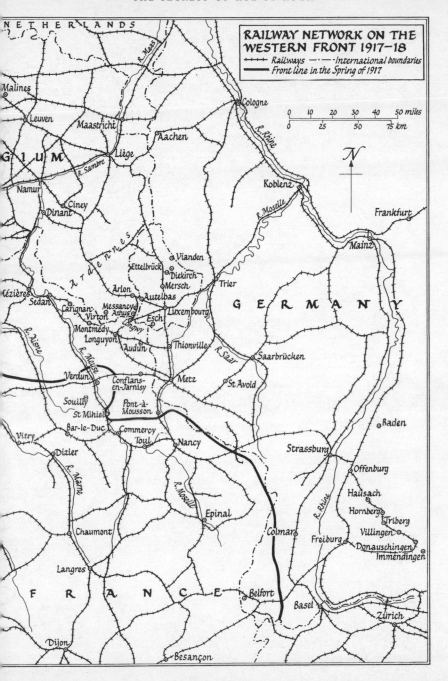

RAILWAY NETWORK ON THE
WESTERN FRONT 1917–18
╂╂╂ Railways ──·── International boundaries
▬▬ Front line in the Spring of 1917

Introduction

A Far-off World

On certain winter days in the high alps between Switzerland and France the traveller sees in the valleys below a vast lake of cloud, its surface lit by the sun. Cloud covers everything: meadows and woods, churches and farms, knots of houses strung along roads, rivers and railway lines. Beneath that heavy canopy people go about their business but from above they are invisible, the hum and movement of marketplace and factory, school and office, sawmill and dairy, all the life of town and village, unheard, unseen.

The veil divides – it is only air and water – and the onlooker sees roofs, streets, a spire. Another fissure and a station is revealed, a water tower, a bridge. Sound carries upward with startling clarity: church bells, children's cries, a hooter, the driver's fanfare as the postbus rounds a bend. Piece by piece the observer fits together a map of the world below, as fragments emerge, vanish, reappear, in a constantly changing configuration, intermittent impressions of lives and landscapes, altered by distance and perspective into something elusive and extraordinary.

In the years after August 1914 much of Europe was similarly obscured. War closed borders, normal traffic was suspended, censorship distorted the exchange of news. The men and women who worked in military intelligence for the Allies – Britain, France, Belgium and Russia – on the one hand, and the Central Powers – Germany and Austria-Hungary – on the other, were charged with finding out and making sense of what was happening in countries that were now cut off. Listening and watching, each side painstakingly collected scraps of information, rearranging, revising, re-considering, in the hope of understanding the intentions of the enemy. Incomplete and inaccurate though reports might be, strategies were based on them, operational decisions influenced by them. Intelligence was inevitably patchy and, fed back to the planners, reinforced assumptions that were sometimes incorrect. Imperfect communication and misunderstanding, not smoke bombs and grenades, produced and perpetuated the fog of war.

In dim-lit rooms in London and makeshift quarters at the front, the battles fought by Britain's intelligence chiefs were as much about bureaucracy as soldiering. How were instructions to be given to officers in charge of networks? Who was to receive scarce funds, expertise and equipment? Although these arguments took place in meetings and correspondence, this was not an intellectual game. The documents that piled up in the wire baskets concerned the work of identifiable individuals, agents and informers who were running immeasurable risks and needed skilful handling. It was on these men and women that the intelligence services depended. Every morsel was important, for even the most innocuous item added to the overall picture of the enemy's strength and objectives.

Over the chiefs' desks were spread the maps of Continental Europe. To the north and stretching far to the east was Germany, menacing, inaccessible, holding in its fortresses prisoners whose information would be invaluable. In the centre of the map lay Switzerland, uncomfortably close to Germany, and, because of its neutrality, a surreptitious meeting-place for adventurers of various nationalities and temporary allegiances. Across the Channel was Holland, also neutral, packed with refugees and humming with spies. The borders of Switzerland and Holland were open. Allied agents operated there, alongside their German counterparts.

Barred to the Allies was the wide band of country running down the middle of the map, extending from Belgium and Flanders in the north to Luxembourg in the south. These were the lands beyond the Western Front, invaded by Germany in the summer of 1914, their borders shut, their people isolated. Luxembourg had been taken over in a single day. Belgium was entirely occupied, except for a small area on the Channel coast to which the King and the Belgian army had retreated. Flanders was reduced to a storehouse and foraging-place for the German army.

West of that boundary, France remained free. In the first month of the war German troops had come within twenty-five miles of Paris before they were beaten back in the Battle of the Marne. East of Dunkerque, the rival armies faced each other in a continuous line, stretching from north to south, dug into foul trenches cut from the mud of the low-lying, waterlogged plain. Behind the allied lines lay unoccupied France, the *zone de l'intérieur*, a great expanse of free country in which, despite the privations of war and the surveillance of the police, people came and went as they pleased. Among these were British officers and British agents. Behind the German lines was closed country, from which the Allies desperately wanted news.

Who was to send it?

Those who lived in the occupied countries suffered moral anguish as well as physical hardship. The instinct to protect their families, friends and neighbours – self-preservation, too – told them to submit to the alien régime that Germany had imposed. Their duty as citizens and subjects – and their self-respect – encouraged them to resist as best they could. Open frontiers had made it easy for the enemy to march in. Those borders were now sealed but, with daring and ingenuity, people and information might be sent across. The risks were great but some were prepared to take them.

It is with these people that the present story is concerned.

I

The Office in Rue St Roch

In the late summer of 1914, when the Germans were advancing through Belgium, Flanders and Picardy, Alsace and Lorraine, it had seemed that Paris itself would fall. On 22 August French troops had been ordered to retreat from the Vosges, on the 23rd from Flanders. On the same day the British Expeditionary Force had fought its first battle, at Mons, south-west of Brussels, south-east of Lille, on the border of Belgium and France. But when the French withdrew, the British had been ordered to do likewise. They had come under heavy attack as they retired, one corps being overwhelmed at Le Cateau. In Paris refugees from the invaded countries streamed into the great railway stations that served the north and east. Parisians, remembering the siege of 1871,* queued for seats on trains leaving for the west and south. The Bank of France sent its gold to Brittany, on 2 September the French government moved to Bordeaux. The governor of the Paris garrison, General Galliéni, had been instructed to defend the capital to the last. Bridges over the Seine were to be blown up, avenues of trees cut down, houses demolished along the boulevards, guns positioned to rake the streets with fire. Ammunition had been sent to gates and barricades around the city walls, men stood by to destroy the Eiffel Tower and the wireless transmitters that were attached to it. The city was an armed camp.

On 4 September 1914 the Germans were less than thirty miles from Paris. Four more brigades had been hastily sent out from Britain, French reinforcements summoned from Alsace and Lorraine. Volunteers were ferried from Paris to the front by lorry, charabanc,

* In the Franco-Prussian War.

4

motor-car and 600 Renault taxicabs.* Astonishingly, in an imprudent manoeuvre, the German armies had weakened their front east
of Meaux, on the River Marne, and the Allies were able to divide
them. That engagement, the Battle of the Marne, saved Paris. On
9 September the Germans withdrew. Chased by the Allies, they
had retreated as far as the Aisne. There, on the far bank, they had
remained.

The threat removed, Parisians had returned to their homes. Galliéni
proclaimed that a city without entertainment was as good as
conquered: at his urging, theatres, cinemas and music-halls reopened,
flaps were unlocked on the bookstalls on the *quais* by the Seine. In
the first week of December 1914 the Sorbonne began the university
year that had been delayed by the outbreak of war. Buses reappeared
on the streets, trading restarted at the Stock Exchange. Captured
German weapons were displayed in the courtyard of the Invalides
and that winter fashionable women honoured the troops by wearing
jackets and tunics cut on military lines. In solidarity with the army,
the hat worn by Parisian policemen bore, instead of a feather, a gilded
grenade, fixed with gold braid and a golden tassel.

Succeeding months had brought less to celebrate. A generation
was lost in the first four months of the war alone. The Battle of
Ypres in November 1914 resulted in a quarter of a million British,
French and German casualties. Of those who came back from the
front, many were blind, or bandaged, or had lost their reason.
Paris was home to thousands of *mutilés*, with stumps for limbs.
Beyond the city, the *zone réservée* was ravaged ground. Pleasant
houses fell into disrepair; good walls tumbled into ruins. With the
passage to and from the front of so many thousands of men, carts
and guns, of motor traffic and horses, roads became dust. Wheels
crushed the meadows. In summer soldiers had trampled the banks
by the reedy streams in whose waters they tried to rid themselves
of trench-foulness and lice. Now trees were being cut too young
for firewood. Towns and villages had seen their schools turned into
hospitals and dressing stations; officers dined and slept in once

* The legendary 'taxis of the Marne'. Each driver made two trips, taking five men
each time.

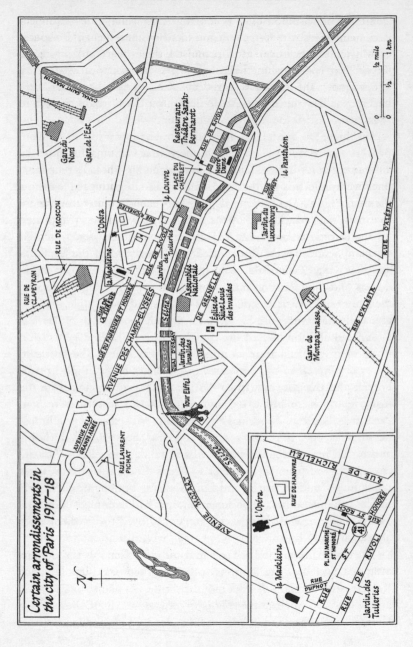

Certain arrondissements in
the city of Paris 1917–18

comfortable farmhouses. Rooms that had been quiet had been commandeered by map-makers and tacticians and men who shouted into telephones. Local girls promised their hearts to strangers. Brothels were flourishing. The best wine was disappearing, even if the officers paid for what they drank, and in the *estaminets* – the British soldiers called these little drinking places 'just a minutes' – newcomers asked for 'the usual' and monopolized the tables to play cards before the fire.

In late December 1914 a French offensive in Champagne had made little progress. At Neuve-Chapelle in March 1915, heavy preliminary shelling by the British, followed by two days' fighting, killed thousands on both sides and produced small gains. A month later the Germans had attacked the front north-east of Ypres, trying a new weapon: toxic chlorine gas. Having condemned its deployment in April, in September the British used gas, 'the accessory', in the Battle of Loos. The results had been appalling. Spanners did not fit the cocks of cylinders; drifting chlorine blew back over the British trenches; newly issued tube helmets had given no protection. The 1915 campaign ended in November. The cost: 144,000 French and British dead and wounded, 85,000 German.

As men were called up, women had taken their places in factories, garages, chemical companies and steelworks, in the postal service and the railways. In Paris *remplaçantes* – female substitutes – drove trams, shifted wood and coal, emptied sewers. *Munitionettes* filled shells. Newspapers were censored, sugar, meat and fuel rationed. Stocks of German-made goods – motors, tools, thermometers, glass eyes – had been used up long ago. People fought over supplies of potatoes, hoarded small change. Police watched clubs and bars, hoping to catch profiteers, gamblers and foreign agents preying on people of doubtful reputation. Hotels and restaurants could not find staff, linen, china or glass. War distorted every aspect of daily life.

The first major battle of 1916 had come in February with a German attack at Verdun; 20 million shells had been expended in a long and terrible confrontation. For six months the armies had struggled until, at the end of August, the German onslaught ceased. France and Germany together had over a million dead and wounded. Further north, along the River Somme, the British had led a joint offensive, pitching waves of men against the German wires. By nightfall on 1 July, the first day of the battle, there had been 41,000 British wounded, 19,000 dead. When fighting subsided in mid-November 1916, the Allies had advanced eight miles. The price had been high: 615,000 allied casualties, between 400,000 and 650,000 on the German side. More than 150,000 men had paid for each mile.

The combatants were trapped in a war of attrition, on a front that ran from the Channel coast to the Swiss border. British and French were dug in on one side, Germans on the other. The lines were works of unceasing excavation. Behind the forward trenches were support lines and, to the rear of these, reserve lines, all connected by networks of communication trenches. Duckboards lined the bottoms and at intervals sumps were hollowed out of boggy ground, in a hopeless attempt to drain water seeping out of clay. Planks and corrugated iron held up walls that zig-zagged along the length of trenches, dividing them into sections.

In some stretches of the front line, troops spent days and nights within whistling distance of their opponents, elsewhere they were separated from their enemies by half a mile, a mile, of no man's land: tangles of barbed wire, piles of discarded shell-cases, helmets, scraps of torn uniform, unburied remains. In preparation for offensive action, each side had to know the nature of this ground. To those who crept, inch by inch, through no man's land, the journey between the lines was a long-drawn-out immensity of fear. It was easy to jump at shadows, slip into ditches, lose oneself in indistinguishable flatlands. Crawling forward, scouts listened for voices speaking a language other than their own, for the click of enemy telephones, the slipping of soil in tunnels beneath, the beating of their own hearts. Sensitive hearing and quick reactions did not always prevent a scout from being shot. The more often a man was sent out, the greater his fear that, on the next night, his nerve might go. By day each side watched the other, sometimes no more than fifty yards apart. A cough or a careless light might betray a man to a sniper. Observers crept forward along shallow ditches, 'saps', to sketch an exhausted landscape of cavities and clumps. Staring from firing-trenches, standing on steps carved out of the earth, peering through loopholes in armour-plated shields, behind parapets of soil and sandbags, men waited.

The war had its own rhythm. For three autumns, two springs, two summers, the cycle had been the same: skirmishing in foul weather between November and the end of January, advancing and retiring over drier ground from February to October. Which side would be first to attack in the spring?

January 1917, the third winter of the war. Cold, tired, in mourning, Parisians saw in the new year at home. Ice floated in the Seine. Bone-chilling winds blew from the north but domestic stoves and boilers could not be lit. What coal there was had gone to factories and the military. In these short days, shops, laundries and bakeries opened late and closed early. Places of public entertainment were unlit, unheated. No underground trains or omnibuses ran at night. Gas lamps stuttered, electricity came on and off erratically. Paraffin could not be got. A candle, at forty centimes, cost as much as an ounce of butter.*

On such a January morning, having shaved in unheated water at his lodgings in the Hôtel Wagram, Rue de Rivoli, Captain George Bruce set out for his new office, two streets away. He was long-limbed, with a quick stride, and it took him no more than three minutes to cross Rue St Honoré into Rue St Roch. This quarter had long been favoured by the British – the Embassy was nearby – but two years of war had diminished the once smart shops in the enclave between the Tuileries and the Louvre. The houses were gaunt and lustreless.

No. 41 Rue St Roch, a narrow, five-storey building, had a discreet front door, guarded by an orderly. Bruce, who was not in uniform, was expected. The orderly managed not to salute: neighbours might be watching, or the landlord, Monsieur Baud, who had an olive-oil business at No. 24, near enough to keep an eye on the maintenance of his building but not so near that he would know what was going on inside it. Monsieur Baud was unaware that No. 41 was the head-quarters of an espionage mission.

Officially, the establishment in Rue St Roch had been set up as

---

* The average salary at this time was between three and nine francs a day (£2.80 and £8.50 in today's money).

an 'Inter-Ally Permit Office', to assess applications from French civilians wishing to travel to Britain. No. 41 was a genuine Permit Office, one of a number established by Major Walter Kirke, chief of I(b), the section of British military intelligence responsible for covert operations behind German lines on the battlefield, in enemy-occupied countries and Germany itself. Kirke, who had been in France since 1914, was based at General Headquarters, at Montreuil, between Paris and the River Marne.* Here he worked alongside the Head of Intelligence on the General Staff, Colonel George Macdonogh, to whom he supplied a daily report. Drawing on this, Macdonogh in turn briefed General Sir Douglas Haig, the Commander-in-Chief.

One of Kirke's principal concerns was counter-intelligence. Just as he sought to infiltrate allied agents into Germany and the occupied countries, so, he was sure, the enemy was trying to lever its own spies into the free part of France, and thence, perhaps, into Britain. During the first year of the war civilians had been able to cross certain frontiers if they could produce visas obtained, before departure, from local consular officials. Although both Germany and the Allies used this screening system, they knew that it was porous. Passage between Switzerland into Germany and France, for example, or in and out of Holland, was relatively easy. The Channel gave some extra protection: to keep spies out of Britain, Scotland Yard detectives boarded steamers at points of entry and asked passengers for their documents, a precaution Kirke thought feeble. In his view, any traveller with a plausible story might acquire a visa. He had little respect for the consuls who represented Britain in various European towns, believing that in some cases they found it more convenient to work for the enemy, 'a large proportion', he pointed out, being 'unpaid, and not even British'.[1]

In late 1915 Kirke proposed that the Allies should develop a network of Permit Offices, staffed by military intelligence officers who could make inquiries and who would be more skilful than the consuls at distinguishing between foreign agents and respectable travellers. His recommendation had been accepted and at the end of

---

* The British Commander-in-Chief and his staff were housed in the Château de Beaurepaire and its grounds. In April 1917 they moved to the Château de Bavincourt, between Doullens and Arras, north of the River Somme.

that year new arrangements had been put in place. Entry into Britain was regulated by a British Permit Office in Paris, with subsidiary offices at main ports on the French side of the Channel and along the 'Line of Control' between the *zone des armées* and the *zone de l'intérieur*. In return, the *Sûreté Générale*, the French security service, was invited to establish a French Permit Office in London. 'Special arrangements' were made for Switzerland and Holland, which, as neutrals, forbade the setting-up of offices staffed by soldiers, even in plain clothes. Instead, the Allies used the military attachés installed in their various legations, a device which all parties understood. Indeed, once the allied scheme was in operation, the Germans set up a parallel system, a development that was to hamper one of the most critical operations to be run from Rue St Roch. When the Germans introduced their scheme, however, Kirke was delighted. As the enemy had copied his idea, he said, it must have been a good one.*

Kirke had a connection, consolidated in restaurants, with his counterpart at the *Sûreté*, Commandant Richard,** and co-operation between their two services was close. Officers from I(b) were posted to large French towns, such as Amiens and Hazebrouck, on attachment to the *Sûreté*, to help keep order, prevent treachery and maintain security, duties that required them to discover who in the locality was, and who was not, to be trusted. Intelligence and counter-intelligence work went hand in hand, the attachés being well positioned to identify potential agents and informers, some of whom might be persuaded to insinuate themselves into neutral or occupied territory.

The intelligence services looked particularly at the refugees and repatriates who had streamed into France from devastated towns and

---

* So good that in 1919 the Permit Offices were converted into a Passport Control Department, formally responsible to the Foreign Office but in fact supervised by a subcommittee of Sir Basil Thomson, Head of the Directorate of Intelligence at the Home Office, and representatives of the Home Office Aliens Branch, MI5 and MI 1(c).

** Commandant Richard had a distinguished record of public service. A former *préfet*, in charge of the policing and administration of a *département* (the equivalent of an English county), he had then been appointed a *conseiller d'état*, responsible for investigating complaints against government departments and agencies. In May 1914 he had become director of *Affaires Communales et Départementales* for the *Sûreté*, reporting directly to the Minister of the Interior.

villages in Flanders and Picardy and been taken in at receiving stations for allocation to communities in central, western and southern France. The handling of these unfortunates showed the French administrative system at its most efficient. When they arrived at the places where they were to settle, refugees and *rapatriés* were required to register themselves and lodge a description of their recent experience at the local *mairie*. Mayors sent these reports to the *préfets* in charge of the *départements* and *préfets* forwarded them to a special office, the *Direction du Contrôle*, in the *Ministère de l'Intérieur* in Paris. Using this material, officials were able to decide what funds should be provided to each locality to support the new arrivals. The dossiers were copied to the *Sûreté*, guardian of the security of the Republic and its citizens, for consultation by Commandant Richard and his colleagues.* From time to time Kirke's officers and their counterparts at the *Sûreté* exchanged information from their respective registries of suspected enemy agents and likely candidates for their allied service. Recruits selected by Kirke's people were sent for training to the office in Rue St Roch.

Kirke had another powerful friend in the French intelligence establishment, Colonel Jean Wallner, head of the Paris branch of the French secret service, the *Deuxième Bureau*. The rivalries of this organization were as complex as those of the underworld that was Wallner's other habitat and the Colonel was as shrewd and experienced a politician as he was a policeman. His office in Rue de Grenelle was near the National Assembly, the Foreign Ministry and the Ministry of Defence; his men had connections in all three. Wallner's interest in the Paris Permit Office was sustained from a distance; he had been posted to an inter-allied espionage office in England at the beginning of 1915, and during his absence his office in Rue de Grenelle was being managed by his colleague, Commandant Ladoux, head of French civil intelligence and counter-intelligence. Although Ladoux

---

* Records were kept of the arrival and departure of strangers and the inhabitants of each place, a requirement dating from the French Revolution, when a system of internal passports had been introduced into France. The *Sûreté* had long used these arrangements for the surveillance of suspected spies, criminals and agitators; during the First World War the registers were also an important instrument for tracing evacuees and reuniting them with families and friends.

described himself as a '*modeste officier subalterne*', he was influential.[2] With Richard, Wallner and Ladoux behind it, the Paris Office could not have had better support.

The first officer to be put in charge of affairs at 41 Rue St Roch had been Lieutenant S. H. C. Woolrych. A volunteer, rather than a regular soldier, he had been commissioned in a hurry into the military intelligence side of the British Expeditionary Force in the late summer of 1914. After training he had joined a regiment that was not expecting him: 'I was posted to 7th Division shortly before Christmas. On my arrival they looked hard at me and said, "Who do you say you are? Intelligence? We had one of them, and he was such a dud that we put him to man the Divisional Laundry."'[3] This reaction was not unusual: intelligence officers were few and the commanders to whom they were sent not always well briefed. The Intelligence Corps was a new phenomenon, assembled by Kirke and his chief, Macdonogh, in the week after the expiry of Britain's ultimatum to Germany. Sure that war was imminent, Macdonogh had made a note of the names of officers he thought suited to the sort of intelligence work needed for a British military operation in France. An indefatigable walker, he had also taken Kirke on a fortnight's tramp along the French and Belgian frontiers.

At midnight on 4 August, when war was declared, he and Kirke had begun a chain of telephone calls to the dozen or so astonished officers on Macdonogh's list, directing them to look for civilian volunteers, people who knew at least one foreign language and, ideally, were familiar with Continental Europe. Schoolmasters and university tutors had been approached, businessmen working as importers and exporters, and a handful of police officers, seconded at a special rate of pay from the Criminal Intelligence Department at Scotland Yard. Artists, actors and musicians had also been sounded out, these being the type of people who, it was thought, understood foreign ways. Those unable to accept a commission themselves often knew friends, relations, recent acquaintances, who were ready for adventure. Some who had joined were honest but amateurish, others adroit but shady. After a few days' instruction in map-reading, repair of motorcycles and management of horses and stables, this improvised troupe had embarked at Southampton for Le Havre. Once in France, each had been issued with a rifle and 100 rounds of ammunition. Lieutenant Woolrych had been among those who went to confront the enemy. Had he but known it, German military intelligence arrangements were even more sketchy.[4]

Woolrych had distinguished himself during his first assignment,

Black and white photograph of a pass issued by Commandant Richard of the French Secret Service to Lieutenant Woolrych, in plain clothes.

control and mapping work with I(a), the section of the Corps that went forward with the fighting troops to collect intelligence 'by direct contact with the enemy', on and about the battlefield and from German soldiers, living and dead. In January 1916 Woolrych had been extracted from the *zone des armées* and ordered to 'cross the floor' to I(b). His task, Kirke told him, was to open a Permit Office in Paris and then to run it. To help him do so, Woolrych was given a special warrant card, bearing Monsieur Richard's signature, entitling him to go wherever he wished in France, at any time of day or night, without explanation. Thus equipped, the lieutenant went in search of premises. Having found and furnished the *immeuble* at 41 Rue St Roch, he assembled his team. In the first-floor drawing room, now an office, he put himself and Lieutenant Monthaye, a young Belgian interpreter, 'full of ideas and enthusiasm', but who, Woolrych said, 'had to be recalled to earth several times a day'.[5] In espionage work, however, imaginativeness was no handicap. The budget allowed for an office manager and, after discreet inquiry, a bilingual secretary, Mademoiselle Andrée Dorgebray, had been taken on. How they found her is not known; she was perhaps a relation of Monsieur Jean Dorgebray, Monaco's honorary consul in Barcelona. One of Jean Dorgebray's duties was to issue visas to people wishing to travel from Spain to Monaco, some of whom, having got there, intended to make their way quietly into France. Dorgebray, who was French and had links with the intelligence services, kept a close eye on such movements and, when appropriate, notified his friends.

Woolrych and Monthaye had next considered how, having identified likely recruits, they were to test and, if found satisfactory, train them. As it was too risky to bring a stream of apprentice spies to a residential building in Rue St Roch, Woolrych looked for accommodation elsewhere. In the university quarter on the Left Bank, near the Jardin du Luxembourg, he was shown a large schoolroom on the top floor of a shabby building in Rue Soufflot. Nothing could have been more suitable. Students pressed through these streets, early and late, and no one, however odd, looked out of place. To furnish the schoolroom, Woolrych put together a set of demonstration materials, including a collection of tailors' wooden dummies. These he dressed in German infantry, cavalry and artillery uniforms, with appropriate badges. On the walls he hung canvas-backed maps and a set of drawings, showing, in profile, the types of train used by the Germans to transport troops, weapons and supplies. He also prepared a comprehensive examination paper for his prospective pupils.

Within weeks the two officers had identified a number of potential agents, refugees from Belgium and Flanders and civilian *rapatriés* with French nationality, stranded in occupied country but allowed to go home. Some were prepared to return under cover to German territory. Before recruits were taken to Rue Soufflot for training, Woolrych and Monthaye tested their resolve by outlining

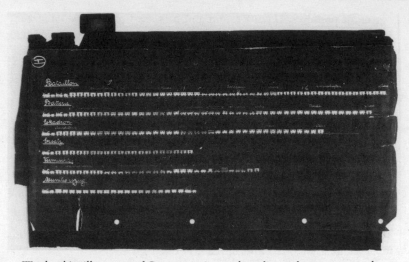

Woolrych's silhouettes of German trains – a battalion, a battery, a squadron, etc. – for recruits to practise identification.

what would be expected. This was enough to deter all but the most courageous.

Take the sending of reports. I(b)'s procedure was this. Information had to be set down succinctly, using scraps of *papier pelure** and a mapping pen and Indian ink for writing in very small characters. Each paper, no more than three or four inches square, was tightly rolled into a very small package and enclosed in a piece of rubber (cut, for instance, from a contraceptive). This could be hidden in a bicycle valve or a pessary. Agents took their reports to local chiefs, for amalgamation with those produced by other members of the same network. They were obliged to move on foot, which was slow, by bicycle, which was conspicuous, or by train, where they might be challenged. Few had cars and petrol was scarce. Some preferred to entrust themselves or their packages to bargemen, but travel along the canals took many days. The quickest way was overland into Holland, with the help of '*passeurs*', professional smugglers. This was dreadful work. In the spring of 1915 the Germans had erected a high-voltage electrified fence along the line from Flanders to the

---

* Thin, tough tissue paper.

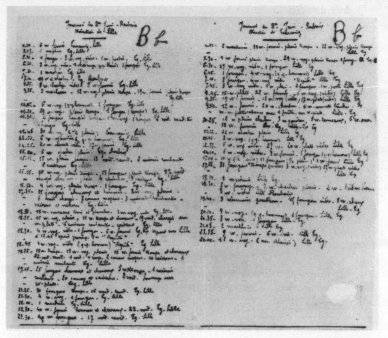

Train-watcher's report of movements on the Roubaix–Lille and Roubaix–Tourcoing lines. Written with a mapping pen on papier pelure. *Each column is the size of a matchbox.*

Belgian/Dutch border. While the agent waited, the *passeur*, in rubber boots, crawled towards the fence to an appointed crossing-place, the *tuyau*,* carrying a lightweight insulated frame. The *passeur* was followed by an assistant holding two strings, each attached to a lookout, one posted fifty yards to the right of the *passeur*, the other fifty yards to the left. The lookouts watched the sentries patrolling the fence, meeting in the middle and turning again to march away from one another. When the two lookouts simultaneously tugged the strings, indicating that the respective sentries had reached the furthest point from the centre, a signal was made to the *passeur*, who then hoisted the climbing frame, and the agent, over the wire. One slip and the agent was electrocuted.[6]

* *Tuyau*: pipe, or funnel.

Attempts had been made to improve message-delivery systems. Local labourers tilling fields near the border were persuaded to hurl packages, placed in slit turnips, across the wire at prearranged points. Agents did not favour this procedure, believing it dangerous to rely on untrained local peasants, who liked it even less. Model aeroplanes were tried, bows and arrows, and trained dogs. Carrier pigeons were employed, a fast but expensive way of getting information back as, however compact, only a little packet could be strapped to a pigeon's leg. This method also endangered innocent people: the Germans kept a sharp lookout for pigeon-fanciers, confiscating equipment and displaying warnings that anyone handling trained birds would be shot. Delivery of homing pigeons to recipients had also become more difficult, the Royal Flying Corps being increasingly reluctant to drop intelligence personnel (pigeons were so defined) more than fifteen miles behind German lines, restricting such sorties to nights when there was no wind and no moon.

All this Woolrych and Monthaye described to those whom they sought to recruit. Volunteers still came forward. Once trained, they were sent by sea or overland behind the lines. Agents who arrived without mishap embedded themselves in towns and villages and then enlisted others. Each community knew when one of its own had been caught on the high-voltage wire, or captured, imprisoned, shot. People continued to offer themselves. Men and boys came forward to take the place of fathers, sons and brothers, women and girls followed mothers, daughters and sisters. Neighbours trusted each other not to talk, although pressure was severe. In families and communities throughout Belgium, Holland, Flanders, Picardy and Alsace-Lorraine, there was much heart-searching. Those responsible for recruiting and managing agents dreaded the silence that told them there had been an arrest.

Some nine months after the opening of the Paris Office, Kirke decided to send Woolrych to Berne, capital of the Swiss Confederation. The military attaché at the British legation there had been recalled to London and for months there had been no one to control the issue of passports and visas. Before Woolrych could be moved, someone had to be found to fill his place at 41 Rue St Roch. This took many weeks. Kirke's first choice was Captain Francis

Verdon, a middle-aged officer in the Montgomery Yeomanry, who in civilian life had worked in a cotton-broking firm in Liverpool. It was soon clear that he would not do. 'He evidently works hard,' Kirke said, '. . . but cannot get agents and is rather helpless.'[7] The Major sent a more experienced officer, Lieutenant Hazeldine, to replace Woolrych – and Verdon, who was still there. Hazeldine's connections were well known and after three weeks he told Kirke that if he remained at 41 Rue St Roch, outsiders would soon guess that this was not just an ordinary Permit Office. 'He does not want to be there permanently,' Kirke wrote, 'as he knows too many people who think he is "*embusqué*".'*

'So,' Woolrych said, 'they tried again with a Captain Bruce.'[8]

George Bruce was thirty-four. Before the war he had worked in banking and insurance and in August 1914 had joined the Argyll and Sutherland Highlanders, the regiment in which his elder brother, Captain Robert Bruce, served as a regular soldier. Robert Bruce had been killed at Le Cateau in the first month of the war. George was luckier: an encounter at Neuve-Chapelle in May 1915 put a piece of shrapnel in his head but he had recovered from the wound. The War Office would not allow him to return to the front. His name had been on Macdonogh's register of people with skills necessary for intelligence work: knowledge of French or German, experience of driving a car or motorcycle, the ability to remain on horseback for a 'reasonable' time. (The exact period was not specified.) George Bruce fitted perfectly. There was no doubt about driving and riding, nor about the languages, for he spoke and wrote both French and German. In the late summer of 1915 GHQ put him into the Intelligence Corps.

In May 1916 Bruce, code-name 'Cairnesse',** was in Amiens. Ostensibly, he was no more than an assistant provost marshal in the military police, attached to the office of the local French commandant,

---

* By '*embusqué*', Kirke probably meant 'an undercover operator'. The alternative meaning, a shirker, is less likely here.
** The name of a house in Aberdeenshire, built in 1792 to a design by Charles Playfair, in a style that, but for the Revolution, might have been favoured in France. Was 'playing fair' in the mind of the officer who chose Bruce's code-name – or was he an architectural historian?

but his real work was to manage a secret service post for I(b). His network was a good one: many from that neighbourhood were to receive British decorations after the war. Bruce and his team were watchful; no strangers wandered about the place for long before being brought in for questioning. Hazeldine had been impressed when, on a surreptitious visit to buy French soldiers' uniforms, he and a colleague had been summoned for interrogation within ten minutes of their arrival in the town. At some point in the summer of 1916 Bruce contracted jaundice and had been sent home to Scotland to rebuild his health. He returned to duty in late 1916, doing work that earned a Mention in Dispatches in the New Year of 1917.

The usefulness of the Intelligence Corps was now recognized, at least in London. In November 1915 the Chief of the Imperial General Staff, Sir William Robertson, had created a Directorate of Military Intelligence in the War Office, separate from the existing Directorate of Military Operations. The CIGS, the Prime Minister's adviser on army strategy, had been Chief of Staff to Sir John French, Haig's predecessor as Commander-in-Chief, and understood the value of what Macdonogh's I(a) and I(b) produced. To reinforce the new structure, Robertson brought Macdonogh home to London and put him in charge of the new directorate. French recommended that Kirke should succeed Macdonogh but Haig preferred Brigadier-General John Charteris, a man of cheerful temperament, reflected in the appraisals he gave his Commander-in-Chief. (This optimism was not always helpful.) In the General Staff at GHQ the work of the Intelligence Staff was now known to be as relevant as that of Operations, a change in attitude Robertson had helped to bring about during his time in France.

From January 1916 British and French intelligence staffs at their respective GHQs telephoned each other every night to exchange up-to-date reports on German troop movements. Information came from battlefield reconnaissance patrols, forward observation posts, and wireless and telephone operators, using listening sets,* augmented by intelligence from prisoners and informers. From this material allied

---

* Introduced by the French in February 1916.

Captain Bruce, drawn by the war artist Muirhead Bone in November 1916, two months before Bruce left the Assistant Provost Marshal's post at Amiens for the office in Rue St Roch. Bone sent this to Bruce through the military post. Book, chair and overcoat give nothing away, and Bone's drawing was 'Passed by Censor 13/4/18'.

intelligence staffs derived their picture of the German Order of Battle, reported, daily, to their Commanders-in-Chief. These briefings described the actual battlefield situation. As important was advice about the enemy's further plans: where reserves were coming from, when they would arrive, to which part of the front they were being sent. For this, GHQ looked to I(b). Demand for military intelligence increased, and with it, the need for trained agents.

Six months had passed since Kirke had first thought of transferring Woolrych to Switzerland and an experienced officer was still required for the post in Paris. In December 1916 Kirke fixed on Bruce. The Major made two proposals to Charteris: that Verdon be transferred to The Hague, to help sift reports, and that Bruce be posted to Paris. Charteris agreed and on 6 January 1917 Bruce was summoned to GHQ to see Kirke.

Paris was not what Bruce had in mind.

'Bruce came in,' Kirke wrote in his diary, 're his application to go to Welsh Guards. He was very insistent on going though I and B.Gl. [Brigadier-General] told him we wanted him specially for a job for which it is hard to get people.'[9] Bruce was determined to go back to the front. He had been overruled when he had made a similar request after Neuve-Chapelle but the Welsh Guards' urgent need for officers seemed to offer an opportunity to return to the trenches.* Kirke sympathized with Bruce's wish for active service; he himself had been trying for months to leave the Intelligence Corps for a post that was more exposed and, as he was ambitious, more visible. Only a day or two before he saw Bruce, Kirke had heard that his own application had been successful and that at the end of January he was to join a regiment on the Somme. Meanwhile, he had to persuade Captain Bruce to accept what, compared with the trenches, must have sounded to the junior man like an unheroic posting.[10]

Neither Kirke nor Charteris could persuade Bruce to agree to go to Paris. The Brigadier-General, therefore, referred Bruce to the Commander-in-Chief. On the following day, 7 January, Bruce was invited to join Haig for luncheon. He was the only guest. The

---

* The Welsh Guards had been founded two years earlier, in February 1915, and their Commanding Officer, Colonel William Murray-Threipland, a Scot from the Borders, was recruiting officers, a number from Scottish regiments.

Commander-in-Chief liked to meet young officers but such private access was unusual. Had the staff advised him that the brother of this obstinate young officer was the Robert Bruce who had fought with Haig in South Africa and had been killed after only twenty-two days of the present war? Perhaps no reminder was needed. The Commander-in-Chief may have known that Captain George Bruce was the surviving son of a neighbour in Scotland, Lord Balfour of Burleigh. It had been the recommendations made by Lord Balfour, a former cabinet minister, that had ended a potentially disastrous strike of the Clyde munition workers in the winter of 1915, at just the time when Haig was taking over as Commander-in-Chief.[11] Haig, to whom such things mattered, would also have been aware that Captain Bruce's father was, like himself, a friend of the King.

The discussion between the General and the Captain ended in a compromise. 'He wishes to join a Battalion and go into the trenches . . . I decided that he must go to Paris but will be given a Commission in the Guards, and allowed to join in 4 months time, by which time a suitable officer should be found to replace him in Paris.'[12] There was no arguing with a direct order from the Commander-in-Chief and so in the second week of January 1917 Captain Bruce introduced himself to the old hands at the Permit Office.

2

Peculiar Arrangements

The Paris Office was not managed directly by GHQ. Kirke's hours were taken up with appraising intelligence and deciding what was relevant to current operations and the Commander-in-Chief's routine briefing. Paperwork concerning the Paris and other Permit Offices was not sent straight to GHQ but via a section based on the other side of the English Channel. This was reasonable: it would have been absurd for Kirke to try to supervise basic administration from a collapsible desk at the front. Surprisingly, however, for traffic across the Channel was slow and insecure, this procedure applied not only to correspondence, minutes and signals but also to secret intelligence material.

The origins of the arrangement were as follows.

By the winter of 1914 it had become evident to the War Office that the Allies had too many rival secret service organizations. Since the beginning of the war at least five networks had been engaged in collecting intelligence on the Continent: two British services – one working for the War Office, the Admiralty and the Foreign Office, the other for the army in the field – plus a French, a Belgian and a Russian service. Mutual trust was often lacking, the French and British believing, for example, that the Russians had been ordered to spy on them, as they, in turn, spied on the Russians.

Each secret service reported to its own GHQ – British, French, Belgian and Russian – although in the latter case the lines were long and tenuous. In late 1914 the War Office had suggested that there should be a pooled arrangement to ensure that each GHQ knew what its counterparts were being told, and at a conference of allied military intelligence chiefs in Belgium in November 1914 this was agreed. Folkestone on the Channel coast was selected as the site for the new organization; reports could be brought there by boat, military couriers carrying intelligence material having disguised themselves as ordinary ferry passengers. Each allied army appointed a senior representative to this central bureau, officers who met at least daily to prepare a single bulletin for transmission by telegraph to their respective GHQs. This was not their only task; each representative continued to deploy his own nation's agents in occupied France and Belgium, in Holland, Switzerland and Germany. As the participants in the central bureau soon discovered, this mixture of independent and collaborative activity was not ideal.

French GHQ had chosen as its representative Colonel Wallner from the *Deuxième Bureau*: it was to Folkestone that he had gone when he left Rue de Grenelle at the start of 1915. As his deputy, Wallner had taken a naval officer, Commander Béliard, in civilian life director of a ship-building company based in Anvers. They were a wily pair, Wallner a man of pavements and police stations, with a connection in every town in France, Béliard, steeped in fog and salt water, a familiar of the hiding-places along the Channel coast, its sandy indentations and its tides. Belgium was represented by Major Mage, the British by Captain Cecil Cameron, formerly of the Royal Artillery.

The Russian service had no delegate at Folkestone but the French had agreed that an experienced Russian officer should be attached to a small inter-allied bureau in the French Ministry of War in Paris. Colonel Comte Paul Ignatieff of the Imperial Guard had been chosen for this task.* The French had also provided a Russian-speaking French officer to assist Ignatieff, a man known to outsiders only as 'Marcel B'. From the Ignatieffs' residence the Colonel and his deputy managed a network of Russian agents in France, Holland, Belgium, Spain and Switzerland. Old quarrels were not entirely forgotten. On a visit to French GHQ at Vitry-le-François, Ignatieff had almost been shot on the spot when, insulted by the reference to Napoleon's victory over

---

* In December 1915 Ignatieff had exchanged his hussar's uniform for civilian clothes and, in the guise of 'Mr Paul Istomine', war correspondent for a St Petersburg newspaper, had come to Paris with his wife. See Colonel Comte Paul Ignatieff, *Ma Mission en France*, Paris: Editions du Masque, undated, and Major-General Sir Edward Spears, *Liaison 1914*, London: Heinemann, 1930.

the Russian army, he refused to reply to a sentry's request for the pass-word: 'Austerlitz'. The story was amusing – Ignatieff had dined well – but it illustrated the sensitivities that made liaison difficult.

The existence of two British services complicated an already complex arrangement. In London a non-army organization, the Secret Service Bureau, set up by Macdonogh in 1909, also handled espionage and counter-espionage, acting jointly for the War Office and the Admiralty. (Aviation was too new to have its own department.) The Foreign Office, the Bureau's paymaster, also took an interest. In the years before the war and the setting-up of the Intelligence Corps, Commander Mansfield Cumming, the SSB's chief, had energetically seeded the Continent with agents, whose reports he sent in, for the most part, to Macdonogh, via Kirke, then at the War Office. Cumming presented himself as a flamboyant intriguer, star of anecdotes about swordsticks and disguise. (Some of these tales were true.)[1] He was, Kirke told his wife, 'the cheeriest fellow I've ever met, full of the most amusing yarns'.[2] In peacetime the two met nearly every day and from August 1914, when the Intelligence Corps went to France, Cumming sent extracts from his agents' reports to Kirke at GHQ, signed, in green ink, 'C'. These were then matched against intelligence obtained by I(b). Such duplication was dangerous. Kirke's officers did not know the identity of the agents who were providing the SSB with intelligence; Cumming's agents did not know the names of agents who were working for I(b). Security was constantly jeopardized. 'Circular reporting', for instance, led each service to believe that information was being corroborated, whereas often the same story was being heard from agents supplying two clients at once.

Early in 1915 the War Office had attempted to clarify the responsibilities of the two services. The SSB was instructed to concentrate on 'strategic' intelligence, to underpin the long-term thinking of policy makers in the War Office, the Admiralty and the Foreign Office, and I(b) to direct its energies to the acquisition and appraisal of 'tactical' intelligence for GHQ. On paper this sounded straightforward but, in so far as it existed, the distinction made little difference to problems in the field. The two services competed for local recruits from the limited pool of those able and willing to serve. The system wasted time and money; worse, it endangered lives.

The strategic/tactical separation was almost entirely ineffective. At the end of 1915 the War Office tried a new approach, this time geographical. A map of Continental Europe was produced and each of the two secret services made responsible for certain regions. Switzerland, neutral, was allocated to Cumming; all of France, occupied and free, to Kirke. Belgium, occupied, was divided by a line roughly extending from Antwerp in the north, through Brussels, to Namur in the south. Eastern Belgium and Germany were reserved for Cumming. Everything west of the line – the rest of Belgium and the whole of occupied Flanders – was given to Kirke. Spain was left to the Admiralty, which had a special interest in the Atlantic coastline.

Holland, neutral, had even more complicated arrangements. Here I(b) and the SSB had been working in parallel and sometimes at cross-purposes. Kirke had agents there and I(b) also used Holland as a receiving-point for information from network chiefs in Flanders and Belgium. Cumming's Dutch operation was organized on different lines. It was run by one man, Captain Richard Tinsley ('T'), a naval reserve officer who before the war had been manager of the Uranium Steamship Company and now managed a number of SSB's networks. Reports collected by Tinsley's agents were sent to him and, rather than giving this raw material direct to the SSB, he passed it on to the British military attaché at the British Legation at The Hague. Having identified and extracted information he considered 'strategic', the attaché dispatched it to the War Office in London. This unenviable responsibility had been given to Major Laurence Oppenheim, a scholar, whose job, already taxing, was made more difficult by interruptions from representatives of both the SSB and I(b), each complaining about the other and asking him to arbitrate.[3]

One of those who most irritated Oppenheim was Captain Cameron, British representative at the central bureau in Folkestone. At the beginning of the war Cameron – code-name 'Evelyn Edwards' – had been responsible for all I(b)'s secret work in Holland, Belgium and France.* Kirke believed in dividing and subdividing authority to

* His French colleagues called him 'Miss Evelyn'. For an affectionate picture of Cameron, see Robert Boucard, *La Guerre des Renseignements*, Paris: Editions de France, 1939.

maintain security and when Cameron was posted to the Folkestone bureau in 1915 some of his original duties were allocated to another officer. Cameron resented the transfer of part of his empire, more especially because it was given to a man whom he did not like: Major Ernest 'Peg Leg' Wallinger, a gunner who had lost a foot at Le Cateau. Wallinger's section, based in No. 7 Lincoln House in Basil Street – a fourth-floor flat near Harrods – was given charge of secret work in Belgium and monitoring travellers on the ferry between Tilbury and the Netherlands. In practice it was impossible to avoid interplay between the two operations. Cameron and Wallinger were unable to work together, making matters worse.

Cameron was an uncomfortable colleague, jealous and thin-skinned. His father, Colonel Aylmer Cameron, had won the Victoria Cross for killing three sepoys in the Indian Mutiny, only moments after his own left hand had been cut off. Although desk-work did not suit him, Colonel Cameron had served as acting head of military intelligence during an interregnum in the 1880s. At eighteen, young Cameron followed his father into the Royal Artillery. Ten years later all seemed to be going well. But Lieutenant Cameron had married and Mrs Cameron was his downfall. In December 1910 an insurance policy for £6,500 was taken out in his wife's name to cover a pearl necklace;* three months later she claimed that the pearls had been snatched from her outside an Edinburgh jeweller's while she was alone, her husband having gone to a chemist's shop to purchase a hypodermic needle.** The Camerons had gone straightaway to the police and shortly afterwards had sent in a claim to the insurance company. At the end of February 1911 both Camerons were arrested and charged with attempting to perpetrate a fraud.

The trial took place in Edinburgh. There were oddities, including the fact that two days before the alleged theft Cameron, not a wealthy man, had written to his bankers, proposing to pay in some £6,000 to his account and asking for advice as to how to invest it. After a week of humiliating evidence, Ruby Cameron's story was declared to be a fiction. Not only had there been no robbery but the pearls

---

* Good pearls were rarer then. £6,500 was the equivalent of £365,000 today.
** Mrs Cameron had become dependent on morphine, the result, it was said, of treatment given for an illness she had contracted in India.

had not been Mrs Cameron's own. Husband and wife were both found guilty and each was sentenced to three years in prison.* Cameron, personally ruined and professionally dishonoured, was stripped of his rank. In the army, among the family's friends and neighbours in Scotland, and in the London clubs, everyone talked about the 'Pearl Necklace Case', and Cameron knew it.[4]

A year later Ruby Cameron was freed on medical grounds. Her husband, she declared, had been entirely innocent. Cameron was released in late 1912. As an ex-convict, ex-officer Cameron had no job and no prospects, except for one: military intelligence. As soon as he was freed he spoke to Cumming about a scheme to post agents and scouts to Belgium and, equipped with a four-horse-power motor-bicycle and several hundred pounds, was sent to Brussels.** From January 1913 until the outbreak of war Cameron remained in Belgium and northern France. He was conscientious and occasionally imaginative and, shielded by an alias, rebuilt his reputation. When war came Kirke took him on and, to give him the necessary authority, recommended that he be made an honorary captain. In 1915 Cameron became a major; meanwhile, Kirke encouraged various influential people to press the case for a free pardon. Cameron's supporters asked the authorities to remember how distinguished his father had been, doing little to restore the son's self-esteem.*** A pardon was eventually granted but the damage was done.

Cameron got on well with Kirke, who applauded his suggestions for penetrating enemy territory: hiring a pleasure-boat, for example, to land agents on the Channel coast (not a success) and digging tunnels to tap German telegraph lines. Cameron's most significant innovation was the introduction of a system of train-watching services. Railways had become the arteries of war, carrying troops,

* See the Lord-Justice General's charge to the jury, reported in H. M. Advocate v. Camerons, Adam's *Reports of Cases before the High Court of Justiciary in Scotland*, Vol. VI, p. 456, Edinburgh.
** See Alan Judd, *The Quest for 'C'*, London: HarperCollins, 1999. The motor-bicycle cost £60. In the winter of 1913, an application was made for a side-car, but Cumming was reluctant to put it before Macdonogh, who supervised his budget.
*** For example, Lord Cromer's letter to *The Times*, 25 June 1914: '. . . some 45 years ago I was at the Staff College with Mr Cameron's father. A finer officer never lived.'

horses, weapons and supplies to the front, taking the wounded to clearing stations and hospitals, carrying survivors home on leave. Under Cameron's direction, train-watchers were recruited to monitor junctions along selected railway lines in France, Holland, Belgium and Flanders. By mid-1916 many hundreds of observers were reporting to network chiefs employed by Cumming's SSB and Kirke at I(b).

Cameron's promotion was built on real achievement. From Folkestone he supervised I(b)'s operations in the whole of France, as well as managing the exchange of information coming in to the central bureau from the various national secret services. Bruce respected him; equally, when Bruce moved from Amiens to the Paris Office, it was with Cameron's approval. Courteous messages went between them. The Paris Office was an important post and Cameron looked forward to visiting 41 Rue St Roch. The honeymoon was brief.

3

Qualifications

Inside No. 41 it was colder than the street. The wooden stairs and banister were smoothed by years of polishing, tall doors opened on to a room lit by piercing winter light. He trod on something, heard an exclamation: 'The cat's saucer!' Looking down, Bruce saw a spreading pool of milk, looking up, a tall, grey-eyed young woman.

This was the first surprise.

The salon was crowded with furniture. Four officers were accommodated here: Woolrych, still waiting for his Swiss posting, Monthaye, the Belgian, and two recent arrivals, 'Interpreter' Chocqueel, French but with honorary British rank, and Captain Lewis Gordon Campbell. An adjacent room housed the so-called Secretariat, Andrée Dorgebray and Dorothy Done, the latter brought in to help subdue the paperwork, and for other more mysterious tasks. It was Miss Done who had dared to reproach the new chief about the milk.

Like Bruce, Campbell was a volunteer. In January 1915 the Intelligence Corps had sent him to Russia to teach telegraphers on the Eastern Front, an assignment endurable only by one used to harsh conditions. Campbell was then thirty-one years old, adaptable, experienced and resilient. From Russia he had been moved to Annemasse, on the French side of Lake Geneva, to manage I(b)'s local networks and look out for German agents crossing from Switzerland into France. By November 1915 he had become so frustrated by the lack of effective liaison with GHQ that he had gone to Kirke to tell him so. It was impossible to discover what intelligence the military required, Campbell said, or whether what he delivered was of value. For example, his agents had supplied full details of the transfer of eleven German divisions from the Eastern to the Western Front. He had heard nothing to confirm whether use had been made of this information or whether it had turned out to be accurate.* Kirke brought Campbell to GHQ for a full briefing but it came too late to be effective. The Swiss police were watching him and in January 1916, alerted by the arrest of someone else of the same name, Campbell escaped across the frontier into France.

Although secret service in Switzerland was reserved to the SSB, Kirke had operators in Zürich and Geneva, working under ingenious forms of cover. One, for instance, was appointed as member of a British Commission looking into the manufacture of aniline dyes, another – Somerset Maugham – claimed to need Swiss peace and quiet to write a play.[1] Their operations were amateurish: in one disaster, reports from Zürich, wrongly addressed, were delivered to the Berlitz Language School in Paris. Kirke also tried to use the local consuls. Although he did not trust them to issue visas, he thought they might serve as postboxes, especially as many worked from their own houses. This too was not a success. When the Swiss police accused Sir Henry Angst, British consul general in Zürich, of espionage and forced him to retire, the Foreign Office complained. Diplomatic channels were not to be used for secret service operations.

Two exceptions were made: the military attachés' offices at the British legations in The Hague and in Berne. Oppenheim's counterpart in Switzerland was Major Hans Vischer, recruited in April 1915 from the Colonial Office, which continued to pay half his salary, the whole being more than the SSB could afford. But the Swiss were anxious to reinforce their neutrality and the police were vigilant. In April 1916 Cumming and Kirke decided that if there were to be a continuing British intelligence presence in Switzerland it would be best to run it jointly. Responsibility for pulling the Swiss service together was given to Campbell; he was told that he had two months to do it. But reviving the depleted and demoralized Swiss networks was next to impossible. Agents and funds were better used elsewhere and in August 1916 Kirke removed I(b) from the joint arrangement. For a time Cumming maintained a Swiss

---

* 'As he knows nothing of the Order of Battle or situation, he never knows when he is being done down by his agents.' Kirke, Diaries, 23 August, 15, 29 and 30 November 1915, 10 January 1916, Imperial War Museum, London.

operation from his own budget but at the end of 1916, MI 1(c), as the SSB was now called, also withdrew.* Major Vischer returned to London.

A quick-witted officer could not be lost to the service. Kirke knew that Campbell was interested in an assignment that was of immediate use to GHQ and that, as an expert in codes, he might be able to find ways to expedite the delivery of intelligence from behind the lines. It was thus that Campbell had arrived in Rue St Roch.

Jean Chocqueel had joined the Paris Office at about the same time. A *notaire* in the small town of Bergues in northern France, he was, at forty, the oldest of Bruce's new colleagues. Chocqueel had belonged to a local regiment of territorials, the Eighth Infantry Reserve, mobilized when German troops invaded the flat and open country west and south of Belgium. In the *képi* and scarlet pantaloons of the Second Empire, water bottles and mess tins dangling from their haversacks, each with rolled blanket, small spade and pike, untrained, armed only with iron poles and the rusty carbines last used in the Franco-Prussian War, the reservists had marched to defend the Citadel at Lille.[2]

There, in October 1914, Chocqueel's regiment was overwhelmed by a force of besieging Germans. As the survivors left the battered ramparts, a French officer had told them that they were relieved of fighting duties. Take to your heels, he said, if your heart tells you, if you get the chance. They had fought hard and had been honourably defeated; now, words Chocqueel never forgot: 'Face to face with adventure, they would be free again.'[3] That night, one by one, the lightly guarded captives slid into the shadows. To his surprise, for he was a lawyer through and through, weighing every argument before taking a decision, Chocqueel hesitated for only a moment. He too slipped away.

He found refuge in a monastery but hiding became increasingly risky. Vouchers were required for the purchase of food and other necessities; people were arrested if they had no identity cards or if papers were incorrectly stamped. Light-headed with hunger, the notary thought he must have imagined his former life. A friend

* Its name had been changed in January 1916.

provided forged papers and, presenting himself first as a store-manager in a thread factory, then as a travelling victualler in potatoes, Chocqueel escaped from Flanders and, in a train full of German soldiers, made his way to Brussels. There he found Belgian agents, who gave him a package for delivery to the Allies and introduced him to a gang of smugglers who guided him through treacherous marshes into Holland. This journey, through thick mist, was the one point at which Chocqueel nearly lost his nerve.

The British navy took him to England and dispatched him to the central intelligence bureau at Folkestone for an interview with Major Mage, the Belgian representative there. Chocqueel explained about the package. A Madame Poucques had given him a password which would make sense to her husband, Major Poucques, commander of a Belgian unit at Dunkerque. Hearing this, the Folkestone office furnished Chocqueel with accreditation and an alias, 'Monsieur Michel', and sent him to Dunkerque. His route allowed a brief stop at Bergues for a reunion with his family, who had thought him dead, fallen 'in a beetfield'.

Jean had been spared and so had they, for Bergues was just inside the *zone réservée*. Little news reached Bergues from occupied country across the line, the region the invaders called the *Etappengebiet*: the foraging zone. The name was apt. Desperate for labour and provisions, the enemy had ransacked farms and villages in the *départements* of the Aisne, the Nord, the Marne and the Meuse, subjecting their inhabitants to continuing demands for milk and wine, money and manpower, machinery, tools, clothing, household goods. Crops were requisitioned, beds and mattresses taken. There was no paraffin, no flour, no bread. Chocqueel's people had heard rumours of repression and starvation and sometimes news was brought by evacuees permitted to leave the *Etappengebiet* on payment of a fee. Little was said officially. The French government suppressed news that might undermine morale; censorship prevented French newspapers from describing the degradation endured by the civilian population in Flanders and Picardy. On his return to Bergues Chocqueel brought not only the story of the fall of Lille and the fate of his fellow reservists but also a description of the other France, as he had seen it for himself.

His next call was on Major Poucques in Dunkerque. The packet, when opened, was found to contain a complete set of plans of the German coastal defences at Ostend. The success of the mission suggested that Chocqueel would make a useful agent. Within a week he was attached to the Folkestone bureau, equipped with a new rank, 'assimilated officer', and the title of 'Interpreter', though it was not for knowledge of foreign languages that Chocqueel was recruited. I(b) wanted his hardiness, daring and skill in deception, resources that until October 1914 had been unsuspected by all who knew him – indeed, by Chocqueel himself.

Instructed in British military intelligence techniques and armed with a diplomatic passport, Chocqueel spent the first months of 1916 travelling in and out of occupied France, seeking recruits for Kirke.[4] Who better to interrogate potential agents than a shrewd and knowledgeable lawyer? In the summer of 1916 Kirke had sent him to the Paris Office.

And then there was Miss Done. Her history was as vivid as that of Campbell and Chocqueel. She had often been taken out of school by her parents, who lived in Cheshire but liked foreign travel. On one such expedition the Dones had become acquainted with the great French *tragédienne*, Gabrielle Réju, whose daughter, Germaine, was about the same age as Dorothy. 'Réjane' suggested that Dorothy should stay with her as company for Germaine. The English girl was carried off to France. From that time she hardly came home at all. Paris in the early 1900s was artistically the most exciting city in Europe and Réjane's friends – Proust was one – were among the most interesting people in it.* Wherever she went, the actress was acclaimed. When the President of the Republic saw her carriage, he raised his hat. Everyone knew her gig, drawn by a pair of snow-white mules – a present from the King and Queen of Portugal – with bunches of violets in their silver studded bridles. Réjane sat for Sargent and Lautrec, Cocteau and Beardsley drew her, Doucet and Poiret made her costumes, Reboux her hats.

---

* Proust drew on Réjane and her friend and colleague Sarah Bernhardt for his portrayal of the *tragédienne*, 'La Berma', in *A la recherche du temps perdu*. In 1919, when he was obliged to leave his quarters in Rue Haussmann, Proust moved to an apartment that belonged to Réjane, next door to her own at 8 Rue Laurent-Pichat. See François Baudot, *Réjane, La Reine du Boulevard*, Paris: Editions 71, 2002.

It was a dazzling introduction to grown-up life. How much did Dorothy describe in letters home to Cheshire? The Théâtre de Réjane, with its electric chandeliers and seats of white and gold brocade? Nijinsky's dancing, Bakst's sets, Stravinsky's music? Réjane's Italian lover and the apartment in Venice, overlooking the Grand Canal? And what did the actors make of the self-assured English girl who came with them to the provinces and the *territoires et départements outre-mer*? Dorothy absorbed the taste of Parisian sophisticates: the colour violet, delicately coloured wine glasses, cigarettes. She expected to find a bidet in every bathroom. She had her own flat in Rue de Moscou, in the newly fashionable '*quartier de l'Europe*'. Her habits became those of her adopted country: thinly sliced roast beef with flageolets for luncheon on Sundays; heated *antiphlogistène* clay as a treatment for boils.

Dorothy was twenty-six when the war began. Wanting to contribute, she wrote first to the Red Cross in London and, when they did not reply, to the *Croix Rouge Française*, which sent her to one of its thousands of '*hôpitaux temporaires, hôpitaux complémentaires, hôpitaux auxiliaires, hôpitaux bénévoles*'. Hers was a converted casino; from their beds, lined up in the *salons de jeu*, moustachioed French soldiers gazed at the huge canvas bags protecting the chandeliers, hanging like wasps' nests from frivolous ceilings.* The railway wagons that brought in the wounded were also used for taking men and horses ('*Hommes 40, Chevaux 8*')** to and from the front. By the time casualties were delivered to hospitals in the rear they had lain for hours in mud and dung-infected straw. The nurses cut away ripped uniforms and blood-soaked dressings, cleaned wounds, attended at the operating table. Dorothy's father had given her a set of whetstones, oils and strops and, when

---

* Possibly Le Touquet. Archives, *Croix Rouge Française* and *Hôpital de Val de Grâce*. The *Croix Rouge Française* had brought together three national societies: the *Société de Secours aux Blessés Militaires*, the *Union des Femmes Françaises* and the *Association des Dames de France*. There is no record of Miss Done's having acquired from the first two of these bodies the diploma that was needed for nursing the wounded. It may have been the *Association* that engaged her.
** The number each wagon could take ('Forty men or eight horses') was painted on the side.

she was found to have discreetly sharpened the surgeons' tools, looking after the knives became her responsibility.

Kirke suspected that there might be spies among Red Cross and *Croix Rouge* volunteers, overhearing secrets revealed by delirious soldiers.* The Permit Offices watched the lists. As an Englishwoman working for a French relief organization, Miss Done stood out. Her family's patriotism was unquestioned – her two brothers were regular soldiers, one of whom had worked closely with Kitchener – her skills and connections unmatched. The interesting Miss Done was just the sort of agent for whom Kirke was looking.

Her first post was in the *Bureau Central Interallié*, in the French Ministry of War, an office for the exchange of information about suspected German spies. There she took on a special duty, the management of a 'Parcel Fund'. There were many such schemes for the preparation and dispatching of soldiers' comforts: long flannel under-things, woollen mufflers, mittens, socks and nightcaps, writing paper, flea powder, soap and cigarettes.[5] Miss Done's parcels were not like these. They went not to the front but to Germany; their contents were unusual.

In the summer of 1915 Kirke had heard about a French intelligence scheme for communicating with French prisoners in German camps. The British, he thought, should introduce something similar. Would-be escapers already possessed a large repertoire of stratagems; in every camp were people who knew how to write home in code or sympathetic ink ('Heat this letter'). Friends and relations had become experts in concealing escaping kit: converting compasses to lids for pots of anchovy paste, or – a device thought up by the mother of Captain A. J. Evans of the RFC – baking maps into the paper that encircled a fruit-cake.[6] Successful escapers passed on tips: what to send – fabric for making into civilian clothes, meat cubes, malted milk lozenges, chocolate, condensed and concentrated foods – and how to camouflage it.

* See Kirke's note after an exasperating conversation in London with the Secretary of the Red Cross: 'Now whole country full of neurotic females with fancy Red X outfits subject to no sort of control. Many undesirables must be included amongst their retinues, and it is an obvious means of access for hostile agents.' Diaries, 1 January 1915.

Invited to follow the French example, the British Red Cross refused. If the Germans were to find maps in prisoners' packages, they would not accept Red Cross parcels in future. 'Question reserved as too difficult,' said Kirke, but he did not abandon the idea.[7] Someone must be found to run an independent scheme. What sort of person were the Germans least likely to suspect? Miss Done might be able to masquerade as the sort of civic-minded Englishwoman who in peace took on the administration of charitable bazaars and in war the knitting of socks and pullovers, managing voluntary relief from her sitting room.

Writing paper was ordered:

MISS DONE'S PARCEL FUND
38 RUE DE MOSCOU
PARIS

ADDRESS: ALL COMMUNICATIONS TO THE SECRETARY

and postcards were prepared, pale green, with a tear-off section for prisoners to acknowledge that packages had been received.

When Miss Done was transferred to 41 Rue St Roch in 1917, the management of the Parcel Fund went with her. The chief business of the Paris Office, as Bruce had understood it, was the finding and training of agents. This sideline was his second surprise.

4

Tangled Webs

Cameron's emphasis had been on watching trains to plot the move-ment of enemy troops, intelligence that was critical in determining the German Order of Battle and deciding when and where to strike or to expect an attack. Train-watching networks were tightly organ-ized: agents recruited sub-agents into self-contained cells, each member working to an agreed procedure for identifying, noting and reporting the composition of trains and the nature of their cargo. Lines were watched round the clock. Observers devised their own methods of coding. Housewives shelled peas and beans of varying sizes into different bowls, recording hospital trains, leave trains, trains carrying stores. Knitters encoded observations in plain stitch for wagonloads of men, purl for horses.[1] All observations were poten-tially significant. Reports that replacement troops who were being brought to the front looked noticeably younger or older than those who had preceded them indicated, for example, that the Germans were conscripting boys and grandfathers to make up the reserves.

Particularly important was information about 'constituted units', the long snakes, as many as fifty-two trains, required to transfer an entire German division.* Each train was made up of *voitures*, passenger coaches holding officers; *wagons*, cattle trucks and wagons for the men; and *wagons plats*, flat trucks carrying guns and ammunition. A constituted unit took days to pass through a railway junction and the further the division had come the longer the interval between trains, as those behind waited for those in front to travel

* From March 1917, when the size of battalions and other units was reduced, only thirty or forty trains were needed.

over points, minutes of delay turning into hours. Further pauses were needed to allow trains carrying foodstuffs to catch up. Trains carrying troops from the Eastern to the Western Front took longest, up to six days, as they had to stop on the Russian–German frontier for the men to be de-loused at disinfecting stations.

Each train-watching network chief managed a separate set of couriers, *passeurs* and agents, some – '*promeneurs*' – roving across country, others watching from fixed posts. It was thought that the more train-watching networks there were, the easier it would be to confirm reports, a dangerous assumption.* Little empires were created and accountability was unclear. Refinements made things worse. Artificial frontiers were introduced, circumscribing the area in which each network operated, although information about enemy activity in one place was often vital to agents next door. The loyalties of agents and informers did not always coincide with organizational boundaries. Issues affecting more than one network were disputed or, because no single individual had responsibility for them, forgotten or neglected.

I(b)'s system was deficient in other ways. Agents produced complex reports needing expert interpretation, descriptions of anti-aircraft batteries, for instance, information about stockpiles, camps, movements of aeroplanes and ships. Intelligence collected for Cumming at MI 1(c) was sent for assessment to Oppenheim at The Hague but I(b) relied on network chiefs. Key points were overlooked or misunderstood, the chiefs, often civilians, being unaware of current military requirements. The roundabout journey from posts to network headquarters to Folkestone to GHQ meant that summaries arrived too late for operational use. Furthermore, reports were not encoded before they were sent across the Channel, an oversight that greatly increased the risk of exposure for those working in the field. Valuable agents were arrested, some shot. A series of incidents badly damaged both Cumming's and Kirke's services; in June 1916, for example, the Germans seized a British steamer, *Brussels*, on which Oppenheim's courier was travelling with reports for the SSB, and in November

---

* '*Renseignement unique, renseignement nul*' ('It is not intelligence if it is unconfirmed'), a maxim of the *Deuxième Bureau*.

1916 the enemy intercepted the Folkestone–Flushing boat, on which reports were being brought to Cameron, an affair that led to the suspension of the commercial cross-Channel ferry service for the rest of the war.* Change was clearly necessary.

Bruce spent his first hours in the Paris Office asking about train-watching. 'He admitted that he knew little,' Woolrych reported, 'but he soon learned. He had formidable powers of concentration and was obviously a first class man.'[2] The new chief asked many questions. Agents were being lost at the *tuyaux*, burnt bodies left as a deterrent, fused into the electrified fence. Why was the delivery of reports so dangerous? Answer: there was a limited supply of the 'real tough nuts' who made good *passeurs*.[3] Was there not a more efficient method? Letters were allowed between occupied countries and Switzerland; why not use the post? Answer: letters were heavily censored and unpredictably delayed. Why was intelligence not delivered directly to the Paris Office for onward transmission to GHQ? Answer: reports from network chiefs had to be assessed at Folkestone. Many observers were experienced railway employees, who consistently supplied their chiefs with detailed and accurate reports; was it impossible to train them to concentrate on constituted units? Answer: it had not been tried.

If the Paris Office was to have a different approach Bruce had to move fast. Having obtained his command, Kirke had moved to the battlefield; his successor, Major Reginald Drake, was already making changes.** One order had gone out straightaway: all transmissions were to be in code. Drake was now considering how to sharpen the content of reports. They should be edited at The Hague, he decided, alongside MI 1(c)'s intelligence, rather than going to Folkestone. Network chiefs could attach a note of what they considered to be key points and if clarification were needed Oppenheim and Verdon

---

* A replacement ferry service, with a naval escort, was provided between Harwich and Hook of Holland but it had no regular timetable and was not run commercially.
** Drake was an experienced intelligence officer. Lady Kell, wife of one of the first joint heads (with Cumming) of the SSB, described him as 'a most able man and most successful sleuth – small hope for anyone who fell into his net'. Constance Kell, *Secret Well Kept*, Imperial War Museum. Quoted in Christopher Andrew, *Secret Service*, London: Heinemann, 1985, p. 59.

could send for agents' detailed observations. This would help to identify inconsistencies and duplication. Oppenheim should referee, 'on
the spot', all disputes about posts, couriers, agents and other
resources.[4]

Drake's proposals cut out Folkestone, direct communication
between agents and Paris – Bruce's idea – would cut out The Hague.
Drake's authority was needed if reports were to be sent straight from
the network chiefs to Rue St Roch and Cameron would have to
agree. This was awkward. Drake had diminished Cameron's authority
and he did not like it. Kirke had supported him but Drake was less
sympathetic. He could not stand him, he told a colleague, and would
never have employed him, had he not inherited him from Kirke.[5]

Cameron was possessive and obsessional. He was already fussing
Bruce about the budget for the Paris Office. From the Folkestone
office, No. 8 The Parade, he asked for accounts and supporting
invoices. Why the expenditure on curtains (200 francs) and gas-fires
(548 francs, 15 centimes for installation)? The weather was arctic,
they told him, and the office not run extravagantly. The lease (225
francs a month) was for six months, renewable, in case the operation had to close at short notice, typewriter hire only 15 francs for
half a year. Maison B. Maurice, from which Woolrych had got the
furniture (460 francs), had agreed to buy it back at half price at the
end of the war.[6]

And now Bruce had produced these fanciful ideas: 'Why not
use the post?' Cameron refused point-blank. Letters were too slow
and irregular. Ask agents to identify constituted units? They could
not be taught to distinguish trains with sufficient accuracy.
Cameron's twitchiness was understandable, for, if things went
wrong, agents died and the service was damaged. But he had no
sense of proportion and could not entertain suggestions that challenged his experience. Like his father, he was better at active service
than at administration. In the first year of the war, when he had
been working in the field, slipping into Channel ports, lurking in
smoky backstreet cafés in Holland and France, Cameron had been
ready to try all sorts of schemes. His foreign colleagues respected
him; to Wallner and Mage he was 'Oncle Edouard'. With his
compatriots it was a different story. Cameron was proud and

mistrustful. He was not prepared to discuss the proposals from the Paris Office.

Bruce was not deterred. If he could try just one operation, he might be able to persuade Cameron to change his mind. Flanders was out of the question. The inhabitants of the *Etappengebiet* were allowed to send and receive nothing but *cartes-messages*, no more than twice a month. Belgium? Letters could be got in and out but the division of the country between MI 1(c) and I(b) was a complication and in I(b)'s half 'Peg Leg' Wallinger was in charge. Belgium was not promising for an experiment that was meant to win Cameron over. Germany was ruled out. No post came from there. There was one other possibility: Luxembourg.

The Grand Duchy of Luxembourg sat at the centre of a web of railway lines. I(b) knew that the marshalling yard at the central station was a key junction, from which trains from Germany and Russia were directed to various sections of the Western Front. In late 1915 Cameron had suggested that a Belgian agent, Afchain, active in Liège, should start a Luxembourg network.* Kirke had said no, on the grounds that it would be difficult for I(b) to supervise such an operation at such a distance.** Shortly afterwards, in the dividing-up, Luxembourg had been allocated to the SSB.

For years the Grand Duchy had been marched over by one army after another, its people pulled this way and that, subjects not so much of a state as of a geographical expression. Since 1839, when the French-speaking part of the Duchy had split away and joined up with Belgium, German influence had become all-pervasive. The railway network was an example. A French-owned company, the *Guillaume/Luxembourg Société de l'Est*, had constructed lines

---

* Afchain may have been a member of the family that had invented and manufactured – '*Afchain seul inventeur*' – the hard peppermints, Bêtises de Cambrai, issued as part of French troops' rations.
** Kirke had also doubted Afchain's efficiency. He told Cameron to move him to Holland, where the French might want to use him. 'If Wallner would take over Afchain so much the better,' Kirke wrote, 'but in any case he should clear out of Liège and Germany.' Kirke, Diaries, 13 December 1915. In February 1916 Afchain's instructions to one of his train-watchers were intercepted. The observer, Lambrecht, was caught, tortured and shot; he betrayed no one, but Afchain's network had to be disbanded.

running north–south and east–west, to exploit important coal and steel works on the Saar and in Alsace-Lorraine. In 1872, after the Franco-Prussian War, management of the lines had been transferred to Germany. The railway was a vital tool for commerce and industry – and for war. By 1909 the network had been extended between Luxembourg and Longwy, a link for the carriage of German traffic – military traffic – towards the Meuse and into France.

The German army marched into Luxembourg on 2 August 1914. (A tentative incursion on the previous day was a mistake, notification of a twelve-hour postponement having failed to arrive.) Marie-Adélaïde sent an enquiring telegram to the Kaiser, *gendarmes* tried to block the road, and a protest, hurriedly drafted by the President of the Council of Ministers, Monsieur Eyschen, was presented to the officer in charge of a German armoured train that had drawn into the station. (The officer signed for the document but the train remained.) To no avail. Luxembourg had only the 188 men of the Company of Volunteers, making up the honour guard and the royal band, and as many *gendarmes*. By teatime on the 2nd, Germany controlled the whole country. The Kaiser and his supreme command set up headquarters there, en route to France. The frontier was closed, surveillance tightened, censorship introduced. As a concession the invaders declared that the elected government could continue to manage the Grand Duchy's internal affairs. Landlocked Luxembourg had been comprehensively embraced by its powerful neighbour. The War Office and the Foreign Office thought of it as monolithically German. As far as they were concerned, the Grand Duchy was infertile ground for allied military intelligence; the complications of history had left its inhabitants without the 'moral cohesion' necessary for resistance.*

In the Paris Office they were not so sure. The people of the Grand Duchy spoke, variously, French, German, Luxembourgeois, Walloon. Some Luxembourgers took their politics from Germany, half a day away on one side of the country, others from France, half a day away on the other. History suggested that cultural and linguistic

---

* At Christmas 1914 there was much agonized discussion in London as to the propriety, in the circumstances, of the King's sending the Grand Duchess his customary New Year telegram. The greetings were not sent.

divisions ran deep. Levers could surely be inserted between the cracks. Captain Bruce came from a family whose line descended from Robert the Bruce, King of Scots, who had overcome the English six centuries before, and he knew that the citizens of a small country do not generally like being ordered about by a bigger neighbour. He wanted to know more of the Grand Duchy, its people – and its railways.

5

Miraculous Arrival of
Father Cambron

On 4 February the temperature in Paris dropped to minus fifteen Centigrade. Windowpanes were frosted on the inner side, pavements were treacherous. At No. 41 everything froze: cans of water for coffee, tea and washing, the cat's milk. Breath became visible. Miss Done and Mademoiselle Dorgebray struggled with gloved fingers at the typewriter keys. Bruce, Campbell and Chocqueel were lucky to have thick socks and greatcoats. Battle was impossible; at the front, officers and men kept themselves up to the mark by forming reconnaissance and raiding parties. The air was crystalline, the moon too bright, as they crept across no man's land, wrestling to cut the tangled wire, pliers and freezing barbs sticking to the skin.

War devoured the country. Blockades and shortages reduced supplies. Granaries, dairies and abattoirs in the occupied countries were emptied to feed the enemy. The local population eked out what remained. Starvation in Belgium and Flanders was averted only by a massive relief effort, largely funded from America.* Zealous bureaucrats made things worse. To neaten their fields, people were told to remove cow-pats and level molehills. Hens and eggs could not be moved without authorization.[1] Useless mouths being burdensome, proclamations were posted, announcing that the old, ill and infirm, and young children with their mothers would be allowed to leave. Evacuees were taken by train to Germany, quarantined to give time for information about the occupied zone to become out of date, and

---

* Devised by Herbert Hoover, Head of the Commission for Relief in Belgium, later US Food Administrator, and, after the Armistice, Allied Director of Relief and Rehabilitation. Secretary of Commerce to two American presidents, he was himself elected President of the United States, 1928–32.

then sent south through Switzerland to France. They were forbidden to leave trains when they stopped at stations, but in Switzerland food and water were handed in to them by the Red Cross. Trains crossed the frontier at Annemasse, where evacuees were allowed to disembark. Released from German supervision, refugees and *rapatriés* were registered by the *Direction du Contrôle*. As the queues moved forward, they were scrutinized by representatives of the allied secret services. Among these was Lieutenant Julian Fuller, I(b)'s man in Evian, looking for refugees and *rapatriés* for the Paris Office. Sooner or later, Chocqueel now suggested, '*un jour ou l'autre*', a candidate would turn up from Luxembourg.

Chocqueel knew an official in the French Foreign Office, Charles Jubert, with an interest in the movement of evacuees. Before the war Jubert, a Luxembourger, had been attached to the office of Armand Mollard, French Minister in Luxembourg and, when the Grand Duchy was invaded, he had accompanied Mollard to Paris. At the beginning of March Jubert told Chocqueel that a convoy was expected to reach Annemasse on the 8th, bringing people from towns near the Luxembourg border. On the evening in question Chocqueel and Campbell mixed with the watchers at Annemasse, keeping their distance from Fuller, who was known.

As the evacuees left the train, Chocqueel caught sight of a man of about thirty, serious and ascetic. Chocqueel, educated by Jesuits, thought he might be a Jesuit priest. Within minutes they had established '*la confiance la plus aimable*'. Yes, Chocqueel's new acquaintance was a Jesuit. Wonderfully, he had come from Luxembourg. In August 1914, he explained, he had been a patient at a clinic in the Marché aux Poissons in Luxembourg. Despite immediate and repeated applications to the local commandant, General Tessmar, he had not been allowed to go home to France. Eventually, however, Tessmar had concluded that if the priest stayed any longer he would become a focus of disaffection and that it was better to expel him. The German Chief of Police had been instructed to produce a visa, with conditions. Cambron could go to Switzerland but no further. He was asked to give his word of honour that he would not move on to France.

Curious though it might be to make such a pledge to the

representative of an occupying power that had broken all treaties, guarantees and agreements, Cambron had given his word and a German policeman had escorted him out of Luxembourg. Along the way they had met the convoy of evacuees and, to save himself the trouble of continuing, the escort had put Cambron with the others on the train and told him to get out in Switzerland. But the officers in charge insisted that no one could get off until the train reached the French border. Cambron had been obliged to breach his undertaking, but temporarily, for he intended to stay in Evian only while the French Minister of the Interior considered his case. If the Minister could give him a permit to return to Switzerland, he would be able to keep his promise to the Germans. Meanwhile, here he was, available to answer questions.

German military trains, Father Cambron said, were constantly moving through Luxembourg. He was sure that most of the railway staff were pro-French and that train-watchers might easily be recruited. Infiltrating an agent into the Grand Duchy might be done in various ways. Although the Germans inspected the passports of everyone entering or leaving, they were less strict with some travellers than with others. Citizens of neutral countries went in and out more easily, representatives of Swiss metal-working concerns, for instance, whose knowledge was necessary for the continuing operation of the steel industry. A person claiming to be, say, a chemist or an engineer might bluff his way in. From Switzerland travellers to Luxembourg had to go via Germany, which was risky, but the Belgian frontier was less tightly controlled.

Once in Luxembourg, an agent should be able to move about reasonably freely. Neither the Luxembourgers themselves nor foreigners, 'even French', Cambron said, needed identity cards or permits; controls were looser than in Belgium and in the *Etappengebiet*. Permission was not required to change one's place of residence. Movement of workers essential to the economy was regulated but its management left to the local Luxembourg police. Cambron was sure that, given good cover, an outsider who knew the country would be able to live there undetected.

He suggested that, if they wanted to find an agent with legitimate business in Luxembourg, his new friends should consult three people whom he could recommend. One was Monsieur d'Hannoncelles, who had taken over as acting consul when Mollard was recalled to France in August 1914. A devout Catholic, he was close to Father Cambron. D'Hannoncelles was being watched by the German authorities but, Cambron knew, this did not prevent his corresponding with Mollard in code. Another was Monsieur de Gargan, one of the chief managers of the Hayange steelworks in Lorraine, d'Hannoncelles' brother-in-law and French by birth. De Gargan lived in the Château de Rodemack in France, just across the Luxembourg border, but when the Germans had invaded the Grand Duchy he had been forbidden to return until hostilities ended and for the present was residing in Lausanne. The Allies could trust him; one of his relations by marriage was a major in the Royal Sussex Regiment, another a captain in the RFC. Cambron could give Chocqueel a letter to de Gargan, asking him to introduce Chocqueel to his third recommendation, Monsieur Mollard at the French Foreign Ministry. The Paris Office already knew Mollard through Charles Jubert. An independent introduction from de Gargan would enable them to test Cambron's credentials.

Cambron also gave names of several potential train-watchers, some of whom lived close to the Luxembourg main station. The Grand Duchess was not universally popular and anti-German officials might be prepared to supply false papers. As for himself, Cambron would let Chocqueel know what the Minister of the Interior decided. If he were able to keep his bargain and return to Switzerland, he could join the game himself.

Here were the makings of a network. Armed with Cambron's letter, Chocqueel went to Lausanne to find de Gargan. By mid-March he was back at 41 Rue St Roch with de Gargan's introduction to Mollard and the names of various Luxembourg nationals in France. It was not de Gargan, however, who was to become the pivot of the Luxembourg operation. The person Bruce wanted was already in Paris.

6

Rose and Réséda

At No. 137 Rue d'Alésia, a substantial house in Montparnasse, Madame Camille Rischard was staying with her cousin, Madame Vanvers. She had been there for weeks and longed to go home to Luxembourg. Madame Rischard had a son, Marcel, her only child, born during her first marriage to a Frenchman, one Pelletier.* When the war started Marcel was studying in Paris, and in the summer of 1916 he had sent word to his mother, asking to see her before he was ordered to the front. Madame Rischard had applied to the German commandant in Luxembourg for a pass to travel to Switzerland and from there she had crossed into France. When she arrived in Paris, she found that her son had not been mobilized. The consequences of Marcel's summons were to be far-reaching.

France and Germany had by that time adopted the system of Permit Offices and, during Madame Rischard's stay in Paris, new regulations had been introduced. To go back to Switzerland she needed a visa. The French authorities refused to give her one, particularly when they discovered that she intended to go on to Luxembourg, a route that would take her through Germany. How were they to know that she would not give away sensitive information once she had left French soil? Madame Rischard appealed directly to the former French Minister in Luxembourg, Armand Mollard, who knew her from his posting in the Grand Duchy. Madame Rischard also had a family connection with Mollard's

---

* Marcel was good at sports and in 1912 had been a member of the French team at the Olympic Games in Stockholm. His achievements had not been glorious: thirty-first out of forty in throwing the discus – although it was the best French score – and eighteenth out of twenty-two in putting the shot.

colleague, Consul d'Hannoncelles, through the consul's brother-in-law, Monsieur de Gargan.

Each time that Madame Rischard called at the Quai d'Orsay, Mollard regretted that he could not help her but that she should not hesitate to call again. When she did, he told her that, alas, as yet nothing could be done. Madame Rischard began to think that she would never see Luxembourg again. In January 1917 her father died. Settling his estate was complicated and she was even more anxious to return. Then Mollard announced that he had a solution.

This was in mid-March, just after Chocqueel returned from Lausanne. When Madame Rischard arrived at the Quai d'Orsay, strangers awaited her. They were not immediately visible. Mollard – did he enjoy this theatricality? – pulled aside a heavy curtain and opened a door. Imagine Madame Rischard's astonishment. Two officers presented themselves; to reassure her, they were in uniform. Their names were as charming as they were unlikely: Campbell was introduced as 'Réséda', 'mignonette', Bruce as 'Rose'.* They must have been confident that she would not betray them: then and there, they came to the point.

They were British. Would she help them?

Madame Rischard was appalled. Respectable persons regarded the world of intelligence with distaste, if they thought about it at all. Agents were professional deceivers and espionage was despicable.

What did they want her to do? The officers produced a message, written on thin tissue, rolled into a ball. Would she take this to Luxembourg? She could conceal it in her ear. This was dreadful. Madame Rischard thought of the risk and not just to herself. She refused to do anything of the kind. The officers were persistent. Would she reflect on it? A visa could be provided.

For months Madame Rischard had sought the means to go home. The opportunity had come but the price was high. Agitated, unhappy, she made her way back to Rue d'Alésia. While she was out, the maid told her, two gentlemen had called. They had been shown into the

---

* 'Rose' was an ancient and unsubtle code-name for a spy, the rose being the sign of secrecy (as in *sub rosa*) and, crowned with laurel, the insignia of the Intelligence Corps. Curiously, Louis Aragon took these flowers as the theme of a poem, *La Rose et le Réséda*, written to encourage resistance in the Second World War.

salon. There they were: Rose and Réséda. Again they asked for her assistance. Again she said no.

How could they have expected anything else? Lise Rischard was forty-nine, her society conventional. She was a person of undisputed propriety and good family. Mollard knew its history: her father, Jean Meyer, an industrial chemist, was one of those who had brought prosperity to Luxembourg and Lorraine. In the late 1870s Meyer had secured for his firm, Metz et Cie, the exclusive licence for local use of the newly discovered dephosphorization process, enabling Luxembourg to exploit huge deposits of iron ore. Until that time the country had been so impoverished that half its menfolk had regularly left to look for work in America. Prospects had been transformed in agriculture as well as industry, the extracted phosphates being used to fertilize formerly unproductive land. In the Grand Duchy the Meyer family was respected for its modesty and philanthropy. But espionage? That would be another thing entirely.

A more unlikely agent could hardly be imagined – but, if Madame Rischard could be recruited, she would be a great prize. No disguise would be necessary for her cover was already complete: a Luxembourg housewife, of impeccable reputation, immersed in the routine of domestic life. And her husband would be as valuable as his wife. In 1900 the former Madame Pelletier, had married into another well-regarded Luxembourg family, the Rischards. Her husband's father, at one time Minister of Public Building and Works, had been commemorated by a representation of his head, in stone, mounted on the front of Luxembourg's main railway station. It was of this station that Bruce and his colleagues had been thinking.

They had fixed on the marshalling yard, halting-place for trains from the east, en route to Belgium and France, and from the west, to Germany and Russia. The railwaymen who managed the yard belonged to a close-knit community; many had worked together for years. A nod, a gesture, was all that was required to orchestrate the lifting and lowering of the heavy levers in the signal-boxes. The railwaymen were on duty at all hours and out in all weathers. Accidents and illness were not uncommon and, to deal with them, the railway company employed a medical adviser.

Circumstances had presented the Paris Office with the means to reach him. The medical adviser to the Luxembourg Railway Company was none other than Dr Camille Rischard, husband of the woman Bruce and Campbell were now pursuing. If Dr Rischard's services could be secured, he would be the ideal intermediary. He knew the railwaymen and was trusted by them. He saw them regularly, unhindered, and talked to them in private.

Finding Madame Rischard had been an unimaginable piece of good fortune. Marcel Pelletier's desire to see his mother; her despair when she found herself stranded in Paris; the instinct that had persuaded Jubert and Mollard to introduce her to the British officers; the laziness of the escort who had abandoned Father Cambron en route to Switzerland; the quickwittedness of Chocqueel that led him to the priest: all these threads had woven themselves together. Luxembourg was the place for the espionage operation, Madame Rischard was available for training. But would Bruce and Campbell be able to recruit her? And, if so, would she be able to enlist her husband?

When Madame Rischard next called at the Quai d'Orsay, Rose and Réséda were there. They asked her a third time, a fourth. Still she resisted. Did the officers dislike their task? Too courteous and too wise to bully her, they tempted her to do something she was afraid to do and that she thought might be wrong. Madame Rischard knew that, forty years before, when her father and Emile Metz had travelled to London to obtain the licence for the steel-making process, they had used secret channels to outwit their German rivals, hot on their heels. What she was now being asked to do was infinitely more dangerous but was there any moral difference?*

Rose and Réséda continued to press. The more Bruce reasoned with Madame Rischard, the more he knew that this intelligent, unyielding woman was the agent he wanted.

---

* Some experts said there was. A key requirement in the doctrine on which the Hague Conventions of 1899 and 1907 were based was that both the occupying power and the inhabitants of occupied territory should behave 'honourably'.

7

Stiff Tests for Madame Rischard

During February 1917, losses of allied merchant ships almost doubled. If German submarine warfare continued on this scale, Britain would be unable to survive. The British Expeditionary Force would collapse, cut off from reinforcements, munitions and supplies; at home people would starve. In the spring General Nivelle, newly appointed French Commander-in-Chief, had declared that a massed attack along the River Aisne would end the war in forty-eight hours.* Haig thought Nivelle's confidence misplaced. He advocated an offensive to break the German hold on the northern sector of the Western Front and recapture Ostend and Zeebrugge, used as a base for assaults on allied transports and warships in the Channel. To argue the case, GHQ needed intelligence about enemy positions in Belgium.

It was not immediately forthcoming. The seizure of the *Brussels* in mid-1916 had brought great trouble to the allied intelligence effort in Belgium and the north of Holland. Reports captured from the steamer had allowed the Germans to identify a number of Belgian train-watchers; interceptions and arrests led to the breakdown of one of Cumming's principal networks in Belgium and the severing of links with associates in Holland. In Rotterdam, meanwhile, Tinsley's espionage connections had been exposed by a Dutch newspaper – this was in June 1916 – and the Germans had demanded his expulsion

* He had replaced General Joffre as French Commander-in-Chief in mid-December 1916. At the end of that year, Lloyd George, former Minister of Munitions and Secretary of State for War, had ousted Asquith as Prime Minister. Making no secret of his antipathy towards Haig, whom he held responsible for the slaughter on the Somme, he manoeuvred with the French to give Nivelle overall command, subordinating Haig.

from Holland. Cumming had allowed him to remain but Tinsley's increased vulnerability hampered the service. The Intelligence Staff at GHQ did not trust Tinsley. His reputation was not improved by his attempts to block Sigismund Payne Best, sent to Holland by I(b) in early 1917 to set up a service for Wallinger. Best had been offered a room on the floor above Tinsley's own office in Rotterdam but was warned by a junior colleague, from naval intelligence, that all telephone calls and letters would be monitored by his host. When Best was assailed in the street by a man with a cosh, this same naval officer explained that Tinsley had commissioned the attack.

The operations run by the Intelligence Staff were more successful. In late 1916 Wallinger's principal Belgian agent, van Tichelen, had approached a priest, Father Buelens, a friend of Cardinal Mercier, Archbishop of Malines, ecclesiastical capital of Belgium.* Mercier had encouraged his countrymen to resist the German occupiers; his priest's sympathies were the same. Assisted by van Tichelen, Father Buelens, code-name 'Lux', had set up a train-watching service, based in Antwerp; his brother, Father René Buelens, had organized a second, at Malines. Other agents were recruited for posts on railway lines serving Brussels and Mons. The network was tightly managed, reliable and efficient. Reports from eleven network chiefs, including the Buelens brothers, were sent to Wallinger every week, brought by bargemen or taken by *passeurs* across the electrified fence. But the canal route was slow, crossing the fence too dangerous, and the reports, careful and comprehensive though they were, had been prepared by civilians who had no means of knowing which observations to include and which to leave out. By the time the Lux reports reached GHQ and relevant intelligence had been extracted, the information that the Buelenses' network had so bravely supplied was often superseded.

Bruce was determined to try his Luxembourg scheme but, if Madame Rischard were to agree to work, her training had to start immediately. German forces might be already on the move, bringing up reinforcements for battle in the spring. Authority to move the Luxembourg project forward had to be obtained with the utmost

---

* Mechelen in Flemish. It is halfway between Brussels and Antwerp.

speed. So far Bruce had said nothing to Folkestone. If Cameron had known what was being planned, he might have forbidden it. He could not be kept in the dark – inquiries would be made about the allocation of funds for unapproved expenses – but asking for permission might delay the whole enterprise. Cameron might go to the Head of the Intelligence Staff. It would be a nuisance if Charteris were to be drawn into the discussion: while committees deliberated, Madame Rischard might change her mind.* Bruce decided to approach Drake directly. In late March he asked him to approve the installation of a train-watching service in Luxembourg.

Drake did not veto the idea but his reply, stamped SECRET, was lukewarm: 'I have obtained the consent of all persons interested in the establishment of this service, in view of the fact that nobody has up to now been able to get posts there.'[1] He had consulted Cameron, who was not pleased that Bruce had gone above his head. Helpful though it was to have Drake's blessing, Bruce needed something more precise. Which lines in Luxembourg would I(b) like to be watched? Drake consulted Folkestone. Additional posts would be useful, Cameron replied, if they were in Belgium. He cited a memorandum prepared by French Intelligence: schemes south of Belgium would be premature.[2] One day, 'ultérieurement', observers might be posted along more distant lines but not yet. Only in extraordinary circumstances – 'des circonstances extraordinaires' – would it be possible to establish regular and uninterrupted links so far away. It was difficult enough to handle reports coming from Belgium and Holland. Why trouble with the Grand Duchy, hundreds of miles from the front, on the other side of the Ardennes?

Bruce knew that Madame Rischard and her connections offered an opportunity that it would be irresponsible to ignore. A sketch of the Luxembourg railway network might do the trick. 'It would perhaps help matters,' he suggested to Drake, 'if you could very

---

* The Head of the Intelligence Staff was one of those who had worked to restore Cameron's reputation. Charteris had been delighted when Cameron received the DSO in January 1917. 'He has done extraordinarily good work for the Secret Service, but there were many difficulties in getting him rewarded.' Brigadier-General Sir John Charteris, At GHQ, London: Cassell, 1931, a memoir based on his own records of each day's events.

kindly have the through routes marked on it, as well as any other point at which observation would be useful.'[3] Inking in the lines would show GHQ that the Luxembourg marshalling yard was a place to watch. When the drawing came back to Rue St Roch, railway lines in Luxembourg had been marked up. Drake's reply was terse: 'I return sketch map.'[4] It was enough.

As Madame Rischard walked about Paris, anxious and despairing, she found herself passing the Madeleine. She was not a believer but the great church drew her in. At least she would be able to sit down; her nights had been troubled and she was exhausted. She could not decide what to do and there was no one in whom to confide. As her eyes became accustomed to the gloom, she began to make out the shapes beyond the flickering candles. Confessionals: each a curtained refuge. She found one with a priest, unseen, anonymous, on the other side of the screen. A priest, like a doctor, was a keeper of secrets.

She took her place.

This was the moment when all the hopes of Bruce and Campbell might have been cast adrift.

'What should I do?' she asked the priest.

'Are you a Frenchwoman?'

'I became a Frenchwoman when I married my first husband.'

He was unequivocal.

'Not only may you work with our Allies' Secret Service. As a Frenchwoman it is your duty.'

No one overheard the low-voiced conversation. No one met her gaze. The nave was filled with murmuring and whispers, the air with incense and beeswax. If the priest was not a spy, she was safe.*

From the Madeleine it was twenty minutes' walk to the Foreign Ministry. Behind the Quai d'Orsay rose the golden dome of St Louis-des-Invalides, the soldiers' church. Beneath the dome was Napoleon's tomb. It was said that, when his coffin was opened, they found the Emperor's body, nineteen years dead, perfectly preserved.[5]

'As a Frenchwoman, it is your duty.'

When she saw the officers, she said yes.

---

* Madame Rischard told this story to her nephew in 1940. Did the officers ever know?

It was the beginning of April. Drake's reply had arrived, *circonstances extraordinaires* had coalesced. Now Bruce told Madame Rischard exactly what he had in mind. They wanted her to recruit her husband. Together the Rischards were to set up a network of train-watchers in the marshalling yard and along the lines leading from the station. Through Dr Rischard, she would be responsible for managing these observers. What was wanted, above all, was news of 'constituted units' travelling through Luxembourg to the Western Front. Information was to be coded and 'Réséda' would teach her how to do it. Her reports were to be sent to Paris by a route they would explain. Messages from Paris would tell her whether her reports were reaching them, give instructions and, if anything unexpected happened, warn her. Funds would be provided for payment and expenses.

If only she could think it over. She asked for time:

Monsieur le Capitaine,
La mission que vous voulez bien me confier . . .
The mission you wish to entrust to me is so heavy with responsibility and in its implications that I beg you to give me a few days for reflection before I take my preparation any further.[6]

The request, sent through the Parisian air-pumped letter-delivery service, came from one new to spying. Madame Rischard sent her '*pneumatique*' to Captain Bruce at 41 Rue St Roch, signed it and put her name and address on the outer cover. The new recruit clearly needed instruction in the techniques of secure communication – and she must be given a code-name at once. She could have all the time she needed, Bruce told her, but from now on they would address her, and she must describe herself, as 'Madame Léonard'.

Four days later she was ready.

Remembering the code-name was the least of it. There was much for her to learn. She had to be able to recognize German uniforms and insignia, transport and weapons, to identify every type of train and its components, to understand all letters, symbols and numbers on carriages and wagons. Monthaye undertook this part of Madame Rischard's education. He was used to coaching civilians, and in the fifth-floor schoolroom at Rue Soufflot were materials to help her make sense of this strange curriculum. Every day she made her way from Rue d'Alésia to Rue Soufflot. It was a steep haul up to the schoolroom and soon, she said, she knew each tread by heart. The cracks in the wall became old friends, greeting her as she climbed past unremarkable doors, long-established cobwebs and – a reminder that ordinary students had used this place – a sign taken in fun from the side of a No. 8 bus and strung up over the stairwell. 'Porte d'Orléans': the service for her own *arrondissement*.

Lists of German regiments, ranks and formations were given her to memorize. She was shown railway networks, silhouettes of trains, drawings of weapons. Round the room were Woolrych's tailors' dummies, displaying bits and pieces of uniform collected from prisoners of war and from the fallen. Was it from dead men's pockets that her tutors had obtained the handbooks she was required to study? One, a teaching device for the German army, included a compendium of technical terms in French and English, with German equivalents. '*Nur für Dienstgebrauch*', said a warning on the cover: 'For Service Use Only'. Madame Rischard was now a member of the Service, though not the one the authors had in mind.

Before Woolrych left for his new post in Switzerland, he looked out the questions with which he and Monthaye had tested the first recruits. Madame Rischard now addressed herself to his examination paper.

UNIFORMS

1. Give the most important characteristics in identifying units from uniforms.
2. Give the details of the uniforms of the most common units, infantry, artillery etc.
3. Describe the colours of the cocades of as many states as you can remember.*
4. Ditto for monograms.
5. Give any signs of uniforms which shew whether an unit is active, reserve, or landwehr.**

---

* The kingdoms and city states of the German empire. 'Cocades' is a typing error for the English word 'cockades'. (In French, '*cocardes*'.)
** Soldiers of the Austrian national army. Spelling and grammar here are as in the original text.

6. Describe a typical landwehr uniform.
7. Give all the signs you know of shoulder straps which at once indicate which army an unit belongs to.

There were dozens of cockades, some with gay embellishments, others with death's heads of ominous appearance, a ghastly study for a peaceable, middle-aged woman.[7]

Weapons:

MACHINE GUNS

1. Describe fully Machine Gun organization in the German Army, with details of the uniform of each different Machine Gun unit.
2. Which are the identifications in Machine Gun Corps Units which are of most value?

TRENCH MORTAR

1. Describe in detail Trench Mortar organization in the German Army, with details of the uniform of each unit.
2. Which are the most important Trench Mortar units from the point of view of identification?

By day Madame Rischard studied with Monthaye; by night she dreamt of bayonets and howitzers, of spectral *Alpenjägern*, water bottles and ice axes attached to their rucksacks, of *Uhlans* and *Attila Hussars*.* Flame-throwers and thunder-flashes illuminated her sleep; *Minen, glatte 150 mm.-Böller* transformed themselves into *mortiers Louis-Philippe*.

Then there were the constituted units.

CONSTITUTED UNIT

Describe exactly what a train carrying a constituted unit looks like. Approximately how many such trains go to a division? Draw a chart shewing the composition of a normal German infantry and cavalry division, giving all the names of the units with their organizations which go to make up a division.

---

* *Alpenjägern* were mountain troops, *Uhlans* were lancers, and *Attila Hussars* cavalrymen wearing the single-breasted grey tunics known as *Attilas*.

Give approximately the number of men in each unit.

Artillery:
How can field guns be distinguished from any other sort of guns?
Give a list of all the most common guns and howitzers with a short description of each and the means of distinguishing the one from the other at sight.
In describing guns and howitzers of the same calibre, what are the most important points to consider in order to distinguish the absolute indication of the gun or howitzer?
What useful information can be obtained from Range Tables?

Infantry:

FOOT ARTILLERY

Describe in detail the organization of Foot Artillery in the German Army, and explain what is required from the point of view of identifications.
Besides the actual movement of troops, what other information is of value?

And for good measure:

Describe the depôt system in Germany.

This was not Madame Rischard's only task. Campbell had devised a code, whose intricacies and manipulations needed hours of practice. Where was she to find a quiet place to study? She could hardly spend whole days in Rue Soufflot and her lodgings in Rue d'Alésia had nowhere to hide secret papers. There was another complication. Bruce and Campbell had to be able to visit her but repeated calls at Rue d'Alésia would endanger her hosts and betray the project. If she came to Rue St Roch, her cover and that of the Permit Office would be as good as gone. Rented rooms would not do. Parisian *concierges* were notoriously vigilant. What would a hawk-eyed doorkeeper think of an unchaperoned woman, receiving men at a place where she did not live? It would be unhelpful if Madame Rischard were to be embarrassed.

A refuge was found: Miss Done's apartment. Bruce and Campbell could come and go by one of two entrances to the courtyard, from Rue de Moscou or via Rue de Clapeyron, an alley busy with cab drivers, black marketeers, commercial travellers, encyclopaedia salesmen.* No questions would be asked. The *concierge* who presided over the Rue de Moscou entrance, Madame Aviez, was discreet and had good relations with her counterpart at No. 15 on the Rue de Clapeyron side. Part of No. 38 was occupied by a *fournisseur des dames* and it would be quite natural for a well-dressed, respectable-looking woman to be coming regularly to the house. Anyone who noticed the gentlemen who came and went would be encouraged to assume that they were friends of the Englishwoman in the fourth-floor apartment and that their visits were connected with the running of the Parcel Fund. From Rue d'Alésia it required only one change to get to Rue de Moscou by bus or métro. On the afternoon of 18 May Madame Rischard collected a key from Madame Aviez and prepared for Rose and Réséda to test her on her work.

Campbell's code had already been refined three times. Madame Rischard had spent the last days of April trying to understand it and, having learnt it by heart, had been presented with an improved version. Memorizing this, she had been given another. Forgetting what she had already learnt was as difficult as remembering each variation. Campbell had explained that, as well as being straightforward to operate, the code had to fulfil other important criteria. In the first place, it had to produce ordinary sentences with a plausible meaning, so innocuous that no one would give them a second glance.** Parsimony was the second requirement. The code must enable a great deal of matter to be compressed into very few lines. Long and cumbersome compositions were not wanted. Third, the code must allow Madame Rischard's reports to be conveyed in whatever language was necessary to send them through to Paris. To do this, the code had to have its own dictionary and grammar. It must not matter whether the mother tongue of the person using it was French, English or German. Being able to shift easily out of one language into another would not

---

* Runaways, too, according to the daughter-in-law of the *concierge*: '*le passage . . . a permis à toutes sortes de gens en 1914 de s'esquiver – disparaîtres, taxis, voleurs, bandits, marchés noirs, colporteurs d'encyclopédies . . . etc.*'
** Like Edgar Allan Poe's 'Purloined Letter', which did not attract attention because it sat with others in the letter-rack.

only save time but reduce the likelihood that text would be corrupted along the way.

Campbell, an engineer with training in mathematics, was good at simplifying complex material and expressing it algebraically. In the code he devised for Madame Rischard letters stood for concepts. 'A', for example, represented 'Name of a place or a person'; 'E', 'Movement of empty trains in a constituted unit'. Bruce, the linguist, understood that a code was not just packaging but a private language with rules for its consistent application and a vocabulary.* The two officers were a formidable combination.

Campbell's code was based on standard principles. Each concept was represented by a number from 1 to 19. A battalion, for example, was 3. Each number was matched by a corresponding letter: 1 = A, 2 = B, 3 = C, and so on. A word beginning with C thus represented 'battalion'. Some concepts were represented by zero, matched by not one but seven corresponding letters: H, K, V, W, X, Y and Z. It did not matter that there were so many, none being much used in French.

Typing the lists of concepts was an achievement in itself. On flimsy sheets Mademoiselle Dorgebray and Miss Done hammered away in French and English, pencilled additions and amendments pinned to the text. Campbell appended neatly inked catalogues of military terms, each with a code number: '14 *Fuss-Artillerie Regiment* . . . 17 *Jäger Zu Pferde* . . .' Bruce corrected his own corrections: '*Escadrons* 2, *Batteries* 1, *Divers* 4 . . . alter the order . . .' Mademoiselle Dorgebray's notes were a frantic *mélange* of French, English, numbers, shorthand and crossings-out: '. . . Tables follow . . . ~,/ (b). La ~ l contiendra aussi le ou les mots la ou les lettres en question . . .' Miss Done wrestled with the typewriter to produce a seventeen-column table, its purpose elucidated in a desperate addendum:

In spelling, letters are taken twice in the same line it beiing [here the keys jammed] understood that the lines being divided into twonparts [her fingers had slipped] the first 20 letters forming the first part and the 21st letter

---

* A fuller explanation, with examples, is given in the Appendix.

counting as the 22nd [corrected by Bruce in red pencil to 21st] letter of the 2nd part . . . The system is quite simple . . .*

It was a nightmare. On 22 May Madame Rischard sent Bruce her first exercise, with an apologetic covering letter. She was so nervous that, although she remembered to use her code-name, 'L. Léonard', she overlooked the ornamental monogram, *LR*, engraved at the top of her writing paper:

Faisant suite à ma lettre vous trouverez un des exemples donnés par vous hier mis en rédaction. Quel charabia déplorable . . .
Attached to this letter you will find one of the examples you gave me for translation yesterday. What a deplorable lot of gibberish and when you read it how you can sense the heavy and laborious effort it needed . . . Alas, Captain, it isn't easy . . . the French translation doesn't fit easily with the English key. The W s are particularly ominous and Watteau and Whisky are dreadfully awkward . . .[8]

This coded effort was in the form of a letter from one 'Jacques'. The censor would certainly have thought it peculiar. 'Jacques' was telling a friend about a journey:

<u>Une réelle</u> merveille . . .
A true marvel this panorama which <u>W</u>atteau painted so admirably, what infinite horizons! . . . Passing <u>F</u>igeac, I thought of the promised <u>w</u>hisky, I will bring several bottles . . .[9]

Underlining relevant letters in his red pencil, Bruce unveiled the message, '*un véritable tour de force*'. Campbell was delighted and so was he. Her reward: more homework.[10]

Madame Rischard was not their only pupil. Chocqueel was to be responsible for composing and coding messages to Madame Rischard from Rue St Roch. He now showed himself worthy of his title, Interpreter, as he formulated acknowledgements and instructions, straining to express himself, '*en termes apparemment aussi naturels que normaux . . .*'[11]

The code was also put through a practical examination. Test

---

* Spelling referred to the procedure by which code-letters were inserted in a particular order in a sentence, to be 'spelt out' by writer and reader.

- 5 -

Sujet

11.- OBJET 3, c'est-à-dire ENONCE C. - Secteur de ligne et deux dates.

entre deux dates / c.à.d. pour

S'il s'agit de signaler les mouvements de trains vides, de même que s'il s'agit de signaler qu'il ne s'est produit aucun mouvement d'unités constituées entre deux dates (voir instructions N°), on se sert du même moyen suivi des chiffres qui représentent :-
1.- la date où l'observation a commencé,
2.- la date où l'observation s'est terminé.

Exemple.

L'information à transmettre porte sur:
Le secteur LONGUYON - LUXEMBOURG.
L'observation a commencé le 18.
    -         s'est terminé le 22.
Le rapport est du 23.

Enoncé C   , la 1° ligne commencera par   C
LONGUYON   - 7, - 2° -   -   -   G
LUXEMBOURG - 8, - 3° -   -   -   I
Date du commencement-5, - 4° -   -   -   E
- de la fin   - 1, - 5° -   -   -   A

Sujet

12.- OBJET 4 c'est-à-dire *par* ENONCE D.- MOUVEMENT D'UNITES CONS-
TITUEES AVEC INDICATION DU NOMBRE DE TRAINS; OU BIEN SAVOIR *ABSENCE*
DE MOUVEMENT D'UNITES CONSTITUEES.

Tout

S'il s'est produit quelque mouvement d'unités constituées,
il faut le signaler jour par jour. Cette information doit être donnée immédiatement après la "phrase" qui contient
l'information annoncée par l'énoncé C. *ainsi le sujet 4 suivra toujours le sujet 3*

Les unités constituées doivent être signalées dans
l'ordre suivant qui est à retenir par coeur :-

1. Nombre de trains de bataillons d'infanterie.
2. -   -   -   -   d'escadrons de cavalerie.
3. -   -   -   -   de batteries d'artillerie.
4. -   -   -   -   de divers, en ce compris toutes les
                    autres sortes d'unités constituées de
                    même que toute unité constituée qu'elle
                    serait pas en mesure de décrire suffisam-
                    ment (voir instructions).

Pour traiter cet objet 4, il faudra toujours réserver 4
lignes pour les unités constituées ci-dessus, même s'il n'y a
qu'une de ces 4 catégories d'unités qui aura passé; cette uni-
té-là, si elle est seule, sera représentée par le chiffre qui
lui correspond, les autres par une des lettres représentant
des zéros.

Exemple.

L'information à transmettre porte sur le passage de:
15 trains transportant des bataillons.
0   -   -   -   escadrons. 2
8   -   -   -   batteries. 1   ← *alter the order.*
6   -   -   -   divers. 4

Enoncé   D   - , la 1° ligne commencera par   D
Bataillons d'infanterie - 15, la 2° ligne commencera par Q
Escadrons   - 0, la 3° -   - quel-
                    qu'une des lettres égales à 0
                    (H, K, W, X Y, Z).-
Batteries   - 8, la 4° ligne commencera par
Divers   - 6, la 5° ligne   -   F

Extract from the code, in draft, typed by the Secretariat, amended and corrected by Bruce and Campbell.

messages were exchanged with the code-breaking unit in the War Office and the code-breakers in the *Service du Chiffre*, the office in the Ministry of War in Paris run by the legendary cryptologist, Major Marcel Givierge. Experts were unable to break it.

Even Cameron approved: 'The code seems to be a good one.'[12] Bruce had sent Campbell to see him at the beginning of May to report that the Paris Office had recruited a civilian, 'Madame Léonard', of special aptitude and persistence. The visit to Folkestone had been surprisingly successful. Campbell took pains with Cameron, asking his advice about methods of summarizing and transmitting reports and his views on the location of posts. The Major was charmed by this attention. 'I think that it has been a considerable advantage to Campbell seeing all the difficulties we have about our train reports . . .' He began to speak more warmly about the Luxembourg project. He called it 'Campbell's scheme'.[13]

Cameron had been thinking of moving Campbell to Holland but changed his mind. As for Bruce, the plan agreed with the Commander-in-Chief in January had clearly been overtaken. The four months in the Paris Office had expired but this was the wrong time to send him back to the trenches. His presence in Rue St Roch was critical.

Meanwhile, as spring turned to summer, Madame Rischard applied herself to her studies. Her coding became swifter, her scripts more fluent. Mortars and machine-guns, gas and grenades: phrase by phrase she learnt the deadly vocabulary of war.

8

Appearances and Disappearances
of Baschwitz Meau

Bruce had moved from the Hôtel Wagram to 21 Rue de Surène, just west of the Madeleine and five minutes' walk from the Permit Office. One way of reaching Rue St Roch was to cut through Place du Marché St Honoré, also known as Place Anglaise. In that quiet square No. 27 was to let. The Permit Office was becoming crowded and taking a second building would not only ease the pressure but would also give somewhere to see people who were better kept away from 41 Rue St Roch. He took the rooms.

Here, on the last day of May, there arrived a letter:

Hôtel de Strasbourg　　　　　　　　　　　　　　*Paris, le 30 mai 1917*
50, Rue de Richelieu,
Entre le Louvre, l'Opéra et la Bourse,
Paris (1er)

Ascenseur – Electricité
Chauffage Central – Bains
Toilettes à Eau chaude et Eau froide
Téléphone Gutenberg 44–95

Mon Colonel,
　　D'après les indications qui m'ont été données par Monsieur Berthe, je me permets de vous adresser une demande d'incorporation dans le service du Contre-espionnage . . .

In accordance with a suggestion from Monsieur Berthe, may I send you this request to enlist in the counter-intelligence service. I am at present a sub-lieutenant, deputy to the Commandant of the Wulveringhem cantonment (Belgian army) and I would be glad to be able to lead a life that is

67

HOTEL de STRASBOURG
50, Rue de Richelieu, 50
Entre le Louvre, l'Opéra et la Bourse
PARIS (1er)

Ascenseur - Électricité
Chauffage Central - Bains
Toilettes à Eau chaude et Eau froide
Téléphone dans les Chambres

Téléphone GUTENBERG 44-95

PARIS, LE 30 mai 1917

Mon Colonel,

D'après les indications qui m'ont été données par Monsieur Berthe, je me permets de vous adresser une demande d'incorporation dans le service du Contre-espionnage.

Je suis, à présent, s/lieutenant, adjoint au Commandant du cantonnement de Wulveringhem (armée belge) et serais très désireux de pouvoir mener une existence moins monotone et plus conforme à mon tempéra-

Baschwitz Meau's first letter to Captain Bruce,

68

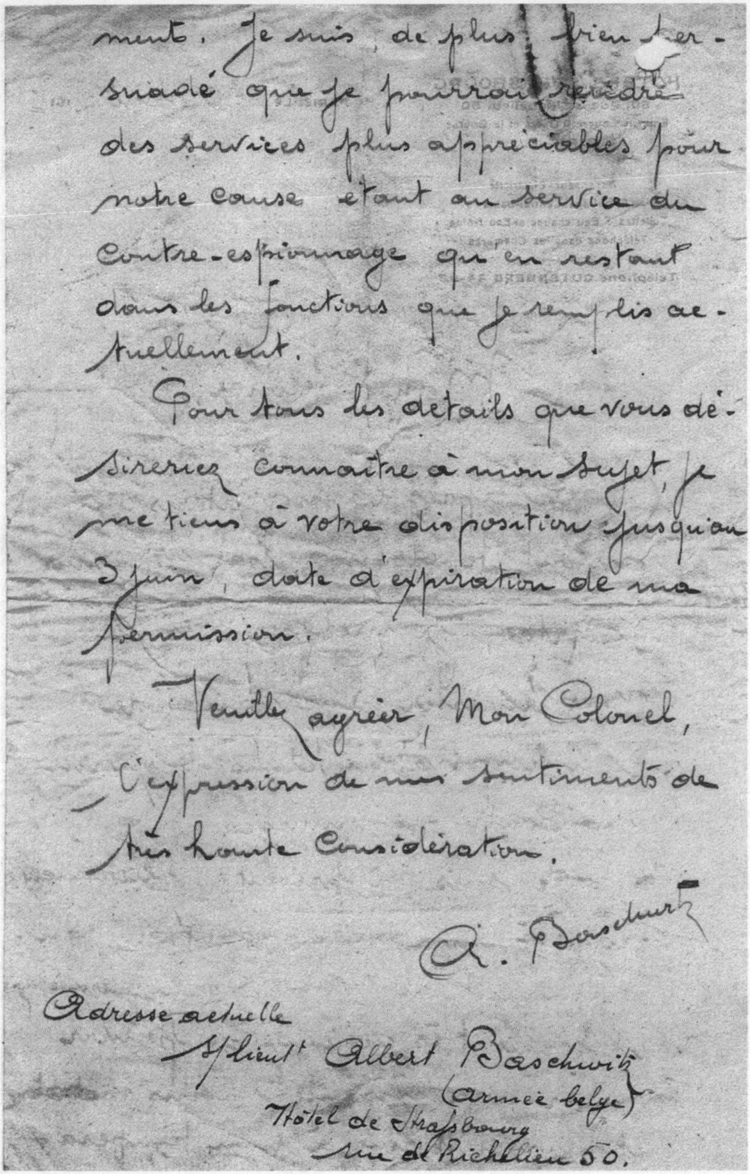

ment. Je suis, de plus, bien per-
suadé que je pourrai rendre
des services plus appréciables pour
notre cause étant au service du
Contre-espionnage qu'en restant
dans les fonctions que je remplis ac-
tuellement.

Pour tous les détails que vous dé-
sireriez connaître à mon sujet, je
me tiens à votre disposition jusqu'au
3 juin, date d'expiration de ma
permission.

Veuillez agréer, Mon Colonel,
l'expression de mes sentiments de
très haute considération.

A. Baschwitz

Adresse actuelle
S/lieut Albert Baschwitz
(armée belge)
Hôtel de Strasbourg
rue de Richelieu 50.

asking for a job in the British army's Secret Service.

less monotonous and to which my temperament is better suited. I am, moreover, convinced that in the counter-espionage service I could be of greater
use to our cause than by staying where I am. If you would like any information about my situation, I can make myself available to you until June
3rd, when my leave expires . . .

*Veuillez agréer, mon Colonel, l'expression de mes sentiments de très haute
considération.*

Then the signature, neat, with the suspicion of a flourish:

A. Baschwitz.

The document was written on good paper in an attractive italic
hand. With it came a letter of introduction, on a lined sheet, the
pen blotchy, the handwriting uneven:

Mon Colonel,
  Je suis en relations avec Monsieur le Capitaine Carr . . .
I am acquainted with Captain Carr, for whom I have been engaged on
matters connected with his service. Some time ago I was master of works
with the British engineering corps at Abbeville, which is where I became
known to Captain Carr. I now send you the attached request in the hope
that it will interest you . . .

Veuillez recevoir, mon Colonel, l'expression de mon parfait dévouement.

This letter came from the person to whom Baschwitz Meau referred:

Alfred Berthe,
128 Boulevard Ménilmontant, Paris.

Carr was a long-serving member of I(b). A. Baschwitz had been
careful to introduce himself through the right channels. Someone
had supplied the address of the new office and the name of its chief.
Not knowing Bruce's rank, the courteous Baschwitz had made him
a Colonel. The writer was obviously a well-educated man with sufficient funds to stay in a good hotel in a smart *arrondissement*.
'Baschwitz' sounded neither French nor German; he could be Russian
or Polish. How had he come to be serving with the Belgian army?
  If this Baschwitz were to be interviewed, it would have to be done
before his leave was up. On 1 June Bruce replied; on 2 June, a

Saturday afternoon, he received him at Place Anglaise, where he had a conversation so promising that he invited him to return on the following day. Bruce made a memorandum:

BASCHWITZ

BASCHWITZ, Albert, Belgian, Sous-Lieutenant Adjoint au Commandant du Cantonnement de WULVERINGHEM, (near DIXMUDE). Born 16th December 1882 at BRUSSELS of Belgian parents: Alexandre BASCHWITZ & Louise B. née MEAU. He was liberated of all military service by having drawn a good number.*

BASCHWITZ left BRUSSELS in 1901 to go to the colonies; has spent 10 years in Africa and two in South America, was with the Compagnie du Kasai, Congo Belge, (Rubber Co); returned from Africa in November 1913 to BRUSSELS where he was at the outbreak of war when he joined the Corps des Volontaires Congolais. This was a Corps raised by Colonel CHALTIN who was charged by the Ministère de la Guerre with the formation of the 'cadres'; BASCHWITZ was appointed sous-lieutenant.

He was taken prisoner with the rest of the Corps on 23rd August at NAMUR. His subsequent history is given in the attached newspaper cutting.** BASCHWITZ is very keen to be employed on a mission to Germany or invaded territory. As an escaped prisoner from Germany the authorities will not send him to the front and he finds his work at the cantonnement at WULVERINGHEM intolerably monotonous. He is unmarried, entirely independent and is confident that he could escape detection in Germany. He speaks German very fluently.

He gives as a personal reference Monsieur GODDEFROY, Inspecteur chef de groupe de la Sûreté Belge at ROUEN (*auditorat militaire*); also his cousin Monsieur Charles W. BASCHWITZ, Jesmond, Cranes Drive, SURBITON.[1]

Bruce next wrote to Captain J. H. Leche at I(b)'s office in Rouen:

I wonder whether you would be so very kind as to make a small but very confidential enquiry for me.

---

* In the years immediately prior to the Great War, conscripts in Belgium were chosen by lottery. Baschwitz Meau was not selected. At the outbreak of war, however, he volunteered, aged almost thirty-two.
** The newspaper cutting was returned to Baschwitz. His exploits as a prisoner of war are recorded below.

For your private information, I enclose a memorandum with regard to one BASCHWITZ who might possibly be of use to us. I know nothing whatever about him, except what he has told me himself and, before going further, it is important to have independent information about him. Could you possibly first find out what sort of a man GODDEFROY is and then, if he is thoroughly reliable, obtain his personal opinion of BASCHWITZ. The latter tells me that GODDEFROY knows all about him and his family.

The points I am specially interested in are of course BASCHWITZ' personal reliability and, particularly, whether he either drinks or talks too much. If he is absolutely all right in these two respects and naturally also 'au point de vue national', nothing else really matters very much.

As it is of course essential that GODDEFROY should not talk, it is preferable, from my point of view, that he should not be approached at all unless he is himself entirely to be trusted. If, however, GODDEFROY is sufficiently sound for us to act on his opinion of BASCHWITZ, he is probably sound enough for it to be safe to speak to him on the matter.

It will be a great kindness if you will do this for me.[2]

Bruce did not ask Folkestone for a report from Major Mage. Cameron was already nervous about Madame Rischard. The suggestion that a strange Belgian should be added to the Paris team might be the last straw. There was another reason for caution. If Baschwitz were to be recruited by British military intelligence, he would first have to be extracted from the Belgian army. It would not do to embarrass him at this stage by asking his seniors about his character and antecedents.

Bruce's letter to Leche suggested that he had already made up his mind about Baschwitz. Was he sober, discreet and loyal to his country? 'Nothing else really matters very much.' Bruce was already fairly certain that Baschwitz was reliable but not so certain that he could recruit him without asking for a second opinion. If Baschwitz were an enemy agent, bringing him into the Permit Office would undermine the whole Paris operation. Baschwitz had declared himself to be an escaped prisoner of war. If his captors suspected that the Parcel Fund was being used to assist prisoners to get out of German camps, they might have sent Baschwitz to Paris to investigate. Until Bruce was sure, Baschwitz must be kept away from Rue St Roch and Rue Soufflot, from Campbell, Monthaye and Chocqueel, from Miss Done and Mademoiselle Dorgebray. Above all, Madame Rischard must be protected. As far as Bruce was aware, Lise Rischard and Albert-Ernest Baschwitz Meau did not know each other. If so, there must be no accidental introduction.

Leche replied within the week:

. . . I know Goddefroy very well and have great confidence in him. He says that he has known BASCHWITZ for some 16 years, and looks on him almost as his best friend. He is, Goddefroy thinks, of Polish extraction. At all events, his people are bankers; he is a most patriotic man, with great pluck and physical strength, colossal cheek, and very 'roublard'.* He is not a man to talk, and though not an abstainer, Goddefroy says he has never seen him, or heard of him, being drunk. He says he is a man 'qui sait faire griser les autres'.** In short, a man one could have every confidence in.

If any further details are wanted, let me know.[3]

This was all Bruce required. He wrote to Baschwitz at Wulveringhem, assuring him that he was not forgotten. Sooner or later, 'tôt ou tard', an opportunity would come for him to be of service. The valediction was fine-tuned:

Recevez, Monsieur, mes salutations empressées,
G. J. G. Bruce, Capitaine.[4]

'Tôt ou tard': but how was Baschwitz to be deployed? And how was Bruce to ensure that any such arrangement would not become entangled in arguments with Cameron?

---

* 'Cunning'.
** 'Who knows how to befuddle others'.

9

Doubt and Delay

At their first meeting, Rose and Réséda had promised to help Madame Rischard to return to Luxembourg. This was difficult. Her case was complicated and as the weeks passed her position had become increasingly dangerous.

When she had applied for permission to leave Luxembourg in the summer of 1916, Madame Rischard had not told General Tessmar, the German Commandant, that she wished to go on to France, a request that would have been refused. She said only that she was needed in Lausanne to nurse her husband's aunt, Madame Auguste Fresez-Settegast. To guarantee that Madame Rischard would not leave Switzerland without authority, she had been instructed to deposit her Luxembourg passport with the German legation in Berne. The German legation being temporarily closed, the Swiss police had told her to leave her passport at the Dutch legation instead. Madame Rischard had remained for some time at Madame Fresez-Settegast's house, 33 Avenue Edouard Dapples, although 'Tante Marie' herself was not in residence. The illness had been a fiction, concocted by the two ladies to extract Madame Rischard from Luxembourg. That achieved, Madame Fresez-Settegast had left for the Waldhotel Bellary at Grindelwald.[1]

When Madame Rischard moved on to France, she had notified neither the Swiss nor the German authorities. She had asked officials at the Dutch legation for the necessary permit but she did not offer it for inspection at the Swiss frontier. It seems surprising that a sensible woman should have been so imprudent. Was it because she was in a hurry to see her son or had she not realized that in wartime travel between the countries of Continental Europe, once so easy, would eventually become impossible?

Having seen Marcel, Madame Rischard had tried to return to Lausanne, intending to go on to Luxembourg. Instead, she found herself in no man's land. The French authorities had no record of her arrival, the Swiss none of her departure. She had no passport, having left it at the Dutch legation in Berne, and no stamps on the document provided by the Dutch. It was to catch such unauthorized travellers that Kirke had introduced his Permit Office scheme. Madame Rischard had fallen between its cracks.

Mollard could do little. France might be able to give her a passport and visa on the strength of her marriage to Pelletier but this might not get her past the Swiss police at the border. Introducing Madame Rischard to Bruce and Campbell was a master-stroke. Unlike Mollard, they had ways of getting a person into Switzerland. Madame Rischard could either be smuggled in – by boat, perhaps, across Lake Geneva – or they could see her through the frontier. The first route would be more uncomfortable but the second was not without hazard. Although Campbell had friends among the Swiss frontier guards, any fuss might lead to an arrest. Bruce and Campbell had made her aware of the risk and she had accepted it.

Jubert had advised Bruce that it would be best for Madame Rischard to apply for a passport and visa in the ordinary way. At the Swiss frontier she need say only that she had come from France to look after a relation in Lausanne. Jubert would make sure that his colleagues in the Foreign Ministry understood that they were to approve Madame Rischard's application. She would be told when to collect her papers from her local *préfecture de police*; before they were handed over, a police officer from her own *quartier* would ask one or two questions to confirm her identity. In April 1917, as instructed, Madame Rischard had delivered her application to the Quai d'Orsay. Since then, she had heard nothing.

The first weeks of May were taken up with memorizing and practising the code. By the end of the month Bruce and Campbell were ready to make preparations for her departure. No word had come from the *préfecture de police*. Jubert made inquiries. At the *préfecture* they said they knew nothing about a passport. At the Quai d'Orsay the answer was the same. In any case, Jubert was reminded, the Swiss had closed the frontier to people trying to come in from

France. If an application had been received from this Madame Rischard, it would have been disregarded. Rules were rules. What was to be done? Jubert was not to blame. The middle levels of the bureaucracy were full of the self-righteous and unbending.

And not just in France. From across the Channel came a succession of impatient letters. Cameron wished to come to Paris. 'I should like to see the lady before she starts,' he declared. 'I presume this will not unduly frighten her.' He intended to be gracious but the 'not unduly' sounded ominously like the Wolf, considering how to introduce himself to Red Riding Hood.[2]

Bruce ignored the proposal. Cameron wrote again, attaching a personal message expressing displeasure. If he were not welcome in Paris, Bruce must come to Folkestone, at once, with all the paperwork relating to the Luxembourg project. Bruce had to squash the idea. If Cameron came to Paris and upset everybody, it would wreck everything. It was simply not convenient: 'I am extremely anxious to get Madame L. pushed off at the earliest possible moment. She is all ready to start as soon as her passport is granted, which should not now be long delayed; it seems better not to intervene directly to accelerate matters if it can be possibly avoided.' The closure of the frontier meant they might have to smuggle her in: 'it might be advisable to send her into Switzerland *en fraude*, which we can quite easily arrange.'[3]

He would come to Folkestone as soon as he could. He did not specify a date. Bringing the documents would be difficult. One of the dossiers Cameron wanted to see amounted to fifty folders, 'some of them bulky'. The files were in constant use. Transporting them to Folkestone was imprudent as well as impracticable, although Bruce did not say so. What if the boat were to be intercepted or sunk? That Cameron did not think of this indicates how intemperate he was becoming. He felt he was losing control of the Paris Office.

Bruce advised Madame Rischard to write again to the Quai d'Orsay, saying nothing about her earlier application. Jubert would ensure that her request was dealt with quickly and she should expect a visit from the local police within the next ten days. The Swiss had reopened the border and, all being well, she should be able to leave Paris by the middle of June. The letter in which Bruce gave this news crossed with one from Madame Rischard, written for practice in German and in code. Deciphered, it told him she was frightened, unhappy and dead tired, '*totmüde*'. For weeks she had risen early to be drilled in military vocabulary and the intricacies of the code, for a mission she found increasingly daunting. 'Too great emotions, all the sombre thoughts & the almost intolerable mental worries of the past weeks have unnerved me . . .' She would not give up but she longed for the pace to slacken.[4]

She had many fears. Would the passport ever arrive? If it did, how far would it take her? Would it stand up to scrutiny at the frontier? Would the guards believe her story? If she got into Switzerland, would she be watched en route to Lausanne? Would the Dutch legation return her Luxembourg passport? If they did, she would have to travel through Germany to get home. Once there, would she be able to do what Bruce wanted? How much easier it would be to return to being Dr Rischard's wife, looking after her household, living quietly until the war was over. Delay and uncertainty ate into her confidence. The prospect of questions from a policeman at the *préfecture* was almost too much to bear.

Would others have been as honest? Madame Rischard was prepared to admit that she was afraid; a professional soldier or a professional agent might have been too proud to do so. Bruce knew that he had to restore her morale. It would be a disaster if she gave up now. If he lost his star recruit, it was unlikely that he would be allowed to try again. Questions would be asked about his judgement and about the extent to which Madame Rischard's discretion could be relied on. She already knew too much. The Paris Office might be closed; if it were, Cameron would not be sorry.

Bruce replied at once. She need no longer worry about her passport – he had been told that her application had been approved – and she should try to rest. When the time came to cross the frontier into Switzerland, he would ensure that there was no impediment: '*on s'arrangera par des amis là-bas pour que vous ne soyez nullement ennuyée*'.*

---

* 'Matters will be so arranged that you will not be in the least bit troubled.' Bruce to Madame Rischard, 5 June 1917.

As for Folkestone, Bruce knew that leaving Paris at this juncture was out of the question. Madame Rischard would see it as desertion and her nerve would crack. He sent Cameron a holding letter:

Everything is now fixed up with Mme. L. . . . She hopes to start on Wednesday or Thursday . . . I do rather feel it would be prudent for me to be here up to the last moment in case of any difficulty with the French authorities, in order that if necessary the red tabs* may be brought to bear. On the other hand, I know you want me over as soon as possible and I realize the impossibility of too prolonged delay.

I hope to know definitely how matters stand on Monday evening when I will send you a wire.

This on its own was enough to infuriate Cameron. The next two paragraphs made things worse:

Regarding financial arrangements, it is not anticipated that the service will be one requiring any regular payments. There may, however, be some expenses and for these, subject to your approval, the following arrangements have been made: Madame L. will advance the necessary money in order to avoid the difficulties of remitting. The amounts can be placed to her credit here from time to time.

Madame L. is prepared to advance up to 10.000 frcs. or even considerably more if need be, but it is clearly understood that she will not commit us to anything other than minor expenses without previous consent from us. Mme. L., although a very wealthy woman, thoroughly understands the value of money and will regard expenditure from our point of view.

I hope this arrangement will meet with your approval.[5]

Cameron did not approve. The proposal was irregular, its consequences were unforeseeable and would probably be catastrophic. He replied at once, firing in all directions.

Your 317.** I note Madame L.'s departure is imminent. You can understand that in view of the present urgency of circumstances my tolerance has

---

* Officers on the General Staff displayed red tabs on their collars. Bruce was using the term figuratively. Tabs worn by officers in the Intelligence Branch, when in uniform, were green.
** The number of Bruce's most recent communication, to which Cameron's message was the reply.

been stretched considerably over this matter as regards your not coming to
FOLKESTONE.

I trust that the returns from her will be proportionate to the trouble you
have taken.

As regards the financial arrangements, I would prefer to supply
Madame L. with a certain sum of money to start a Service with, say 3.000
francs, which should be sufficient for installation. If it is functioning when
this sum has been expended we can then pay into her account in PARIS
other sums. It is to be presumed she will let you know how much per month
she will require, that, I think, is a more satisfactory method. You will also
understand that she will render to us, when occasion permits, an account
of how this money has been spent. I understood that you would be able to
communicate with her as well as hear from her and, therefore, there should
be no difficulty about informing her as to financial arrangements.

I enclose 3.000 francs in this letter to hand over to her.

I have no doubt that if the Service shews no sign of functioning she probably will not spend this sum, but from various points of view I do not like
to contract Official debts.[6]

When he received these unfriendly paragraphs, Bruce had much on
his mind. He was trying to calm the increasingly insecure Madame
Rischard and to arrange her transfer across the Swiss frontier.
Tiresome though they were, however, Cameron's letters had to be
answered. Now there was no comradely 'Dear Cameron':

Dear Major Cameron,

I have to acknowledge your 246 of 12th June and enclose receipt for
Frcs. 3000.

Reference finance . . . the circumstances are not such as permit of Mme.
L. letting us know beforehand how much per month she will require.

I note you do not like the idea of paying in arrear, and I will therefore
endeavour to pay an amount of say Frcs. 500 to Madame L.'s account here
immediately. It is quite impossible to hand her money directly, especially
such a sum as Frcs. 3000. I am absolutely certain that you will agree with
me when I have the opportunity to see you and tell you all about it.

Regarding Mme. L.'s departure, this will be on Saturday evening next . . .

Various little points have cropped up in the last two days for which I
am extremely glad to have been here; more will undoubtedly crop up between

now and Saturday. I can only say that it is jeopardizing the work of the last two months if I leave before she actually starts. When you hear various interesting details which I shall have to tell you, you will I think understand, but it is impossible to write these things in detail.[7]

How could Bruce explain Madame Rischard's state of mind? She was like a highly strung racehorse, nervously awaiting the start. This was not the time to talk about double-entry bookkeeping.

He knew that she was brave – her admission that she was afraid made her courage the more striking – and believed that under pressure she would be steady. Why had she become so full of self-doubt? If he mishandled her, he might lose her altogether. It was difficult for a British army officer of thirty-four, unmarried, to understand the emotional state of an edgy, exhausted Frenchwoman in her late forties. Bruce was an exacting teacher – Campbell was kinder – and time was pressing. He had to be sure that she had memorized every detail of the code, that she was drilled to the point at which, if arrested and interrogated, her responses would be automatic. The lessons at Rue de Moscou were difficult for them both, especially when Campbell was not there to share them, and it was hard to maintain the atmosphere of the schoolroom in the domestic surroundings of Miss Done's apartment. Bruce had to keep Madame Rischard up to the mark and, in doing so, his manner had become not less correct but more. She did not like it and at their last meeting at 38 Rue de Moscou she made her feelings clear. Confronted with the unexpected, Bruce listened intently, betraying nothing. That, too, seemed unsympathetic to a woman overwhelmed.

Next day she sent a letter, written in her dramatic hand on the mourning paper, half an inch of black around the margin, ordered after her father's death.

Mon Capitaine, Je vous ai fait de la peine hier et j'en suis désolée . . .

Captain, I gave you much pain yesterday and I am sorry. In speaking as freely as I did, I was thinking only of how my remarks might help you. I told you that, whenever I came to Rue de Moscou, it was with every confidence, complete devotion to our cause, enthusiasm even, and that when I left I was always more troubled, more out of sorts, asking myself whether I should continue with the dangerous course on which I had embarked and whether I would be better to give up the task with which I had been entrusted, a task thankless to the point of making it impossible to inspire in you the understanding that would have produced during our hours of work together a little of the confident camaraderie which would have sustained and encouraged me.

Je vous ai dit encore que nos séances de travail me laissaient chaque fois une impression de blâme et de désapprobation . . .

I also told you that at every one of our sessions you gave me an impression of reproach and disapproval which paralysed my energies and left me wretchedly anxious – and the only reason for all this was my loyalty to an obligation that I had knowingly accepted. That, in essence, was yesterday's conversation, Captain.

I made these admissions to show you how detrimental this has been, because I strongly believe that in a matter as serious as this 'morale' needs to be treated with as much care and intelligence as the work itself, considering that it is this which gives the strength and enthusiasm that is necessary to sustain the immense effort that is required.

Allow me to add in this letter that ever since our meeting at Rue d'Alésia I have respected and felt for you. In all our dealings, I have never altered that judgement. Completely, almost sublimely, devoted to your vision and your duty, you show loyalty and greatness of spirit, but you are cold and unfeeling. You are capable of great and wonderful things but you lack gentle persuasiveness and delicate flexibility.

Have confidence in yourself, Captain. You can succeed because you have the qualities that are essential to, and are a part of, your present task. I have admired your initiative, your patient tenacity, your stamina and your devotion to such a thankless cause and this will remain, indelibly, among my greatest memories.

A friendly handshake to your charming friend, who with such persuasion so often restored my flickering courage by his kind words.

Don't think of me with bitterness, Captain, and do believe you have my complete loyalty.

L. Rischard.[8]

'*Froid et insensible.*' Cold and unfeeling. Alone with Bruce – Campbell was not at this final meeting – Madame Rischard had been frank. It cannot have been easy for Bruce to listen to these hard words.

His reply:

Madame, J'ai la conscience très nette de ne pas mériter les choses si aimables que vous me dites . . .

I am keenly aware that I do not deserve the friendly things you say about me; may I suggest that perhaps I am a little less deserving than you think of the other, less flattering, observations to which you have done well to expose me? In any case, do believe, Madame, that I am grateful to you for being so frank and so sincere. What is more, you may be sure that your criticisms will be good for me, for in some way or other there must have been error on my part for leaving you with the impression you describe.

Je ne puis vous écrire, Madame, sans tâcher de vous exprimer tant soit peu l'admiration que nous ressentons, mon camarade et moi . . .

I cannot write, Madame, without trying in however small a way to express the renewed admiration which we feel, my colleague and I, for your great act of self-denial and of devotion to the cause which has become your own, because it is the right cause. We strongly believe that the difficult and honourable decision you have taken will allow you to give great service not just to the allied cause but to that of all humanity, for our joint effort has but one aim: the eradication of Evil and the urgent restoration of lawfulness and peace. We will both retain the most precious recollection of your sympathetic and gracious presence; be sure that your fine example will constantly inspire us anew. I beg you to believe, Madame, this expression of our entire esteem and of our deepest respect.[9]

With this dignified response, things were put right. Although the exchange was painful, it had been necessary. She had admitted that she was vulnerable; he had acknowledged that he had been severe. Each was now committed to the other. But if things went wrong she would pay the higher price.

The meeting on 11 June was the last before Madame Rischard left Paris. On the 14th, in a note about financial arrangements, she asked him to forgive her for not saying a proper farewell: 'I could not find the words, emotion had extinguished it all.'[10]

Three days later she was on her way.

10

The Escapers' University

If all went smoothly, she would be in Luxembourg at the end of June. Reports from the marshalling yard could not come soon enough. When the ground began to dry out at the end of March the Allies had renewed the offensive on the Western Front. Elements of Haig's strategy were retained: at the beginning of April the British attacked at Arras, in the northern sector of the front. Five days' assault in the infamous bulge of the Ypres Salient gained 7,000 yards, at a cost of 160,000 killed and wounded. In the first week of June the British GHQ moved from Bavincourt to the château of Blendecques, lent by a local paper-maker, south of St Omer, Haig's objective being to move the British front forward to secure the Belgian coast. Nivelle's offensive in Champagne and along the Aisne, in mid-April, was a disaster, not least because the Germans had acquired a copy of his plans, carelessly carried to a forward position. In four days the French suffered 118,000 casualties; despite these losses, Nivelle had pressed on. Over the next six days another 22,000 men were killed or wounded.

On 29 April a battalion of French infantry refused to go back up the line and, although the ringleaders were arrested and in some cases shot, spontaneous mutinies began to spread. In mid-May Nivelle was sacked. General Pétain, the new French Commander-in-Chief, had immediately decreed that major attacks should cease. Measures were taken to improve conditions and discipline was restored but commanders were shaken. Red flags had been seen at the training camp at Etaples, on the coast. Were Bolsheviks at work?

On the Eastern Front morale in the Russian army was so poor and desertions so frequent that generals could no longer rely on their troops. The country was a ferment of agitation: the Tsar had abdicated in March, attacks from left and right undermined the Provisional Government, the Bolshevik Party pressed for an immediate end to the war. The Russian intelligence section in Paris had been ordered to continue its work but Ignatieff suspected that secret information was being passed to the Germans by supporters of the Russian Revolution.

If Russia collapsed, Germany would be able to withdraw divisions from the Eastern Front. These troops were used to hard attacking tactics and, brought to France, would be available for a renewed offensive. For the previous two and a half years, the enemy had allowed the Allies to pitch their troops against the guns, a wearing-down strategy Germany intended to continue. As the Allies ran out of men and munitions, their politicians would be forced to ask for peace. But the balance was about to tip in the Allies' favour. Attacks on American supply ships and evidence of enemy subversion in the Americas had persuaded President Wilson to bring the United States into the war.* The decision had been announced on 5 April. Weeks were required to bring troops, weapons and machines across the Atlantic but once they were in place Germany would be crushed – unless she moved first. The months from July to October were crucial.

While he waited to hear from Madame Rischard, Bruce sought to repair the widening breach between himself and Cameron. If his chief was still unsure about Lise Rischard, a reluctant recruit with impeccable credentials, it was hardly likely that he would share Bruce's enthusiasm for taking on Baschwitz Meau, a Belgian officer of mysterious origin, eager to work with British Intelligence. A meeting at Folkestone was the only way to find out. Bruce might not be able to convince Cameron but at least he could not be accused of ignoring him. As a precaution, Bruce asked to see Drake. If Drake considered that the Belgian could be trusted, it would be difficult for Cameron to disagree. As soon as Madame Rischard started for Switzerland, Bruce went to Blendecques. His visit to GHQ could not have been

---

* A cable composed by the German Foreign Minister, Arthur Zimmerman, had been sent to the Mexican government, proposing an alliance to help Mexico regain its 'lost' territories in Texas, New Mexico and Arizona.

more fortunately timed. Someone who knew a great deal about Baschwitz had preceded him.

The story had begun a year and a half earlier. Towards the end of November 1915 an observer in the RFC, Lieutenant Sidney Buckley, was shot down with his pilot over northern France and taken prisoner. Buckley became a regular escaper. At last his exasperated captors sent him to Fort Zorndorf, in the valley of the River Oder, east of Berlin. The fort was surrounded by high, sloping walls and a moat; prisoners' quarters were mostly underground. Time spent at Zorndorf, the Germans believed, would cure even the most inveterate prison-breaker. So many experts passed through the Fort that it became known as the Escapers' University. Here, according to one such virtuoso, Captain J. L. Hardy of the Connaught Rangers, were men 'who could make a pair of wire-cutters out of a safety-razor, a metal saw out of an officer's epaulette, a complete German uniform out of a Russian greatcoat and a Frenchman's breeches'.[1] The illicit contents of the packages sent by the Parcel Fund were designed for just such recipients as these. Eight months at Zorndorf was the maximum sentence, for damp and cold made men ill and low-spirited. When a prisoner's time was up, he was moved elsewhere. At the next camp, he passed on all he had learnt.

The Germans were punctilious in keeping to the rules for the treatment of prisoners of war, for officers at least. A prison-breaker who was recaptured would be tried; if found guilty, the maximum sentence was two weeks' solitary confinement. That is, for trying to escape. Other offences – easing locks with stolen pork fat, dismantling bedsteads to make ladders – could be classed as violating official property and carried additional penalties. Worse, in attempting to escape or avoid recapture, a man might be bayoneted or shot. One of Buckley's fellow-inmates at Zorndorf was the above-mentioned Hardy, whose reputation as a prison-breaker was widely known throughout the camps of Germany. Buckley and Hardy exchanged escaping stories; in Hardy's case the tales were not so much about himself as another man, a Belgian, bold and *insouciant*. His name? Baschwitz Meau.

Hardy and Baschwitz had met at Halle in 1914 but as each had soon moved on they had not had time to get to know each other.

In March 1916 Hardy had been transferred to a prison camp at Magdeburg, between Berlin and Hannover, where he found Baschwitz, who had been there for the previous eight months. The impression he made upon Hardy was profound:

a man in a thousand . . . short and slim and muscular, about thirty, with blue eyes, a turned-up moustache, a fine chin, and possessed of a most acute sense of humour. He had spent most of his life in Africa and South America, and spoke fluent English and perfect German, for he was the real soul of adventure, this man: nothing in life could satisfy his craving for excitement and danger, and I knew that he felt his captivity indescribably.

Baschwitz and Hardy decided to work together.

Next to an outer wall of the Magdeburg camp courtyard was a roofless wooden shed, its outermost side giving on to a river-bank. If they could jump into the shed from a nearby ledge and saw through the planks, their road would be open before them. A prisoner who did a little carpentering persuaded the Germans to let him buy a keyhole saw for cabinet-making but to do the sawing the would-be escapers had to be able to occupy the shed without interruption. They hit on the following scheme: Baschwitz disguised himself as an orderly, not very well, so that he was bound to be noticed. Emerging from the shed when he knew a sentry was looking, he dashed back to his room, face averted. The impersonator was not found. The shed was boarded up.

Ideally, the escapers would not be missed for at least two roll-calls, the first in the evening, the second on the following morning. The problem of morning roll-call was to be addressed with an old stratagem. Two officers undertook to report sick. They would insist on remaining in bed but would surreptitiously join their fellow-prisoners on the parade-ground. The count would be two short, Baschwitz and Hardy being gone, but the officer in charge would be reminded that two had been unable to rise from their beds. The accomplices would then sprint back to their rooms. When the duty officer came to check, he would find them lying quietly under the blankets.

Managing evening roll-call was more difficult, as routines for inspection varied from room to room. In Baschwitz's quarters the duty officer merely looked over the beds. This gave Baschwitz an idea. From a fellow-prisoner, a sculptor in civilian life, he obtained some plaster of Paris and fashioned a dummy face, 'a wonderful bit of work,' Hardy said, 'with a pink complexion, an aquiline nose and a fine head of hair, made of clippings from the barber's shop'. The mask had a well-tended moustache and its eyes were closed. Baschwitz arranged the replica atop a lump of blankets and hid behind a screen. The duty officer saw nothing unusual. This was encouraging. In Hardy's room, however, the procedure was more thorough. A sentry prodded each bed, to ensure that its occupant was not a fabricated clump. After much thinking, Hardy had a revelation: *they did not count the beds.* He dismantled bedframe and bedding, redistributing them among the other beds, which were shifted to fill up the gap, and hid. The experiment worked: at evening roll-call the inspecting officer failed to see that the room was minus a bed and a prisoner.

On a wet, grey day in April 1916, the time came. In the event of a break-out, sentries had been instructed to fire without warning; as Hardy prepared himself, his fellow-captives assumed, he said, 'a peculiarly considerate and commiserating air . . . for this is always how one feels towards a prisoner who is just about to "go in off the deep end"'. All went well: vaulting into the shed; cutting the planks, saw silenced with a lubrication of raw bacon fat; creeping through the gap; replacing the timber; exposed edges rubbed with mud to delay detection. The fugitives had a compass, a small map and a fragment of railway timetable. For speed, they had decided to use a local service from Magdeburg station. Hardy chose a non-smoking compartment, in case soldiers invited him to share their tobacco ration, Baschwitz sat with the smokers. 'He spoke such perfect German,' Hardy said, 'and was such an accomplished liar that it was a matter of indifference to him with whom he travelled.'

Their first objective, astonishingly, was Berlin, where they hoped to find a German businessman, now in the Foreign Ministry, known to Baschwitz's brother Conrad. Although his acquaintance with this man was indirect, and the governments they served were at war, Baschwitz thought he might help them. The weather was fine, it was exciting to be escaping, and the expedition was like a holiday. In Berlin Baschwitz and Hardy took a tram to Charlottenburg, where the official lived. Baschwitz went ahead to reconnoitre. The maid told him her master was not at home; when her mistress came into the hall, she told the stranger her husband was in Constantinople. Even in a tight spot, Baschwitz was too chivalrous to embarrass a lady by asking for help she might not wish to give. Murmuring a false name and something about a letter he had to deliver personally, he turned to go. But why was he not in uniform? 'Invalided out,' Baschwitz replied. Looking at him oddly, she took a handful of cigars from a box in the hall and thrust them into his hands. Was she sorry for the visitor or was it a sign that she would not betray him? At any rate, she did not call the police. What she told her husband and whether he asked what had happened to his cigars, Baschwitz and Hardy never knew.

In case the Berlin plan failed, the runaways had prepared an alternative scheme. Hardy's first break-out had been from Neu Brandenburg, a camp north of Berlin, from which he had got to Stralsund, on the Baltic coast. After he had been recaptured, he had been told by a man who knew that part of Germany that from Stralsund he should have taken a steamer to Rügen Island, where there were ships for Sweden. Hardy and Baschwitz now took up this recommendation. By tram and train, they moved toward the coast. Night came. Back at Magdeburg, the replica face was placed on Baschwitz's pillow and in Hardy's room the bedframe disassembled. The escapers, having got to Stralsund, settled down in a field. In the morning, having tidied themselves as best they could, they made for Rügen Island, only to find that there were no ships in the harbour and none expected. If they wanted passage to Sweden, they must go to Arcona, a busier port, fifteen miles along the coast.

Now Baschwitz and Hardy met disaster. As they tramped through the rain, they realized they were being shadowed. With a confidence they did not feel, they turned round and looked their pursuers in the face. Where might they find a night's lodging, Baschwitz asked. But though his German was fluent and colloquial, he addressed these locals in a dialect other than their own. They were immediately suspicious – and excited, for a lookout was being kept for two other fugitives, Russian prisoners of war. Hoping for a reward, they directed the runaways to an inn. As soon as they entered it, Baschwitz and Hardy knew that they were trapped. The room was full of German soldiers and, when the cross-looking woman who managed the place demanded the newcomers' papers, a *Landsturm** sentry stepped forward. 'And then,' Hardy said, 'quietly and fluently, without a trace of nervousness, this splendid pal of mine started to lie.'[2] Having been found unfit for service, Baschwitz explained, he and his companion had been sent to work in a factory in Stettin and were now going home to Sweden to their families. The local police wanted to check their papers and were keeping them until morning. The soldiers seemed persuaded, until the woman who kept the inn said something Baschwitz could not follow. A triumphant shout; she had spoken as people did in Stettin, she cried, and they had not understood it. More lying by Baschwitz – but the damage was done. An *unteroffizier*** announced that Baschwitz and Hardy should consider themselves under guard. In the morning he would telephone the police. That did not prevent their being allowed to sleep, said Baschwitz. The *unteroffizier*, a decent man, agreed. The adjoining room had a couple of iron bedsteads in a corner; there, on thin mattresses, Baschwitz and Hardy laid themselves down, watched by the under-officer and two men with loaded rifles.

At first light Hardy woke, stiff, sore and dejected. The sentries and the under-officer were asleep. With an inch of wire Hardy set about picking the lock of the door – and found that the soldiers had forgotten to secure it. Waking Baschwitz, he pointed to the slumbering watch-keepers. Boots on, out of the door, across the yard. For a mile they ran, then another three, through a wood, over heathland and scrub. If they could reach the coast, if they could steal a boat, they might get back to Stralsund and lose themselves there. A man came past on a bicycle. He stopped, challenged them, cycled furiously to a nearby house. From the building a telegraph line ran ominously to the road. 'Oh for a pair of climbing-irons and some wire-cutters,' said Hardy, as if he were escaping in a dream; 'we knew that the very wires over

* Soldiers mobilized from the Austro-Hungarian reserve.
** A rank between a corporal and a sergeant.

our heads were carrying the news . . .'³ Scrambling up a tree, he looked over the surrounding country. Soldiers with rifles and civilians with shotguns were already closing in. 'I climbed down and told Baschwitz how things stood, and he laughed, and pulling out his case offered me a cigarette. We lit up, and then with one accord linked arms and walked towards the edge of the wood. We should indeed be lucky if there were no firing, but if we had to stop one, we felt it was better, here in the open, than tangled in the wire of a prisoners' camp.' Within minutes Hardy and Baschwitz were being marched away. They bore themselves proudly. 'We had sworn to each other that we would not put up our hands under any circumstances, and it was a relief to both of us that we had not been called upon to do so.'⁴

The next days were black. Within five minutes of their flight from the inn, the *unteroffizier* had woken to find the prisoners gone. Without a word, he had removed a boot and, toe on trigger, rifle muzzle in his mouth, had blown his brains out. Some, who did not think a man could be so courageous, suggested that the escapers had murdered him and made it look like suicide. Hardy and Baschwitz were locked up in separate cells in the town jail at Stralsund while the matter was investigated. Their outrage and isolation were almost unendurable: 'no one to speak to,' Hardy lamented, 'nothing to read and nothing to smoke, with the prospect of many months' confinement before us, and the memory of our lost chances to vex and distress us . . .' At last, after five days, there was an inquest. The examiner was punctilious: Baschwitz and Hardy were cleared. The return to Magdeburg began badly. In Stralsund a sergeant who had failed to spot them when they first came through the town now exacted a price for his embarrassment, insisting on searching them and, as he escorted them to the railway station, inviting people to come and jeer at them. There was nothing they could do. It was, Hardy said, their worst day in Germany: 'Never during my captivity have I felt so acutely the shame of my position . . . and Baschwitz and I could not look each other in the face during that journey.'⁵ At Magdeburg, the officers in charge were anxious to reassert their authority. A fortnight in solitary confinement, the penalty for attempting to escape, was considered too lenient for this unbiddable pair, and, among other crimes, they found themselves charged with conspiracy, a much more serious matter. For two months, hungry and, until parcels and clean uniforms arrived, infested with lice, the two friends languished in a military prison. But at the court-martial, as at the inquest, the Germans followed the rules. Baschwitz and Hardy were given copies of the charges and the services of a lawyer and, after a fair trial, the conspiracy theory was dismissed. Furthermore, a sentence imposed for damaging government property – sawing the planks in the shed – was reduced by the amount of time they had already served. At exactly eight in the evening, on the day and to the hour that the remainder of their term expired, the doors of their cells were opened.

Baschwitz and Hardy talked the whole night, walking up and down the passage. They had expected to be separated, for it was unusual to leave escape partners together, but as they were released from their cells, they had been told that they were both to be sent to a nearby camp at Burg. In that case, they intended to try again. Next time they were bound to succeed. It seemed impossible, Hardy said, 'with the experience we possessed and with the intense confidence we had in each other, that we could ever fail again. No matter how hard the camp, or how great the distance to be covered we would do it – most certainly we would . . .' Together they were transferred to Burg, together they looked for its weaknesses. Then bad news came. The War Ministry in Berlin had sent orders that Hardy was to be moved to Zorndorf. The two adventurers were to be separated after all. Hardy was to go very early in the morning, while the other prisoners were still confined to their rooms. On the night before he was to go he walked with Baschwitz across the yard. The bugle sounded for evening roll-call. It was time to part. 'We shook hands, and I left him standing there under the arc lamps – the best man I ever knew.'[6]

So in the summer of 1916 they parted, the practical Hardy, aptly named, uncertain about his German but able to fashion a spanner from a metal spoon, and the exotic and ingenious Baschwitz, with his bright eyes and curling black hair, always ready with a ruse or a lie.

Hardy and Baschwitz were in many ways alike. Both longed for freedom and the chance to rejoin their fellow-soldiers in the field. Both were anxious to 'give a good account of themselves', to be shot, if it came to it, facing the enemy, in the open. Mocked at Stralsund station, each knew how the other felt. Hardy trusted Baschwitz completely. How, otherwise, would he have agreed to fall in with the plan to go to Berlin, on the off-chance that an official in the German Foreign Ministry would help them? Baschwitz and Hardy were elated by their success in breaking free, by the summer morning and the open road, but calling at the house in Charlottenburg had been madness.

Yet there was something particularly wonderful about Baschwitz Meau. His essence was romantic, devil-may-care. When Hardy climbed down from the tree, what did Baschwitz do? Laughed and lit a cigarette. Baschwitz knew that though they might catch him they would never keep him. He would slip through their fingers again and again, fluid and dazzling, quicksilver. Baschwitz had a sort of magic. Bruce was to discover it. At his first meeting with Baschwitz, at Place Anglaise, he too had been captivated, immediately and irrevocably.

This was the story Captain Hardy told Lieutenant Buckley when they were brought together at the camp at Zorndorf in 1917.

These two made numerous attempts to break out of Fort Zorndorf, scaling walls with a ladder made of wood from deckchairs and iron supports from bedsteads, slithering in white camouflage dress over the snow-covered moat. New people arrived, bringing their own apparatus, secreted in false-bottomed boxes or stuffed into socks. Equipment, skills and experience were pooled and further experiments made: with tunnels, grappling hooks, aerial ropeways, punts. The Germans were right. At Zorndorf, habitual escapers learnt their lesson but it was not the one they were sent there to acquire.*

Conditions began to tell on Buckley's health and he was duly moved, this time to Fort 9, a camp at Ingolstadt, south of Nürnberg in Bavaria. In June 1917 he was sufficiently recovered to be returned to Zorndorf. He and his travelling companions had been told to wear

---

* Hardy was eventually transferred to Schweinitz, north of Leipzig. He escaped from that camp in April 1918 and after 450 miles reached safety in Holland.

uniform for the journey, this being the rule when prisoners were moved by train, but they had persuaded the Germans to allow grey flannels, saying that when on duty British officers were so attired. To alleviate the constipating prison diet, Buckley's mother sent dried prunes, the stones replaced with maps of the Continent, in miniature. With these and other provisions – compressed raisins, Oxo cubes, cheese, malted milk lozenges and chocolate – he boarded the train. Among the party was Captain Evans, the officer whose mother had devised the method of baking maps into fruit-cake. Buckley had advised Evans that, though the presence of so many experienced escapers made Zorndorf intellectually stimulating, as a residence it was uncomfortable. The two of them decided to escape together. In his haversack Evans had a Tyrolese hat, bought from a Frenchman; Buckley's headwear had been fabricated from a piece of cloth and an old straw. Their compasses were in their pockets. Toward midnight the train neared Nürnberg and slowed down. Evans asked the sentry if he too would like to eat and at this prearranged signal the prisoners stood up and began, in a confused mass, to pull their bags from the luggage rack. Out jumped Evans, then Buckley.

It was 200 miles to the German/Swiss border. For cover, they kept to the forests, scattering pepper in their tracks to confuse the dogs that might be set on their trail. Repeatedly accosted by locals, they bluffed their way out: 'Just because we don't speak your dialect . . . Good day.'[7] On the fifth night, having eluded a party of a dozen men beating the woods, they almost ran into a sentry posted outside Gunzenhausen. Here at last a sign told them where they were, fifty miles from their starting-point. They dare not catch a train or, though it would have provided a direct route to their objective, walk beside a railway line. Villages and hamlets were full of barking dogs. Fields of hop-poles entangled them at night; in marshland, cut with steep canals, water came up to their thighs. Three times they crossed and recrossed a bridge over the Danube, north of Donauwörth, nailed boots striking iron girders, until they were sure they had the road they sought. By the tenth day their clothes were filthy, hair and beards unkempt, arms and faces red with insect bites, toes swollen and blistered. Sharing Buckley's slippers, 'almost an essential part of one's equipment',[8] they tried to dry their boots during rest periods in ditches and bracken. They longed for a smoke, forbade themselves to talk about food. From the twelfth day they lived largely on seed potatoes, eaten raw, knowing they were taking peasants' precious stock, and that, if seen, they might be shot. After seventeen days, delirious from hunger and fatigue, they were sure they must have left Germany behind, until Evans saw a frontier guard at least a mile away, bayonet glinting in the sun. Buckley was by now almost too weak to walk. Desperate for information, Evans approached a girl in a sunbonnet who was making hay. She gave him the name of her village – and did not betray the wild-looking stranger. On the eighteenth night, sticks discarded, Burberry raincoats tied on their backs with string, they crawled up the bank of a stream, under the nose of a sentry, and fell into Switzerland.

This was on 9 June 1917. Buckley and Evans were taken to the British legation in Berne and then were driven to GHQ for questioning. Their interrogation over, they were sent home to England. Evans reported to the RFC for retraining, Buckley returned to GHQ for an interview with Drake. When Bruce came to see Drake a fortnight later, Buckley had already told his story. It is pleasant to imagine how the conversation went when Bruce introduced the subject of the remarkable Belgian. Baschwitz had told Bruce about his adventures with Hardy, Hardy had told Buckley about his adventures with Baschwitz. All was now corroborated.

11

Letters from Lise

Madame Rischard was about to be placed in a situation more dangerous than she realized. When last in Switzerland, she had been an innocent visitor, her mission personal. She was returning as an agent of a foreign power. For security, she had been allowed to believe that she was I(b)'s only agent in Switzerland. She did not know that if she got into difficulty their duty to her would have to be balanced against other liabilities. To date, I(b)'s Swiss record had been spectacularly unsuccessful. Madame Rischard had not been told about this unreassuring history; it would have shaken her to the core.

All the belligerents ran secret services in Switzerland; all energetically denied it. The presence of so many foreign agents gave an edge to every transaction: in hotels and restaurants, on trams, trains and omnibuses, on the steamers plying the lakes, in shops, stations and post offices, someone was always watching. Bruce had decided that Madame Rischard should cross the frontier at Annemasse. Campbell could arrange it. That is, as long as he was himself not caught by the Swiss police, whose embrace he had so narrowly escaped eighteen months before.

Getting Madame Rischard back to Lausanne was just the beginning. Her request for the return of her Luxembourg passport might attract attention – as far as she knew, it was still at the Dutch legation in Berne – and while her application was being considered the Swiss police might decide to look more closely at this woman who had been away from Luxembourg for so long. They might want to know whether Madame Fresez-Settegast's condition had improved and, if so, what her visitor had been doing during these past months. Madame Rischard had to be ready with plausible answers.

For communication with Rue St Roch, a secure channel had to be set up between Paris and Lausanne. The precedents were unhappy. When Kirke had taken I(b) into Switzerland in late 1914, he had set up two networks, one based in Zürich, the other in Geneva, a dangerous duplication. In Zürich he had put Lieutenant George Pollitt, an industrial chemist with a doctorate from the University of Basel, who had worked before the war at Brunner Mond, the chemical company.* When the first agent he recruited turned out to be a fraud, Pollitt decided that he was not suited to espionage and in July 1915 had asked for a transfer to the new 'Special Brigade' for gas warfare. It was Pollitt's successor, E. B. Harran, another former Brunner Mond employee, who had misaddressed reports to the Berlitz Language School in Paris. In August 1915, when Sir Henry Angst was accused of spying and obliged to retire from the British consulate, I(b)'s Zürich office had been closed.

Kirke's Geneva network had been equally unsuccessful. To run it, he had chosen Captain John Wallinger of the Indian Police, younger brother of Major Ernest 'Peg Leg' Wallinger. At this time, early 1915, the latter soldier had just taken over from Cameron as chief of I(b)'s operations in Holland and Belgium. A number of John Wallinger's agents were based on the French side of Lake Geneva (strictly, this was Cameron's territory); they and their colleagues on the Swiss side used the lake to take information, money and instructions between the one country and the other. The Swiss police had begun to investigate and in the late summer of 1915 one of Wallinger's key recruiting agents had been seized and had given the police the names of two colleagues who were working in Germany. Kirke had suspected the consul and pro-consul at Geneva, neither of whom was British, of being German informers, a suspicion that was increased when Baron Brault, John Wallinger's principal agent on the French side of the lake, was warned by an associate that attempts were being made to lure him into Switzerland to arrest him there. Brault had left at once, changing his name to avoid pursuit and consigning the agents for whom he was responsible to the care of his counterpart on the Swiss side, Dr Condom.

---

* Pollitt was the agent who was appointed, as cover, to the British Commission into the manufacture of aniline dyes. See above, p. 32.

Then Condom heard that he too was being watched. He had fled in a motor-boat to the French side of the lake and disappeared, smuggled away by the very agents who had looked to him for protection.

It was to revive the Geneva network that I(b) had recruited Somerset Maugham, a French and German speaker, who had been serving with an ambulance unit on the Western Front. But the complications of Maugham's private life were a distraction; in the winter of 1915 he was cited in an undefended suit for divorce, brought by Sir Henry Wellcome, the pharmaceutical magnate, whose former wife, Syrie, had then come to live with Maugham in Geneva. These domestic arrangements were tense, not least because at the same time Maugham's homosexual lover, Gerald Haxton, was being tried at the Old Bailey on six counts of gross indecency. In May 1916 Kirke brought Maugham's Geneva assignment to an end. Another playwright took over in Geneva, Edward Knoblock, an American, fluent in German and French, who had become a British subject in order to fight. Knoblock was enthusiastic and creative but it was too late to enliven the performance of Wallinger's network.*

Kirke had already been instructed by the War Office to remove all I(b) operations from Switzerland, as part of the clarification of responsibilities decided upon in London at the end of 1915. From January 1916, Swiss secret service operations in Switzerland were officially reserved for Cumming. Like Maugham until he was sacked, John Wallinger had remained in Geneva. Arguably (just), he did not trespass on Cumming's ground, his main activity being negotiations with Danish expatriates whom he thought might help him find recruits for espionage work in Germany. When his discussions with the Danish intermediaries came to nothing, he had turned to Holland, but this was his brother's territory and people had been confused. Kirke had now had enough: 'JAW's Swiss show,' he observed, '. . . is a waste of money.' At the end of May 1916 there was 'a parting of the ways' between himself and the younger Wallinger.[1]

Cumming's Swiss network had also attracted the attention of the

---

* Before taking the plunge, Knoblock consulted Henry James, who had also applied for naturalization. 'You are right,' said the novelist, and, in an echo of the priest's words to Madame Rischard, 'Your first duty is to this country.' Edward Knoblock, *Round the Room*, London: Chapman and Hall, 1939.

Swiss police and in mid-January 1916 many of his agents in Switzerland had been rounded up. This was the trap from which Campbell had luckily escaped, only to be sent back with instructions from Kirke and Cumming to try to organize a joint Swiss operation. The legacy of complication had made it impossible. It was then that Kirke withdrew I(b) from Switzerland, Cumming brought MI 1(c)'s Swiss connection to an end and Major Vischer, military attaché at the legation, was ordered home to London.

It was now six months after the departure of I(b) and MI 1(c) from Switzerland. Alone and untested, Madame Rischard was being sent by the Paris Office into that same arena. Knowing something of the misfortunes of 1915 and 1916, it was clear to Bruce that an entirely new line of communication had to be set up between Lausanne and Paris, using only people approved by Campbell and himself. There was no one at the legation on whom they could rely. Woolrych was recovering from an appendectomy and had not yet gone to Berne as the military attaché; the intelligence establishment at the legation consisted only of Professor Thomas, a meteorologist, employed in climbing nearby mountains, twice daily, to appraise the wind.* Bruce approached Drake, who went to the War Office, the Foreign Office and MI 1(c) but, after the earlier débâcle, officials thought it unwise to change existing policy. Switzerland remained off limits to I(b). Drake tried again. A concession was obtained. Bruce was to be allowed to run his operation in Switzerland – how much Drake disclosed is not known – on condition that no agent was to be recruited without prior clearance by Drake himself, nothing done to imperil existing sources and to the extent only that 'current work' required it.[2] Lieutenant Fuller, at Evian, was to organize the carriage of messages across Lake Geneva, and Cox and van den Heuvel, two reliable men associated with a training school for agents in Bellegarde on the French/Swiss frontier, were to look after Madame Rischard if she had to be urgently removed from Switzerland by train.** Expenses could legitimately be paid from sums held by Paris for operations in France.

* Observations needed for flight planning and gas warfare.
** J. D. 'Jim' Cox belonged to I(b). He worked with Frederick van den Heuvel of MI 1(c), 'Fanny', a director of Eno's Fruit Salts and a Papal Count, with whom Campbell occasionally stayed when crossing in and out of Switzerland.

This would make use of the money Cameron had insisted on sending, of which the greater part was still to hand.

At the beginning of May Campbell had gone back to Annemasse to see old associates. Two visiting cards were pinned to his report:

ELEUTERIO PALADINI
ARCHITECTE–GEOMETRE DIPLOME
Annemasse (Haute-Savoie)

And, larger (but there was more to say),

Mme. Léonie Montvuagnard
Massage et gymnastique médicale
Massage vibratoire
Système suédois
4 Avenue du Mail Genève

Discussions with the electrotherapist had been fruitful:

I have known this woman (age 33–36) for over a year, and she has on several occasions done odd jobs in Switzerland for me, and has always carried them out without a hitch. She is a good-looking, well-dressed woman and very *débrouillarde*.* She is French of birth, but married a Swiss (JEMY). They were subsequently divorced, and she has the custody of the child, a daughter. I believe it was she who obtained the divorce. She is a qualified masseuse, and is fairly well known as such in GENEVA.**

I sent over to GENEVA for her yesterday (9th) afternoon, and met her in ANNEMASSE last night. She is very willing to do all that is necessary.

I suggest that about a fortnight before M. R.*** goes to Switzerland, Madame MONTVUAGNARD should start putting a weekly advertisement in the *Suisse*, for massage work. M. R. could answer this upon her arrival, and could be massaged by Madame MONTVUAGNARD a few times. Upon M. R.'s departure for Luxemburg, correspondence on medical and other matters could thus perfectly naturally string up.

I arranged that Madame MONTVUAGNARD should receive 10 Swiss

---

* Resourceful.
** Madame Montvuagnard's medical 'massage work' was a sort of physiotherapy, or what the French call *kinésithérapie*. In John Buchan's novel, *The Three Hostages* (Edinburgh: Thomas Nelson, 1924), published six years after the end of the Great War, 'Madame Breda' uses Swedish massage for more sinister purposes.
*** That is, Madame Rischard.

francs a month when receiving letters. I think she should also be paid for her massage treatment as she is hard up at present owing to the war.

NOTE: I was put in touch with the above through M. PALADINI (card enclosed). I saw him yesterday and he made the necessary arrangements to bring her over. Mme. MONTVUAGNARD is making out a list of the doctors who would recommend her so that M. R. could also get in touch with her through this natural source.

This information, and how much the advertisement would cost, will be forwarded to the PLACE ANGLAISE shortly.[3]

Campbell also consulted Monsieur Antoni, recruited at the beginning of the war to take messages between Switzerland and France.[4] Antoni's daughter, Emilie, lived in Geneva; her husband, Signor Cerutti, an Italian, had been mobilized and was serving in Italy. 'In peace time,' Campbell told Bruce, 'his wife just looks after the home, and family (2 children), but at present is *ménaging* for a retired French officer in Geneva.' Cerutti, Campbell explained, was 'a very sound fellow, and worked for me for several months passing people backwards and forwards across the French/Swiss frontier . . . Mme. Cerutti is absolutely reliable, and Antoni is very keen that she should be allowed to act as the intermediary . . .'[5]

'Reliability' implied not just efficiency and trustworthiness but also a brave and willing heart. There were, however, other considerations. In the small, status-conscious society of Lausanne, an association between two women from such dissimilar circles might catch the eye of inquisitive neighbours. Campbell did not wish to run the risk. If a second go-between were required, Madame Cerutti was available but for the time being he recommended that they rely on Madame Montvuagnard-Jémy. He was sure that she and Madame Rischard would be able to keep up a sustained, easy and, as he put it, 'natural' correspondence, Swiss censors being, he surmised, more suspicious of correspondence about dressmaking than about the Swedish method of vibratory massage.

Bruce had promised Madame Rischard that as she crossed the frontier his colleagues would look after her: '*on s'arrangera par les amis là-bas pour que vous ne soyez nullement ennuyée*'. There was reason to be anxious. Swiss officials might ask questions for which she had not been rehearsed. German agents might be masquerading as customs officers. Her luggage might be opened, her clothes and person searched. Bruce and Campbell knew what caught the eyes of the police: corsages of artificial flowers that might have documents in the stalks, parasols whose handles might contain secret papers.* Madame Rischard's boxes might be examined for false bottoms, her luggage labels for messages written in invisible ink. The enemy used these devices and expected the Allies to employ them too. Rumour said that a woman working for the Germans had been caught with a report pasted on to her bare back, thickly varnished.** Surely the frontier police would not suspect Madame Rischard of anything like this?

No one knew how she would be received.

The test came on 17 June, a Sunday. Madame Rischard made her way toward the barrier and stepped into Switzerland. As the police stamped her new French passport, she saw a familiar figure, watching from the Swiss side. It was Réséda. Bruce had assured her that friends would be on hand when she went through; for Campbell himself to appear at that moment was a miracle.

He could not stay. He had to return to Evian to telephone the Paris Office. Next morning he made out his report.

Everything went off all right yesterday morning. I had everything arranged in advance and Madame L. passed through perfectly normally, like any other passenger. She was just asked the two questions: 'Where do you come from?' and 'Where are you going to?' and her passport was then *viséd*.

She looked awfully tired, but a smile of gladness came on to her face when she saw me the other side of the room.

Unfortunately, she was the last through, and it being then 8 o'clock, it was too late to catch you before you left Paris. I just managed to catch the train to EVIAN; I telephoned from there and Mademoiselle did the rest.

ANTONI met me on Saturday morning at ANNEMASSE and I took him

---

* In 1916 Captain Carr had circulated a description of these and other tricks.
** In another version, the messages were said to have been written in invisible ink. In her two-volume memoir, *Toute Ma Vie* (Paris: René Juillard, 1954), Mistinguett, the music-hall star, claimed the back was hers.

to EVIAN yesterday morning after seeing Madame L. off, gave him her gear which is going to be delivered at her address by ANTONI on Tuesday.[6]

In Paris Madame Rischard had been apprehensive but safe. Although Bruce was a hard taskmaster, he had been there to protect her. Campbell had calmed her, Miss Done's apartment had been a refuge. She had left all that behind. She had no idea when she would be able to leave this temporary stopping-place but she knew that in Switzerland she was vulnerable. She was alone, a bird that had alighted on a ledge, surrounded by enemies with keen eyes and quick ears. How long would she have to wait, here in Lausanne, between two worlds?

Bruce had left for Madrid, on business so pressing that he was unable to wait for the call from Evian.* Before going back to France he made the long-deferred visit to Folkestone to see Cameron. The discussion at No. 8 The Parade was frank, its outcome a truce. Cameron understood that Bruce must sometimes use his discretion in deciding how to respond to orders from Folkestone. Indeed, he said, he was surprised, even annoyed, that Bruce should have thought his directives unfriendly. Bruce did not forget this conversation.

He spent only two days in England. Madame Rischard had been in Lausanne for more than a week and he was anxious to know whether she now had her Luxembourg passport. When Bruce returned to Place Anglaise on 28 June two letters were waiting from Lausanne.

Before she left Paris he had told Madame Rischard how their correspondence was to be conducted. She was to place letters to Rue St Roch in sealed envelopes and enclose them in an outer cover – she had been provided with a stock – labelled only with the name and address of a Swiss intermediary. There were three: Madame Gardiol, Monsieur Bathet and Monsieur Trimollet, all of whom lived in Geneva. They would ensure that her letters reached an I(b) agent

---

* 'Germans intriguing hard in Spain', Haig, Diaries, 25 July 1917, National Library of Scotland, Edinburgh. Drake had secured Admiralty and Foreign Office permission for Bruce to work there alongside French Intelligence. See Drake, *History of Intelligence (B)*, PRO WO 106/45, paras. 26–28 and Commandant Gusthal, *Les Héros sans Gloire du Deuxième Bureau*, Paris: Éditions Baudinière, 1932.

who would get them by dispatch rider to Paris. Letters going in the other direction would be transmitted via one of the agents in Geneva for onward posting to Lausanne.

As letters might be intercepted, sensitive passages were to be put into Campbell's code. Messages of a general nature – about the state of the sender's health, for example – could be written *en clair*. Aliases were to be used. Not for Madame Rischard herself: as the Swiss police knew who she was and where she lived, she would have been foolish not to revert to her real identity. 'Madame Léonard' was therefore dropped. At 41 Rue St Roch, however, a Swiss family was created, 'the Garlands'.* Bruce, thinly disguised as 'Georgette', became a female cousin, the same age as Madame Rischard, Campbell took the role of Georgette's husband, 'Jacques', a doctor, Chocqueel that of 'Nicole', their tempestuous seventeen-year-old daughter.

Madame Rischard had followed these instructions but, unused to subterfuge, she was careless. An uncoded passage in her first dispatch, composed on her third day in Switzerland, told 'Georgette' that as soon as she returned home she would lay everything before her husband, 'in the hope of winning him over', adding that she was sure that the seeds would be sown on fertile ground. Worse, she appended an extract from a letter from her husband, complaining about the brutishness of the German occupation.** Attaching any cutting to a letter was unwise. It was lucky that the censor had not felt the pin through the envelope.

This was not the only disturbing feature. Madame Rischard had worked hard to encode secret information but her attention had wandered. In one sentence she had introduced an F, an L, an M and an O by writing about a stroll with Tante Marie and an imaginary dog, one Floc, from Lausanne to Montreux via Ouchy. A censor with local knowledge would have known that this would have been

---

* An odd choice of name, there being no such word in French. When the garland was assembled, were 'Rose' and 'Réséda' – rose and mignonette – thinking of the Arcadian gardens of home?
** Madame Rischard to Bruce, 21 June 1917. 'I don't know what I'd give to be rid of the sight of these swaggering figures with all the trappings of their stupid and ridiculous arrogance', Dr Rischard to Madame Rischard, June 1917 (no other date given).

impossible for an invalid, the walk described being a stiff haul of at least fifteen miles. Furthermore, in her penultimate sentence, written *en clair*, Madame Rischard had unguardedly suggested a quick method for identifying whether letters were or were not in code: 'each time you write me an ordinary letter with nothing hidden in it, leave the year out of the date . . . Good idea?'* Errors such as these might betray them all.

Another worry concerned the number of letters. She said she had sent four via Monsieur Trimollet. Had two been intercepted before Trimollet had received them? They might have been discarded by a disapproving censor. Although Madame Rischard had enclosed everything in the prepared covers supplied by Bruce and Campbell, she had affixed her own wax seal to the inner envelopes. The seal was thick, heavy and embossed and the censor would have felt it. Enclosures of this nature were suspect, especially from a correspondent who wrote four letters to the same address in a single week.

Madame Rischard did not know that Bruce was away – he had written twice from Spain but his letters were delayed – and when she did not hear from him fear made her flustered. She became more frantic and imprudent. Her fourth letter had a postscript, *en clair*, asking for Antoni's address in case of emergency, a fifth an inquiry about burning papers when she left Switzerland. She was delighted, she added, to report that she had been able to convince the officials at the Dutch legation that she had not left Switzerland.[7]

There was consternation in Rue St Roch. Explaining to Madame Rischard where she was going wrong needed a delicate touch. A tactfully worded letter would be best, uncoded, to avoid misunderstanding. Campbell could go to Evian, give it to Antoni to take by hand to Lausanne and wait there for Madame Rischard's reply. This would also enable Campbell to look into the question of the missing letters. On the morning of 29 June Bruce composed his letter to Madame Rischard and in the afternoon Campbell left hotfoot for Evian.

* Letters containing secret information were to include the year, 1917, say, or '17, in the date at the top of the page. Ordinary letters were to give only day and month of writing. Madame Rischard to Bruce, 21 June 1917.

Agents crossed Lake Geneva in the following way. The steamer that circled the lake began and ended its round in Switzerland and no stamps were required for passengers who did not intend to leave Swiss territory. The boat not only called at Geneva, Vevey and Lausanne but also at two stops on the French side, Evian and Thonon. Someone on secret business, like Antoni, could board the steamer at a stop in Switzerland, disembark on the French side, catch a later boat and finish the journey in Switzerland. Undercover journeys from France to Switzerland could be made in a similar way. The route was neither safe nor easy. Ticket collectors on the boats noticed people who regularly made interrupted journeys, police monitored the quays on the Swiss shore and German spies were stationed on the French side. The police were less likely to question local people but strangers expected to be challenged, especially if they had heavy luggage. If Madame Rischard had tried to re-enter Switzerland by this means, she would have been stopped.

Antoni came to Evian on the Saturday morning. Back he went to Lausanne, carrying the letter and a large bouquet. Had Bruce and Campbell been so advised by Miss Done and Mademoiselle Dorgebray? The Secretariat knew how unsettled she was, for they typed out copies of all the correspondence. Presenting himself at 33 Avenue Edouard Dapples, Antoni sent in flowers and letter, saying that he would return next morning. Madame Rischard must have had a wretched night, worrying about missing letters – she had now sent seven altogether – and her own imprudence. Her reply was imploring. She must talk to Campbell, face to face and at once. '*Fixe-moi un rendez-vous*', in a boat on the lake at ten a.m., at the foot of the Avenue d'Ouchy at three p.m., on the next day, the day after, at the same time on the same days at 14 Avenue Fraisse, where there was a quiet path, anywhere but her own house, but he must telephone, please telephone, ask only for her, speak as if to a stranger: '*Il faut que je te voie.*'[8]

It was impossible. At the German legation in Berne, now reopened, Madame Rischard had been instructed to obtain a certificate of good character. She hoped to collect it when the police station in Lausanne opened on Monday morning; the testimonial was probably being prepared at this moment. If Campbell went to her now, they might both be trapped. He would have to say no. Antoni took another letter to Avenue Edouard Dapples, telling Madame Rischard that Trimollet had sworn that all letters from Lausanne had been forwarded according to instructions. She was horrified. Not knowing that the letter with the cutting had got through to Paris, Madame Rischard believed that she had betrayed her husband Camille as well as everyone else. To and fro Antoni went. Campbell could not leave Madame Rischard in this state. Before he returned to Paris, he told her, he would arrange to come to Lausanne. Madame Rischard could not understand why there had to be delay. 'A la grâce de Dieu . . . For God's sake! . . . I despair!'⁹

Silence. Until Campbell was sure that letters were not being intercepted, he dared use neither Antoni nor the post. Madame Rischard was in torment. Had they deserted her? It was a hard test and a vital part of her apprenticeship. Meanwhile, with the help of other agents, Scheinsciss, Bathet and Kunz, Campbell and Antoni experimented with letters to Geneva, tracked and timed. Trimollet was watched. After four days, Campbell decided that it was safe to move. This time Madame Montvuagnard took his letter to Lausanne: 'If I come over, I am Mr T. Sinclair.'¹⁰ Madame Rischard's reply was a mixture of pathos and bravado. She reproached him for being so calm about the missing letters. If Campbell were such an optimist, why was he so slow in coming? She was not afraid, although sure she had been betrayed. The Germans would give her the passport and then arrest her at the frontier: 'Better death than captivity! . . . the worst tortures will never make me abandon my duty . . .'¹¹ If she were prepared to place herself in such danger, surely Campbell could have risked a journey to Lausanne?

Was Madame Rischard thinking of the time when she had caught sight of Campbell on the Swiss side of the frontier? Perhaps she thought that he could come and go as he pleased. Did she not know that the boat and the quays were watched and that for Campbell, even more than for Antoni and Madame Montvuagnard, expeditions between France and Switzerland were not to be undertaken without good reason?

That night Mr Sinclair took the boat from Evian. By half past nine on the 9th he was at Avenue Edouard Dapples. He found

Madame Rischard 'very much in the depths'. For three weeks she had been living a double life. Bruce and Campbell were at the far end of a line of unknown agents; what was she to do if the chain had one weak link? And there had been the frightening time when she thought herself deserted. Campbell's visit was a huge relief. 'I convinced her at once that there was no question of T. playing false. He was perfectly sound, and the whole difficulty was that the postal authorities had felt the inner seal and had opened and possibly confiscated the letters.' The incriminating enclosure? 'Madame L. told me she had only sent one letter with a cutting from her husband, which we had received. I looked through copies of her letters . . . One was a morbid outburst, which might refer to any personal matter, and the others were of little interest.'

All the summer morning Campbell remained with Madame Rischard, in the placid little town, between the shining flatness of the lake and the grassy meadows that ran up to the mountains. War had brought them together, mining engineer turned soldier, gentlewoman turned spy. In the apartment in Rue de Moscou Campbell had guided Madame Rischard through the intricacies of the code, helping her along when she was 'un peu découragée'. On the night when she crossed the frontier, he had been there, 'the other side of the room'. Now he calmed her fears. He and Bruce would support her. 'We had a long talk about things in general and she became perfectly all right and confident again.'

They turned to the question of her papers. Madame Rischard had told the Dutch she had destroyed the permit they had given her. It was not easy to convince them but at last her Luxembourg passport had been handed back. She had next presented herself at the German legation, taking the Luxembourg passport and documents showing that she had been in Switzerland for the past six months: a certificate from a doctor in Lausanne, saying that he had been treating her since December 1916, and her Swiss permis de séjour, which Madame Fresez-Settegast had prudently renewed on her behalf in January 1917.

'They seemed quite satisfied,' Campbell told Bruce, 'and asked her no awkward questions.'[12] German record-keeping was exemplary. Madame Rischard had gambled on that exactitude. There was no entry in her dossier, so she could not have gone anywhere.* As far as the Germans were concerned, Madame Rischard had been in Switzerland all the time.

But rules had changed. She now needed a visa to go home and for that she must apply to the Foreign Ministry in Berlin. She could expect a reply within three to six weeks. If Berlin moved quickly and there were no further questions she might be able to leave at the end of the third week of July.

Campbell knew that too long a delay would undermine Madame Rischard's confidence. Was there anything the Paris Office could do for her? She had only three requests. Would Miss Done be good enough to send the names of the *corsetière* at 41 Rue de Moscou and the *fournisseur des dames* at 38? Would Campbell take a letter to Marcel? And, most serious, if the espionage operation went wrong and she and Camille were not shot but interned in Germany, would the British undertake to press for their release at the end of the war? Campbell could not possibly give an honest answer to this last. No one knew what the circumstances would be. Germany might have won (Campbell hardly allowed himself to think this) and intervention by a defeated Britain might do more harm than good. He could only assure Madame Rischard that everything he and Bruce could do for her, Dr Rischard and their associates, would be done. He had to go. At one o'clock Mr Sinclair left Lausanne. When the boat reached Evian he disembarked and Captain Campbell took the afternoon train to Paris.

* Just as Hardy had done when he and Baschwitz planned their escape from the camp at Magdeburg. Hardy had removed his bed from the dormitory. There being no bed, the German duty officer knew there had been no occupant.

12

Der Landwirt

In early June 1917 a long-planned attempt was made to break through German defences. For a year British, Australian and Canadian sappers had been tunnelling beneath the German front lines, filling shafts 100 feet down with ammonal explosive, sealed in metal containers to keep it dry. At dawn on 7 June nineteen mines exploded below Messines Ridge, south of Ypres. The blast woke Lloyd George in Downing Street; the Professor of Geology at the University of Lille got out of bed to observe what he took to be an earthquake. The explosions were followed by a wave of attacks, planned by General Sir Herbert Plumer, Commander of the Second Army. Thirteen thousand German troops were killed or wounded, more than 7,000 prisoners taken. The Germans lost 48 guns, 218 machine-guns and, significantly, confidence in the invulnerability of their front-line trenches. The cost to Plumer was 25,000 officers and men.

How would Germany respond? The collapse of Nivelle's offensive in mid-April 1917 had left the French unable to do more on the Western Front than mark time until the arrival of support from the United States. Haig was left to pursue his own strategy. He thought it folly to wait for the Americans. As Russia fragmented, quantities of hard, experienced enemy troops were pouring into France. In Haig's view, the Allies' best hope was to press forward with an unrelenting series of limited attacks over the old battlegrounds of Ypres, pushing up to the Belgian ports where German U-boats had their forward bases. The surprise at Messines was the prelude to the Ypres campaign. Intelligence about German railway movements would be of great value – but could the Luxembourg scheme be launched in time? It would be three to six weeks before Madame Rischard's visa arrived. Three days to get home, seven to set up a network, five for information to reach GHQ – no, it was impossible. But the Ypres assault might continue into autumn, winter even. There was time for reports from Luxembourg to make a difference.

An eight-week forecast was ambitious. Dr Rischard was as yet unaware of the role assigned to him, train-watchers had to be recruited. These uncertainties would be dealt with once Madame Rischard got home. Meanwhile, the Paris Office addressed the question of reporting lines. The original idea had been to use the ordinary post. If Campbell's code was sufficiently secure, the censors would not only fail to decipher Madame Rischard's letters but would not even realize they should try. But there were drawbacks. Censors worked slowly, their decisions were arbitrary and often capricious. Suspicious phrases were simply blanked out, enclosures thrown away. Correspondence considered too verbose was destroyed. Rules were strict. Letters and non-picture postcards were allowed between Luxembourg and Switzerland but at any time regulations might be changed. Cameron was right. It would be a mistake to depend on the post.

Printed matter was also censored but more expeditiously, type being easier to read than handwriting. Regular publications – newspapers, journals, calendars – were often only casually inspected. For this reason intelligence was often conveyed via 'For Sale' and 'Wanted' columns. Transmission was fast, as newspapers, classed as perishable, were delivered by the quickest possible means.

That was what Bruce wanted: an innocuous publication, sent routinely to subscribers, censored cursorily, if at all. In the spring of 1917 he found what he was seeking: *Der Landwirt.**

The masthead gave the name of the publisher:

Verantwortlicher
Herausgeber u. Drucker
Paul Schroell
Diekirch

Diekirch was a small town about thirty miles north of the capital of the Grand Duchy, lying on the edge of thick woods, through which

---

* *The Agriculturalist.*

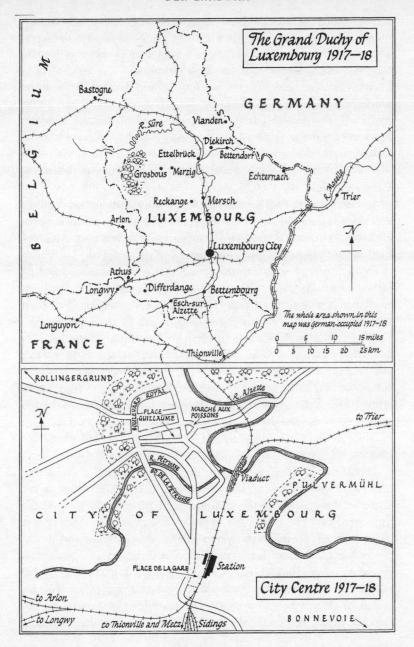

The Grand Duchy of Luxembourg 1917–18

GERMANY

BELGIUM

Bastogne

Vianden

R. Sûre

Diekirch

Ettelbrück

Bettendorf

Grosbous

Merzig

Echternach

Reckange

Mersch

R. Moselle

Trier

Arlon

LUXEMBOURG

Luxembourg City

N

Athus

Longwy

Differdange

Bettembourg

Esch-sur-Alzette

Longuyon

FRANCE

Thionville

The whole area shown in this map was German-occupied 1917–18

0   5   10   15 miles
0 5 10 15 20 25 km

ROLLINGERGRUND

R. Alzette

N

BOULEVARD ROYAL

PLACE GUILLAUME

MARCHÉ AUX POISSONS

to Trier

R. Pétrusse

BD. DE LA PÉTRUSSE

Viaduct

PULVERMÜHL

CITY OF LUXEMBOURG

PLACE DE LA GARE

Station

to Arlon

to Longwy

to Thionville and Metz

Sidings

BONNEVOIE

City Centre 1917–18

ran the Luxembourg/German frontier. The Schroells, a local family, owned a bookbinder and stationer, three printing houses and several newspapers. Paul was young for a newspaper proprietor; he had inherited the family firm in 1898, when he was eighteen. He and his older cousin, Emile, ran the newspapers and the Diekirch printing works, Paul's mother – 'Amama' – and sisters, Maisy and Lily, managed the bookbinding and stationery business. A dozen employees put the papers together, working long hours while the town slept. In that small rural community, workmates and their families knew each other, an intimacy that was important when the Germans came.

Jeanne Schmitt, Paul's wife, was part-owner with her sister of the second printing house, at Ettelbrück, ten miles south-west of Diekirch. A manager, Peter Thein, supervised this business. After the birth of her children – two, Alice and Gabrielle, survived – Jeanne played an increasing part in the production of the *Landwirt* and by late 1912 the direction of the Diekirch publishing and printing business was largely in her hands. Since 1910 the *Landwirt* had been edited by Emile Schumacher, a family friend, Paul being preoccupied with the establishment of the third printing house, Maison Caffaro, at Esch-sur-Alzette, fifty miles from Diekirch. In June 1913 the *Journal d'Esch* made its first appearance. From that time the *Landwirt* was effectively put together by Jeanne, although Paul's name continued to appear on the masthead. All day she worked in the office at the Diekirch works. Her housekeeping was done by a local girl and a German governess, Käthe Müller, looked after Alice and 'Gaby'.

Useful, industrious, provincial life: father, mother, grandmother and aunts working in the family business, well-ordered house in the Esplanade, daughters in the schoolroom. Four times a week on the appointed day, the *Landwirt*'s subscribers enjoyed their newspaper over their good breakfasts. Contributors were friends and neighbours. Articles voiced local concerns and interests. The businesses prospered and, although Paul had much to think of, he found time to practise the cor anglais – the alto oboe – and play music with his friends at Victor Schramm's café in Diekirch town square. Jeanne devoted herself to her family, her household, the *Landwirt* and the works. People thought her the perfect wife. No woman was as wise or as discreet.

In 1914 the Germans came. The August day was hot. People put out skins of water for the horses and the young men who tramped singing through the town. Alice and Gaby sat on the doorstep:

> *Die Vöglein im Wälde, die sangen, sangen,*
> *Sangen so wunder-wunderschön,*
> *In der Heimat, in der Heimat*
> *Da gibt's ein Wiedersehn.*

> The little birds in the forest, singing, singing,
> Singing so wonder-, wonderfully,
> In our homeland, our homeland,
> We will meet again.

Poor lads – but the children were unmoved. At the tops of their voices they chanted:

> *In der Heimat, in der Heimat,*
> *Da gibt's **kein** Wiedersehn.*

> . . . They will **not** meet again . . .

Alice and Gaby knew it would upset their Fräulein but even at nine and seven they were angry that soldiers had marched into their country.[1] Three days later Käthe Müller's brother Richard was killed in the battle for Liège.

The next blow fell on 14 August, eve of the Feast of the Assumption of the Virgin. On that day it was the custom of the Schroells to celebrate their own two Marys: Amama and Maisy. To honour his mother and sister, Paul had chosen his favourite dish, '*Filetsbifsteack, le plat préféré de Papa*'. In the evening they gathered at the house on the Esplanade, Paul and Jeanne, Alice and Gaby, Amama, Maisy and Lily, to address themselves to the feast. They had just taken their places when a German officer arrived, asking for Schroell. Yes, Jeanne told him, her husband was at home. He was here to eat a delicious piece of beef. Gretchen was at this very moment carrying it in from the kitchen. Could she not persuade the visitor to have a mouthful? They had more than enough. Alas, there was no space for an extra chair but the children's playroom had a table. Their guest could make himself comfortable there.

Was it the aroma that rose from the dish, or Madame Schroell's commanding kindness, that encouraged the officer to sit down among the children's toys, unfold his napkin and partake? As the children went off to bed, Gaby peeped round the door. The soldier could not take Papa away, after Mama had gone to such trouble to make him feel at home. Paul finished his steak, potatoes, carrots, onions, last pieces of gravy-saturated bread. A private word with Jeanne – and he was ready.

For ten days she did not know where they had taken him. She tried to concentrate on the business and reassure the staff. On 26 August a telegram came from the President of the Council of Ministers, Monsieur Eyschen, saying that Paul had been imprisoned in the Château Collart at Bettembourg.* He and the editor-in-chief at the *Journal d'Esch*, Franz Clement, had been arrested, with a contributor, the director of the College of Commerce at Esch, for *deutschfeindliche Betätigung*, anti-German activity: the *Journal d'Esch* was alleged to be pro-French. Curious: the *Journal* mentioned Goethe, Heine and Schiller so often that joking readers called it the *Journal de Boche*. From Bettembourg the prisoners were moved to Koblenz; Jeanne and Clement's sister visited them, with Commandant Tessmar's permission, driving into Germany in a car draped with a Red Cross flag. The papers were appearing as usual, Jeanne assured her husband; there was plenty to draw on from German publications, now available in quantity. Alex Paquet, the family lawyer, was doing his best to secure their release.

These days were hard. A German officer with an awkward name, Dr Ernst Arnzt, was billeted in the house, an order Jeanne could not refuse. Fräulein Müller collapsed with grief at the loss of her brother and the strain of looking after two little girls who had become rebellious and anti-German. Jeanne nursed her through a fever and sent her home. Minister Eyschen wrote to the Kaiser and at the end of September the prisoners were freed. The arrest had been a warning.

At Christmas the *Landwirt* received a copy of a pastoral letter, written by Cardinal Mercier, Archbishop of Malines, condemning the destruction of his country. In Leuven, 1,800 medieval buildings and the university library had been set on fire.* Paintings and manuscripts had been lost, hundreds of civilians killed, others forced to leave. Occupying troops claimed to have been fired on by armed civilians, *francs-tireurs*; panicking, young soldiers had torched everything they saw. Villages and towns had been laid waste. Malines was bombarded, the cathedral damaged. So were the Archbishop's palace, the church of Notre-Dame, streets of sixteenth-century houses. Faith was a comfort, the Cardinal declared, but looking heavenwards was not enough. The invasion was not only un-Christian, it was illegal. The title of the Christmas letter – 'Patriotism and Endurance' – was unprovocative but its contents were a rallying cry. The Cardinal enjoined his readers, clerical and lay, to redouble their support for soldiers at the front and demonstrate their loyalty to Belgium and their King. Cardinal Mercier encouraged his priests, Father Buelens and his brother Father René among them, to oppose the enemy, by whatever means they and their parishioners could devise.

Cardinal Mercier not only condemned the invaders, but incited resistance. Copies of his letter were circulated in France, Holland and Luxembourg, as well as Belgium, among Catholics and non-Catholics alike. Paul Schroell published it in the *Landwirt*, in full.**

To drive the message home, he placed above it, in heavy type, the censors' prohibition:

> Darf nicht im *Landwirt* erscheinen.
> Not to be printed in the *Landwirt*.

This asked for more than five weeks in a cold cell.

Did Schroell think that a self-respecting editor could do no less? It was not the first time that the family newspapers had been in

---

* Louvain, former capital of the Duchy of Brabant.
** No issues of this edition of the *Landwirt* have survived but a copy of the relevant sheet is included in Alice and Gaby Schroell's memoir. The Cardinal's letter is printed in a narrow column, the ink is smudged and there is a typographical error in the title: '*Patriotisme et Endurange*'. Servas Bettendorf, the *Landwirt*'s master typesetter, must have been trembling with excitement as the letters were picked out.

trouble. Paul's grandfather had been accused of anti-clericalism, his paper denounced from the pulpit. Paul's father had been arrested for publishing criticism of church schools. He had been given clearance by a local bishop but, rather than betray his sources, chose jail.

Paul Schroell did not publish the Cardinal's letter out of respect for the Church. An unbeliever, he refused to go to Mass. Priests were too influential, he said; their parishioners, particularly the women, too deferential. Jeanne had adjusted her practice to suit her husband's views. She had gone to her mother's for the children's christening; it was understood that Paul's work kept him away.

The Cardinal's letter appeared in the *Landwirt* because Paul Schroell agreed with what it said and because he refused to be told what was and was not to be printed in his own newspapers. What did Jeanne think? Though a good Catholic, she did not advertise her religion; was it essential for Paul to advertise his patriotism? She agreed with Paul's decision. The family and the businesses were at risk but the Cardinal had told them that the Germans had broken the laws of God and man. Amama was especially vigorous. During the Franco-Prussian War she had taken a wounded French prisoner into the house. Nursing him had increased her sympathy for the French. She had not liked Prussians then and she disapproved of Germans now. She had backed her husband when he defied the law and she would support her son.

There was a small chance that the Germans would disregard the *Landwirt*'s provocation. So far the invaders had behaved officiously but not tyrannically toward the people of Luxembourg. It was Christmas, when religious articles were bound to appear in country newspapers. The censors might be indulgent; they might even be on holiday.

But there was the superscription:

Darf nicht im *Landwirt* erscheinen.

Someone warned Paul that he was about to be arrested.

On 15 February he escaped to Switzerland. There was no time to say goodbye. He spoke to Jeanne on the telephone but they were all aware that Germans listened in. Hubert Flohr, conductor of the orchestra at Victor Schramm's café, worked the Diekirch telephone exchange and knew what was going on. Aunt Maisy had been so irritated by clicks on the line that she had smashed the mouthpiece against the wall. From the apparatus she had been reproached by a third party, deafened in the line of duty.

Paul went first to the Schweizerhof in Basel. A fellow-lodger made no secret of being interested in Monsieur Schroell's visitors and Paul knew that he was watched. He moved on to the St Gotthard Hotel in Zürich. Jeanne was left to look after the two newspapers and the three printing houses. The Ettelbrück business was in good hands – Peter Thein had run things there for the past ten years – and in Diekirch she could rely on Emile Schumacher. Managing Maison Caffaro was more demanding, Esch being so distant. Jeanne asked Paul's sister, Emilie, and her husband, Josy Hermann, to direct the works and produce the *Journal*. But how was money to be obtained for wages and other bills? Bank accounts were in Paul's name and the manager of the Diekirch bank, Monsieur Bech, refused to give Madame Schroell an advance. He had to think of the depositors, he said. For all he knew, Monsieur Schroell had gone for good. The family did not forget this insult. Emile Schumacher spoke to his father, who lent Jeanne enough for immediate needs, Amama offering her house as security. Even with funds, obtaining newsprint was difficult, as minimal amounts were released by the National Print and Publications Office in Luxembourg. Paul's cousin Emile was believed to have influence but, when Jeanne appealed to him, she was rebuffed. The family thought him soured by years of playing second fiddle in the business.*

Jeanne was afraid that she would be unable to carry on. Without her husband's signed authority she could neither draw on bank accounts nor act in his name. The businesses would collapse, the men be thrown out of work. She asked Tessmar for a pass to go to Switzerland. All she wanted, she told the Commandant, was to be able to put everything on a proper footing. He gave her a permit and at Easter she went to Zürich, crossing the German/Swiss frontier at Lörrach, where she was searched: '*une visite corporelle très désagréable*'. Paul was still staying at the St Gotthard Hotel. Alex

* '*Une vieille rancune familiale probablement!*'

Paquet had prepared a document, giving Jeanne the powers she needed to continue to run the business. This Paul signed. She had not brought his cor anglais, she said, in case it was confiscated, but she had found a carrier, Charles Hoffmann, a Diekirch boy at university in Switzerland. He would bring the oboe to Zürich, claiming it as his own, and hoping that the frontier guards would not ask him to play.

From Switzerland Schroell went to Paris. Although she now had access to the family bank account, Jeanne was allowed to send only a little money out of the country. Paul did not starve. A Diekirch man, Nicolas Treinen, owned the Restaurant Théâtre Sarah-Bernhardt, serving the playhouse in Place du Châtelet.* The theatre flourished – people wanted distraction – and the restaurant's business was good. It was understood that any Luxemburger who needed a meal might lunch or dine at Treinen's establishment as the proprietor's guest, bills to be settled at the end of the war. For four years Schroell ate there daily.

Paul was not idle. Cinéma Gaumont in the Champs Elysées had vacancies in the orchestra that accompanied the silent films: the cor anglais was engaged. Furious sight-reading was required and the repertoire was huge: Monsieur Jamin, the conductor, had to provide every kind of music, including interludes to placate the audience when reels split or the projector failed.** Jamin ran two series of concerts in the Jardin du Luxembourg, Concerts Rouges and Concerts Pasdeloup.*** French musicians were away at the war and there was plenty of work for a cor anglais. By helping him out,

* Now Théâtre de la Ville. Sarah Bernhardt's success in managing her own theatre had encouraged Réjane to do the same.

** Playing in the silent cinema was often a sideline for hard-up musicians: Shostakovich, for example, supported his widowed mother and his sisters by doing so. Sight-reading was excellent training; on this were founded the careers of such celebrated musicians as Albert Sammons, who played at the Gaiety Lounge in London, and Jack Jacobs, Dutch violinist and Musical Director in the tea-rooms and restaurants of J. Lyons & Company. See Eric Wetherell's *Albert Sammons*, London: Thames Publishing, 1998.

*** Jules Pasdeloup founded the Concerts Populaires in 1861, still running, as Concerts Pasdeloup. His aim was to introduce the French public to unfamiliar music by foreign composers, Schumann, for instance, and new work by young French composers. A patron of Bizet, *Carmen* was dedicated to him.

Jamin said, Schroell could practise and at the same time earn extra money.

Among the clients of the Restaurant Théâtre Sarah-Bernhardt were Luxembourg *légionnaires*, volunteers in the French army. They were badly paid; leave money was five francs a day and in Paris that did not go far. In the early summer of 1916 the restaurant's *habitués* decided to do something to support their compatriots, heroes who subsisted on meat extract and biscuits at the front, while they themselves sat over Treinen's dinners. Paul and his friends set up a committee – *Comité de l'Oeuvre des Soldats Luxembourgeois, Engagés Volontaires au Service de la France* – to publicize the legionnaires' contribution to the war.

How were they to raise funds? Jamin thought concert parties would be a draw. Programmes and posters were designed by Paul's Parisian cousins, artists working at the Musée des Plantes and the Sèvres porcelain factory, Jamin supplied the band and Madame Jamin, coached in the Luxembourg language, sang patriotic songs: '*Hemecht*' and '*Feierwon*'.* With much eating, drinking, entertainment and conversation, the *légionnaires*' allowances were augmented and the expatriates' homesickness, if not assuaged, was put to use.

Paul thought he could do more. Thirty thousand of his countrymen lived in France – 40,000 if those serving with the French army were included. They needed a newspaper. The committee agreed to act as a partner in the venture and Paul looked for investors. The *Luxembourgeois* was to come out twice a week; its objective, proclaimed on the masthead, *Luxembourg Libre, Uni Economiquement à la France*.** The first issue had been published on 22 January 1917, just as Captain Bruce arrived in the office in Rue St Roch.

Charles Jubert was now working at the SRRR, *Service de Renseignements sur les Réfugiés et Rapatriés*, at 6 Rue de Hanovre, near the Opéra. The SRRR had recently been put on an independent footing, with Mollard at its head. Formerly part of the welfare service

* 'The Motherland' and 'Little Steam Train', the nation's official and unofficial anthems.
** 'Luxembourg Free and Economically at One with France', a vision of the Grand Duchy as some believed it had once been, before the French-speaking part of the country had joined up with Belgium in 1839.

run by the *Direction du Contrôle*, its real focus was counter-espionage.[2] Jubert knew all about the committee and the *Luxembourgeois*. He also knew the *Journal* and the *Landwirt* and could vouch for the proprietor. Jubert was president of the International Federation of Bicyclists and before the war had pedalled through every town and village in the Grand Duchy. (It was not large.) He understood the life of places like Diekirch, Ettelbrück and Esch, where people were careful about disclosing information to those they did not know. Jubert introduced Schroell to Bruce.

The *Journal d'Esch*, Paul explained, was managed by his sister and brother-in-law, the *Landwirt* by his wife. If Jeanne wanted certain articles to be published on certain pages at certain times, the editor would not object. Schumacher was a friend. His father's loan, secured on Paul's mother's house, had rescued the business, binding the Schroell and Schumacher families even more closely together. Captain Bruce presumably had in mind the sort of articles that must on no account contain typographical errors. The typesetters would not query their instructions; if they did, Jeanne would assure them that the text was correct and check that every letter was placed exactly where it should be. The *Landwirt* was a local newspaper, yes, but it was also sent to subscribers who lived elsewhere. No, it would not take long for the *Landwirt* to get from Luxembourg to Switzerland; the censors understood that readers wanted their news before it staled. Father Cambron, the Jesuit priest who had been expelled? If he would like to receive the *Landwirt*, it could easily be sent to him in Berne.

Paul had complete confidence in his wife. He could sound her out; a friend in Switzerland, Jean Nilles, acted as their '*boîte aux lettres*'. Jeanne understood Paul's elliptical allusions at once. Articles containing coded messages were to be put into the *Landwirt*. Who would write these pieces? Bruce knew that Madame Rischard could not do it. Her time would be taken up with summarizing and coding reports and dealing with correspondence from the Paris Office. In any case, it would have been extraordinary if she suddenly started writing for the newspapers.

Schroell suggested Joseph Hansen, the Diekirch schoolmaster. He would regard it as an honour to be asked to help. The schoolmaster loved Paris – as the boy with the highest marks in Luxembourg, he had won a scholarship to the Ecole Normale Supérieure – and was a thoroughgoing francophile. He wrote for *Voix des Jeunes*, a journal for French-speaking Luxemburgers interested in French art and literature. Hansen was not violently anti-German – he simply preferred French culture – and the authorities had shown no particular interest in him. He was the youngest professor in Luxembourg, a respected teacher at the Diekirch school, one of three in the Grand Duchy where Latin was taught.* People called him 'an idealist'; they did not think of him as a man of action. No one would suspect him.

Hansen had been a regular contributor to the *Landwirt* but since the spring of 1915 had written nothing. The Schroells knew why. The Hansens were neighbours and the children were always in and out of each other's houses: Alice and Gaby, the two Hansen boys, Josy and Georges, and their sisters, Jeanne and Simone. Gaby looked up to Josy; when they had snowball fights, she made it her special duty to keep him supplied with ammunition. In 1915 Josy had been sent home from Scout camp with meningitis. He was put in his grandmother's high bed, his mother watching over him. He had asked for Gaby, and little Jeanne had run to fetch her. Could Gaby give Josy a kiss? Of course, said Josy's mother, too distracted to think of the risk. The boy died two days later. After an anxious time, the families were told that Gaby had not been infected. The Hansens had supported Jeanne when Paul left her in charge of the business; now she tried to console them. They came in to see her almost every evening, after the children had been put to bed, to drink a *tisane* and talk about the day. It would be quite natural for Hansen to offer to write a column for the *Landwirt*. The pieces would not be signed but, if it came out that Hansen was the author, no one would be embarrassed. Hansen had written for the paper before and Madame Schroell was known to need contributors.

In early June Schroell wrote to Hansen, giving as his address the St Gotthard Hotel in Zürich. The letter was in German; an English translation was made for the files at Rue St Roch:

---

* The other grammar schools were in the capital and at Echternach.

My dear Professor,

The announcement of the sudden death of your eldest son has grieved me very much. I sympathize deeply with you in your pain, and all the more as I am under a debt of gratitude to you for the loyal support which my sorely tried wife finds in your valuable co-operation.

We are at the present time passing through a period during which the most revolutionary changes are to be expected. You would therefore do well to resume for the *Landwirt* chosen extracts from the great foreign press. Will you please do your best to have these extracts inserted, so far as possible, before the heading: *'Lokal Neuigkeiten'*?* The extracts could possess a definite character. You will yourself find the form which today is most suitable for the *Landwirt*.

The political situation seems to me discouraging to the last degree. What does the great public think with regard to the future of our small home? I count firmly on you and Fr. Cle. so that later on we shall be able again to work on together. You can both count on my gratitude; you as a Godfather of my journalistic enterprises, Cl. as my boon companion. How pleased I should be to have the latter with me now! I feel the lack of him continually, especially as I have useful employment for him.

Please greet especially Madame Hansen, Alex P. and all friends and colleagues.**

Let us hope that our common work will soon reunite us all.

P. Schroell

Paul wrote in similar terms to Jeanne. Hansen was bound to show her the peculiar letter he had received from her husband, with its formal phrasing and strange references to Clement. Over steaming cups of *camomille, tilleul, verveine-menthe*, she would explain.

Paul's letters were posted by an intermediary in Switzerland on 12 June, five days before Madame Rischard returned to Lausanne.

---

* 'Local News'. 'Before the heading' is a literal translation of *'vor der Rubrik'*, i.e. 'Under the heading'. Schroell to Hansen, 9 June 1917.
** Fr. Cle., or Cl., referred to Franz Clement, editor-in-chief of the *Journal d'Esch*, Alex P. to Alex Paquet, the Schroells' lawyer.

13

Not Singly . . .

Longer days brought leisure. In Paris theatres and cinemas stayed open until eleven. Bread was rationed but tea-rooms still served *pâtisserie* and on meatless days restaurants celebrated new potatoes, radishes, peas, lettuce and shallots. Bruce acquired a gramophone, Campbell golf clubs and a tennis racquet. Boats rested under the willows at Malmaison; did Miss Done and Captain Bruce take fruit and cheese for Sunday picnics on the river? At the end of July Madame Garland told Tante Lise that the family were going to the mountains for a fortnight. While they were on holiday, she would encourage Nicole to write. This was cover: Bruce and Campbell were to be away from Paris, leaving Chocqueel in charge of communication with Lausanne.

For a year and a half Bruce had taken no leave. Since he had arrived in the office in Rue St Roch in January 1917 his duties had been demanding; as well as organizing the Luxembourg operation, he managed agents throughout France – the vice-consul in Lyon was one of his network chiefs – and, as special business, in Madrid. At the end of July 1917 he went home to Scotland for a fortnight, returning to France on 10 August. The weather had broken and it rained non-stop. When the Allies attacked at Ypres on the last day of July, men were up to their waists in water. Tanks sank into mud. In twenty-four hours the Allies gained a mile and three quarters, at the cost of 30,000 killed and wounded. The Germans lost as many. Both sides deployed mustard gas, sardonically christened 'Yperite'.[*] The Allies used tactics tried by the Canadians at Arras in April, rapid

* Dichlorethylsulphide.

artillery fire, using the new light machine-guns, to cover the advance. The enemy withdrew deeper into the battle-zone, the so-called 'elastic defence', leaving empty ground to absorb the bombardment and enticing the attackers forward on to the guns. '*Ici toujours la même chose . . .*' Georgette said despairingly to Lise, 'it all goes on as before.'[1]

Woolrych's desk at 41 Rue St Roch was now occupied by Buckley, seconded to the Paris Office, at Drake's suggestion, to expand the escaping scheme. When their aeroplanes were shot down or their tanks disabled, aviators and tank crews tended to stay by their machines, attempting to destroy them, rather than trying to get away into the surrounding country. So many of these expensively trained officers were being captured that GHQ had asked I(b) to organize escaping courses for the RFC and tank regiments. Infantry officers were excluded from the programme, it being thought that, given a choice, they should and would fight to the last. If they were given escaping lessons, they might suppose that GHQ thought capture preferable to death; though true, this would set a bad example.*

Bruce and Buckley talked more about Baschwitz Meau. If Madame Rischard were unable to leave Switzerland – she had heard nothing from Berlin – should they not try to put the Belgian into the Luxembourg marshalling yard? As if he had overheard, at that very moment Baschwitz appeared in Paris. Having a little leave, he had brought himself to the Hôtel de Strasbourg, round the corner in Rue de Richelieu. On 15 August he saw Bruce. Had the Captain any proposals? 'The good impression he made when I saw him in June is fully confirmed,' Bruce told Drake; 'if he could be attached to us immediately, his prisoners of War [*sic*] experience could be turned to very good account.'[2]

Bruce was further reassured by Meau's answers to two questions. French being the Belgian's first language, why had he not offered his services to the *Deuxième Bureau*? And, having decided to approach

---

* See Drake's memorandum, *History of Intelligence (B), British Expeditionary Force, France, from January 1917 to April 1919*, PRO/WO 106/45, paras. 46–48. The tuition was not forgotten. When Bruce's soldier nephew was captured in the Second World War, one of his letters asked for a supply of 'Uncle George's medicine'. Those at home understood what was meant.

British Intelligence, how had he obtained Bruce's name and the Place Anglaise address? The explanation was this. The last stage of Baschwitz's escape in 1916 had been by boat from Holland to Folkestone. Sent back to La Panne at the beginning of October, he had asked General Orth for permission to return to active service. This was refused. Baschwitz's history of escaping and of inciting others to escape meant that if he were captured again he would be shot. On 21 November he had been posted to Wulveringhem as Deputy Commandant.* There he had languished. In any case, there was no fighting to do. The King of the Belgians declined to engage his army in the next allied offensive, on the grounds that, if he were to do so, the enemy would bear down even more harshly on his people.**

Baschwitz had discussed his difficulty with a colleague, Major Neefs, quartermaster of the Fourth Infantry Brigade. How was he to find something dangerous, something useful? Neefs suggested that he try again. Commanding an infantry platoon generally brought death or glory, often both. Impossible, said Baschwitz. Apart from the first eighteen days, his entire service career had been spent escaping. He was not qualified to command other people. He had been thinking, however, about Intelligence. From what he had heard, the British Secret Service was the one to aim for.[3] But how was he to introduce himself? He could hardly ask his superior officers to allow him to transfer his services to the British. That would be tactless; the Belgian army was an entirely separate command. Neefs had an idea. Prince Alexander of Teck, brother-in-law to King George V, was at La Panne, as head of the British Mission to the Belgian army. Why not confide in him? This Baschwitz did. The Prince and his wife, Princess Alice, were friends of Bruce's parents and Teck suggested that Baschwitz write to Bruce

---

* *Adjoint Permanent du Commandant.*

** In the King's eyes, Belgium remained neutral. He had mobilized his army only to resist invasion. In the winter of 1915/16 the King had asked the Prime Minister, de Broqueville (also Foreign Minister and Minister of War), whether it might not be better to negotiate a separate peace treaty with Germany. The King and his ministers managed to keep discussion private; neither his subjects nor the Germans realized that there was dispute. Only the most senior army officers knew the extent of the King's non-cooperation with his fellow allied Commanders-in-Chief.

in Paris.* Secrecy was paramount. Baschwitz was sure that enemy agents had photographed him as he came ashore at Folkestone. Any mention of his working for the British would attract the attention of German counter-espionage, endangering those he wished to serve. Baschwitz's introduction was private and informal; the mistake in the way he addressed Bruce – in that first letter he called him Colonel – suggests that no ADC was asked to check the rank of the head of the Paris Office.

'I have now discussed the project of a mission with BASCHWITZ,' Bruce told Drake, 'and he is extremely keen. I am quite certain that he would be very useful to us, and I would ask you to apply to the Belgians for him to be attached to the British Army.' The 'project of a mission' had a surprising feature. 'I am quite clear that the best plan would be to put him down by free balloon . . .'[4]

Why had Baschwitz and Bruce fixed on ballooning?

Suppose that a man wanted to soar over enemy lines at night, drift quietly across Alsace and drop down into occupied country. Suppose that Baschwitz had to be sent to Luxembourg. A balloon would be the quickest way to get there. It would be difficult – Bruce was not so mesmerized by Baschwitz as to forget this – but details could be discussed later.

Even at this early stage, a complication presented itself. It would not do to worry Cameron. Madame Rischard's visa might arrive at any time; meanwhile, it would be unwise to propose an alternative plan. One experiment in the Grand Duchy was enough for Cameron. As Bruce's note to Drake would probably be copied to Folkestone, he said nothing about Luxembourg. The allusion to free balloons would allow Cameron to feel that he was being kept in the picture

---

* Prince Alexander of Teck, 'Alge', was married to Princess Alice, Queen Victoria's youngest grandchild. His sister Mary, 'May of Teck', married Queen Victoria's grandson, who in 1910 succeeded his father as King George V. In 1917, when the King decided that his family should put aside their German titles, the Tecks became the Earl and Countess of Athlone. There had long been friendly, but discreet, connections between the royal family and that of Captain Bruce. His father had been one of Queen Victoria's close advisers; Jean, his sister, was maid of honour to Queen Mary (that is, in attendance as a lady-in-waiting when the Queen was in Scotland); and Victoria, Bruce's younger sister, named after the old Queen, had shared lessons with Princess Mary, only daughter of King George and Queen Mary.

but, beyond that, Bruce was careful to be vague: 'I will go fully into the question and work out a scheme.' The most urgent objective was to secure Baschwitz's services.

The Belgian army said no. Sous-Lieutenant Baschwitz would not be released. Bruce begged Drake to use all his influence. Clerical duties could be performed by a substitute. Could Drake not tell the Belgians how hard it was to find intelligent men to go behind the lines? Women with the necessary capacity and judgement could still be found, Madame Rischard being one, but men with the right quali-fications were scarce. Fit adult males had all been called up; British military officers known to be willing to work behind enemy lines had already been extracted from the army. If secondment from the French and Belgian armies was ruled out, I(b)'s work would become impossible.[5]

Persuaded by the urgency of Bruce's arguments, Drake agreed to plead his case via a direct approach to Orth, who was now at GHQ as head of the Belgian Military Mission. The General was 'person-ally quite well disposed' towards Drake's request. He did what he could, to no avail. Secondments were decided by a branch of the Belgian army that was more concerned with administrative conveni-ence than military intelligence. Although Baschwitz's present job was not important, moving him would require 'a succession of replace-ments all through'.[6] Drake promised to try Orth again but was not hopeful. Some other way would have to be found to conjure Baschwitz out of Wulveringhem.

14

. . . But in Multitudes

On 15 August, the day on which Baschwitz presented himself at Place Anglaise, Bruce had a letter from Lausanne. Berlin had spoken. Permission to leave Switzerland was refused. Madame Rischard was astonished and very cross. She had been in Lausanne long enough. She had already asked Camille to order new curtains for the washstand at home. Repairs were being made to the cover that protected the dining-room table, the gardener had set to work on the flowerbeds. Was she going to miss the begonias for a second summer?*

She was ready for her mission. Hesitation had melted away. In these days Madame Rischard's letters were assured, her coding fluent, even witty. One theme was financial. Funds for the espionage operation were to come from her French bank account; she had accordingly appointed Jubert her representative at the Paris end, with authority to receive and make payments on her behalf. The difficulty lay in getting money into Luxembourg. The Rischards had a friend in Paris, also known to Jubert, a Monsieur Denis, of the Comptoir Métallurgique de Longwy, the office that dealt with the accounts for the Longwy steelworks. Through its books Monsieur Denis was able to get money into the Grand Duchy. Madame Rischard had written to Monsieur Denis, saying that sums were due to her from her late father's French investments, and asking whether he might be able to facilitate a transfer. Denis had offered to send whatever she required. Jubert would ensure that the French authorities asked no questions

---

* Dr Rischard's report on housekeeping matters appeared on the reverse side of the cutting, enclosed with his letter of early June, in which he complained about the German occupation.

– Denis asked none himself – about this 'private arrangement' between the Rischards and an intimate family friend.[1]

Madame Rischard had begun to enjoy her correspondence with the Paris Office. Lausanne was dull but her letters to the Garland family were full of incident. She let her imagination run, decorating her sentences with fantastic flourishes. Needing a six-letter word beginning and ending with a, followed by a j, she reported that Tante Marie had been savaged by a fly, requiring applications of arnica and a jeweller to saw the rings off the victim's swollen fingers. A neat deployment of g and z was managed by slicing off a neighbour's legs with a sharpened scythe, *'abattant l'herbe des gazons'*.[2] Cutting grass was code for train-watching – and as dangerous.

Were Bruce, Campbell and Chocqueel startled by these cadenzas? It was not long before they began to match them. Bruce gave Georgette strong views on the Philosophy of history, a dizzy interest in the works of Taine and Michelet. Campbell turned Jacques into a worrier, fretting about his mother and his health. It was on Chocqueel that Madame Rischard's elaborations had the most profound effect. Wanting an R, he had created Robert, a son for the Garlands. Competing for her parents' attention, Nicole became wild and unmanageable.[3] Georgette and Jacques introduced a governess, Mademoiselle Testu, bringing a much wanted u, and Tante Lise gave advice: 'See that she keeps Nicole busy with a needle in the afternoons . . .'[4] But Nicole preferred the cinema to mending linen, tennis parties to the schoolroom. Chocqueel gave her an unsuitable admirer: *'nos sentiments n'ont encore aucun aspect dangereux, ils sont uniquement amicaux; nous sommes occupés beaucoup moins de flirt . . .* nothing dangerous in our feelings for each other . . . not really flirting . . . he is the same age as me . . . a perfect friend . . .'[5] Mademoiselle Testu was determined to discipline her charge and, when Nicole would not submit, punishment was severe. Their relationship mirrored that between France and Germany, their battles coincided with those between the Allies and the enemy, a device to keep Madame Rischard in touch with the progress of the war.

Now, just as they were getting into their stride, there came the refusal from Berlin. Madame Rischard demanded an explanation. The Germans had no right to keep her in Switzerland: 'We will see who gives in, these gentlemen or me . . ."[6] She did not encode these protestations. If the Germans read them, so much the better. They would understand that she would not put up with this. Camille would have to go to the German Commandant, General Tessmar. Bruce made the best of it. The delay gave time for Campbell to come once more to see her in Lausanne. There were important matters to discuss and this might be their last opportunity.

The most urgent issue concerned the *Landwirt*. Madame Rischard thought well of Paul Schroell – Emile Metz, her late father's business partner, had been the principal investor in the *Luxemburger Zeitung*, founded by Paul's uncle – and approved of the plan to incorporate her reports in articles by Joseph Hansen. But although Schroell's invitation had been posted three months ago, Hansen had not replied. In mid-August Schroell had asked Jeanne to investigate. He was still waiting for her answer.

He knew from earlier letters how things were at home. Luxembourg was greyer, poorer. People lived from day to day, dreading unpleasant surprises. Men were taken away at no notice, women left to labour in the fields. Workshops and factories were busy but ordinary goods were nowhere to be found. There was no leather to patch boots and shoes. Canvas could not be obtained, nor barrels, nor saucepans. Hours were long but there was little to show for them. People on low wages could not make ends meet. Food was expensive and even milk, butter, bacon, bread and eggs were hard to obtain. Miners and factory hands got what they could at canteens. Children went hungry to school. Jeanne had arranged for milk and rough bread to be kept for her at farms outside Diekirch, sending Alice, Gaby and Aunt Lily on foot to fetch it back under their skirts. Emile Schumacher had taken a horse and cart to a distant farm to collect half a salted pig, travelling by night. The children went too, sleeping as inertly as they could manage on top of the place where the ham was hidden.

Thirty-three months of occupation. People could stand it no longer. At the end of May thousands of miners and metal-workers came out on strike, demanding more food and higher wages. The authorities cracked the whip. Canteens were closed. Distribution of provisions was stopped, collection of emergency funds prohibited. Union leaders were weak and divided and their protests were ignored. Many strikers were imprisoned; those living in tied housing were evicted. When the strike collapsed – it lasted a week – all who wished to return to their former jobs were forced to re-apply. Men who had taken an active part in demonstrations were blacklisted.

Esch-sur-Alzette was in mining country and the strikers' grievances were reported in the local newspaper, the *Escher Tageblatt*, as the *Journal* was obliged to call itself. All eyes were on Esch. The town council had supported the strike, the only local authority to do so, and councillors' speeches had been brave. When the censors read them in the *Tageblatt*, they had not liked them. The Hermanns were told to be more careful. Jeanne understood the implications. There was no need to close troublesome newspapers by force. Starvation would do. The National Print and Publications Office demanded a high price for newsprint, especially from proprietors whose newspapers were out of favour. Jeanne could see that a time would come when she would have to close down altogether. She could not charge readers or advertisers more – newspapers were already a luxury – and only just managed to pay a decent wage. No more savings could be made and there was no one from whom to borrow. Emile Schumacher's father had come to the rescue in 1915 but she could not go to him a second time. All this she conveyed to Paul.

The *Landwirt* was a crucial element in the espionage scheme. Somehow the Paris Office had to subsidize its publication, secretly and indirectly. How were they to manage it? The sum required was large and, until Madame Rischard's network had proved its worth, Cameron would never agree to use the Secret Service budget to prop up a country newspaper in Luxembourg. Might Madame Rischard provide funds? When Bruce had spoken to her about her own expenses, she had offered to advance what was necessary. Remembering that earlier conversation, and encouraged by her businesslike approach, Bruce asked Campbell to put Jeanne Schroell's problem to her.

On 8 September, a Saturday, 'Mr Sinclair' called at 33 Avenue Edouard Dapples. Madame Rischard's nerve was steady and she was in good spirits. She was willing to assist in every way. The *Landwirt* need only send someone along to her bank in Luxembourg, from which, her account replenished by Monsieur Denis of the Longwy steelworks, money would be made available. She was sure the bank manager would be discreet. Perhaps, but Campbell was more cautious. 'I told her that this was not necessary . . . all we asked her to do was to post money in a double envelope to an address in Luxemburg of which we would inform her from time to time in code.'[7]

On that same morning Schroell called at Rue St Roch, bringing a postcard from Jeanne. Hansen had not received Paul's invitation to contribute to the *Landwirt*. Knowing little herself, Jeanne had been unable to tell him very much. Madame Rischard would have to speak to Hansen when she got home. The schoolmaster would be worried about security; anticipating this, Jeanne had shown him the postcard. If Madame Rischard could see it and memorize its contents, it would serve as a password between herself and Hansen. A dispatch rider was immediately summoned to carry the postcard to Evian. All day Bruce tried to telephone instructions to Lieutenant Fuller at I(b)'s post at Evian but the line was so crackly that it was impossible to leave even the briefest word. At last he got through to Scheinsciss and so to Fuller. The postcard was delivered to Campbell on 9 September; next day he took it to Lausanne.

In her message Jeanne had emphasized that Hansen would need payment for his articles: '*H n'a plus de repos* . . . H has had no rest since the death of his son. He is on the road all day looking for provisions.' Bruce took up the point in a covering letter to Campbell:

You should tell Madame that she is empowered to agree to pay H. rather more a month than we had hitherto imagined necessary . . . I think that, provided that he can get in everything she wants, she could go, without reference to us, to Frs. 500 a month salary.

Her discretion was not to be unlimited.

PS. Impress on Madame that she must be sure to keep me informed of expenditure and that she must see to it that she gets acknowledgement from us of our agreement to the expenditure. Otherwise we may have her incurring big liabilities we know nothing about; at the same time one does not want to risk her not doing things which would be valuable for fear of our not paying![8]

This was the essence of Campbell's conversation with Madame Rischard. Now they had to wait while Camille went to General Tessmar.

15

Strafes

Relations between Bruce and Cameron, never warm, were cooling fast. Cameron worried unceasingly about finance. Every outlay had to be justified, every transfer explained. Expenses caused particular difficulty, so much so that at the end of July Bruce had taken matters to the top:

MEMO

Expenses

Submitted question of expenses to Colonel Drake on 29.7.17.* He agreed to the following arrangements for the officers of the Paris Bureau, subject to future alterations should the arrangements be found to work unfairly for or against the officers:

We will draw bare travelling expenses, i.e. railway fare when not on warrant, wagon-lits, taxis and porters, plus 15Frs. a day to cover hotel expenses, it being understood that we continue to draw our Frs.3 billet and Frs.6 ration and Paris allowance while we are travelling on duty.[1]

Referring the issue to Drake settled the argument about expenses but made the underlying conflict worse. The differences were only superficially about money. In that respect, Cameron's vigilance was understandable. Secret Service funds sometimes found their way into the wrong pockets – in the worst cases, those of people who were working for more than one master – and unexplained payments might be evidence of more serious deficiencies. Bruce did not need to be reminded of this nor that every centime spent at Rue St Roch was unavailable for expenditure on his agents elsewhere. He took as much

---

* Drake had been promoted in the late summer.

trouble with his accounts as with drafting letters. The quarrel between Cameron and Bruce went deeper.

The flashpoint came in the latter part of August, when Bruce went to Havre to see Captain Priestley, who directed I(b)'s section there. Priestley's reporting lines were complicated: I(b)'s French operation was supervised by Cameron but the transfer to Havre of the Belgian government had made the town into an extension of western Belgium, Wallinger's territory. Haig had been in Havre on 10 August for discussions about the respective roles of the British and Belgian armies in a proposed coastal attack on German defences at Ostend, arrangements in which Cameron and Wallinger were both involved, stoking the antipathy between them. Priestley was caught in the middle. When Cameron learnt that Bruce had seen Priestley, he complained in a fierce cable from Folkestone. For Bruce, this was the last straw. When he returned to Paris, he wrote to Cameron to say so.

Personal
Dear Cameron,

You have always told me to be as frank as I like in private letters & I therefore write to protest against your 2 recent letters on the subject of my trip to Havre.

On receipt of your wire No. 251 of the 20th I was placed in a difficult position. I did my very <u>damnedest</u> for you without any thought of any kind but to do the very best I could.

So far as I can judge on the facts in my possession, my mission to Havre was successful; all I have got from you is 2 severe rebukes, written, the first without knowledge of the facts, the second in a way which seems intentionally nasty.

You will perhaps remember that on the occasion of our last conversation at Folkestone I told you that when I had a direct order I always hesitated to use discretion for fear you should send a strafe, to which you replied 'of course, my dear Bruce, I should never do that' & you were quite annoyed at the suggestion. I am driven to the conclusion that you are deliberately out to be offensive – I cannot imagine why – & I write this letter in the hope that there may be some other explanation.[2]

Cameron had encouraged Bruce to be direct. They were contemporaries, with a similar background and connections, associations that were doubly precious after all that Cameron had endured before the war. Bruce had taken him at his word. He had written man to man – but there was no friendship in his letter.

Bruce had addressed Cameron as an equal. This stung, the more so for the following reason. War honours were to be announced on 13 September and Bruce and Cameron knew that the French government intended to recognize their work. Cameron's espionage operation had been running since 1914. Train-watching had been his idea, set up long before Bruce had appeared on the scene. Bruce had done well at Amiens and in Paris but, except for the escaping scheme, overall direction of everything in France had been Cameron's responsibility. Now both were to be recognized together, both entitled to wear the slip of ribbon of a *Croix de Chevalier* of the *Légion d'Honneur*. There was to be no difference in rank.

If Cameron answered, Bruce did not keep his letter. The next item in the file was a crisp message from Folkestone.

Kindly let me know how the matter of Madame L. who is en route for Luxemburg is progressing and if you have any news of her.[3]

The answer from Rue St Roch was evasive.

There is as yet nothing fresh to report. Madame L. has received a refusal from the Germans to allow her to return into Luxemburg; there is, however, reason to hope that the decision will be reversed.[4]

Not good enough. Cameron shot back a reply.

Kindly state when you heard of this refusal from the Germans; such an important matter should have been reported.[5]

The second 'kindly' sounded even more menacing than the first.

Bruce was caught. It was three weeks since Madame Rischard had heard from Berlin. Of course he should have told Cameron straightaway. More urgent issues had intervened: negotiations over Baschwitz; the mission to Havre. There was no point in saying so. He had failed to take Cameron into his confidence or to acknowledge his authority. He no longer respected Cameron's judgement and Cameron knew it. Instead, Bruce looked to Drake. No wonder Cameron was aggrieved. Repeatedly Bruce defied him. When he vetoed the idea of a Luxembourg operation, Bruce applied to Drake. When he expressed doubts about Madame Rischard, Bruce went to Drake. Bruce had disregarded Cameron's advice about funding this ludicrous operation, preferring to rely on arrangements of his own. The request to see the files had been refused. When he, Cameron, had suggested that he should come to Paris to meet Madame Rischard, he had been deflected. Bruce and Drake had cut him out. Drake and Bruce were in France, communicating by dispatch rider between Rue St Roch and GHQ, while he sat on the sidelines. He hardly saw his subordinate. For months Bruce had said that he was too busy to come to Folkestone and, when he had eventually looked in at 8 The Parade, the conversation had been unsatisfactory. Having made his remark about 'strafes', Bruce had returned to Paris.

Cameron's complaints could all be reduced to one: 41 Rue St Roch was out of control. As Cameron and Kirke had envisaged it, the Paris Office was responsible for the recruitment and management of agents in France and Holland. Since February 1917 its *raison d'être* had changed. Bruce had embarked on the Luxembourg venture, sanctioned by Drake. Bruce and Campbell had organized networks in Switzerland and Spain, supported by Drake. Then there had come the recruitment of Buckley and the elaboration of the escaping scheme, assisted by Drake. And what had the Luxembourg operation produced? Nothing. Bruce's agent had got as far as Lausanne, where the Germans were probably on her trail. If she were arrested, the Paris Office would be responsible. How much did she know about I(b)? A great weight of grievance and anxiety had settled on Cameron's mind and he could not shake it off.

Cameron's question about the timing of the refusal from Berlin had been sent on 8 September, a Saturday. Bruce did not reply. By now Dr Rischard would have gone to Tessmar and at any minute Madame Rischard might have better news. Cameron followed up his letter with the dispatch of another reprimand, this time in human form. On 10 September Lieutenant Tangye arrived at 41 Rue St Roch with a special order from Folkestone. This young officer, a barrister before the war, was used by Cameron as a go-between, fetching and carrying between Folkestone, Paris and GHQ. He was now in a most uncomfortable position. The order he brought from Cameron stated that the Lieutenant was to be installed at 41 Rue St Roch as Folkestone's representative. He was to be given his own office, a letter-numbering system, T. P., for Tangye Paris, a separate budget and 500 francs for immediate expenses. Further instructions – 'Kindly note . . .' – were on their way. Bruce referred the matter to Drake.

Drake seized his chance. It sounded, he said, as if the activities of Bruce and his team had little connection with what Cameron was doing. In that case, there was no reason to retain the Paris Office as an annex to Folkestone. It should either be shut down or allowed to go its own way. Closure was premature: it would not be right to refuse Bruce the chance to show what he could do. He should be given that chance but henceforth the Paris Office would report directly to GHQ. The link with Folkestone should be severed.

Drake had no doubt about the cause of the friction but, when he came to write up his decision, he was restrained: 'personalities' were responsible, he observed, but so was the English Channel. Intelligence operations could not easily be managed at long range and the distance between 8 The Parade and 41 Rue St Roch was greater than had been supposed. If Cameron and Bruce had been able to meet regularly, face to face, there might have been less misunderstanding:

Secret Service is not a matter which can be organised or controlled entirely by correspondence. In this work above all other the personal touch and inspiration are what are most required.[6]

This was charitable.

Bruce had won – but Cameron did not give up. Further orders came from Folkestone. Before management of the Paris Office was transferred to GHQ, all documents and correspondence relating to Folkestone were to be handed over to Tangye, with all reports, 'both Railway and General', all questionnaires and codes, account books and vouchers for expenditure. A statement was to be drawn up, 'showing the approximate value of Furniture, Fittings, etc.'. Rent covering the balance of the current period was to be repaid to Folkestone. Nothing was to be assigned to Cameron's budget for work done at 41 Rue St Roch after 18 September, the date of severance. These matters were complicated. I(b) had more than 1,000 agents in France, many employed directly by Folkestone but paid through the Paris Office, and funds for some French operations were also channelled through the account at Rue St Roch: 'Frs. 200', for example, 'on behalf of Cameron, namely the fee of the Belgian lawyer in connection with the *affaire* Logiest'.[7] Cameron had given Bruce and Tangye only seventy-two hours to prepare and close the books. Mademoiselle Dorgebray and Miss Done typed heroically and by the night of 17 September the accounts were done. A memorandum of unexpired assets was attached. No repayments were due from Paris to Folkestone. On the contrary, a significant sum – 1,929 francs 20 centimes – was owed in the other direction.[8] Cameron sent a line of thanks to the team in Rue St Roch and took trouble to write to Chocqueel and Mademoiselle Dorgebray, whom he had recruited. He had no wish, he told Bruce, to call at No. 41. The formal handing-over of the office – the army took such occasions seriously – would have to occur without him.

However maddening, the accounts were a side-issue. The chief sticking-point had concerned Tangye. Bruce had not wished to turn him out but Cameron continued to insist that, while posted to Paris, Tangye was to communicate directly with Folkestone, a correspondence from which others were to be excluded. Messages between Cameron and Bruce were to be sent via Drake. This was ridiculous – and embarrassing for Tangye, whose relations with the team in the Paris Office had been friendly and constructive.

Once again Bruce wrote a personal letter to his chief. The idea of having an independent officer in Paris was, he told Drake, absolutely impossible. Dual control would be bound to lead to friction. Tangye had better things to do; such a role was a waste of an officer. In any case, there was no space for an extra man at 41 Rue St Roch and certainly no room for a separate office. Drake had broken down the 'watertight compartments' that had proliferated under Kirke. Installing a special Folkestone representative in Paris would be the first step in recreating them.[9]

Bruce's answer to Cameron was more gentle. The proposed arrangement, he pointed out, would be awkward for the whole team and particularly for Tangye, 'in this office but not of it', with no means of getting a letter typed except as a favour. There was no reason why Cameron should not continue to use Bruce as his representative in

Paris: 'Colonel Drake I know has no objection to this.' After all, the purpose of organizing I(b) in one way rather than another was not to satisfy the *amour propre* of members of the Service but to win the war: 'I am convinced that this plan is both workable and is in the best interests of the show . . .'[10]

The row made black days blacker. The Luxembourg project seemed to be petering out. The efforts of the Paris Office had got Madame Rischard only halfway home. Baschwitz Meau's energies were being spent on the allocation of flood-management duties in the Belgian army. More disappointments: Charteris and Cumming could not agree on reporting lines from Berne and Woolrych's appointment was dropped: 'absolute and final'.* Buckley's future became entangled in administrative disputes. The War Office had discovered that Cumming was also running an escaping service and that other sections were involved. Drake advised Bruce that 'some sort of central organisation' was to be set up in London; as a key ex-escaper, Buckley was ordered to return to England to direct it.[11] The loss of the scheme undermined the case for bringing Baschwitz to Paris – and the argument that there was no room for Tangye at No. 41.

To top it all, Cameron now sent Tangye to Switzerland to collect material from a French agent. When Bruce asked the young man whether it had been explained to him that, just as the Paris Office did not interfere in Folkestone's operations in Holland, so Folkestone had no authority to venture into Switzerland, Tangye replied that 'Cameron had told him that he had no knowledge of any demarcation.'[12] The timing of this intrusion could not have been worse. Bruce was about to send one of his own people into Switzerland with instructions for Father Cambron. It would be disastrous if there were to be any mix-up. Cameron should have known better.

Was Bruce always to be enmeshed in correspondence about administrative disputes? Cameron wanted cash and account books from the Paris Office. Copies would not do. He had noted the cost – 502 francs, 65 centimes – of Bruce's journey to Madrid, a mission, he declared, unconnected with work for Folkestone.[13] Backwards and

---

* I(b) realized that it would put Woolrych under Cumming. Charteris objected: 'if we supply the man, he will report to us'. Drake to Bruce, 13 September 1917.

forwards went a stream of counterfoils. Folkestone's debt to Paris went up, down, up again. At last, having arranged with Drake that GHQ would absorb small outstanding items, Bruce told Cameron they were exactly square. Drake had arranged to come to Paris for the ceremonial transfer of the office but on the appointed date he was called to London. Bruce was anxious to close the Tangye question. His proposal for an informal understanding had been rebuffed: Cameron's experience led him to distrust *'relations officieuses'* . . . 'back-channels': 'You know that I have been brought up in a very stiff school as regards this matter.'[14] He had forgotten the stiff schooling when he had ordered Tangye to go to Switzerland.

Drake gave his ruling and Cameron surrendered. He had spoken to Tangye and had concluded that 'for the general good' he should give Bruce's suggestion a trial. He would continue to correspond directly with Bruce; Tangye would provide liaison between them, as before. The last sentence of his signal had an error – 'I shall be glad if you would **communication** with Bruce accordingly' – but Cameron, the perfectionist, did not bother to correct it.[15] He was sick of the whole pack of them. One crisis over, the Paris Office was left to its own devices.

16

Snakes and Ladders

Madame Rischard's training had been thorough but it had not prepared her for the peculiarity of her present life. She knew few people in Lausanne and trusted only Tante Marie and the doctor. Since mid-July she had enjoyed almost no society: Madame Fresez-Settegast was in Grindelwald all summer. Making new friends was out of the question. Women who seemed quite respectable might be foreign agents. Was she not one herself? They would talk about what they read in the newspapers and watch her reactions. A chance word, a tensed muscle, would betray her. Not that she wanted to sit with other ladies at little tables, eating little cakes. In accepting this burden, she had cut herself off from ordinary pleasures and ordinary people. She walked alone in the Botanical Gardens and the park beside the lake, with too much time to think.

After Campbell's visit, she felt more isolated. She began a course of English lessons, to fill her empty days, and in halting sentences tried to describe her state of mind. 'I fear you will call this a weakness on my part but I hope you will never have to struggle with opposite sentiments and that you will never be placed between two duties, both imperious and high, and have to decide for one or the other.'[1] Working in English brought her closer to her colleagues but she knew that at 41 Rue St Roch and 38 Rue de Moscou their lives went on without her. Although her English rapidly became fluent, for clarity Bruce and Campbell continued to write to her in French. This too was a disappointment.

Loneliness made her jumpy. To reassure her, Bruce sent Campbell back to Lausanne. When he called at Avenue Edouard Dapples, on the evening of 8 October, Madame Rischard showed him a letter from General Tessmar, forwarded by Camille. The Commandant had no objection to her returning to Luxembourg. But officials at the German legation now had told her that Tessmar's opinion was irrelevant. Berlin had refused permission; any change of policy must therefore be communicated from Berlin. No, she was not allowed to make a second application. Still shocked by this rebuff, she had asked Camille to go back to Tessmar.

How could she explain these refusals? The Germans must suspect her. She thought she should warn Camille. She could hide a message in a large ball of silk and wrap the whole in a piece of crochet-work, to be taken to Dr Rischard by a former patient who had been convalescing in Switzerland. Madame Rischard did not seem to understand the risk. The unfortunate carrier might be stopped as soon as she set foot across the frontier, her luggage searched. The Germans would find the ball of silk and unravel the entire espionage operation. Campbell managed to dissuade her from trying anything so imprudent.

Other than practising the code and her English, Madame Rischard had nothing to do. For all her knowledge of guns and howitzers, the war went on without her. Descriptions of the skirmishes between Nicole and Mademoiselle Testu gave her some indication of how things stood but allusions were a poor substitute for an extended conversation. Otherwise, she depended on censored accounts in *Le Matin* and *La Suisse*, and, even allowing for bias, what she read was chilling. It was said that the Germans intended to make a concentrated attack before the winter, that they might come through Switzerland. Why had Bruce and Campbell not mentioned this? The more neglected Madame Rischard felt, the more anguished she became. Were they preparing to abandon her? Bruce read her accusations with dismay. She had called him 'cold and unfeeling'. To dispel that impression – and for the benefit of any third party who might intercept Madame Garland's letters to her unhappy cousin – Bruce shed his own skin. The language he adopted was as extravagant as Madame Rischard's own: '*Qu'est-ce que je puis te dire* . . . What can I say to chase away the black serpent that slides into your thoughts, eating at our friendship?'[2] The controlled and formal British officer became an impassioned Frenchwoman. This fluency was dangerous. Hearing these echoes, Madame Rischard lost her bearings.

The rumours in the newspapers were cited elsewhere. At GHQ every intelligence briefing included a calculation: so many German divisions on the Western Front, so many on the Eastern Front and in the Balkans. Charteris advised Haig that German morale was evaporating and that there were stories of insubordination in the German army, information contradicted by reports from French GHQ and from Macdonogh in London. Haig wondered whether Macdonogh was, 'perhaps unconsciously', inclined to believe his co-religionists (Macdonogh was a Roman Catholic, Haig a devout adherent of the Church of Scotland).[3] This was naïve. Although their views diverged, the two intelligence chiefs respected each other. The DMI's opinion, Charteris said, 'is the only really valuable one with regard to Germany's intentions'.[4] Temperament, not rivalry, made the two men draw different conclusions from the same information. The situation was too serious for squabbling. Thousands of soldiers were being killed, thousands maimed, allied and German, pierced and splintered, caught on barbed wire, sucked into mud and slime, east of Ypres, in the darkening days of autumn.

The year was running out and there was still no word about Madame Rischard's permit. At the end of October she told Bruce that General Tessmar had referred her case to Berlin, as had – 'Quelle ironie!' – the Grand Duchess Marie-Adélaïde. Madame Rischard had no idea how this had come about: 'N'importe! . . . Who cares! Success is what matters.'[5] This was the last chance. If the Germans refused a direct application from their own Commandant in Luxembourg, the war would be over before she got home.

The alternative scheme had also stalled. It seemed impossible to extract Baschwitz from the Belgian army. Drake referred the matter to the War Office. There the file moved upwards until it reached the desk of the Chief of the Imperial General Staff, Sir William Robertson, the Prime Minister's military adviser. Robertson's answer was unhelpful. 'He considers that the proposed employment of officers is objectionable and that he cannot approve of it,' Drake told Bruce.[6] The CIGS gave no reason for this magnificent reply. Bruce offered one, in order to knock it down.

Is it any use urging that it is presumably the employment of officers in
<u>enemy</u> territory which is considered objectionable (as officers are of course
sent every day to neutral territory on special missions) and that it is neutral
territory [here 'Luxembourg' was inserted in Bruce's hand] in which I want
to employ BASCHWITZ. He would not have to set foot on enemy territory
at all, as we should put him down by balloon.[7]

Drake was kind. Luxembourg was occupied. It was perhaps safer
than Germany but not much:

the contingencies foreshadowed by the War Office in arriving at the decision they did would clearly be involved, that is to say [lest Bruce had missed
the point], these officers would run the risk of being shot by the enemy.[8]

Bruce was undeterred. Sending Baschwitz into Luxembourg was now
vital to his scheme. A soldier who understood the needs of
commanders and the state of the front, Baschwitz could be relied
upon to notice items of operational significance that Madame
Rischard and her informants might not think important. He would
be able to build on the Rischards' connections, extend them to parts
of the railway network where Luxemburgers could not go. (Bruce
already had in mind Alsace and Lorraine and, in time, Germany
itself.) Baschwitz would be living under cover, espionage his only
task. The Rischards could not work full-time; Camille had his medical
practice, Madame Rischard the supervision of her house and garden.
Nor could the Rischards train and manage agents. Carrying information home, extracting from it intelligence about constituted units,
coding reports and letters: this would take all their private hours.
Baschwitz's skill and experience made him a 'force multiplier' without
parallel. With such a professional as catalyst, Madame Rischard's
contribution would be increased a thousandfold.

The war could not go on for ever. If the Germans succeeded in
breaking the front before the Americans came, in sweeping the British
out of France altogether, I(b) would still have, in Baschwitz, a trained
and resourceful agent behind the lines. If, on the other hand, the
Allies prevailed, driving the enemy back beyond the Rhine, Baschwitz
could be sent forward to reconnoitre. Furthermore, if, while the
present operation was under way, the Rischards were betrayed,

arrested, shot – such things had to be considered – the Paris Office could look to Baschwitz to close down the network. If Baschwitz himself were to be captured – unpleasant thought – his escaping skills might bring him back alive.

Bruce sent Baschwitz a copy of Drake's letter, with a private note. There was a way out, if Baschwitz would agree.

Mon cher Baschwitz,

   . . . Je vous demanderais de considérer ceci comme absolument confidentiel . . . I would ask you to keep this absolutely confidential. No need to tell you how disappointed I am by this decision and I know how distressing it will be for you. That is the official decision. One last suggestion occurs to me, which I make unofficially to you. It seems to me that, if you were ready to give up your rank of Sous-Lieutenant and if you were able to persuade your General to do without your services, the remaining obstacles to your assignment would be set aside . . .[9]

Other officers might have been surprised at the suggestion that they should renounce their rank, but not Baschwitz, who had already discussed something on these lines with Major Neefs. If he were to be seconded to British military intelligence, Baschwitz thought that as little as possible should be put in writing. His escaping record had marked him; once the Germans knew he was no longer with the Belgian army, they would be on the lookout and he would be useless as an agent. It would be best, Baschwitz thought, if his papers stated only that he was on indefinite, unpaid leave. Bruce's proposal was no more than an extension of this idea. What did rank matter? Baschwitz was not a professional soldier; he had joined the Belgian army to help win the war. If other means were required to attain this end, so be it. As far as he was concerned, resigning his sous-lieutenancy was simply an administrative move to release him for espionage.

While he waited for Baschwitz's reply, Bruce prepared the ground. The timing was fortunate: in mid-October Charteris came to Paris for discussions with his counterpart from the United States, who was setting up an intelligence briefing system for General Pershing, the American Commander-in-Chief. When he met Charteris, Bruce tried him on the Baschwitz issue. The Brigadier-General was not encouraging. The French might agree to let an officer renounce his rank, 'and so be employed by us for a special mission', but he did not believe the Belgians would do likewise.[10] This was a reasonable assumption. Relations between the British and Belgian Commanders-in-Chief were uneasy, although the King of the Belgians had made an official visit to Haig at the front at the beginning of September and their talk had been friendly. The King regarded a separate, negotiated peace as the best hope for his devastated country. The wreckage he saw at Ypres had not changed his mind.

Baschwitz jumped at Bruce's plan. 'I am afraid you may think me unduly pertinacious,' Bruce told Drake, 'but I hope you will not mind my sending you the enclosed letter from BASCHWITZ, which I think shews a very good spirit.' A reproof might have been expected – junior officers were not supposed to bend the Brigadier-General's ear – but Drake forgave Bruce for seizing his chance. He sent Baschwitz's letter to Charteris. Again the correspondence made its way up the hierarchy. For Bruce it was one of the most important issues in the world, to his superiors an insignificant addition to the piles of reports, digests and memoranda moving between War Cabinet, War Office and General Staff. Drake's application disappeared from view.

The fighting continued, and the rain, as the Allies struggled towards Passchendaele. At the end of September Haig's generals advised him to end the campaign but, after so much had been invested, it was difficult to resist the urge to drive on. Autumn produced only rotting fruit. 'It was the saddest day of the year,' Charteris wrote on 9 October, after the battle of Poelcappelle. 'It was not the enemy but the mud that prevented us doing better.' What had become of the high purpose with which this work had started? 'Somehow one sees and thinks of nothing but the awfulness of it all.'[11]

No news from the War Office about Baschwitz, nothing for Madame Rischard from Berlin. The talk at GHQ was of a German offensive in the spring. If the Luxembourg scheme were to make any sort of contribution, an agent must be trained and put into the marshalling yard by the beginning of 1918. Desperate for ideas, Bruce turned to Buckley, who suggested sending coded messages to officers held in camps next to major railway lines, inviting them to report on the movement of constituted units. Put to Drake, the proposal was rejected. It was unfair to ask prisoners of war to do anything so hazardous.[12]

Other ideas came from a colleague in Macdonogh's department, Major Claude Dansey, who was on his way to Switzerland to do a job for Cumming. Dansey had been head of MI5(e), the section that controlled civilian passenger traffic through British ports; when Bruce consulted him, he could think only of solutions that involved complicated journeys by sea. Could I(b) not send people into Luxembourg on papers saying that they had returned from the Congo? For verisimilitude, an agent could be sent out to Dacca on a French boat and brought back openly from there. Or an agent could travel from Dacca to America, back to Vladivostok and across the trans-Siberian waste to Stockholm. Once in Sweden, an application could be made for permission to go home to Luxembourg via Germany.[13] Bruce did not take these propositions further. As far as Baschwitz was concerned, the difficulty was to get him out of the Belgian army, rather than into the Congo, from which he had already extricated himself in the summer of 1914. The idea of presenting Madame Rischard as an expatriate returning from Africa was even more preposterous. Not only would such a disguise be implausible but the Germans already knew who she was. In any case, sending people to Luxembourg via Africa, America, Russia and Sweden would take months.

Fuller suggested a more conventional route. He had read in *La Suisse* that a Luxembourg *chargé d'affaires* was being sent to Berne to look after the Grand Duchy's interests in Switzerland. The nominee was Monsieur Antoine Lefort, Minister of Public Works. Could he not expedite matters in Berlin? Hopeless, said Madame Rischard. Camille knew Lefort – Dr Rischard's father had been minister in the same department – and had spoken to him about her case. Nothing had come of it.

Wheels were turning, nonetheless. The intervention of the Grand Duchess was now explained. Dr Rischard had been attending to her sister, Princess Charlotte, and, when she asked him about Madame Rischard's whereabouts, he had told her that his wife was stranded in Lausanne. The Grand Duchess had taken an interest and, as a result, a minister of state had been instructed to write to Berlin, insisting on Madame Rischard's repatriation. But it all took so much time.

When it came, the breakthrough was unexpected. On 16 November Madame Rischard wrote to Campbell about her niece, Mademoiselle Madeleine Vanvers, the daughter of the cousin with whom she had lodged in Rue d'Alésia. Mademoiselle Vanvers – or van Weers, as she had to call herself under the German régime – had been caught in Luxembourg when the frontiers closed. She had been given permission to leave, would be put on a special train for *rapatriés* on Sunday afternoon, 18 November, and would arrive at Annemasse next day. With Fuller's help, a surprised Mademoiselle Vanvers was whisked out of the queue, transported to a quiet hotel and, next morning, luggage neatly stowed, installed in a reserved seat in the train for Paris. Mademoiselle Vanvers, who had been staying at the Rischards' house, brought with her a letter from Camille, telling his wife that a Luxembourg neighbour, Pierre Huss, was in Lausanne. Dr Rischard suggested that a meeting would be a good idea.

Madame Rischard saw Pierre Huss. Afterwards she wrote urgently to Bruce, in code: '*Avons des renseignements importants* . . . Vital intelligence. Come as fast as possible.'[14] Bruce and his colleagues knew little about Huss, more about his son. A report of espionage cases was regularly circulated within I(b) and the name of young Huss had appeared in one of the lists. According to the report, while studying in Switzerland, Norbert Huss had been recruited by 'an Allied S.S.' (the country was not specified) for a mission in Germany. The French Secret Service had become aware that the young man had a link with the German Consul in Zürich and, suspecting that he had been 'turned', French police arrested him as he crossed the frontier at Bellegarde. Documents he had with him suggested that he was being used by the Germans. In June 1917 he was given a life sentence by the Conseil de Guerre in Lyon. He was twenty-five.[15]

Norbert's father was distraught. He was determined to know who had entrapped his son and how Norbert was being treated. As he was not a French *rapatrié*, Pierre Huss could only obtain a permit for a temporary stay in Switzerland. He was wealthy and well-connected – he was a chemical engineer by profession – and had little trouble finding people to help him. One was Monsieur Blun, Zürich correspondent of *Le Matin*, another a Monsieur van Claparede, who, although Huss did not know it, had a connection with Campbell. Blun promised to consult the *Deuxième Bureau* and the Ministry of War in Paris, van Claparede to be in touch with associates in France. Huss had promised Dr Rischard that, while he waited in Switzerland, he would look up Madame Rischard in Lausanne. Hitherto, Huss and the Rischards had been no more than acquaintances. The war had brought the doctor and the chemist together – that, and their attitude to Germany. The treatment his wife had received had turned Camille's scorn for the Germans into implacable hostility; Pierre's resentment had become burning hatred. He would do anything to help the French, he said, not just to wipe out Norbert's shame but to damage those who had led him into temptation.

Madame Rischard had more than one conversation with Pierre Huss. On 25 November she wrote to Campbell, enclosing a message from Huss, which she had put into code. She sent it via Monsieur Bathet; if Huss saw the typewritten envelope, he would have known only that it was directed to an address in Geneva. Campbell deciphered the message:

Ravitaillement, charbon et travail suspendus . . .

Reprovisioning, coal and work stopped metallurgical factory by demolition viaduct. Reply if you approve: instruction and terms.

Huss[16]

The team in Rue St Roch knew which viaduct was meant. Lines from Luxembourg's central station ran below the city fortress, on its cliffy outcrop, skirting steep walls. Trains from Trier came into the marshalling yard by that route, for re-ordering and reprovisioning before they were taken on to France. Along other lines came trains from the steelworks at Longwy and from Metz; they too halted in the marshalling yard. Demolition of the viaduct would throw the entire choreography of the railway into disarray. Huss, the chemist, could obtain materials to make explosives. He now took Madame Rischard into his confidence. It was fortunate that he did so. If the viaduct were sabotaged, the Germans would suspect that local people were involved.

They would hunt them down, sweeping up guilty and innocent alike. The viaduct would be out of action for a time but it would be repaired. When spring came and the railway was functioning again, lines and the station would be closely guarded.* Watching the marshalling yard would be impossible. Madame Rischard knew that she must consult the Paris Office and that she had to act quickly.

Faced with responsibility, she showed all her intelligence and nerve. Until Bruce told her what to do, she would trust Pierre Huss. Not completely: she would say only as much as was necessary to retain his confidence and delay the execution of his plan. She reminded Huss that he had come to Switzerland to inquire about Norbert. His son had been tried in France and was incarcerated there. If Pierre told the French about his scheme, it might help Norbert. Indeed, France might be able to accelerate the demolition of the viaduct. Bombing from the air would be just as effective. If French aeroplanes knocked out the railway, German anger would be directed at the French military, rather than at local people. Then Madame Rischard told Pierre something that even her husband did not know. She was in touch with a highly placed man in Paris, a friend of Charles Jubert, who might interest himself in Norbert's case. She could send a secret message; it would not be the first time they had communicated in code.

As soon as Bruce could leave Paris, he took the train to Bellegarde, changed trains and crossed into Switzerland. Madame Rischard had asked for a final meeting; this was the time.[17] On 6 December, a Thursday, he came to Lausanne. Tall and lean, he was noticeable even in plain clothes and as he left the station he realized he was being followed. Dodging through courts, alleys and churchyards, walking quickly with his long stride, he shook off his pursuer. Only then did he present himself at No. 33.

It was six months since Bruce and Madame Rischard had seen each other. There was much ground to cover, notably and most

* Charteris had reported that bombing railway interchanges from the air had so far produced poor results. 'The only two successes we can claim are the destruction of a depôt and damage to Ledeghem junction, which threw out of joint part of the German railway system for two days.' Sir John Charteris, At GHQ, London: Cassell, 1931, 30 October 1917.

urgently, the whole question of Pierre Huss's presence in Lausanne and the use that might be made of him. The chemist was about to go back to Luxembourg, his permit having expired, and as he now knew that Madame Rischard was corresponding with Jubert in code he might as well be asked to give her husband a message to that effect. Pierre might tell other people, too, but if Madame Rischard were arrested as soon as she set foot on German territory, at least Dr Rischard would know why. Before Pierre was drawn in, however, Bruce had to be sure that he was sound. With misgiving, his only insurance being Pierre's anxiety about Norbert, Bruce decided that he should be tested with a request for information about the working of the Luxembourg marshalling yard. Madame Rischard would ask Huss whether he could supply this. Meanwhile Bruce would make inquiries about Norbert. Wallner was working in the Ministry of War in Paris – his attachment to the Folkestone Office had come to an end – and would be able to find out exactly what the young man had done and whether any service his father could give might eventually count in the son's favour.

That settled, Bruce turned to the rest of the agenda. Some matters had already been touched on in correspondence: alterations to the code; the provision of newsprint for the *Landwirt*; the procedure for recruiting Hansen. There was a new subject: Baschwitz Meau. In Paris Baschwitz and Madame Rischard had been kept apart. Now Bruce told her that he had identified an agent who could be sent to Luxembourg to work alongside her, a man of good reputation and integrity, whom he, Bruce, regarded as a personal friend. He told her little more; if she were caught and questioned, she must know nothing that would enable her interrogators to identify her colleague. The agent, Bruce said, was French, his name, or, rather, the name by which he was to be known, Conrad Bartels.* If the agent came to Luxembourg, would he be able to live there under cover? Madame

---

* A playful code-name but unsafe. 'Joseph Conrad', the writing name of Josef Teodor Konrad Nalecz Korzeniowski, was the author of *The Secret Agent*, which had been published only seven years earlier. Bartels was the name of the German who ran secret operations in Erskine Childers' novel *The Riddle of the Sands* (1903). Did the officer who chose Baschwitz's code-name think that German counter-espionage officers were not well-read?

Rischard was sure it could be done. Bartels would need an identity card, coupons for food and other items. Samples of such cards would have to be sent to France so that copies could be made. They would have to find work for him and somewhere for him to live. She thought that Camille would be able to do something.

The lamps were turned up, the curtains closed. The discussion was unfinished when Bruce went out into the winter dark but he promised to call again next day or the next.

She waited. He did not come. He sent no word. In the Friday and Saturday post there was nothing. No deliveries were made on Sundays but letters could be collected from the post office. Madame Rischard took herself there and in her box found an envelope addressed in Bruce's hand. She opened it only when she was safely home. Its contents were extraordinary. There must have been a mistake:

My dear old boy,

No sooner had I got into the hotel bus in this hospitable city, when a stylishly dressed member of the fair sex joined me and inquired as to whether I had met a tall Englishman, who passed out by a special gangway at Bellegarde. I was unfortunately unable to oblige & although a pleasant conversation followed on the way to the hotel, I was unable to induce the lady to let me take her friend's place – in fact she seemed very disappointed & gave vent to her feelings to the *Chef de réception* on arrival. Some fellows seem to have all the luck.

As to business I have not done badly, on the contrary have been very well received & one of my new clients hopes to see me again & take me round.

Strange the mixture of races in this part of the world – he is a Luxemburger by origin & I need hardly add a great friend of the Entente causes.

Our friends tell me that quite a change is coming over many, who until recently were all but hostile to the allies. It is curious how the feelings of some people alter from time to time.

Well, good-bye old boy for the present, will write to you again but I also hope to hear from you before I leave as to how to proceed on my return.

Yours as ever,

Jim

Madame Rischard was shocked. Who was Jim? Worse, who was this woman – clearly not a lady – who accosted men at railway stations, talked freely to strangers and publicly berated the chief receptionist at an hotel? Did this explain why Bruce had failed her, why he had sent neither excuse nor apology? Who was the person from Luxembourg? Could it be Pierre Huss? The author of the letter talked about a mixture of races: Huss had a French first name and a German surname. What did 'Jim's' letter mean and why had Bruce sent it on? Had he been entrapped? Only he could tell her, but did she wish to hear? At least he should know that she had read this miserable scrap. Straightaway she composed a disapproving note. The letter, she said, had presumably been sent in error. It mentioned a person of the same nationality as herself; was this the man of whom she and 'Georgette' had spoken three days before, a Luxemburger with a German name but French sympathies?* Or was it someone else? There were a number of her compatriots in Switzerland, people with French names and German connections. If the author of the letter was engaging with these, the risk to Bruce and his friends was great. As for associating with a woman of this sort, surely Bruce could see that nothing could be more dangerous. If he could not come immediately, she would send the letter back in the next day's post.

She folded the paper, wrote on the outside that it was to be delivered into the addressee's own hands or, failing that, forwarded, and sent it after Bruce.[18] But Bruce had gone. He had received the letter from 'Jim' the day after his visit to Madame Rischard. Someone had been on his trail from the moment he crossed the border at Bellegarde.** He had thought that he had been followed when he left the train at Lausanne; had the shadowing started earlier?

The letter from 'Jim' had been a coded warning.*** No second

---

* That is, Pierre Huss.
** 'Jim' was probably J. D. Cox, the agent at Bellegarde.
*** The message may have referred to an operation run by allied agents based near the French/Swiss border. A Belgian woman, described as being well born, well educated and – this accords with 'Jim's' letter – 'good looking', had agreed to encourage the attentions of a local agent, a German, who enlisted her, as he thought, and equipped her with underclothing impregnated with secret ink. Wallner would have been aware of the scheme. See the reference in Alan Judd (*The Quest for 'C'*, London: HarperCollins, 1999) to *Notes on Instruction and Recruiting of Agents, compiled for CSS by Staff of MI 1(c)*, 31 December 1918. The operation led to the destruction of a sizeable German network.

visit could be made. That night Bruce had written to Madame Rischard to say he had been recalled. In his haste, he put 'Jim's' letter into the envelope, rather than his own. On the Saturday he discovered his mistake. At the first opportunity he posted off the correct letter but, as he was on his way to England, knew it would take several days to reach her. He had alerted Chocqueel; with luck, Madame Rischard would forward 'Jim's' letter unopened to Rue St Roch. Chocqueel had immediately sent word to Luxembourg. 'Just a line to say that Mummy' – he wrote as Nicole – 'posted a letter she thinks to you yesterday which she says was not to you . . . You see my English is good is it not so?'[19]

Too late. Shaken by 'Jim's' letter, Madame Rischard had already sent Campbell the first of a series of urgent messages. Chocqueel's words did not reassure her. '*Pourquoi ces mystères?* . . . Why these mysteries? God preserve me from mixing myself up in other people's private lives. Dear Jacques, stay as you are, simple and true . . .' Had Madame Rischard been less fearful, she would have waited for an explanation. When it came, she did not accept it. Chocqueel told her the letter had come to her in error. In ordinary life she would have said no more about it. But this was not ordinary life. Perhaps someone was watching her and keeping a record of her visitors. The thought made her almost hysterical. She could not go on like this. She must be released. Campbell must tell Bruce to give her up: '. . . *pour que je puisse te prier d'insister* . . . insist to Mummy that she set me free once and for all'.[20]

Brooding over Bruce's absence and his silence – in the apparent circumstances 'Mummy' was horribly inapt – Madame Rischard's trust evaporated. On 12 December she sent another letter to Campbell. Bruce had evidently lost confidence in her: '*mais chut!!! . . .* But hush!!! Let us take no notice!'[21] These pages were scribbled on a pad on her knees as she jolted back from Zürich in the train, having risen before dawn to see Huss before he left Switzerland. The weather was radiant, her mistrust had been allayed, her courage revived. That morning she had received a letter from Camille, telling her that the permit was on the way. She might be home for Christmas.

On her return to Lausanne she found a letter from Bruce, the one he had meant to send. It told her that he had been called away and that he would write. Thinking about it all, she asked herself whether she could really carry out her mission:

. . . *je succombe à nouveau au plus sombre des découragements* . . . I have fallen once more into the deepest despair. I have lost confidence in Georgette and therefore in myself and in that state can I really do what you wish me to do? Would it not be better to give me up?[22]

Before sending this letter, Madame Rischard went to the post office – it was a Sunday – to see if there was anything for collection. There she found another letter from Bruce, written after his return to Paris. Again he apologized for being unable to continue their conversation, again he promised that, if he could, he would return to Lausanne. About 'Jim' he said only that she would understand that she need not be concerned. He could not tell her who had written the letter or why but she would be able to read between the lines. Madame Rischard was furious. How could she not fail to be concerned, she exclaimed? 'Jim's' letter referred to an unnamed person from the Grand Duchy. How could she decide whether these entanglements mattered or not?[23]

Bruce had worked with Madame Rischard for almost a year. Had he misjudged her? Her moods changed by the hour, her expectations were often impracticable, she needed constant reassurance. He had been sure that once she began her mission she would settle down. On balance, he thought so still. Her instability was understandable. It would have been hard for a professional agent to endure the solitary, secret life she was leading in Switzerland. For an amateur, waiting to go into enemy country, it was terrifying. Had they asked too much? He did not think so. Madame Rischard was volatile but she had shown that she could be firm and capable. Whatever the difficulties, she had addressed them. She had mastered the code and the management of correspondence. The only mishap had been the one he had just caused himself. When they discussed money she had been straightforward. She had dealt sensibly with Pierre Huss. She was sometimes thrown off course but when Campbell spoke to her face to face she reacquired her composure. At his own meeting with her, less than a fortnight ago, he had found her competent and collected. The mysterious letter from 'Jim' was bound to have upset her, especially the references to the person from Luxembourg. Explanations were no use. A calm exchange of letters would restore her confidence, the prospect of the journey home reinvigorate her. It had been a piece of misfortune, that was all.

17

Bifurcation

To be home for Christmas Madame Rischard would have to leave Lausanne by 21 December at the latest. Bruce could not go to her; the War Office had ordered him to London for more meetings. In the second week of December there had been an upheaval in the Intelligence Staff and changes were being made that affected all sections. The War Cabinet had become increasingly doubtful about the advice Haig was receiving from his head of Intelligence. Charteris held to his belief that Germany's confidence was weakening. He hated the war: 'I thought I had lost the power to feel,' he said, when he lost his closest friend. 'I almost wish I had.'[1] Unceasing pressure on the Western Front would, he thought, bring capitulation. In the autumn he had encouraged Haig to order one more offensive. Pausing now would give Germany time to bring experienced men from the Eastern Front and another winter in which to train a new intake of conscripts. When Churchill visited the front in the second week of September, as Minister of Munitions, what he saw made him doubt that the Allies would be able to beat the Germans. The Prime Minister, Churchill said, thought the same.

The Ypres campaign had been halted on 20 November – what remained of Passchendaele had been captured a fortnight earlier – but the enemy had shown no disposition to retire. Charteris was right: Germany's manpower was draining away. The autumn onslaught had cost her more than a quarter of a million men. But the Allies' story was the same. This was where the Brigadier-General's diagnosis failed. Why should either side go into hibernation when a final thrust might bring victory? On 19 November Haig ordered an advance on the German lines at Cambrai, against some of the strongest and most elaborate defensive works on the Western Front. The early stages of the attack were so successful that in England church bells, silent since 1914, were rung in celebration. By 29 November the British had moved forward 7,000 yards. Next day the enemy caught the Allies unawares. When battle ended on the night of 4 December, the ground acquired had been lost again. Each side had sacrificed some 40,000 men. The destruction of tanks was enormous.

On 30 November, allied commanders had been ordered to hand over to their seconds-in-command and get some rest. After the battle critics said that, as the German counter-attack came at this vulnerable time, the enemy must have known about the change.* Although investigation showed that bad luck rather than poor security was to blame, Charteris's enemies seized their moment. On 7 December Lord Derby, Secretary of State for War, told Haig that ministers thought the Brigadier-General's advice should no longer be relied upon. On the same day news came that the Russians had dropped out of the war. Darkness was closing in. Charteris knew what this meant: 'The hard facts are that we face the new year without Russia, with Italy almost on her knees, with France exhausted, with America of little help until June, and with the initiative again with Germany.'[2] Haig accepted that Charteris had to go.** On 13 December his successor was identified – Major-General Sir Herbert Lawrence, Commander of the 6th Division, a soldier with no intelligence experience, from the same cavalry regiment as the Commander-in-Chief. It was to Lawrence that Drake now reported.

There was another parting. Cameron had applied to join the army in the field. His train-watching systems were 'at a low ebb and practically non-existent' and he felt himself incapable of reviving them.[3] Wallinger's London service took over Folkestone's work; Tangye, a

---

* Spies were busy on all sides. In mid-September Charteris reported that a Chilean had been arrested in England and had confessed to having been promised £10,000 by the Germans if he could find out where Haig's next attack was to be directed. Sir John Charteris, *At GHQ*, London: Cassell, 1931, 7 December 1917.
**'. . . to avoid friction and to maintain confidence in our Intelligence I am obliged to change him. I am sorry to lose him.' Haig, Diaries, 13 December 1917, National Library of Scotland, Edinburgh.

success, remained at 41 Rue St Roch. As it turned out, Cameron did not go to the trenches. For all his awkwardness, he was an experienced espionage officer, whose skills were needed at the centre. After some weeks of sick leave, he was transferred to MI 2(d), the War Office section responsible for intelligence relating to Russia, Persia, Afghanistan and India.

These were the developments that took Bruce so hurriedly from Switzerland to London. On the eve of his departure, he asked Chocqueel to write to Lausanne to explain. Once again Nicole took up her pen. 'Mummy is very upset . . . she say she cannot understand why you say that you lost confiance in her.' The errors were intentional. Chocqueel had been polishing his role: Mademoiselle Testu was trying to teach Nicole to write in English. Her letters were studded with self-conscious slang, not always plausibly: the colloquialisms Chocqueel's colleagues suggested – 'Mummie bagged all the ripping chocolates' – were an out-of-date mixture of Angela Brazil's boarding school stories and RFC *patois*. But as she pleaded for Georgette, Nicole's style was perfect: '. . . she was awfully pleased to see you . . . she thinks more of you than nearly anybody else in all the world'.[4]

Madame Rischard was not comforted. It was nearly Christmas and her visa had not arrived. She longed to be with her husband or, failing that, her son, anywhere but Lausanne. On the 22nd she wrote sorrowfully to Bruce. To avoid misunderstanding, she did not encode her letter; to reassure the censors, she put it into German. Her unhappiness had been increased by a letter from Camille, who had been distressed by the message Pierre Huss had delivered: 'He now knows about our secret relations . . . and wishes you over the mountains, even to the devil.' Camille had asked her not to destroy their lives. She told him that she could not break her promise. Hating the idea that his wife was mixed up in this, he had nonetheless accepted that it had become a duty. His generosity made things worse: Camille had agreed to advance any money that might be needed for Hansen and to purchase newsprint for the *Landwirt*. Bruce was surprised to read this. How had Dr Rischard heard about the arrangement with the *Landwirt*? Had Madame Rischard spoken about these matters to Pierre? But there was no doubt about her turmoil. '*Also, Georgette, ich muss Klarheit und Gewissheit haben . . .*' the letter ended, 'I must have clarity and certainty, and that as soon as possible, or let me go free.' She had signed herself, in fading ink, 'In loyalty yours, Elisabeth'. Then – what had gone through her mind? – she had crossed out the name, and, refilling her pen, substituted 'Lise'.[5]

This composition arrived in Rue St Roch on 26 December, the day Bruce returned from his second visit to London. He answered immediately; the much-corrected draft suggests that he typed the letter himself. He was, he said, completely at a loss. Having re-examined 'Jim's' letter, he could only suppose that Madame Rischard had been upset by the reference to the woman at the station. If she were to reflect on their correspondence, she would understand that the text of the letter from the so-called 'Jim' might have another meaning. Even now Bruce did not say who 'Jim' was or what his letter had meant. Instead, he gave Madame Rischard his word of honour 'as a Scot' that he had done nothing that should destroy her faith in him. He was puzzled by what she had written about her husband. Dr Rischard's help would be invaluable – but how had he heard about Hansen and the *Landwirt*? Could she explain? Bruce kept the most important question for the last. Why did she want him to give her up? She had begged him to set her free; did she not know that he would never dream of forcing her to continue with her mission, although he could not understand why she no longer trusted him and why she had lost sight of the great objective for which they had both been working.[6] He must have an answer. She need not write to him in code or in a language that was not her own. If she enclosed her letter in two envelopes, the inner one marked 'Personal', no one else would read it. Bruce wrote as Georgette; even so, in sending such a letter and in asking Madame Rischard to answer in similar fashion, he took a great risk.

She saw that he was serious. No, she had never lost sight of their shared purpose. That alone had sustained her. Why was she in such despair? He had asked her to tell him exactly what she thought. For all the references to '*Ma chère Georgette*', all the feminine endings to adjectives and verbs, it was now to a male friend that Madame Rischard addressed herself, a man, moreover, whom she thought had erred. His surmise was correct. She had been upset by the references to the woman at Bellegarde. Was she Bruce's intimate, who knew all his secret comings and goings? 'Some people have all the luck', 'Jim's' letter said: what sort of woman was this? If she was as indiscreet as it appeared, Bruce had been inexcusably foolish. Such a person would give them all away, Bruce and Campbell, Camille and herself, the whole network. After this, how could he expect her to trust him? There, she had said it all. It was distressing to have to probe; if she were mistaken, would he forgive her?[7]

And, Madame Rischard said, there was another reason for doubt. Briefed by Wallner, Bruce had encouraged her to indicate to Huss that in any post-war review of Norbert's case, Pierre's service would be taken into account. She had since heard 'on good authority' that Norbert's release was unlikely. Bruce had been guilty of bad faith and, in consequence, so had she. It pained her to have to put all this on paper but, as Bruce would not come to see her in Lausanne, there was no alternative. As for his questions about Camille, Pierre had told her husband only that she had offered to communicate with a friend of Jubert. She was now waiting for a letter from Pierre. They had agreed that he would not write to her until he had found someone who could supply regular reports about activity in the marshalling yard. From what Camille had written since, Pierre had already applied for permission to return to Switzerland, which suggested that he now had the information they wanted.

She had told neither Pierre nor her husband that she was working for the Allies. Camille was quick and from what he knew of Jubert had guessed that she had aligned herself with some official operation. She had told him nothing that was compromising, only that money would be needed for a friend and to buy paper for a purpose that would become apparent. Although she had given no names, she had said something about Marcel's former teacher of French literature, so that Camille would see that she was alluding to Hansen. He had evidently understood that the money was for the *Landwirt*. Camille's interpretation of other points had also been correct. He had understood that it must be Georgette, this hitherto unknown cousin to whom Lise had formed such a close attachment, who was Jubert's friend and, thus, his wife's new colleague: 'and he is not exactly thrilled by the extent of your influence'. Camille had tried to persuade her to disengage; when she had written back to say that her commitment was irrevocable, he had told her that he would come to Switzerland himself, not to hinder but to help her, and that he had already applied for a passport. He would stick by her to the end and, if she were betrayed, would sacrifice himself to save her. '. . . There, Georgette, is your clarification.'[8]

It was not the first time that Bruce had been rebuked by his *protégée*. But, unlike the letter Madame Rischard had sent him at the end of their sessions in Rue de Moscou, this was not brisk and self-assured. Then she had spoken as a candid friend. Now she sounded cynical and disillusioned. She believed that he had failed her. As chief of the operation, his duty was to protect her. He had been distracted, as she thought, by another woman. He had neglected her and now she repudiated him. Dejection had become defiance. For the sake of the cause, she declared that she would continue. Bruce had been weak and fickle but waiting for her was her husband, heroic in his loyalty, patience and devotion.

How was Bruce to make things right? He could not give operational details: that there were other agents in Switzerland, that 'Jim's' letter had been a warning. How was he to dispel Madame Rischard's assumption that he was close to the woman at Bellegarde? In different circumstances, this could have been laughed away. Not here. In a succession of plain statements, Bruce tried to make things clear. He had known neither the woman at the station, nor, at the time, the person who had sent the message. The warning had been a disagreeable surprise. He had not explained this earlier, not wishing to alarm her. Nor should such matters be discussed in correspondence. He had looked into the matter and there was no reason for her to be frightened. As for his own safety, he knew what precautions to take. She would understand, however, that it would be unwise for him to visit her too frequently.

The rest of his letter was equally firm. As far as Norbert Huss was concerned, she had not been misled; nothing had yet been decided about pardoning people after the war. He knew that Pierre was anxious to communicate directly with a lawyer who could help his son; this was being arranged. And Camille, for whom Bruce had such sympathy and admiration? Perhaps they would meet one day.

For the present, could he count on having her complete confidence? If not, he would prefer her to consider herself completely free of all obligation, for they could not continue in this manner. '*J'espère, chère amie, que nous n'aurons plus besoin de nous écrire de cette façon* . . . I hope, dear friend, that we have no further need to write in this way, as it endangers us all.'[9] So saying, with hope of a word to tell him that she realized she had misjudged him, he ended his explanation.

With this letter, sent on New Year's Day, came a fresh beginning. Once Madame Rischard understood that her suspicion had been misplaced, she put her doubts behind her. Resolute and energetic, from now on she could not do enough. Even her handwriting was bolder – helped by a tortoiseshell fountain pen the Garlands had sent her for Christmas. Her letters to Nicole were playful. The girl's English was so modern and striking, Tante Lise exclaimed, quite unlike that taught in Lausanne by old-fashioned Mrs Chapuy. Indeed, she observed, deftly deploying an f, two bbs and a t, that dear lady 'would be flabbergasted' to read such exoticisms.[10] Much drafting was needed before Chocqueel could reply in kind: 'Mummie want me to apolgize which I won't as I am thoroly tired with these questions in the morning and questions in the afternoon about verbs and tenses . . .'[11]

More wonderful, Madame Rischard's good temper brought her husband round: '*Raccommode-moi avec Georgette,*' he told his wife; 'Mend matters with Georgette.' As Camille had joined the Garland family, Georgette's grandmother had become his mother-in-law: 'If she looks after Grandmother, I forgive her everything.' Madame Rischard was delighted: 'Don't you think that nice of him?'[12] Camille had given up the idea of coming to Switzerland. Getting a passport would take too long and by the time he had it his wife might be on her way home. Could Nicole not come to see her instead? Arrangements were made but at the last minute Chocqueel was unable to travel, prevented by 'that viper . . . Oh, I do <u>hate</u> old Testu.' Campbell went in Chocqueel's place.

A visit was necessary, to agree on modifications to the code. In letters between Paris and Lausanne there had been much cryptic discussion of locked boxes and impenetrable rooms: counting letters and words took too long and Campbell had replaced the 'spelling' method with a system using a prearranged key. Agreed references had been identified in a Baedeker's *Guide* and in 'Lieber's *Code*', a choice both witty and apposite, 'Baedeker' being a handbook for excursionists, as Madame Rischard had now become, and 'Lieber' a manual of practice for conduct in war.[13] The *Code* made disagreeable reading: Section V reminded non-uniformed inhabitants of invaded countries that spying on their occupiers was a breach of trust; death, it said, was a justifiable punishment for civilian spies, 'war traitors'.

Campbell left Paris on 19 January, crossing into Switzerland at Annemasse on the afternoon of Saturday the 21st and going straight to Avenue Edouard Dapples. Madame Rischard had important news. On the previous day she had been called to the German consulate in Lausanne, to be told that Berlin had agreed to her repatriation, in response to a request from the Luxembourg government. The Grand Duchess's intervention had done the trick. A visa was on its way; Madame Rischard would be able to set off in two to three weeks. She was absolutely certain, Campbell said, 'that there would be no further hitch'. Although he did not like to spoil her pleasure, he knew they had to decide what to do if she were prevented from leaving.

Huss was available, should they need him. He had returned to Lausanne only on the 19th, having been detained at the border by the Swiss frontier police. His report was promising. He had approached an acquaintance who might be able to provide information about the marshalling yard but, knowing Norbert's story, the man had refused to have anything to do with espionage. As he did not wish to be rebuffed by others on the same grounds, Pierre had gone straight to Camille and explained what was required. Camille, in turn, had spoken to an employee in the Luxembourg station, a known francophile, 'whose business' – this was from the report Campbell afterwards made to Bruce – 'is the "receiving and despatching of trains"'. The railwayman was indebted to the doctor, who had saved his child's life, and was eager to help. Furthermore, 'this man's friend, who is in the same service in the station, is also willing to work, and as they take alternate 12 hours shifts, all should be well'.[14] Neither man wanted payment, only reimbursement of expenses.

Pierre had done all he had been asked to do. As well as looking for potential train-watchers, he had also examined the marshalling yard and the surrounding topography. From his description Madame Rischard had made an annotated map:

La bifurcation est immédiatement après le viaduc, direction Trèves . . . The fork comes immediately after the viaduct, going toward Trier. There is a little stream that runs beneath . . . In the direction of Trier at a distance of 600 to 800 metres from the viaduct trains go between rocks which form a wall to the left and right . . .

All railway lines were shown, with other details. To the north and east the Germans were laying another track, to avoid having to take trains through the central station, work that was to be completed by the end of the month. Directed by Pierre, Madame Rischard had marked this new route on her sketch. Emplacements had been built nearby so that the railway could be covered by small fire and there were heavy guns on the hilltops in the south-west, around Differdange and Esch. Pierre had suggested that, if aeroplanes were sent in to bomb the lines, it would be best to approach at first light and to ensure that, when the machines dropped into the valleys through which the railway ran, other pilots remained above to give cover.

According to Pierre's notes, many German divisions had recently been transported via Autel-Bas, south of Arlon, along the line that went from Messancy through Athus to Longwy. It was thought that they were making for the front at Verdun or the Aisne. Troop trains generally took this route, in some cases going on north to Belgium. Pierre had done his work well and it looked as if he could be trusted. Within hours of the receipt of this report, his information was corroborated. According to a briefing for the Commander-in-Chief, some twenty German divisions, hitherto unidentified, had recently been moved to France.*

Madame Rischard was convinced that Huss was playing square: 'she told me that she had reminded him several times . . . that he

---

* 'All information points to great railway activity on lines S. of Liège into France during last month. The French information is bad in this area, as compared with our arrangements further North.' Haig, Diaries, 23 January 1918.

could be sure that his son would never leave France if he whispered a word of what she said to a soul.' Campbell thought they might as well give Huss the complete picture, 'since he already knew enough to boil the whole show', but Madame Rischard had not thought of sharing as much as that. After all she had gone through with Bruce and Campbell, she was possessive about her mission. When Campbell expanded on his proposal, she was even more doubtful. If her permit did not arrive, he and Bruce would like her to remain in Switzerland to receive correspondence and act as intermediary between Paris and Luxembourg. Campbell would take Pierre through the code; Pierre, in turn, could teach it to Dr Rischard. As her husband had access to the railwaymen, he would be the ideal person to prepare reports for Pierre to deliver to Hansen. Madame Rischard did not like this suggestion and was not sure whether her husband would like it either. Camille had no time for coding and decoding, she told Campbell, and Hansen might refuse to deal directly with Pierre. Norbert's arrest cast a long shadow.

Even if she were allowed to remain in Luxembourg for only a few months, she could still make the necessary arrangements. If she had to come back to Lausanne, she would like Bruce and Campbell to arrange for her to be brought from time to time to France. The monotony of life in Switzerland was half killing her, she told Campbell. The doctor had been giving her arsenic injections to keep up her spirits. Campbell could make no promises. After much persuasion, Madame Rischard agreed that Pierre should be introduced to the code. Campbell was ready to start lessons immediately, until Madame Rischard reminded him that she had allowed Pierre to believe that she was associated not with the British but with the French. It was therefore arranged that she should do the teaching herself: 'I should not be surprised if there would be a small *crise* and Madame may put up a fight not to tell Pierre everything, but I think it would blow over.'[15]

On Sunday, 22 January, having stayed the night with Antoni in Geneva, Campbell went back to Lausanne. Pierre's coding lessons had already begun. Time was short. To be home before his permit expired, he had to leave Switzerland no later than 7 February. Madame Rischard was certain that by then she too would be on her way.

First page of a letter from 'Lise' to 'Georgette', received at Annemasse, via
the intermediary in Geneva, three days after its dispatch from Lausanne.
The year – 1918 – is not included in the date, indicating that the letter is
en clair. The last sentence of the first paragraph alludes to a difference of
view between the cousins; Bruce, but not the censor, would have understood the reference to the 'Jim' episode. Madame Rischard assures her cousin
that, nonetheless, she will not neglect the Garlands' interests when settling
her late father's estate: '. . . don't worry about anything, I beg you, my
honour is at stake and everything will be done as if you were dealing with
it yourself.'

The second paragraph begins by asking 'Nicole' to write more clearly.
The girl's letter of 27 January, like that of the 26th, is an enigma: 'I despair,
we normally understand each other so well!' Madame Rischard had evidently
found Chocqueel's coding confusing.

Future arrangements for transmitting instructions were as follows. Correspondence from Paris would be sent, as before, to Bathet in Geneva. He would post it on to Madame Fresez-Settegast, for forwarding to Luxembourg. Similar arrangements would apply in the opposite direction. Tante Marie would keep a note of dates on which letters addressed to the Garlands arrived from Luxembourg and were sent on to Geneva, in case there were inquiries about delayed or missing correspondence.

In these last days, Madame Rischard had become a model of professionalism. Efficient and inventive, she thought of everything. The delivery of letters, for example. Her dressmaker, a francophile, lived at Arlon and often came to the city to see clients, as Luxembourg itself had no one to make fashionable clothes. She might agree to carry messages from train-watchers. Then there was Conrad, whose situation Madame Rischard had promised to consider. She suggested that as soon as he arrived in the Grand Duchy, by balloon or otherwise, he should come to her. She and Camille would be able to supply false papers. She made one condition. Neither Jubert nor his father – the latter was still in Luxembourg – was to be told that Conrad and the Rischards were connected. Who knew what pressure might be put on any member of the circle?[16]

Campbell returned to Rue St Roch on 25 January. Two days later Madame Rischard sent a long letter to Bruce, saying that she had her visa, hoped to leave Switzerland on 5, 6 or 7 February and to be home by the 10th. She had been considering various aspects of their arrangements. First, Conrad. It would be best, she thought, if he were to stay with Camille and herself at their house in Luxembourg, 20 Boulevard Royal. Conrad could have Marcel's old room. Camille would be able to give him 'everything he needed' – that is, the railwaymen's reports. Next, Gilbert. It was he – that is, Jubert – who had helped her take the first steps in her journey home. If there was anything she could do for his father, he had only to let her know. Then, Nicole. Madame Rischard would like her to continue to write in English, using the English key, but *legibly*. It would be practice for them both.

There followed much about the code. Recent modifications had made the whole ciphering and deciphering procedure much easier, although Pierre had been finding lessons difficult and she had been obliged to give him a new key. Michel – Camille – would be able to help her with coding and decoding; as they knew, he was good at riddles. When she got home, she would ask Hansen for a course of private lessons, as a pretext for his making repeated visits to the house. She would start with Hugo's *Châtiments* (Lieber's *Code*) and the *Fables* of La Fontaine (Baedeker's *Guide*).

If they wanted her to come back to Switzerland for a time, she would do so. Some things could not be said in letters. Might she look forward to a visit from Nicole? There was plenty of space; her house had many rooms. Five doors gave on to three different streets; a sixth door, unknown even to the servants, had been sealed to prevent rats emerging from the eaves but could also be opened up. Nicole could go in and out as she pleased and Mademoiselle Testu would never know. In other words, the house was just the place for any games of hide-and-seek in which Conrad might find himself engaged.

She would send a photograph of the house, so that the Garlands would be able to think of her in her own surroundings – and Conrad to find it without asking passers-by. She had been considering her own journey. She would not be able to take a dog home to Luxembourg, even an imaginary one, so Floc, having served his purpose, was allowed to expire. Pierre had mastered the code; here was a sample letter, addressed to Nicole's brother Robert. And thinking of these boys, could Bruce find out whether Norbert was allowed to receive money for books and extra food? She would like to send regular sums but it might be difficult to do so from Luxembourg. As for the code, she was now completely satisfied with the operation of the new version. Could she suggest one or two additional refinements? Repetition of letters, words and phrases should be avoided. (She made this point via a seasonal recommendation about double flannel vests.) Words that might arouse suspicion should not be used in their letters; instead of 'confidence' or the lack of it, for example, she would speak of fine weather and rain.

She had her tickets. She would leave Lausanne on 7 February and on the 8th meet Madame Fresez-Settegast in Berne, where the latter was staying en route to Villa Allmer in Grindelwald. (Waldhotel

Bellary was closed for the winter.) On 9 February Madame Rischard would start for home. As she travelled through Germany, she would try to send a postcard, addressing it to Madame Garland, care of Madame Fresez-Settegast at Villa Allmer. As she packed her boxes, she felt, she said, as if she were setting off for a holiday of her own. In these last letters, Madame Rischard made only brief reference to the misunderstanding between Bruce and herself. Her faith in him was intact – but she had suffered greatly. Some of the best in herself, she said, had been depleted. She was glad she could go home knowing they were in accord.

Better than that. Bruce told her he would try to come to say goodbye. She was overjoyed – but still remembered practicalities. He need not give his name when he came to Avenue Edouard Dapples. The servants had overheard a conversation about a French lawyer – the advocate in Lyon who was dealing with Norbert's case – and knew that Madame Rischard was being advised on the disposition of her father's estate. They would not be surprised if a French-speaking gentleman were to call on her at home. On 4 February Bruce came to Lausanne, not, this time, from Bellegarde but from Annemasse. So that Madame Rischard would not forget her old Parisian friends, Rose and Réséda, he presented her with photographs. How like he was, she said, to her brother.* He also gave her a supply of envelopes with typed addresses – and a *cigarette-étui*, to keep beside her as she wrote her letters. 'If the key failed to turn', its contents would be a comfort.[17] Did the cigarette case hold a cyanide pill, in case the scheme went wrong? And Bruce gave her a watchword, the motto of his family: *Omne Solum Forti Patria*. Every Country is a Brave Man's Land. She would adopt it, she said, as her own device.

He returned to Annemasse that night and waited there. Something might yet go wrong. On 6 February, the eve of Madame Rischard's departure for Berne, he wrote to her care of Madame Fresez-Settegast, who sent the letter on to Luxembourg. That afternoon, the 6th, he

---

* Léon Meyer, a charming and talented boy, had died at fifteen. The director of the Luxembourg Athenaeum published a memoir, with some of Léon's poetry. Sister and brother had been close and one of the poems was dedicated to her.

told Madame Rischard, he had gone into the high country above Annemasse, taking the path to the summit of the Grand Salève. As light faded, he reached the outcrop above Monnetier and looked down over the cloudy sea that covered the neighbouring country. The sun was setting; before him the Petit Salève stood out – *'une île entièrement entourée de vagues'* – an island surrounded by waves of mist. To the right rose Mont Blanc, magnificent in pink and gold. Above, the sky was intensely blue and clear. He saw the old world, before the war, the world that, if they succeeded, would return.[18]

Then, as night came, he descended into the obscurity of the town.

18

Pigeons and Balloons

The War Office machine cranked slowly – Drake had submitted his second memorandum about Baschwitz in late October – but liaison between the British and Belgian armies improved during the winter and a different mood at the top made it easier to reopen the question of the sous-lieutenant. The change had begun in the aftermath of King Albert's tour of the front. He had been appalled. Fighting on such ground would swallow up his troops, leaving him nothing with which to bargain for his country. Even Prime Minister de Broqueville – Prime Minister, Foreign Minister and War Minister in one and staunch believer in a just war – found himself coming round to the King's view that a negotiated peace would be less dreadful than this slaughter. Other ministers disagreed and there were murmurings about betrayal. De Broqueville found it hard to keep the confidence of the Cabinet and, although he remained in office, the King was obliged to appoint both a new Foreign Minister and Minister of War.

Resistance was robust. Urged on by disrespectful articles and cartoons in *Libre Belgique*, Belgians mocked their German masters. Children copied the military goose-step and fell over, women rose when soldiers sat next to them on the bus, waiters ostentatiously swept the floor after taking orders from German officers. Outraged, Commandant von Bissing tightened the screw. While civilians resisted, led by their priests, the Belgian army waited at La Panne. The King knew he could not keep it there indefinitely. Morale was slipping and there were tensions between French-speaking officers and Flemish-speaking troops. Confined to a narrow piece of coast, frustrated by inaction, all longed for resolution of the war that kept them from their homes and families. General Anthoine, Commander of the French First Army, told Haig that King Albert had admitted that his troops were in 'a sad state'.[1]

After the King's visit to the front, the British and French Commanders-in-Chief were asked to receive other guests from Havre and La Panne: de Broqueville; General de Ceuninck, the new Minister of War; and General Rucquoy, the King's Chief of Staff. Lord Athlone accompanied the party and General Orth was in attendance. In discussions, Haig and Pétain suggested various operations that, while collaborative, would not draw the Belgian army into the trenches. It was now too late in the year to attack German-held Channel ports from the sea but, if an offensive were launched during the spring tides, Belgian support would be essential. In the meantime, Belgian experts could help French and British troops divert the swollen rivers and streams that had engulfed the Western Front, saturating fields, seeping into trenches, undermining the roads and light railways that fed the lines. Orth and Athlone were invited to find out whether a joint flood-control exercise would be feasible and, if so, who would be responsible on the Belgian side. Administrators were told to co-operate. In the last week of December 1917 the first Belgian work parties arrived, led by teams of engineers experienced in draining ground, siting pumps and constructing dykes. By mid-January some 12,000 men were working to safeguard the rearward defences in Flanders.

These developments encouraged Bruce to make another attempt to obtain Baschwitz Meau's release. The opening came with the announcement of Charteris's departure from the Intelligence Staff. On 13 December the Brigadier-General's successor, Major-General Lawrence, arrived in France for an initial briefing on I(b)'s activities. Five days later, from his office at Havre, Captain Priestley wrote on Bruce's behalf to the new Belgian Minister of War, a direct application that must have been approved at the highest level. This may have been the Brigadier-General's doing – Charteris had not yet officially handed over his functions – or the product of neat footwork by Bruce and Priestley during the interregnum. Whoever drafted it, the application was elegantly phrased. Baschwitz's services were much needed, his commanding officer had agreed to do without him and, if it would help from an administrative point of view, the writer understood that the sous-lieutenant was ready to resign his commission: 'In consideration, therefore, of the very great importance that British GHQ attaches to this mission, I beg to submit the case to your judgement . . .'[2]

On 31 December Charteris left the Intelligence Staff, not, as Haig had envisaged, to reorganize French agriculture, but to run day-to-day business at the Transport Directorate. Major-General Lawrence took over on 1 January. There had as yet been no reply from de Ceuninck's office, but on 3 January Bruce told Baschwitz he was coming to Wulveringhem. Baschwitz was ecstatic: 'I have an idea that this time it will be successful and that – at last! I will be able to set to work. It can't be soon enough!'[3] Wulveringhem was not far from Dunkerque and, having spoken to Baschwitz, Bruce went on to La Panne to see Athlone. It was arranged that Bruce should put in an official request for Baschwitz's transfer to British Intelligence, the candidate having resigned his rank in the Belgian army, as he himself desired. Beneath Bruce's signature and title, Captain, General Staff, was typed 'For Major-General, Intelligence', indicating that Major-General Lawrence had approved the application.[4] The timing was lucky. A fortnight later Lawrence was gone, promoted from I(b) to replace Lieutenant-General Sir Launcelot Kiggell, who had retired, ill and exhausted, after two years as Chief of Staff. Starting the stately dance again with Lawrence's successor would have taken at least another month.

Each day counted. For the time being, the enemy was outnumbered. Information acquired by I(a) – from observations in the field, interrogation of captives and informers – and from I(b)'s agents behind the lines suggested that Germany now had 169 divisions on the Western Front. Taken together, Britain, France, Portugal, Belgium and the United States had 175, plus 4 in Italy. On the Eastern Front, however, Germany had a further 58. Even if 20 remained there, 38 would be available to reinforce divisions in France, giving a total of 207. Unlike young conscripts coming straight from Germany, the men who had fought in Russia needed no training. They were already on their way. On 21 January Haig learnt from his intelligence briefing that by the beginning of February – that is, within ten days – Germany would be able to mass a new force of some 30 divisions at any point along the line. By 1 June, if Germany were to wait that long, as many as 70 divisions would be available for a concentrated attack.[5]

This was bad enough. Two days later, on 23 January, came the report from agents in the field, corroborating Huss, that some 20 German divisions had already moved up to the line; on the 25th, the new Head of Intelligence, Brigadier-General Cox, told Haig that over the past eight weeks 126 field batteries, 100 heavy batteries and 14 infantry divisions had been brought from Russia and that German artillery regiments had been re-armed with light field howitzers.[6] Before Christmas Charteris had predicted that 'the Enemy's big blow would not fall until March'.[7] Now it looked as if he had been too sanguine.

On 30 January the Belgian Minister of War gave his answer. Sous-Lieutenant Baschwitz Meau had been placed on indefinite leave, without pay, to enable him to give his services to the British army. Next day Priestley sent Bruce a copy of the Minister's letter, with a brief covering note (one line only, the typewriter ribbon being nearly finished). This was swiftly followed by the arrival in Paris of Baschwitz himself.

There was no time to be lost. Handshakings with Bruce, Campbell, Chocqueel and Tangye, with Miss Done and Mademoiselle Dorgebray, and Baschwitz was off to start his training. He was in plain clothes now. As he made his way through the streets, only his alert eyes and light step betrayed him. To the casual eye, he might have been a banker or a lawyer, en route to an office with a mahogany desk. Out of Rue St Roch and into Rue St Honoré, toward the river. Fog hung in the streets, thickened by smoke from domestic fires. Near the Seine the mist was heavier and the Restaurant Théâtre Sarah-Bernhardt enticing; was Paul Schroell's committee conferring within? Trees in the Jardin du Luxembourg were black and leafless. Jamin's concerts had finished for the season, his musicians had dispersed to warm cinemas and tea-rooms. Woolrych's uniformed effigies still guarded the schoolroom in Rue Soufflot; his maps were there, his photographs of engines and wagons. No one had yet removed the destination board from the Porte d'Orléans bus, hanging over the stair. Settling into a cloud of cigarette smoke, Campbell at his side, Baschwitz began his lessons in code and constituted units.

By the time Bruce returned to Paris on 7 February, after his final visit to Lausanne, the novice had made great strides. Next came field training. Bruce had chosen as supervisor a colleague from Amiens, Captain Robert Boccard, not least because Boccard and Baschwitz shared a mother tongue. Discussions about secret writing, forged documents, dead-letter boxes, escape routes, suicide pills and the like were complex enough without the added difficulty of translation. A simple telephone call fixed things up and Baschwitz was duly dispatched to Amiens. This being Meau's first excursion as an under-cover representative of I(b), Bruce was anxious to know that he had got there without adventure: 'your "*protégé*"', Boccard assured him, 'arrived to the tick'.[8] Teacher and student liked each other and, when Baschwitz left for practical instruction, he took with him a sleeping bag and two rugs, on loan from Boccard until the apprenticeship was complete.

The comforts were needed, the next stage of Baschwitz's educa-tion being conducted out of doors. Infantry and artillery brigades were shifting south from Hazebrouck to Chaulnes, where Gough's Fifth Army was entrenched, a large-scale movement of the sort Bruce wanted Baschwitz to observe. For six bone-chilling February days and nights the student watched roads and railway tracks. Lithe as a cat, he slid through bushes, padded under the night. It was as well that Baschwitz knew how to make himself invisible. Although Boccard had telephoned the Fifth Army in advance, a shape in the mist, 'a stranger in a soft cap and a trench coat', might have been shot at.[9]

While Baschwitz was so engaged, Bruce had been inquiring about flying him into Luxembourg. The aeronautical side of the intelligence service was an offspring of the Secret Service Bureau. Aeroplanes appealed to two of Cumming's great passions: like Toad in *The Wind in the Willows*, he adored inventions and acceleration.* Room could always be found in 'C's' diary for a meeting to set up a new society

---

* Cumming's enthusiasms had nearly finished him more than once. In the 1903 Paris–Madrid race his car had smashed against a wall; the following year he had almost drowned during a practice run for a motor-boat race down the Seine from Paris to the sea; in October 1914 he had lost a leg – it was believed that he had cut off the shattered remains with a penknife – in a motoring accident in France. In that sad business his son Alistair, commander of the Intelligence Corps motor-cycle section, was killed. Once recovered, Cumming had acquired a modified car, with Chief Constable's number plates, and for use in the Admiralty corridors an American scooter, on which he punted himself at speed, a cork substitute attached to his stump.

for the enjoyment of a faster means of locomotion or for an appointment to examine a new technology: electrical gas-detection apparatus; metal said to be invisible in sunlight. Cumming had been an early believer in the application of aviation to information-gathering. In 1906 he had become a founder member of the Royal Aeroclub and in 1913, at fifty-four, a qualified pilot.* Shortly afterwards, he had presented the Chief of the Flying Department at the War Office, General Henderson, with plans and costings for an aeroplane for Secret Service use, assuring him that, to minimize risk, the machine would be sent out only in fine weather above easy country and, absurdly, that it would 'never fly over any route that the pilot has not previously gone carefully over on his bike'.[10] Despite these precautions, the War Office baulked. If intelligence were to be acquired by flying, officials thought missions should be left to the RFC, newly sprung from the Naval Air Service and the Army's Balloon and Kite Regiment, and to birds. In the South African war Lieutenant Abadie, Staff Officer (Pigeons), had successfully deployed avian assistance at minimal expense and with few losses in action. The Secret Service could surely do something similar.** 'C' did not get sanction for his aeroplane but in September 1914 Kirke had been presented with fifteen pigeons by the French, who had used birds for high-speed liaison between Paris and the provinces during the Franco-Prussian War.

Much of I(b)'s aerial work depended on pigeons. One of the most difficult aspects, getting birds into occupied country, was very like the challenge Bruce faced with regard to Baschwitz Meau; the solutions were instructive. Kirke's pigeons had been allotted to five agents, members of an Italian circus troupe, for smuggling into Belgium. Cameron had arranged the reporting system.[11] The project was less ambitious than the aerial observation schemes 'C' had talked about in the years before the war, when there had been time for Cumming to expound and Kirke to listen, but it was a beginning.[12] Kirke became an enthusiast, solicitous about his birds. 'Pigeon and bomb brought in by RFC,' he noted, when one of Cameron's fleet brought

---

* Flying a Maurice Farman biplane from the Farman School at Etampes in France.
** Abadie's was the first such official post in the British army, although organized pigeon-messenger services had long been used in warfare.

back a message. 'Pigeon all right . . . Bomb taken over to French Mission for expert advice.'[13]

As the project expanded, a regular supply of birds was required. Captain A. Waley, M C, was appointed to manage a carrier pigeon service for the Intelligence Corps; for advice he turned to the president of the Pigeon Association, Alfred Osman, a fifty-two-year-old solicitor's clerk from the East End of London, who, as a *doyen* of pigeon-racing, had connections with pigeon-breeding miners all over the country. Bird-keeping arrangements proliferated throughout the army. This was too untidy for Macdonogh, then in France as Head of Intelligence. In June 1915 he had ordered all carrier-pigeon services to be centralized. The birds, accompanied by Captain Waley and Osman, now a colonel, were transferred to the Signals Directorate.* I(b) retained a specialized service for itself.

Of all the feathered personnel, I(b)'s pigeons needed the most stamina and persistence.** Theirs were long-distance missions, their task the bringing of reports from the far side of the enemy lines. Pigeon-keeping had been forbidden by the Germans but, if birds arrived, how could the tender-hearted not receive them? In the early months of the war I(b)'s agents and birds were flown in by the RFC, a procedure dangerous for all concerned.*** Landing an aeroplane at night on unknown ground was tricky and, although turn-round time was brief, the sound of engines attracted the curious. There were also difficulties of supply. The RFC had no spare machines or pilots and none that could be provided at short notice. As time went on, pilots became disinclined to allow space and weight for pigeons and, after the German Fokker monoplane was introduced in the autumn of 1915 and allied aviators found themselves facing aerial machine-guns, birds, however docile,

---

* Under Waley's auspices, by 1918 more than 20,000 birds were being managed by 380 official handlers.
** The determination of the homing pigeon is legendary. In 2001, for instance, the postal service in the Indian State of Orissa still employed some 400 pigeons, to ensure that mail would be delivered even in the cyclone season. The ancestors of these birds had been handed over to India by the departing British army in 1947.
*** Escapers were sometimes referred to as 'birds'. See Campbell to Bruce, 30 May 1918: 'One of Buckley's birds to whom he lectured has turned up in France.' Bruce's files contain a list of agents, 'pigeons', sent across the lines.

became too much of a distraction. Those in charge of the war in the air disliked the whole idea.

I(b)'s research was hurried on. With help from the Inventions Board of the Ministry of Munitions, a parachute was produced, the 'Guardian Angel', designed to permit descent from an aeroplane in flight. Kirke asked 'Peg Leg' Wallinger to find and select recruits, a responsibility he delegated to Hazeldine. This officer and a Belgian colleague, Joseph Ide – 'Emile' – were based at Bruay, headquarters of the 'Suicide Club', agents training to follow cavalry in a dash through the lines. Some of these men, I(b) thought, might volunteer to go in by parachute instead. As soon as the operation was launched, the Germans became suspicious. They heard the sound of engines overhead, waited for bombs to be delivered, listened for bangs. Nothing: were pilots dropping weapons with time-fuses? There were no explosions, immediate or delayed. Could every fuse be faulty? Then observers saw the parachutists.* New orders were given, search parties dispatched. Calculations based on wind speed and direction told them where to look. Discarded parachutes were dragged from hiding-places, cordons put in place, houses and cottages turned inside out. Parachutes were pulled out of trees, parachutists interrogated, locals sheltering injured men arrested.

German 'Jastas' – single-seaters of the Jagdstaffeln, the hunting squadron – were sent up to intercept the RFC's less agile biplanes, piloted by airmen who were already exhausted after long hours of patrolling and reconnaissance. Pressing through the night into enemy territory required stamina and concentration, and by the time they arrived at the appointed place even practised aviators were drained. Only the fortunate came back in the first light of dawn. There were so many disasters that the RFC was instructed to fly no more than

---

* The Head of the German Secret Service, Colonel Nicolai, marvelled at their daring. When a pilot was above the parachutist's landing-place, Nicolai explained, he would open the floor of a lightweight aluminium side-car, fixed between the wheels of his machine, 'and the spy, who did not know the moment at which this would be done, fell out . . .' Although the timing of the agent's expulsion was not quite so unpredictable, Nicolai was to some extent correct, communication between cockpit and cradle being no more than a mixture of hand signals and whispers down a voice-pipe. Colonel M. Nicolai, The German Secret Service, London: Stanley Paul & Co., 1924.

fifteen miles behind German lines and to go in only when the moon was obscured. Pilots flying up-to-date machines had the best chance of survival but the latest models were considered too precious to send into country from which damaged aircraft could not be retrieved. A two-seater reconnaissance aeroplane carrying a parachutist's side-car could not easily execute the rapid turning loops, lengthways rolls and spinning nose-dives needed for escape. High casualty rates robbed the RFC of experienced men; in April 1917, when a third of the RFC's pilots, navigators and machines was brought down each week, life expectancy was reckoned in days. Charteris was not surprised when General Trenchard, the RFC's Commander, told him at the beginning of 1917 that dropping agents by parachute had become too expensive. Then someone in I(b) had another idea: balloons.

Some said it was Sigismund Payne Best, Wallinger's second-in-command, who first proposed a balloon scheme, having tried it out on Cumming. The official record gives the credit to Wallinger.[14] There was a precedent. In 1870 and 1871, during the siege of Paris, dozens of balloons had taken pigeons to the provinces; the birds were said to have delivered some 25 million letters back to the capital.* Kirke applied to the Royal Naval Air Service for the loan of two balloons and the services of a specialist, and at the end of January 1917 kit was delivered to I(b) by Britain's top balloonist, Commander Pollock. A solicitor by profession, Pollock was reputed to have made more than 500 flights in trials and competitions before the war, including a Channel crossing, solo. He dressed warmly for his ascents and, having once revealed a glimpse of woollen combinations while disentangling himself and his trousers from a mooring rope, was known as 'Pink Tights Pollock'.[15] The Commander was to become one of Bruce's principal supporters.

The Naval Ballooning School was housed at the Roehampton

---

* The idea was suggested by a famous '*colombophile*', van Roosebecke. To provide workshops, railway tracks were boarded over in the station halls of the Gare du Nord and the Gare d'Orléans. Ropes and balloon silk were suspended from the great glass roofs; at trestle tables seamstresses cut and stitched the fabric and sailors knotted nets to contain the inflated balloons. Reproductions of contemporary illustrations may be found in Patrick Facon and Jean-Pierre Debaeker, *Ballons et Dirigeables*, Paris: Editions Proxima, 2001.

Sports Club, at Hurlingham, on the banks of the Thames. Pollock had been in charge here since the beginning of the war, training observers to manage gas-filled tethered balloons. From these sausage-shaped 'captive' or 'kite' balloons, operators scanned enemy trenches, watching for signs of an advance. The balloonists' duty was considered so hazardous that instruction was given only to volunteers declared unfit for other service. At the front the prevailing wind blew from west to east and an observation balloon that broke away from its mooring-ropes, as many did, was likely to drift over the German lines and be shot down by incendiary bullets.* Until the 'Guardian Angel' exercise, observers in captive balloons had been the only personnel to be routinely issued with parachute packs.** Learning to control an observation balloon that had broken free was an essential part of Pollock's course and, before they qualified, observers were required to take a solo trip in a 'free' balloon, inflated, to save hydrogen, with 20,000 cubic feet of compressed coal gas, drawn from the gasometer at the Oval cricket ground in Kennington.[16] Jettisoning enough ballast to avoid the huge gasometer often sent trainees up so far that, caught on high wind-streams, they disappeared into East Anglia, en route to a crash landing.

It was in such free balloons that Wallinger's team proposed to carry I(b)'s agents across the lines. Hazeldine came over from Bruay to take part in a practice run. At the 'air station' – the exercise yard of Wormwood Scrubs Prison in Wandsworth – Pollock demonstrated balloon housekeeping: laying out the fabric on the ground, filling the balloon with gas, deflating it, packing up the skin. The first ascent, by Hazeldine and two colleagues, lifted off from Roehampton, ending two hours later at St Albans with a near hit on the bishop's conservatory.

---

* The skins of these balloons, made of two layers of rubberized cloth, with a layer of vulcanized rubber sandwiched between, were impenetrable by small-arms fire, except at very close range. Incendiary bullets, first appearing in 1916, ignited the hydrogen in an instantaneous explosion. See William Pollock, in *Harmsworth's Universal Encyclopaedia*, London: Amalgamated Press, 1920.

** Many preferred not to wear their packs, in case the parachutes burst out of their own accord and, catching the wind, lifted them out of the basket. See Maurice Baring, *Flying Corps Headquarters 1914–1918*, London: G. Bell & Sons, 1920.

One outcome of the trial was a change in the Best/Wallinger scheme. The original plan required agents to leave balloons by parachute once they reached targeted landing-places. Experiments showed that this was impossible when there was even a breath of wind. Unanchored, a balloon could not be made to hover. Agents should bring balloons to earth, Pollock said, leaping out of their baskets at the moment of impact. This procedure had other advantages. Loss of load sent balloons swiftly heavenwards, where air currents were sufficiently strong to propel them out of sight. Furthermore, having no parachutes to cast off and conceal, agents could make a quick exit, leaving, if they were lucky, only a few bent blades of grass as evidence of their passing.

Eliminating parachutes had another benefit. When an agent hopped out of his basket, he had much to carry: birds in containers, bags of birdseed, maps, compass and electric torch. Some gear could be put in his pockets or strapped round his waist; unburdened by a parachute, he could also take a rucksack. This gave I(b) an opportunity to develop a project hitherto impracticable: dropping wireless transmitting and receiving apparatus into enemy territory. Weight and bulk could be accommodated in Pollock's baskets; in fact, the heavier the load the better. The greater the diminution of load on landing, the higher and faster would be the ballon's re-ascent.

In February 1917 I(b)'s technicians put the idea to Drake.* The Colonel, who had just succeeded Kirke, applied to the chairman of Marconi, the radio communications company, for authority to consult their chief inventor, Captain Henry Round.** This expert already had a connection with I(b): in earlier days, at Cumming's

* Drake was interested in the application of new techniques to military intelligence collection: 'possibilities of signalling by some such system as radiant heat, sounds above the ordinary range of audibility, the use of certain strata of the earth's surface as conductors of some form of electrical or other signalling', Drake, *History of Intelligence (B)*, para. 85.
** H. J. Round, who joined Marconi in 1902, had installed the direction-finding network that enabled the British navy to intercept the German fleet at the Battle of Jutland in 1916. For this and other services, he was awarded the Military Cross; as he had not served in the field, Round insisted on accepting it as a civilian. In 1921 he became the first Chief of Marconi's Research Group. A prolific inventor, he filed 117 patents during his sixty-four years with the company.

suggestion, Cameron had gone to him to discuss the interception of wireless communication between German airships, 'Zeppelins', as they formed up for bombing raids over England. Hearing what Drake wanted, Round produced a portable continuous-wave set, 'weight about 60 lbs . . . far ahead of anything in wireless apparatus'. Signals emitted by this remarkable device were believed to be undetectable.* Sets were assembled, codes devised, agents sought. Candidates were interviewed at Bruay. Once trained, they need only wait for a propitious wind. It was against this background that Bruce had his first discussions with Baschwitz about going in to Luxembourg.

The 'balloon stunt' had other offshoots, the most ingenious being the pigeon-balloon. The principal aim of the balloon exercise was to get agents quickly into hostile territory, its secondary objective the carriage of pigeons. It occurred to Wallinger's people that by balloon pigeons might be sent unaccompanied into enemy country. A 'pigeon stunt' obviously required some sort of ballooning machine; with Pollock's assistance a prototype was constructed. From an eight-foot balloon four curtain rings were hung, each carrying a string from which was suspended a wicker basket, large enough to contain a pigeon. A cross-frame, delicately arranged, prevented the strings from tangling. To each basket was attached a small silk parachute. The baskets were covered with rabbit wire, to protect the birds against rats and ferrets while they waited for someone to chance upon them. A supply of birdseed was included.

The navigation and location-finding aspects of the 'pigeon stunt' were particularly relevant in considering how Baschwitz might be taken in to Luxembourg by free balloon. Pollock had drawn up tables, based on wind speeds, distance, altitude and weight, to work out a range of times at which Wallinger's agent-balloonists could expect to arrive at their designated landing-places. The underlying principle was the same for the pigeon-balloonists. As it was too difficult to train the birds to bring down the balloons, Pollock and his team looked for a mechanical solution. From the neck of the pigeon-balloon they hung an American 'Waterbury' alarum clock, the only type with a rotating winder. A loop of wire was attached to this, curtain rings threaded on the loop. When the bell rang to give the alarm, the winder

* Unless the recipient had the right apparatus.

The determined and capable
Miss Dorothy Done.

(*Below left*) Official writing
paper, although the address
was private and the Secretary
was Miss Done herself.

(*Below right*) Reply form
for prisoners of war.

MISS DONE'S PARCEL FUND
38, RUE DE MOSCOU
PARIS
————◇————

ADDRESS : ALL COMMUNICATIONS TO THE SECRETARY

KRIEGSGEFANGENENSENDUNG

MISS DONE

38, Rue de Moscou

PARIS

Madame Aviez, 'Celestine', concierge at 38 Rue de Moscou, and her husband the drayman survey the courtyard.

Interpreter Chocqueel, a notary in uniform, with the escaper's badge.

Father Cambron, faithful reader of *Der Landwirt* even during his Swiss exile, with Captain Bruce.

The Rischards' house at 20 Boulevard Royal, Luxembourg.
When this photograph was taken in the 1950s, the house looked –
and still looks – much the same as in 1918.

Madame Rischard, photographed shortly after her return
from Paris to Lausanne.

Dr Rischard, 'Camille', Madame Rischard and the dog, dining at 20 Boulevard Royal in the 1920s.

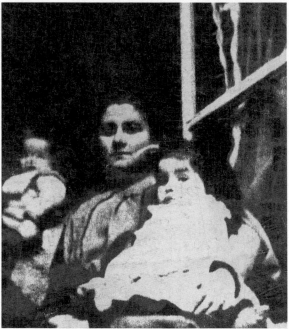

Madame Schroell, acting publisher of *Der Landwirt*. She holds Alice, an aunt (not pictured) has Gaby in her arms.

The extraordinary Baschwitz Meau.

Mobile pigeon loft, converted from a Parisian omnibus.

General Weygand presenting decorations to (*left to right*) Madame Rischard,
Dr Rischard, Joseph Hansen, Paul Schroell, Chef-Manoeuvre Bram and Assistant
Station Masters Rockenbrod and Offenheim.

turned, loop straightened, curtain rings and strings dropped off one by one, the cross-piece detached itself, the parachutes opened and the pigeon baskets floated away.* Ballast was a bag filled with water, hung from the neck of the balloon. A hole was punched through the canvas and calculations were made as to the rate of flow that would compensate for the leakage of gas. When the two were in balance, the altitude of the balloon remained constant. In his balloon research Bruce took notice of this solution, elegant in its parsimony. Ballast had become one of his special interests.

The first demonstration of this magnificent device took place in Drake's London office in February 1917. The actual pigeon-carrying part of the contraption being some twenty feet high, the baskets and their contents were represented by four army boots taken from captured German prisoners. The alarum clock was fixed to the ceiling, the boots suspended from the curtain rings. Bell rang, winder rotated, boots clattered to the floor. It worked. A hundred balloons were ordered and instructions given for the acquisition of 400 pigeons. Again, Hazeldine's office was selected as the headquarters for the operation: being in mining country – most of the coal for Paris and the allied armies was produced there – Bruay had birds and handlers.

The first pigeon-balloonists took off at the end of February and by late spring the project was in full swing. 'Hundreds of outfits' were prepared for deployment by Captain M. G. Pearson of the Suicide Club. Pearson saw the lighter side of this eccentric enterprise. He put it about that he had managed to cross-breed pigeons with parrots, producing birds that could give spoken reports, and was rewarded when a crusty officer asked why he could obtain none of these hybrids. Levity did not undermine efficiency and, although balloons went off course, parachutes crash-landed and pigeons fell into

---

* The apparatus was expensive, balloon and equipment costing £5 the set (£126 today). The balloons were made to measure by the navy; the baskets, commissioned from Lord Roberts's Memorial Workshops for the Blind, were bespoke. Waterburys, no longer imported, had to be tracked down, at seven shillings and sixpence each, from pawnshops. When the supply gave out, someone in I(b) thought of twisting yellow cotton fuse through the wires that carried the curtain rings. Measurements were made to establish how long cotton of varying length and thickness would take to burn from bottom to top, and, using Pollock's calculations, fuse, lit just as the balloons were sent off, proved an effective substitute for the rotating winders on the clocks. Cotton lengths being twopence a foot, it was also a saving.

uncooperative hands and hungry mouths, the scheme was successful. It was fast: in some cases pigeons dispatched late at night returned to GHQ by five o'clock next morning. It also produced results: I(b) had estimated that with luck 5 per cent of birds would be sent back with messages. The average was nearer 40 per cent and of these more than a third brought valuable information.* Belgian, French and Italian Intelligence ordered kits. In France the procedure was known as 'le procédé Pearson' and the Captain became a member of the Légion d'Honneur. The Germans offered large rewards to people bringing in birds and apparatus: twenty marks for a live French carrier pigeon, ten for a dead one, twenty for a pigeon-balloon, fifty for a bird with apparatus and basket.[17]

Experience with small balloons in the spring and summer of 1917 gave Pollock the opportunity to refine his calculations and enabled the Air Board and the army to perfect arrangements for transporting cylinders and pumping gas. Expectations grew. If pigeons could achieve so much, humans should be able to do more. Take reports. At present, these were returned by untrained civilians, who, chancing on the pigeon baskets, had time only to read the instructions and load the birds with random, often unverified information. Professional agents would be able to make exact inquiries about specific matters. Though hazardous, a balloon flight was faster and safer than trying to get agents into Belgium or occupied France across enemy lines and the electrified fence, while smuggling them in via Switzerland, where I(b) and MI 1(c) were in any case forbidden to operate, required additional training and extra cover. Rehearsals with

---

* In May 1917 a young man who discovered a number of pigeons in the Forêt de Mormal, west of Cambrai, gave such precise information about local ammunition dumps and gun emplacements that French pilots were able to put them out of action. See Helen McPhail, *The Long Silence*, London: I. B. Tauris, 1999, p. 126. One report directed the RFC to a town where the Commander of the Bavarian Army, Field-Marshal Crown Prince Rupprecht, was reviewing troops; another gave I(b) the name and location of a château in which Field-Marshal von Hindenburg was staying. Bombs were dropped on both places. The enemy was outraged. An alarmist suggested that tiny clockwork cameras must have been fitted to the tails of pigeons trained to fly in convoy, so that entire stretches of river, road and railway could be photographed in sequence. H. R. Berndorff, *Espionage*, London: Nash & Grayson, 1930.

pigeons were encouraging in another respect. By and large, pigeon-parachutists had been hospitably received; there was no reason why agents on allied missions should not expect an equally friendly welcome. For Drake, Pollock and Wallinger, Hazeldine and Ide – and for the prospective agent-balloonists – this was reassuring. For Bruce and Baschwitz, too, as they discussed their 'project of a mission'. If agents could be dropped with as much accuracy as pigeons, Pollock's estimates could be assumed to be sound. A balloon flight from the Western Front to Luxembourg would be longer, higher, more unpredictable and more dangerous than anything I(b) had organized before, but practice in taking balloons into occupied France and Belgium would help Bruce and Baschwitz assess the risks.

Hazeldine had chosen three Frenchmen to be the first agent-balloonists. In the autumn of 1917 they were sent to Hurlingham for training, with Ide as interpreter. Trials were done at night. Civilian anti-aircraft teams were invited to participate. They practised picking out moving objects with searchlights, the balloonists tested their nerves. Hazeldine remained at Bruay, conferring with meteorologists. At last, after weeks of blowing from the east, the wind swung round. This was in December. A signal was sent to England. Pollock, Ide and the agents were brought by torpedo boat to France, lorries carrying balloons and cylinders, guarded by a 'Special Naval Party', left Wormwood Scrubs for the coast. The plan was this. Two of Hazeldine's recruits, Faux and Lefebvre, were natives of Valenciennes, the lace-making town south-east of Lille, now in German hands. They were to be launched together in the first balloon and dropped near their home town. A third agent, Jules Bar, was to follow. Having made their way home, the three were to set up a local espionage service, communicating with I(b) through Holland. Pollock's calculations had to be absolutely reliable if these men were to be landed in their own neighbourhoods. While the balloons were being inflated, meteorological reports were monitored minute by minute, until the moment when the wind was moving at the right speed to take them, at 3,000 feet, to the predetermined target.

Faux, Lefebvre and Bar were returning to occupied France and, if successful, would report from territory for which Cameron was responsible. Despite this, Cameron had not involved himself in the balloon stunt. Nor had he taken part in consultations about portable transmitters, although in the early days of I(b) he had talked to Round about the use of wireless by agents working behind the lines. Cameron was not only familiar with the idea that agents might be sent in by air; he had been the first member of I(b) to use this method.* Despite his experience – and his anxiety about any activity that seemed to trespass on his territory – he showed no interest in the rehearsals at Bruay. Did he inquire about progress? Apparently not. 'Peg Leg' Wallinger, his rival, had been put in charge of ballooning and, perhaps for this reason, Cameron had either been excluded or had excluded himself. In December, when the wind changed and the launch date for Faux, Lefebvre and Bar was fixed, he did not join Wallinger, Pollock, Ide and Kirkpatrick in France. At the end of that month, when the C. F. service was incorporated into the W. L. service,** he went on sick leave and was eventually transferred. And Bruce? Other business kept him in London – this was just after the 'Jim' episode – and as the three Frenchmen readied themselves for take-off, he was travelling back to Paris. Having got to 41 Rue St Roch, he waited for news.

In a field near Doullens, nine miles from the front, the Special Naval Party laid out the first skin. Cylinders of hydrogen were pumped in, 28,000 cubic feet altogether, and – 'like some gigantic cabbage' – the balloon slowly filled the night.[18] At one a.m. it was ready, swaying gently as it strained at the ropes. Faux and Lefebvre were brought from a local farmhouse. Pollock gave last instructions and the most recent estimate of the time at which they should prepare to land. All shook hands. Pollock tested the lift of the balloon. In a quiet voice, he ordered, 'Go'. As the balloon rose, Lefebvre said 'Vive la France' and in a few seconds they had disappeared into the clouds. Jules Bar was dispatched in the same way on the following night.

* In the first months of the war Cameron had twice sent one of his agents, Demartin, into northern France by aeroplane. On the second mission the pilot assigned to the job had crash-landed but after destroying the remains of his machine got to Brussels, where the Germans, now on his scent, chased him through the streets. Demartin got away from the wreckage and managed to send useful information until he was betrayed. Both men fled to Holland and escaped by sea.
** C. F.: Cameron, Folkestone; W. L.: Wallinger, London.

To inspire him as he was carried upwards those on the ground played *La Marseillaise* on a wind-up gramophone.[19]

The balloons behaved well but the mission was unsuccessful. Faux and Lefebvre arrived safely but were unable to set up a reporting service. They sent only one pigeon message and then there was silence. Jules Bar broke a leg on landing and was captured and shot. Five more agents were dispatched by balloon, the only variation in procedure being the substitution of *La Brabançonne* for *La Marseillaise* when Belgians went up.* Three of the five were caught. Round's wireless transmitters were also a disappointment. Agents had difficulty sending messages, the four-horsepower generators that powered the apparatus being hard to obtain, let alone conceal, at a time when small portable engines were not generally available and petrol could be bought only with German permission. Agents found almost no one to help them; hidden radio receivers were in operation in some towns, receiving allied news broadcasts from the Eiffel Tower, but few country people were familiar with the technicalities of wireless transmission.** Some reports were sent but were unintelligible. Round came out to GHQ to investigate and found that the receiving apparatus was defective: 'in such technical affairs,' Drake observed ruefully, 'one is obviously in the hands of one's experts'.[20] The experiment was brought to an end when an agent made a bad landing and was captured with his transmitter.

There were troubles, too, with the pigeon stunt. German pilots had better things to do than flying low to intercept showers of miniature balloons but on the ground the police were vigilant. Unauthorized birds were sought out and killed, including those

* The Belgian national anthem. The unofficial anthem was a country song, '*P'tit Quinquin*', sung or whistled as a warning when German agents or informers were in the offing. See Ch. Lucieto, *La Guerre des Cerveaux: Le Diable Noir*, Paris: Berger–Levrault, 1928.

** In Lille a young priest, Abbé Pinte, who taught chemistry at Roubaix, assembled a radio receiver in his bedroom, and, assisted by Firmin Dubar, a Lille textile manufacturer, Joseph Willot, a doctor of pharmacy at the university there, and Monsieur Lenfant, chief of police in Tourcoing, ran a news and information service for the citizens of the three towns. Based on information obtained from Paris, they and others produced a news-sheet, *Le Journal des Occupés inoccupés*. Cited in McPhail, op. cit.

used for pharmacological research in the University of Lille, and, on occasion, ludicrously, chickens. For people found with carrier pigeons, the penalty was death. Posters in heavy black, glaring from the walls of public buildings, gave the names of pigeon-handlers who had been shot. Innocents rescuing stray birds from cats were as much at risk as those who persisted in defying German law. In 1917 so many civilians were accused of keeping birds that the French government asked the British to suspend the pigeon-dropping operation. The pause did not last long, pigeon intelligence by now being indispensable.

Another difficulty was to safeguard the supply of trained pigeons. One of the drawbacks of the scheme was that, unless the baskets were found as soon as they landed, birds died of hunger, thirst, exposure and exhaustion. By the latter part of 1917 there was such a shortage of pigeons that it was clear that auxiliaries must be found. Wallinger's team suggested a solution: another mechanical substitute. With Pollock's experts, they assembled an artificial pigeon: a little balloon, about two feet long when collapsed, folded up into a package. Rubberized material was too heavy and unresisting to be parcelled up small, so 'gold-beater skin' was tried. This had been used in the Boer War for the manufacture of observation balloons and, though expensive, was soft and resilient.* An illustrated pamphlet, enclosed with each balloon, gave instructions for assembly and launch. Non-experts in I(b) supposed that a person who found the package and wished to inflate the balloon would be able to do so from a domestic gas-jet but, as those who had filled balloons from the gasometer at the Oval understood, hundreds of cubic feet of coal gas were needed to lift even the smallest craft. For miniature balloons, hydrogen was required. A home-made generator was devised, a round canister, about eight inches tall, like a Bath Oliver biscuit tin, with two spouts soldered on to the top. Chemicals were mixed in the tin, the neck of the balloon was placed over one of the spouts and the tin plunged into a bucket of

---

* Very thin vellum, made from the fibrous membrane covering the flesh of young lambs. This innermost layer of skin stretches when wet and when dry becomes taut, while remaining springy. It is an ideal surface on which to beat gold, a soft metal, to make gold leaf. It was also used to make condoms.

water. This, entering the tin by the other spout, reacted with the chemicals to produce enough hydrogen to fill the balloon. Once the balloon was inflated, the tin was discarded. The contrivance looked odd but, when tested, was found to be satisfactory. A hundred packages were assembled.

In theory, the 'tin pot stunt' was a good idea. Those who found the parcels could hide them until they had something to report and an east wind on which send it. Moreover, unlike cooing pigeons, canisters would not announce their presence to every passer-by. In practice, the scheme was a failure. Mixing the chemicals was complicated and time-consuming. It was not always convenient for people busy with woods, fields and animals to stop to assess the weather. Hazeldine and his colleagues waited in vain for results. Had the balloons floated over allied lines and drifted out to sea? Unlikely, said experts: the gas supply was insufficient and the balloons had been weighted to tip over after a given amount of hydrogen had leaked out, expelling any remaining gas. Had GHQ failed to spot the balloons or depleted skins? Probably not: the balloons had been furnished with coloured streamers, to attract attention when they tumbled from the skies. I(b) watched for weeks but only one message came back. A British soldier noticed a piece of paper, caught on the German wire, and during a night raid managed to retrieve it. The sender, a woman, was lucky; contrary to instructions, she had not only answered the questionnaire but had also filled in her name and address.[21]

The failed experiment was nonetheless useful, especially to Bruce. One of his chief concerns was to find a way for Baschwitz to dispose of his balloon after he had landed. The practice hitherto had been to ensure that, after depositing its load, the balloon retained enough gas to travel onwards. This hope was not often realized. Having drifted further into occupied country, discarded balloons were either shot down or expired for want of gas. The Germans had become expert at using weather records to discover the direction from which balloons had come. By examining deflated skins and working out capacity and range, they could estimate where agents might have disembarked and seal off relevant areas. More than one man had been caught in this way.

For Baschwitz, the risk was very great. Some hydrogen would leak out during the long flight from France and he would have to release more in order to bring himself down. The remainder would be enough to carry his balloon over the Grand Duchy into Germany, on the same west wind that had brought it across the Ardennes. It would not take the Germans long to discover that an agent had been deposited in Luxembourg. They would quickly close in and scour the country. If Baschwitz were to have a chance, his balloon must be got as far away as weather would allow and human intervention could contrive. The tin pot stunt had demonstrated how hydrogen might be replenished; could the procedure be applied on a bigger scale?

The record was not cheerful. None of the agent-balloonists sent into France in December 1917 and January 1918 had been able to set up a network; several had died. Even so, Baschwitz was determined to try it. Ballooning into a heavily guarded country was no more hazardous than escaping out of one – arguably, less so. From reports of arrests and executions, I(b) knew where its balloonists had come down. This showed that for both pigeon- and agent-carrying apparatus Pollock's calculations had been correct. Meteorologically, mathematically and technically, the scheme had proved itself. That was how Baschwitz looked at it. The decision, however, lay with Bruce. He was sure that, if anyone were to succeed, it would be Baschwitz. But was it right to send him?

In mid-February, while Baschwitz was doing field work at Chaulnes, Bruce wrote to Wallinger to ask about balloon training for an agent, 'Meau', whom he wished to put into Luxembourg. Wallinger spoke to Pollock. If the Admiralty gave permission, the Commander said, training could be arranged. He had already looked at the map. Although Luxembourg was well-forested, he thought a landing would be manageable, although hills, 'especially steep sudden ones', should be avoided. This was to some extent encouraging. Pollock had taken out his compass and slide-rule: a flight of seventy miles or so was very long and weather conditions would change as the balloon proceeded. He would have to build in a margin of error of at least twenty-five miles; 'that is to say,' Wallinger told Bruce, 'in

POLLOCK'S opinion, we should be able to hit the Province of LUXEMBURG, and that's about all'.*

If the Admiralty had no balloons for training, Wallinger offered a spare from Bruay. Hazeldine could help with the launch. Admiralty support would be needed to bring kit to France and superintend the filling. If Bruce could draft an official request, Wallinger would put it in. Captain Maitland, Assistant Director of Naval Air Services, was a personal friend and would 'fix up' things immediately. In fact, said Wallinger, more eager by the minute, when the agent arrived at Hurlingham, he might even accompany him himself on his apprentice flight, 'to act as interpreter'. It seems that Bruce wished to perpetuate the assumption that his agent was French: his formal request for Admiralty support, signed by Drake's deputy, Major Stewart Menzies, referred to 'Meau' as a French civilian.** The cover was useful and, as the French military would be involved in the operation, it would be tactful to let them think the agent was one of their own.

Despite his obligations to the Admiralty, Pollock was determined not to be left out. The last sentence of Bruce's application accordingly asked whether the Commander might be spared for three or four days' final instruction before the agent's dispatch. Pollock was already making energetic preparations, asking Wallinger to find out the weight of the Frenchman and his baggage, apart from food and personal necessities, so that he could decide on the size of the balloon. In overcoat and without overcoat, Meau placed himself upon the scale.

As soon as he had Menzies' letter, Wallinger bustled over from Basil Street to the Admiralty. Maitland was entranced. Bruce must send his agent to London straightaway; the Admiralty would provide

* Wallinger was evidently mixing up the Grand Duchy with the Province of Luxembourg, the French-speaking area that had joined up with Belgium when Luxembourg was divided in 1839. The Province was part of the territory for which Wallinger was responsible. Wallinger to Bruce, 13 February 1918.

** Menzies to Wallinger, 18 February 1918. Menzies had joined I(b) in 1915 from the Life Guards, after being gassed. Ambitious and well-connected, he was said by some to be an illegitimate son of Edward VII, a rumour Menzies took no trouble to dispel. In 1939, outmanoeuvring Dansey among others, he became Head of the Secret Intelligence Service, taking over Cumming's green ink and the code-name 'C'.

balloon, gas, labour and other essentials, on account. Pollock was standing by, Wallinger told Bruce, so that training could start without delay. When the agent got to London, he would be met at the station. Everything would be done to make him comfortable: 'my Belgian can if you like take charge of MEAU and get him fixed up in the quiet little Hotel where we always put our men'. If Bruce had time to spare, Wallinger added, and the weather were suitable, he might like to accompany his agent on the first ascent. Wallinger hoped to join them. 'I have arranged this with Captain MAITLAND, who said he would also try and come himself for a joy-ride! I think all of us going up with him would tend to inspire confidence in MEAU and make him look upon the balloon journey as an enjoyable sport, which indeed it is.'[22]

If Baschwitz had not been so high-spirited himself, he would have thought these Englishmen were mad.

19

Madame Rischard's Other Occupation

At first light on a February morning, Zürich railway station was not alluring. Under a staring clock, the anxious, who had risen too early and arrived too soon, looked reproachfully at their watches. Chins hunched into overcoat collars, did they think of influenza? Better to have remained under the covers, with the prospect of sweet rolls and hot chocolate by a bright fire, than to be standing here in a soot-laden draught, waiting for the 5.07 stopping train to Cologne.

Among them was a woman on her own, warmly clad, neatly shod. The train came in, her things were stowed and she took her seat. Once settled, she brought out a *cigarette-étui* and, as the train drew away, began to smoke, keeping the case to hand. She seemed as reassured by it as by the cigarettes themselves. Zürich, Winterthur, the frontier: just over an hour. When the inspectors asked for papers, the well-dressed passenger was ready. She was in transit only; here – she spoke in German – was her passport, issued in Luxembourg, and the permit allowing her to leave by this route. Having appraised the lady and her documents, the police moved on. Gentlemen brought out pocket watches. Germany. On time.

Conscious that the first stage of the journey was behind them, passengers put aside their newspapers and shifted their stiffening limbs. The peckish assessed the timetable and thought about a surreptitious bite. Horsehair bristles, escaping from the seats, spiked through skirts and trousers. The train turned north-east, to Singen, then north-west towards the Rhine. Immendingen, Donauschingen, Villingen, Triberg, Hornberg, Hausach . . . Soothed by the rhythm of wheels against track, travellers dozed. But not the woman with the Luxembourg passport: all day, while she was taken through Germany, she smoked her cigarettes and looked out of the window. She observed the condition of fields and those who worked in them, the appearance of towns, traffic on roads and rivers, activity on railway platforms and in sidings. Other occupants of the compartment came and went. When there was conversation, she was an attentive but non-committal listener. Madame Rischard was at last on duty.

It was nearly six o'clock when the train pulled in to Offenburg. Those who were breaking their journey installed themselves in an hotel. The cost of a porter was, Madame Rischard thought, extortionate. Before she dined, she wrote to Madame Garland, care of Madame Fresez-Settegast at Villa Allmer in Grindelwald. So far all had gone smoothly and she was not fatigued. She had thought constantly of Georgette and Jacques; their '*cigaretten-étui*', she said, had not left her side. Once posted, this message, on a wartime postcard, ready-printed with a ten-pfennig stamp, went to Freiburg, where mail from Offenburg was examined. From there, franked with the censor's mark, it would be taken to Baden for delivery next morning to Madame Rischard's aunt in Switzerland. Bruce's postal experiment was under way.

Madame Rischard had last been in Germany in the winter of 1916. At that time strict rationing was already in force. But now people were starving and angry, rebelling against sacrifice for victory that did not arrive. Germany had become a country where schoolchildren threw stones, mothers heckled outside town halls, factory hands downed tools. Curfews had been introduced, adolescents forbidden to congregate or go to the cinema. People had been ordered to save, housewives to make do, parents to produce more children – contraception was not allowed – to replenish the Fatherland. Special privileges had been granted by the authorities – an allocation of thousands of tons of barley for making substitute coffee, extra allotments of beer for Bavaria – and emergency policies announced: house-owners with gardens and apartment-dwellers with balconies were allowed to keep rabbits and chickens, workers given time off to grow vegetables on designated sites. Such concessions only increased resentment at the war's privations.

There were strikes and riots. Auxiliary police, replacing men who were at the front, sided with demonstrators. While mayors and councillors hesitated, the military intervened. Regulations had been imposed upon every aspect of civil life. Potato consumption was one example: cellars were checked to make sure that potatoes were correctly stored and, if so, that stocks were neither being hoarded nor – a difficult balance – used up too quickly. Violations of the rules were recorded and sent up the administrative chain for analysis. Some measures were ludicrous, the requirement, for instance, that all rumours be reported. A contemptuous population turned to jokes and rhyme.[1]

Madame Rischard had known none of this while she was in Paris and Lausanne. Now, as she looked about the hotel, everything suggested desperation. Fires were miserly, carpets threadbare, furnishings worn. People's faces were gaunt, their shoulders bony. Energy had been drained out of them. Germany was altered. So – but exhilaratingly – was she. The lessons of the past twelve months had given her new competence and authority. She had work to do, colleagues to shield, secrets to keep. Tonight and tomorrow, alone among strangers, she must behave as if nothing had changed. With this in mind, she proceeded to unpack what she needed for the night and, having tidied her hair, went in to dinner.

No one intercepted her as she made her way to her table. No one troubled her as she dined. There was little choice, but the waiting staff was kind and efficient and the food good. No one accosted her as she went to her room. Her suitcase was as she had left it. Had Bruce and Campbell taught her to place a fine thread among her things, so that she would know if strange hands had searched them? Nothing was disarranged. No knock roused her in the night and, when she woke, she knew that within a few hours she would be home. The prospect of going into enemy country had been terrifying but, so far, her journey could not have been more manageable.

It was as well that she was rested. The next day's travels were wearing. From Offenburg the 7.36 crossed the Rhine to Strassburg. That took an hour. Between connections, Madame Rischard wrote another postcard to Madame Garland: 'Beste Grüsse aus Strasburg'. Her message had two signatures: 'Lise' and below, in a different hand, 'Pierre'. Huss, who had left Switzerland three days earlier, had waited to escort her into Luxembourg, and the postcard was to tell Bruce that his two agents had kept their appointment.

The train for Luxembourg left at 10.08. Travelling west toward the Saar, it passed through depopulated country. There were no announcements and for long stretches passengers had no idea where they were. Untimetabled stops were made to suit important people. Madame Rischard saw only straggly hedges, broken-down farms and unkempt fields, a landscape left, season after season, to the care of children, exhausted women and old men. At cheerless stations departure was delayed until supplies of butter, eggs and winter vegetables had been confiscated from the suitcases of disembarking passengers. People began to grumble, although informers were everywhere, ears cocked. Railway compartments were believed to be breeding grounds of subversion and a surveillance system operated on all lines. Even station lavatories were watched, in case users felt impelled to write rude protests on the walls. Madame Rischard's neighbours found much to be cross about: as the day went on, stops grew longer, police more intrusive, food in refreshment rooms less edible. Complaints were outspoken. This Madame Rischard thought encouraging.[2] War had made life intolerable and the Kaiser's subjects were evidently unafraid to say so.

They saw little of the country as they came up through Metz in the darkening afternoon. The train was already more than eight hours late when it reached the border. In peacetime, before invasion swallowed up the Grand Duchy, it had been easy to cross into Luxembourg from Germany and France. Now the frontier was heavily policed. At first there were no surprises. Pierre's papers had been correctly made out and his companion was able to show her Luxembourg passport, retrieved so many months ago from the Dutch legation in Berne. That was only the first hurdle. When she presented the customs declaration, Madame Rischard was ordered to open her suitcase. Swiss chocolate? Not allowed. After so many hours of confinement, so much delay, this was the last straw. The rule had doubtless been invented on the spot. Why should the inspectors want to confiscate sweetmeats, except for their own consumption? Rather than give in, and despite the fact that it had already taken her more than a twelvemonth to get home, Madame Rischard was sufficiently incensed to consider taking herself and her luggage back into Germany. She would try later when other officers were on duty. Sensing a difficulty, the inspectors changed their minds. Chocolate was permitted but only 250 grammes per person. As further protest might be dangerous, Madame Rischard surrendered the excess. By this small affair she was reminded that power was capricious – and that it wore a uniform.

It was past ten o'clock when she and Huss arrived at Luxembourg central station. Camille was not there to meet them. He was recovering from influenza and it would have been foolish to linger in the cold for a train that might not arrive until the middle of the night. Outside, in Place de la Gare, the gas lamps were unlit. The windows of the Hôtel Clesse were dark and in the next street the 'Münchner Kind' was empty. Were there no customers for German beer? Even the Hôtel Starr seemed devoid of life. It was Sunday night and the hour was late. No trams were running, no cabs waited. The streets were quiet. In the blackness, buildings were mere shapes, statues, monuments and fountains indistinct. Cobbles pressed up against Madame Rischard's soles: Boulevard Royal. Five shallow steps up to the porch, stone urns, one on each side of the balustrade. A crack of light as the door was opened. Thus Lise Rischard came out of the night into her own front hall. Camille was on his feet. He was better, he said, but weak. She saw it at once – and that something must be done about the carpet on the staircase.

It took days to put things straight and even then it was impossible to restore the house to the state in which she had left it. So much was unobtainable: beeswax, polishing cloths and feather dusters, washing soda, kitchen soap, vinegar for cleaning windows, new heads for balding mops and brooms. When she looked into her cupboards, she found nothing. There were no glasses of preserved fruit, no jars of jam or marmalade, no stores of sugar, flour or tea. Every box of currants had been consumed. There were no raisins, no bags of flour, no packets of salt and spice. How was she to restock? Everyday commodities had become luxuries, to be bought only in small quantities at high prices. Shops were closed four days out of seven; potatoes, dried beans and peas, rice, yeast, bacon, lard and coffee, intermittently available, were rationed. As for replacing the stair carpet, that would have to wait until the war was over.

Domestic wants were not her only preoccupation. The doctor had settled into his own routine while his wife was away. Now, like the furniture, he needed buffing up. Their first exchanges were not about worn shirt collars or the timing of meals. Madame Rischard had more urgent business to discuss. Her husband was not surprised. From the moment she came into the house, he said, he knew that something momentous had happened. Her letters and the messages brought by Huss had already given him a clue. He understood that she was in touch with a friend of Charles Jubert, one Georgette, highly placed and influential, interested in what went on in the marshalling yard at the Luxembourg central station. To this end, Huss had been charged with finding an informant among the railwaymen; when that proved difficult, he had asked Dr Rischard to help him. He, Camille, had identified two people but, as yet, neither knew what he was supposed to do. Dr Rischard did not know either but he could guess. He thought it was going to be disagreeable.

Lise filled in the gaps. She explained how Armand Mollard had introduced her to Rose and Réséda at his office at the Quai d'Orsay. She told Camille what she had said to the officers. She described her interview in the Madeleine and the priest's response. She talked of lessons in Rue Soufflot and studies in Rue de Moscou, of engines, trains and constituted units. She seemed to know every German regiment, every type of weapon. She spoke about Paul and Jeanne Schroell, Sepp Hansen, the *Landwirt*. Lise was saying all this, his wife, who had come home at last to look after him, and the dog. To top it all, this Georgette to whom she had bound herself was neither female nor French. Dr Rischard had not suspected anything so deep. And yet, instinctively, he had made the right preparations. The railwaymen to whom he had spoken were trustworthy and ready to enlist others, equally reliable. She had mentioned that money would be needed. Funds were in place and could be transferred straightaway. As he had told her last December, he would stick by her to the end.

So they set to work. A week after her return, Lise wrote in code to Madame Garland. Camille was ready and both Jeanne Schroell and Hansen had agreed to play their parts. As Paul Schroell had supposed, newsprint would have to be bought for the *Landwirt* and the schoolmaster to be paid for his articles. When she knew the costs, she would write accordingly. Finally, and crucially, for the past week no constituted units had passed through Luxembourg. A report repeating these points would be inserted in the next issue of the *Landwirt*.

This letter was written on 18 February. Inspected by censors in Luxembourg, cleared for delivery to Madame Fresez-Settegast in Switzerland, forwarded by her to Bathet in Geneva and sent on by him to Bellegarde, it reached Bruce on the 27th, good going, considering the complications of the route. It was not the letter, however, that won the race. On the previous day, 26 February, a copy of the *Landwirt* had arrived at Rue St Roch, delivered from Cambron in Switzerland via the diplomatic bag.

So far Bruce had received only the postcards from Offenburg and Strassburg, which had arrived together on 16 February. There had been nothing to tell him to look for a report in the *Landwirt*. The newspaper he now held in his hands had been published on Thursday 21 February. If Madame Rischard had started transmitting, she had begun quickly. Hansen, too. He would have had no more than a week to learn how to manipulate letters and phrases of the code and to practise his compositions. This edition of the *Landwirt* had news of events that had taken place on the morning of the 21st; it must have been set in type on the afternoon of that day at the latest. Only ten days after Madame Rischard's return: was it realistic to expect anything so soon?

The inky Gothic German typeface was difficult and intimidating. At first sight, the *Landwirt* looked more like an enemy propaganda sheet than a country newspaper. Two thirds of the front page dealt with news about the war, everything seen through German eyes, every sentence approved by Tessmar's censors. A closer look, however – and in Rue St Roch they were looking very closely – showed that the *Landwirt* had lost neither its independence nor its sense of humour. The bottom third of the first page presented episode three of a serialized version of Emil Schweig's fairy-tale, *Die Verwünschene Prinzessin*. Whether the enchanted princess was the Grand Duchess, held in thrall by Berlin, or the German military leadership, deluded by dreams of victory, the *Landwirt* left readers to judge.

According to the masthead, the paper still appeared four times a week. This issue was densely printed over two pages, front and back of a single sheet. Scanning the contents took only a minute. The item Bruce sought leapt to the eye: three paragraphs in the middle of the second column on the back page: *Lokal-Neuigkeiten*. It was under this heading that Paul Schroell had asked Hansen to write. Pencils in hand, Bruce, Campbell, Chocqueel and Tangye pored over the text. Three piglets were for sale in Diekirch market. In air raids over Düdelingen, the barber had been injured and the windows of the Klepper-Landtgens' café blown in. Horses were being taken from Ettelbrück to Germany – just as the ploughing season was starting. The authorities were being asked to release for human consumption the ration of oats allocated to these animals.

Could this hide a report about the marshalling yard?

The officers bent lower over the type. A fractional difference distinguished a Gothic 𝕾 from a Gothic 𝖀, 𝕾 from 𝕳, 𝕬 from 𝖀. Such work could not be done quickly. Phrase by phrase, line by line, they counted out letters, marking them with pencilled dots. A sequence emerged. Decoded, it was a meaningless jumble. Perhaps this *Landwirt* had been sent to see how long it would take to get a newspaper from Luxembourg via Switzerland to Paris, if it could be done at all. But in that case Jeanne Schroell would surely have given them some sort of clue. The pencil marks were erased and they began again. Had Madame Schroell hidden a report in the war news on the front page? One passage stood out: a discussion in the Luxembourg parliament about the trapping of rooks and over-fishing of pike by people desperate for meat and fish. A blank. What about 'For Sale and Wanted'? Old hands would never leave a secret message in so obvious a place but a novice might have done so. On the back page Herr Lickes was asking for a cooper; Widow Hubert Deltgen selling lime. Aerts Garage required tarpaulins and hoses, new or second-hand; the elder Widow Deltgen offered a reward for a lost dog answering to the name of 'Jull'. In Campbell's code, J had a whole variety of meanings, depending on its place in a sentence. The box number, 210, might also be significant.

Nothing there.

Jeanne Schroell had put in a notice of her own: *Dienst-Mädchen gesucht*, Maid-of-all-work required. Applicants were asked to reply to *Madame* rather than *Frau* J. Schroell, although use of French titles was forbidden. Was the anomaly deliberate? Another item in French advertised a billiard table, illustrated with its accoutrements. Again the pencils hovered. Letters and numbers were checked off: nothing. In 'For Sale and Wanted' the whole world of the *Landwirt*'s readers was encapsulated. Bruce and his colleagues had entered it and come out empty-handed.

Whose eye was drawn to *Büchertisch*? An article like no other in the paper, erudite and reflective, it started two inches down the first column on the back page, stopped in mid-sentence to give room for overspill from *The Enchanted Princess* and finished at the top of the second column. It seemed to have been chopped about, this contribution, as if it were not part of the *Landwirt*'s regular furniture. Unusually, the piece was signed – but only with an initial: N. In Campbell's code, N, on its own, told the reader to look for a report of a general nature. Was the signature a coincidence?

From the Library Table

The entire house has been filling up with books, sent by the editor of the *Landwirt* for review . . .

The easy opening was the work of someone who had read much and knew how to write. Might the browser at the library table be Joseph Hansen?

. . . but the distractions of the present time have been so urgent that there has been no time to examine them. Every spare moment has been taken up with the search for bodily nourishment . . .

It must be Hansen: the bookish scholar, torn from his desk by the need to find food for his family. The officers read on. With every sentence the language became more convoluted, as if certain words and phrases had insisted on inclusion. The content was obscure, until they reached a passage, more forceful than the rest, in which there were two familiar references: to Franz Clement, editor of the *Journal d'Esch*, and to *Voix des Jeunes*, house journal of the Luxembourg intelligentsia.* Schroell was connected with the one, Hansen with

* Clement had written a critical review, described by 'N' as 'sensational', of books published during 1917. The essay, in the form of an open letter, had appeared in an almanac recording the previous year's events (on the lines of Britain's *Annual Register*), but 'N' thought that the *Voix des Jeunes* would have been a more appropriate place to publish it.

Die Kammer überläßt es dem Büro, die nächste Sitzung einzuberufen, voraussichtlich für nächste Woche.

Büchertisch.

Zu einem ganzen Haufen sind auf dem Redaktionstisch des „Landwirt" die literarischen Produkte, die seit Beginn des Krieges bis heute aus Luxemburg an unsere Adresse gingen, angewachsen! Wir sind alle unglücklicherweise durch die Nahrungssorgen so sehr in Anspruch genommen, und von dem großen Weltgeschehen gibt es so viel zu melden, daß uns keine Spalte übrig bleibt und wir, trotzdem wir gerne dazu bereit wären, nichts oder so viel wie nichts darüber berichten können; eine Haltung, mit der übrigens unsere Leser vollauf einverstanden sind. Und doch läßt diese imposante Sammlung eine Fülle von Gedanken in uns erwachen! Aufmunternd muß diese Hochflut hochinteressanter Neuerscheinungen für jeden freiheitlich gesinnten Patrioten erscheinen; Achtung gebietet schon die herrliche Kalenderliteratur; als König dieses Genres ist der „Almanach Babert" anzupreisen, welcher denjenigen von Hachette vollkommen und in fast ebenbürtigem Gewande ersetzt! Für unsere Buben gibt es eine eigene Zeitung, welche wir gerne jedermann empfehlen; die schönsten Artikel derselben stellte man zusammen und daraus entstand ein wunderbares Werkchen — für unsere Schuljugend ein köstlicher Zeitvertreib! Doch auch Erwachsene und literarisch Gebildete holen daraus reichlichen Genuß; auch sie gelangen zu einem guten Teil auf ihre Rechnung; einer besonders originellen und schöpferischen Feder entstammt das meisterhaft erzählte Histörchen: „Das Ferienkind".

Auch den diesjährigen Volksbildungskalender unterließen wir zu rezensieren. Und doch enthält er gerade für uns Diekircher so manches Interessante. So wird der erzählende Teil eröffnet durch eine aus überreiztem Mystizismus und krassem Realismus gewobenen Novelle von A. Nickels. Ferner finden wir darin ein Charakterbild des oft genannten Pfarrers München, der zur Zeit der französischen Revolution als „prêtre assermenté" in Diekirch die Seelsorge ausübte und als überzeugter Anhänger der Republik der Klöppelkriegbewegung nach Kräften entgegenarbeitete. Die Intellektuellen Diekirchs aber möchten wohl am meisten durch den sensationellen „offenen Brief", den Franz Clement im Volksbildungskalender an den Autor von „Bärnd Bichel" richtet, angezogen werden. Und dabei muß sich ihnen allen derselbe Gedanke aufdrängen, nämlich daß dieser geistreiche Brief vielleicht in einem draufgängerischen und rein literarisch-satirischen Kampfblatt wie die „Voix des Jeunes" an seinem Platze gewesen wäre, aber in einem Volksbildungskalender nicht hätte aufgenommen werden dürfen. Daß die auf einer bewußt exklusiven Anschauung beruhenden Paradoxe von Franz Clement sogar von vorgebildeten Intellektuellen mißverstanden werden können, das beweist das erquickliche Abenteuer, das den jugendlichen Adepten des „Cénacle des

würdigen Art hatte die Baronin die Unterhaltung bald dahin gebracht, wohin sie sie hatte haben wollen — „Also, lieber Baron, ich weiß, wen Sie

Opening paragraphs of the first column of Madame Rischard's first report – and Joseph Hansen's first coded composition – in Der Landwirt *of 21 February 1918: 'From the Library Table'. The marks of the officers' pencils may still be seen, at the end of the first paragraph, for instance, showing how they checked off the message: We are all ready in Luxembourg.* Aus Luxemburg *[line 4]* . . . Wir sind alle . . . *[line 5]* . . . bereit *[line 9].*

the other. The allusions seemed to have been specially attached, like the gaudy ribbons on Hazeldine's balloons.

The officers picked up their pencils. 'W' in *'Weltgeschehen'* . . ., 'i' in *'keine'* . . ., 'r' in *'wir'* . . . The movement of their fingers fell into a rhythm, pencil marks into a pattern. Until this moment the code had been simply an intellectual construct. Bruce, Chocqueel, Tangye and Campbell, its inventor, knew it as musicians know a score. Now it was full of meaning.

Wir sind alle bereit in 46, 34 und 68 sind einverstanden bis heute nichts zu melden keine 'constituted units' gingen durch.

Code within code: 46 stood for Luxembourg, 34 for Hansen, 68 for the *Landwirt*.

We are all ready in 46, 34 and 68 have agreed. Until today nothing to report, no constituted units have gone through.

It was eleven months since Bruce had first proposed a Luxembourg train-watching project. Drake's reaction had been tepid, Cameron's icy. This proved the doubters wrong. The scheme worked – and fast. Five days to transmit information from occupied territory was phenomenally quick. Bruce's dispatch to GHQ was short but satisfying:

B. P.   No. 1.   26/2/1918.
No movement of constituted units has taken place in either direction through LUXEMBURG station during the period February 10–20.[3]

Did they allow themselves a toast? Or was it thought to be tempting providence? Madame Rischard deserved congratulations and, it being Chocqueel's turn at coding duty, the letter in which they were sent was in Nicole's hand and style. The notary wrote with a swing, rhapsodizing about visitors, presents and successes. Exclamations did double service, stepping up the temperature of the prose and marking off sections in code. A tumbling paragraph about homework (*'félicitations'* and 21st February, *'21 fautes'*), a flourish of family news (Robert was trying to persuade his father to let him smoke), and the composition was done.[4] It went with fond thanks from Maman for Tante Lise's first news from Luxembourg, for Madame Rischard's letter of 18 February had just arrived.

No sooner had Chocqueel sent off congratulations than a third postcard was delivered, telling them that the heavy luggage had come from Switzerland and with it a copy of Garnier's dictionary.[5] Tante Lise had begun her lessons in French literature and was looking in local bookshops for Fontaine's *Fables* and Hugo's *Châtiments*. Finding the latter might be difficult; if she failed, would Conrad be able to bring a copy? The reference to lessons told Bruce that she had arranged for Hansen to come to Boulevard Royal, the mention of the books that, until Baschwitz reached Luxembourg, key words for the code would be drawn not from Baedeker or Lieber but from Garnier. Madame Rischard was applying herself with zeal.

The postcard came in on the 28th, a Thursday. On the same day another *Landwirt* was delivered, the edition for the previous Saturday. It had no *Büchertisch* and no other article by 'N' but *Lokal-Neuigkeiten* looked promising: six inches of coverage about a congress of gymnasts at Esch and details of the week's offer at the Diekirch Cinema Palace (*Journey to the Moon* shown *gratis* at every performance).[6] Code, presumably. Out came the pencils. No, the gymnasts were genuine, and the film. Going through the rest of the paper took hours, Saturday's *Landwirt* being twice the size of the weekday edition. The officers found nothing. Two days later Monday's *Landwirt* arrived in Rue St Roch. This time *Lokal-Neuigkeiten* reported on the selection of a mayor for the municipality of Eich and the allocation of land for spring planting. More activity with pencil and eraser.[7] Again, nothing.

On that same Monday morning another letter from Boulevard Royal was brought in to Bruce's office. It included two important messages. The first, hidden in a complaint about the price of wallpaper, referred to Jeanne Schroell's difficulties with the *Landwirt*. A year's supply of newsprint would cost the equivalent of 11,000 French francs. Madame Rischard's bank would give credit for that amount but could the budget accommodate such a sum?[8] The second point concerned train movements. Constituted units were coming from Trier and were being sent southwards through Thionville. Bruce immediately telephoned this last piece of information, in code, to GHQ. It sounded as if a division might be moving towards the front.

Madame Rischard's only worry, apart from the question of money, was that the Garlands had failed to write. The first sentence of her letter reproached Georgette for her silence.[9] Chocqueel drafted the reply. Letters had been written, Nicole protested, even if they had been neither as frequent nor as long as her aunt might have wished. Tante Lise did not realize how busy they were in the Garland household. She, Nicole, had hardly a moment's peace, what with interruptions and criticism from Maman and Mademoiselle Testu. Tante Lise had no lessons to do and no need to think about style: 'It would be tremendous – épatant – if I could write like you.'[10] 'Epatant' was part of a coded message, conveying an instruction from Bruce: 'Try to keep to the Landwirt as much as possible. It is tremendously important and quicker.'[11] She should keep railway reports for the Landwirt, a faster route than letters. As for the 11,000 francs, she could tell Madame Schroell that the money would be made available.

It was not surprising that the Garlands' letters had been slow to reach Boulevard Royal. Everything they wrote had first to be got to Madame Fresez-Settegast for forwarding. When letters reached Luxembourg, they had to be cleared by the censors' office before delivery. Bruce's message acknowledging the postcards from Offenburg and Strassburg had been sent on 16 February, Chocqueel's congratulations on the 27th, so there had hardly been time for these communications to arrive. Madame Rischard's fears were understandable. She had no idea whether her reports had got through or how they had been received.

Then her letters ceased. At first the officers were untroubled: copies of the Landwirt arrived without fail, a piece by Hansen in every issue. Although Madame Rischard might not always wish to put a report in the newspaper, it seemed that she and Jeanne Schroell understood that Lokal-Neuigkeiten should be a regular feature, always in the same place, halfway down the middle of the second page. It should become so familiar to the censors that they would disregard these trifles, of interest, surely, only to people in a scattering of villages and hamlets – Bettendorf and Eppeldorf, Lintgen and Useldingen, Bövingen and Hovelingen – or to exiles in Switzerland, nostalgic for home.

Lokal-Neuigkeiten was a model of parochialism. On Wednesday 27 February readers learnt that Joseph Clesse-Müller was selling a quantity of white wine, 1911 vintage, and that Madame Schroell had not yet found her maid-of-all-work. Changes were to be made in the rounds of seven postmen. Frau Schiltz at the Diekirch café had beet-root to spare.* Close inspection produced not a single word in code.[12] Next day's paper reported that a bracelet had been found after the concert at the football club and that the Diekirch Democratic Circle had arranged a lecture on constitutional and electoral reform.[13] No code. Saturday brought the four-page weekend issue. A pocket watch had been stolen with a ham and other edibles from the vicarage at Gilsdorf. In Diekirch apprenticeships were available at the barber's, the blacksmith's and the wagon-builder's. One item of news was more than locally significant: an announcement that the railway company required staff for station and freight duties. Appropriately qualified applicants were asked to present themselves for interview on the 1st of April; more posts would be advertised in six months.[14] The marshalling yard had been quiet while the viaduct was being repaired; if new staff were being recruited, work must be almost done. This information was useful – but there were no passages in code.

The absence of reports had become disturbing. During the first week of March the readers in Rue St Roch grew more apprehensive. Had Madame Rischard's first communication in the *Landwirt* been her last? The news they dreaded would need no decoding. Her post-card of 19 February had been open for all to see. She had talked about reading French literature: studying Fontaine and Hugo was not treasonous but an intelligent censor might have thought the message strange. The authorities could have let it go in the hope that subsequent letters would tell them more. Had Madame Rischard's letter of 22 February confirmed their suspicions? All had been well up to that date, the day after the publication of the *Büchertisch* article. Why had there been no reports since then? Why did the woman not write?

---

* At the request of the Imperial Office for Fruit and Vegetables, the Association of German Housewives had published factsheets, with recipes, to encourage root vegetable consumption. The promotional efforts of the Association had evidently been a failure in Diekirch, as elsewhere.

No news for a week. The *Landwirt* for 4 March, a Monday, came in on Saturday, the 9th. The officers took in the headlines, skimmed the columns. *Vom Weltkrieg*: skirmishes on the Western Front, peace negotiations between Germany and Russia, Japanese action in Siberia. *Amtliches*: new regulations for exporting horses, selling machinery for grinding bran and flour, transport, consuming butter and using seed crops. *Lokal-Neuigkeiten*: paragraphs about discarded mangel-wurzels and rationed fats and meat. The pencils ran down the columns, paused. At last. Interwoven among sixty lines of Hansen's prose was a report.

It was strictly factual. The railway line was being doubled over the Pulvermühl viaduct, between the central station and the point where the lines divided. From there one track led to Trier, the other to Ettelbrück. A project to double the line on that section had often been discussed in peacetime but had always been thought too difficult and expensive. Now the scheme was going ahead at full speed. Until it was finished, no constituted units could travel by this route.[15] This was the proposal to which Huss had referred in January in Lausanne. Having read the report, Bruce immediately telephoned Drake at GHQ. Once the doubling of the line was complete, the Luxembourg marshalling yard would be able to handle a very great deal of traffic.

In her letter of 22 February Madame Rischard had indicated that while the viaduct was out of action trains were being directed from Trier via Thionville, bypassing the central station. From Thionville, military traffic was going to Arlon in Belgium. Her next letter – written before she received instructions to send reports only in the *Landwirt* – told Bruce what the trains were carrying:

THIONVILLE–ARLON 2nd–4th
12 trains constituted units artillery
Uniform as follows
Hat band not seen.
Shoulder straps yellow.
Red piping.

The marshalling yard at the Luxembourg main station 1999. The rotunda of the locomotive shed is at centre back. The station building is in front of the

No crown, grenade or monogram.

No. 68.

Two red crossed cannons on shoulder straps.

Grey collar with yellow line forming an angle.*

This coded message, written on the 5th, had evidence of haste. Madame Rischard had dated it incorrectly, February, rather than March, and the ink was smudged. The espionage operation was gathering speed and she had to catch the post.

Although re-engineering on the viaduct was not yet complete, military trains, routed via Thionville, were now crossing the country in great numbers. Those which interested Madame Rischard were convoys of twelve to fifteen trains, each made up of dozens of

---

* Madame Rischard to Bruce, 5 March 1918. Here '68' was not a reference to the *Landwirt*, as in Campbell's code, but the number troops wore on their uniforms.

long rectangular roof below the spire. There would have been many more lines in 1918, and the Place de la Gare would not have been filled with cars.

carriages and wagons, following hard upon each other towards France. It was clear that, while the viaduct was out of use, information would be needed about train movements elsewhere on the network. Furthermore, until Madame Rischard could be sure that her observers were able to identify the convoys that made up a constituted unit, she had to make such decisions herself. To do so, she needed descriptions of all military trains travelling in sequence through Luxembourg. The two railwaymen Camille had recruited covered the Luxembourg central station, each doing a twelve-hour shift, but they could not provide reports on this scale and neither of the Rischards had the time to enlist and manage a large number of observers. Camille therefore suggested a different approach.

It was simple but very risky: Dr Rischard would obtain the necessary information from the railway supervisors. These men saw documents relating to train movements, paperwork that was extensive, for it mapped activity over the whole network. For all traffic, military and civilian, lines had to be assigned, signals and switching of points co-ordinated. Particular trains or convoys of trains were given priority. At stations where trains were required to halt more than briefly, sidings of adequate length had to be cleared; if troops and horses were on board, arrangements had to be made for washing out coaches and wagons and for provisioning. To prepare trains for departure, various procedures had to be gone through – filling the boiler, getting up steam – that could not be carried out at short notice. Instructions relating to the movement of trains were drawn up by the military and telegraphed to senior people at the Luxembourg central station. No train left a station without a wire being sent ahead to alert stations along the next stage of the route. Sheaves of telegrams accumulated on supervisors' desks, scraps of paper piled up on the spike, information that, taken together, made up the railway equivalent of an Order of Battle. At the Luxembourg central station, five men had access to this material: principal assistant station masters Joseph Offenheim and Jean Rockenbrod and assistant station masters Auguste Diderich, Ernest Kraus and Jean Kneip. Dr Rischard spoke to them. All agreed to serve.

By the end of the second week of March, the scheme was working smoothly. On 13 and 14 March *Lokal-Neuigkeiten* gave details of all trains that had carried infantry and artillery through Thionville and Arlon to Cambrai during the previous week.[16] Madame Rischard's information included a note of uniforms and numbers appearing on vehicles. To be doubly sure that the Paris Office had received these reports, of which she was justifiably proud, she also put them in letters, written on the 13th and the 15th, disguised in the first case as remarks about the latest fashions in hats and in the second as observations about hydrangeas.[17] Mirroring train-watching reports in this way contravened her own warnings about repetition. If her message-sending routes were discovered, German counter-intelligence would be able to compare the text in the *Landwirt* and in letters. Duplicates would make it easier to understand the basis of the code, allowing the enemy to penetrate the network, deceive Paris with false reports, sabotage the operation. In his most recent letter, Chocqueel had asked Madame Rischard to put her reports in the *Landwirt*, rather than in letters; he had not thought she would be so rash as to do both. In a coded postscript to her letter of the 13th, she gave the reason. Hansen was slow and his visits erratic. In time he would make an excellent auxiliary; although some aspects of his behaviour were unconventional, he was extremely intelligent.[18] Until he became more reliable, she felt she must underpin anything she gave him for *Lokal-Neuigkeiten* with coded messages to the Garlands.[19]

From this and other allusions, Bruce and his fellow-officers understood that their Luxembourg network chief was not finding it easy to persuade Hansen to work to a routine. This was correct. The schoolmaster had been reluctant to take part. He had to remember his professional responsibility. And then there was his family. If he were caught, who would be the breadwinner? He had listened to the proposition out of affection for the Schroells, his next-door neighbours; he had felt obliged to consider it because he respected Jeanne's courage and determination. Was it Madame Schroell or his conscience that had induced Hansen to say yes? He hated what Germany was doing to his country. Here was his opportunity to do something about it – and to demonstrate that a scholar could also be a man of action.

The pen might yet prove mightier than a service rifle, *Lokal-Neuigkeiten* more powerful than an artillery barrage. Had he been asked to propose his own area of specialism, a parish gazette was not what Hansen would have chosen. Criticism was more his line, reflective articles that gave scope for wit and style. At least he did not have to put his name to these pieces about fatstock and half hoggets. His fellow-contributors to the *Voix des Jeunes* would have been astonished to know what he was writing. Indeed, he knew little enough himself. He had been asked to compose sentences in which certain letters appeared in a certain order but, for security, the basis of the code had not been explained. This was irritating to an inquiring mind. Madame Rischard realized that Hansen was frustrated, understood his pride, felt his distaste for writing about cabbages and turnips. To carry him with her, she had appealed to his love of France and French civilization, reminded him of his true intellectual milieu, not the school in Diekirch or her drawing room in Boulevard Royal, but Paris and the Left Bank of the Seine. Hansen had been educated in France, he was saturated in its culture. Now he could repay the debt. The importance of this work was greater than that of any essay or review, the reader who had commissioned it more exacting than any university professor. Hansen must write these pieces with all the fluency and precision he could command. Trivial though they might seem, the articles must be delivered regularly and on time. Who was this mysterious reader? Madame Rischard could say only that the information was being sent to Paris. Hansen concluded that he was working for the French; she did not tell him otherwise.

Thus Joseph Hansen forsook the literary intelligentsia for military intelligence. By mid-March he was working at full stretch.

Der Landwirt 18 March:
Thionville–Arlon 14th to 16th
7 trains artillery, 8 trains infantry, 24 trains various.

Der Landwirt 21 March:
Thionville–Arlon 17th to 19th
One train artillery, 4 infantry, 2 cavalry.

Der Landwirt 23 March:
Thionville–Arlon 20th and 21st
One train artillery, one train infantry, five trains cavalry.

Trèves–Arlon 20th
4 trains infantry.

And – the importance of this will become apparent –

Thionville–Luxemburg–Longuyon.
4 trains infantry, believed Austrian.[20]

Uniforms were described, when seen, and vehicle numbers given, details amplified by Madame Rischard in letters to the Garlands.

Letter to Nicole, 15 March:

Thionville–Arlon March 12th to 13th
4 trains artillery, 43 trains infantry, 18 trains various.

Uniforms:

1. Hat band black
   Shoulder strap black
   Piping red
   No. 13.

2. Shoulder strap grey
   Piping red
   A crown
   A monogram.

3. Shoulder strap grey
   Piping red
   No. 121.

4. Hat band black
   Shoulder strap yellow
   Piping red
   A grenade.

Arlon–Thionville March 12th to 13th

1 train artillery, 4 trains various.

Uniform:
Hat band black
Shoulder strap red
A grenade.

All in a couple of pages about decorating rooms and planting new varieties of shrubs and flowers: 'I tend them with jealous care.'[21] Madame Rischard's servants would have been puzzled by her allusions to hydrangeas and lobelias and repapering the walls. The gardener wanted a view on pruning, the housemaid instructions for spring-cleaning, but their mistress was always at her desk, writing, writing.

Madame Rischard was now part of an elaborate intelligence-gathering mechanism; her letters were military reports, treated accordingly. The procedure was as follows. As soon as Father Cambron received his *Landwirt*, he gave it to one of Campbell's people, who got it to Major Vischer in Berne.* From there it came in the diplomatic bag to Rue St Roch. The DMI had been asked by Drake to approve this private arrangement between Bruce and Vischer; if the Foreign Office knew, it turned a blind eye.

On arrival at No. 41 Madame Rischard's reports were read, decoded and summarized. To keep things straight, Miss Done and Mademoiselle Dorgebray had set up three registers to track communications between Luxembourg and Paris. One dealt with reports in the *Landwirt*, listing the number and date of each issue and the date on which it arrived in the diplomatic bag. The second covered letters sent by Madame Rischard, with dates on which they were written and received and summaries of subjects mentioned. The third registered letters to Madame Rischard from the Garlands. Again, dates were listed and subjects noted. When a message or *Landwirt* report arrived in Paris, its receipt was acknowledged, with date, in a letter to Madame Rischard. Similarly, when Madame Rischard received a letter from the Garlands, she confirmed its arrival in her next letter. The dates of these acknowledgements were recorded in the respective registers.

Straightforward in principle, the scheme was complex in practice. Letters from the Garlands were written by different people, 'Georgette', 'Nicole', 'Robert' or, more rarely, 'Jacques', depending on whose turn it was for coding duty. 'Tante Lise's' acknowledgement of a letter from one member of the family would sometimes be given in a letter to another, complicating the registers. Communications sent from Paris via Lausanne to Luxembourg were simpler to catalogue than those coming in the other direction. The Paris Office acknowledged everything by letter, there being no other way of sending word to Luxembourg, whereas Madame Rischard could use the *Landwirt*, letters, or both. Timing was unpredictable and the lists were hard to synchronize. Letters from Paris might take as many as eleven days to reach Luxembourg, eight from Luxembourg to Paris. Two letters might be forwarded from Switzerland in the same post, having been held up en route. In such cases, Madame Fresez-Settegast added a note on the reverse, in her old-fashioned hand:

---

* He had been reinstated as military attaché when Woolrych's appointment fell through.

Arrivées toutes deux de nouveau par le même courrier . . . These two letters just arrived by the same courier. Received your letter this morning, the 31st. And that for Lise dated 2nd, forwarded straightaway. Greetings, Aunt Marie.[22]

It was not easy to keep registers in step but filing had to be complete and up to date. A gap in the sequence might be the first sign of an interception, an unusually long delay an indication that somewhere along the way letters or *Landwirts* were being scrutinized by readers for whom they were not intended.

Having extracted material concerning movements of constituted units and other relevant intelligence, 'Cairnesse, Paris', that is, Bruce, re-encoded and telegraphed it to O. B. Ciphers* in the Intelligence Staff at GHQ. As telephone lines were unreliable and weary clerks responsible for unscrambling signals sometimes made errors, GHQ kept copies, on pink 'C' forms, of all transcripts; these were sent back to Rue St Roch for checking. It was GHQ's practice to acknowledge receipt of reports immediately, by telephone, but written confirmation was often slow. The Intelligence Branch by now employed more than 5,000 agents behind the lines and the officer in charge of O. B. Ciphers, Captain A. W. Speyer, had a mass of material to appraise. A week might elapse before a dispatch rider delivered GHQ's formal acknowledgement. With the pink forms came brown paper slips with Speyer's handwritten observations, telling Bruce how signals fitted in with information coming in from the hundreds of other train-watching posts further up the lines that led from Luxembourg into France and Belgium.

To the untrained, some of Speyer's comments might have seemed disappointing: 'too vague', he noted against the report of train movements between Thionville and Arlon on 11 March, a wary 'possible' for a report of three batteries going in the opposite direction. Bruce was not dissatisfied. Even a watery 'too vague' was not a criticism. Professionals knew that at this early stage the objective was to set up a line of communication, a secure system of reporting, an understood procedure. Useful detail was certainly emerging from Madame Rischard's reports, corroborating or contradicting information from

* O. B.: Operations Branch.

other sources further up the railway lines to the front, and already one or two of her messages had alerted Operations Branch to a hitherto unknown troop movement. 'Probable', against reports for 18 and 19 March, for instance, had given much pleasure to the team in Rue St Roch. The underlying aim, however, was to establish a routine, ready for the moment, which Bruce was sure would come, when questions arose to which only the Luxembourg network might provide the answers.

Speyer was not the only recipient of Madame Rischard's intelligence. Although the circle in Folkestone had been disbanded, Drake and Wallner continued to work together, their co-operation being important for the successful prosecution of both espionage and counter-espionage. The boldness of the Luxembourg scheme had captivated Wallner from the first and Bruce had kept him up to date. The connection was direct and private. When *Landwirt* reports were decoded, Bruce sent them to the Ministry of War and, as relevant, their contents were transmitted by Wallner's office to French GHQ.* It would have pleased Madame Rischard to see the larger pattern. But these exchanges were not for her eyes. Bruce could not tell her what became of her reports after they had been fed into the bureaucratic apparatus.

Despite months of practice, Madame Rischard found it a struggle to examine, synthesize and code so much so quickly. Once she had worked out which trains formed part of a constituted unit, descriptions of each convoy and what it carried had then to be translated into the correct sequence for Hansen. Corresponding with the Garlands was almost as difficult. Plaiting letters and punctuation into sentences in the prescribed pattern required skill and imagination. Camille was helping her, she told Georgette: 'I am reading English quite well to Michel and he is even trying to learn the difficult words.'[23] A point had occurred to them about dating letters from Paris. If the censors studied the Garlands' correspondence, they might wonder why these people who lived in Switzerland took so long to take their letters to the post. Should they not build in an interval to take account of

---

* As Bruce revealed to Madame Rischard in a letter written after the Armistice, 18 November 1918.

the time required for delivery to Madame Fresez-Settegast? This precaution had not occurred to the Paris Office; once stated, it was obvious.

As railway traffic increased, the Rischards recruited more observers, identified only by code number, never by name. Camille collected the reports; his medical round took him to the central station and, from time to time, to outlying halts and signal boxes. Petrol was hard for civilians to obtain but the nature of the doctor's work entitled him to an extra ration. No one prevented him from going about his business; used to seeing him, the police did not trouble to search his vehicle. On the seat was his doctor's bag, with stethoscope, bandages, medicines, thermometer and other instruments. Bits and pieces of writing reminded him to see particular people, look for particular symptoms, prescribe particular doses. Or, rather, that is what he would have said had he been asked. To and fro he went. He always had a brisk greeting for whoever was on duty at the station, Offenheim or Rockenbrod, Diderich, Kraus or Kneip. If a paper had to be passed discreetly, a handshake was convenient. The doctor was a busy man and not usually gregarious. These days, however, he sometimes had a minute for a terse exchange. Third parties did not intrude upon these conversations, presuming them to be about the symptoms of influenza or other medical confidences.

At the beginning of the third week of March, the work on the viaduct was finished. This was the special importance of the coded report in the *Landwirt* of 23 March. The four infantry trains that had gone from Thionville to Longuyon on the 20th had been routed via the Luxembourg central station. The marshalling yard, first focus of Bruce's train-watching proposal, was fully operative again. It was time to introduce *chef-manoeuvre* Edouard Bram, superintendent foreman.

20

Sowing and Reaping

Bram had been Dr Rischard's first recruit. His skill and experience were crucial to the efficient running of the station but, unlike colleagues who managed paperwork, he handled rolling stock and track. It was not part of his duties to be recognized by the travelling public. When principal assistant station masters and assistant station masters left their offices to walk up and down the platform, passengers greeted them and railway employees touched their caps. Offenheim and Rockenbrod attracted more deference than Diderich, Kraus and Kneip, being one rank up, but all were noticed. Not so Bram. Ever present, he was invisible. In neckcloth and mended trousers, an oily rag to hand, he walked along the cinders, examining engines, carriages and wagons, prodding covers, lifting tarpaulins. While a train was being readied – it could take four hours for a heavy engine to get up steam – he would have a word with the fireman, the driver, the guard in the brake-van. German or not, all were railwaymen, warming themselves by a brazier in the dawn. When he finished his shift, Bram went home to Bonnevoie, a *quartier* next to the marshalling yard. Senior staff lived further from the station – Offenheim in Boulevard de la Pétrusse, Rockenbrod in Rollingergrund – but Bram could see the track even when off duty. He was the ideal train-watcher.

Meetings between Dr Rischard and Bram were rare. The *chef-manoeuvre* kept odd hours and, not being on the administrative side, when not in the consulting room had no reason for frequent conversation with the doctor. How were they to arrange the delivery of information? To protect the espionage network, reporting lines were kept separate; Bram could not use his colleagues as intermediaries.

It would be dangerous for him to come regularly to the Rischards' house. Just as close acquaintance between Madame Rischard and Madame Cerutti had been ruled out in Lausanne, so it was thought too risky to suggest an alliance between the doctor and the railwayman. Unseen in the marshalling yard, in Boulevard Royal the foreman would draw all eyes. It was Bram's idea to sound out his cousin, Mathias Schmit, a mathematics teacher, who also lived in Bonnevoie. Bram saw much of this cousin – blood being thicker than status – and thought he might be prepared to carry messages to and from the Rischards. Schmit taught at the Diekirch school alongside Hansen. He too now made a habit of calling at Boulevard Royal. Curious neighbours drew their own conclusions: Madame Rischard was said to be studying French literature with Hansen; the doctor must be brushing up his algebra and trigonometry with Schmit. Whatever the nature of their studies, the Rischards were conscientious pupils. On the upper floors of No. 20 lights burned late.

The 21st of March was the first day of spring. Days were milder, chestnut trees breaking into leaf. Madame Rischard talked of flowerbeds and the placing of arbutus, the *Landwirt* of lambing, piglets and ploughing. Hansen wove strings of code into observations about the price of grass seed and clover. At the front March winds carried spring snow that did not last. Dawn came earlier – clocks had been adjusted for summer time at sunrise on the 9th – and, looking up during morning stand-to, soldiers saw that the sky was lighter. But their fields were ploughed with entrenching tools and the earth was sown with wire. In January alone the Allies had planted 20,000 tons of barbed steel; a fence 1,000 miles long protected the forward line.

The cycle was well recognized: halt in the winter, attack in the spring. In other years the Germans had allowed the Allies to strike first and then repelled them with minimal loss of ground. This time the enemy could not afford to wait. Although French and British numbers had been depleted, reinforcements were on their way. In winter 1917–18 American soldiers had been few – only one regular division, supplemented by Marines, was in France – but thousands were expected. Pershing was determined that his troops should remain a distinct and separate army, unamalgamated with allied divisions, but they had not yet been put into fighting formation and their tanks, aircraft, artillery and ammunition were still to arrive. American conscripts were strong and eager but they had not faced gas attacks and guns, heard their own and others' screams, known the sickly smell of blood. Once organized and trained, they would be a formidable enemy. The Germans knew that they must strike before the Americans were present in greater numbers. The confrontation of 1918 had to be early and conclusive.

The 'hard facts' to which Charteris had alluded in December 1917 told the Allies that Germany would attack in April or May at the latest.[1] On 7 January Haig had warned the War Cabinet that the next four months would be critical. He had outlined what seemed to him likely: 'that the enemy would attack both the French and ourselves, and that he would hold Reserves in hand ready to exploit wherever he might have gained a success'.[2] The assessment was correct. This, broadly, was the approach that had been settled upon by General Ludendorff, deputy chief of the German General Staff.

Paris was already on alert. Half an hour before midnight on 30 January German heavy biplanes, 'Gothas', dropped tons of explosive on city and suburbs.* Avenue de la Grande Armée, a métro stop away from Rue St Roch, received a direct hit from a 500-pound bomb. Underground stations and church crypts were measured to see how many might be sheltered there, landlords were told to open cellars to strangers during raids. The blackout was reinforced. Electric sirens, 'ténors', were installed in *arrondissements* that could afford them; others relied on factory hooters, fire-engine bells and whistles. Above Paris, 200 captive ballons held up a curtain of fine wire to intercept the intruders. People were nervous. These bombs, the biggest yet, were designed either to fragment on impact or to penetrate stone walls. Would the next delivery bring something worse? Gas masks were unpacked.

Allied commanders were sure a German attack was imminent. Briefed by I(a) and I(b), on 3 February Brigadier-General Cox reported that the enemy now had 174 divisions at the front; on the 21st that their number had increased to 179; on the 25th to 180. According

---

* These machines, made by the Gotha works, had supplanted Zeppelins.

to Cox, information from captured soldiers, aerial observers and French and British agents indicated that the first thrust would be directed against the British Third Army, north of the Somme, and the Fifth Army, west of the Oise. From what they knew, the Intelligence Staff deduced that Ludendorff had decided not to push further into Flanders, where the battlefield was still sodden, but to concentrate on the middle of the front. Not the sector where the French Fourth, Second and Sixth Armies were defending the Marne and the approach to Paris. That would be a later target, to be struck once the British had been knocked aside.

Each report was a drumbeat. On 3 March, Major Cuffe, standing in for Cox, told Haig there were 182 enemy divisions at the front. By the 11th there were 185 and 77 in reserve. The Intelligence Staff's assessment was supported by news from Luxembourg. 'During the last fortnight of February,' Haig noted, 'the enemy moved five Divisions by the Hirson–Valenciennes railway to our front. This was as much as that line could carry.'[3] The Hirson line led up to the Oise from Luxembourg. German troops and machine-gun units were being delivered to Cambrai and the surrounding area: by the 18th, 187 enemy divisions were in position, with 80 in reserve. At Haig's intelligence briefing Cox referred to heavy traffic being brought from Germany to this part of France. 'We don't know yet what the trains are carrying,' Haig wrote in his diary, '. . . troops are not coming to Flanders but . . . going towards Valenciennes.'[4]

The most vulnerable point in the British line was the section immediately north of the Oise, where Haig had reluctantly agreed to take over some forty-two miles of front, previously manned by the French. Fourteen divisions of the Fifth Army, commanded by General Gough, were all that could be spared to hold this ground. Defences were still being dug, putting additional strain on men already overstretched. Passchendaele and all that had preceded it had reduced the British infantry to little more than half a million men. Further north, near Arras, the situation was slightly better. The Third Army had sixteen divisions to hold twenty-eight miles of front but here too defensive works in the battle zone were unfinished and in the rear zone, where supplies and heavy weaponry were held, much was still unprotected.

The attack came at daybreak on 21 March. At half past four

drifting fog was cracked open by a blast of yellow light, as thousands of German guns sent high-explosive shells into the British line. Trenches were saturated with gas, tearing the eyes of men on watch, gripping the throats of those who woke from sleep. Through fog and smoke came a high, thin sound: bugles, calling the *Sturmtruppen*, storm troops. The wraiths moved swiftly through no man's land, stealing on the trenches, encircling posts before the occupants knew the enemy was come. Then crashing waves of noise, noise that was inescapable, noise that took away the power to hear, to speak, to think. Flame-throwers shot fire, machine-gun bullets hammered into flesh, grenades and trench mortars shattered living and dead. Guns mounted on runners were manhandled forwards; across the shuddering ground the thunder of heavy artillery rolled in from the far distance. Behind this terrifying barrage the infantry advanced, fifty-two German divisions confronting twenty-six British divisions.

By the end of the day more than fifty miles of front had been engulfed. Along one nineteen-mile length the enemy overtook almost the whole allied forward position. Seven thousand British had been killed, 10,000 wounded, 21,000 taken prisoner. On 22 March Gough ordered the stunned remnants of the Fifth Army to fall back to the rear zone, still fighting but undeniably in retreat. German losses were high: 10,000 dead, 29,000 wounded. Even so, the *Kaiserschlacht*, the Kaiser's battle, was a major victory for the Germans, psychologically as well as territorially. None of their troops had been captured and they had made significant gains. The Kaiser declared 23 March a victory holiday for German schoolchildren; Hindenburg was awarded the Great Cross of the Iron Cross, last conferred on Blücher after the defeat of Napoleon in 1815.

The enemy had emerged from its lair. Ludendorff intended to press toward the Seine, cutting off Pétain's GHQ and separating French from British. Having done so, he meant to eliminate the French army and force the British back toward the Channel. His advance was prolonged, steady and relentless. During the next three days the enemy swept over ground it had left in March 1917. Towns and villages were retaken: La Fère, Ham, Péronne. In the north, German troops pushed toward Bapaume, in the south they aimed for Noyon.

Below the Oise German reserve divisions waited for instructions to move against the French.

In Paris there was panic. On 8 and 11 March the Gothas had returned. Shelters gave poor protection; seventy people were killed in a collapse at the Bolivar métro. A 250-pound bomb hit a gas-pipe in Rue de Rivoli, round the corner from Rue St Roch. On 22 March, at half past seven in the morning, there was worse: a series of huge explosions, fifteen minutes between each. No aeroplanes were seen or heard; at ten a.m. an official bulletin suggested that the bombers must be flying at 7,000 metres, perhaps higher. Were enemy pilots supplied with oxygen? An hour later the director of the Paris municipal laboratory asked to see the Prime Minister. Examination of *débris*, Clemenceau was told, showed that the weight of the projectiles far surpassed anything a bomber could carry. These were shells, fired by an immense long-distance gun.

Late in the evening of 24 March Pétain came to see Haig. The French Commander-in-Chief believed that the Germans were about to overrun his position along the Marne. All available French forces must be devoted to saving Paris. This was his government's instruction. Haig thought his French counterpart 'almost unbalanced'. To defend the capital Pétain was ready to abandon Haig's right flank and allow the French and British armies to be divided. The British would have to face the weight of the German army single-handed. Faced with this crisis, Haig asked Lawrence, Chief of the General Staff, to telegraph to London. The Chief of the Imperial General Staff – Sir Henry Wilson, who had replaced Sir William Robertson as Chief at the beginning of February – and Lord Milner, representing the War Cabinet, were asked to come to GHQ at once, to arrange, Haig said with desperate emphasis, 'that General Foch, or some other determined General who would fight, should be given supreme control of the operations in France'.[5]

The CIGS arrived that night. At midday on the 26th a conference was convened at Doullens, north of the Somme. Poincaré, President of France, was present, Clemenceau, the French Prime Minister, Milner, Wilson, Pétain, Foch, Haig and Lawrence. The immediate concern was Amiens, twenty miles south. If that were to fall, the enemy would be positioned to move either north and west, surrounding the allied armies that defended the Channel ports, or south, swallowing the zone between Somme and Seine. Those present agreed that Amiens must be covered at all costs. Clemenceau accordingly proposed that Foch should co-ordinate a shared force to protect the area. This was helpful; a joint operation would keep French and British together. There was one drawback: in this new arrangement, Foch would remain subordinate to Pétain.

The Germans were as yet nowhere near the outskirts of Amiens – their most forward position was twenty miles to the east – and if intervening ground could be held they might not get there. Foch, forceful and resolute, now said exactly that. There should be no retiring, not a centimetre. It was then proposed that Foch should be charged with co-ordinating the action of all the allied armies on the Western Front, a structure that would leave Pétain in charge of the French army and Haig of the British, both under Foch's overall direction. Haig was so sure that Pétain had to be led by Foch that, as he had indicated in his telegram to London, he was willing to give up his own independence of command, a principle on which he had hitherto insisted. The proposal was accepted, to Pétain's dismay. Haig thought he had lost his nerve: 'he had the appearance of a Commander who was in a funk'.[6]

Paris was gripped with rumours about the 'super-canon'. It was given out that there were at least three 'obus de Bertha', perhaps as many as sixteen, that they were mounted on rails, that the shells were charged with poison gas.* Householders stuck paper reinforcements on their window panes, a gesture only, like crossing themselves or touching wood. Bandes de papier did not repel splintered glass. In fact there was only one such gun, assembled in the winter of 1917–18 in the forest of Saint-Gobain. The Germans called it 'La Parisienne': its bore was two and a half feet in diameter and it could lob a 200-pound shell over seventy miles, with such force that after sixty-five firings, the barrel had to be demounted and returned to Krupp's in Essen for re-boring. During these interruptions Parisians persuaded themselves that the super-canons must have been

---

* The gun the British called 'Big Bertha', Bertha being the first name of the wife of Krupp, the German arms manufacturer.

destroyed by sabotage or aerial bombing; when shelling resumed, it seemed even crueller than before.

The enemy was not invincible: 'Friend and foe are, it seems, dead beat and seem to stagger up against each other.'[7] In the broken, spongy swampland of the Somme German artillery commanders struggled to bring heavy guns up to positions now occupied by infantry. The rapidity of advance had strained lines of supply and communication between front and rear. Behind what had been the allied support area, in the bleak villages of the *zone des armées*, famished German troops plundered henhouses and dairies, rounded up ducks and geese, raided kitchens and cellars. Discipline evaporated as rough wine hit empty stomachs. Beneath tables and on doorsteps, men collapsed into sleep, in boots and coats, packs still on their backs, drawn down too deep in slumber to hear their officers' commands. Meanwhile enemy forces were being replenished from the east. Using intelligence from I(a) and I(b), on 26 March Cox reported that there were now 196 German divisions at the front, of which 69 had been identified as being ready for battle. Ludendorff had many in reserve.

More were on the way:

Letter to Georgette, 25 March.

Thionville–Arlon 22nd, 23rd March

3 trains infantry
1 train cavalry

Identifications:
L. I. R. 35
Uniform:
Hat band not seen.
Shoulder strap grey.
Piping not seen.
A crown, a grenade, no monogram.
No. 17.

Shoulder strap marked A. Grey neckband, with the monogram TCM 21 and the ordinary monogram 17.
Equipment marked LIR 35.[8]

As the trains came through the marshalling yard, Madame Rischard grew more apprehensive. Soldiers, guns and horses were pouring into France. Every issue of the *Landwirt* carried a bulletin from German headquarters, announcing another victory. If Paris fell, what would become of the office in Rue St Roch? Her instructors and supporters – Bruce and Campbell, Chocqueel, Miss Done and Mademoiselle Dorgebray – would have to pack up, destroy papers, make for the coast. On 25 March the *Landwirt* printed news from Berlin: 'As the British retreat, they are setting fire to French villages and towns. Fortress Paris has been shelled by long-range guns.'* The first phase of the advance had been successfully completed; massive artillery pieces were being trained on Paris in preparation for the final assault. Had all the efforts of Bruce and his team – teaching Madame Rischard the code, getting her home to Luxembourg, recruiting Hansen, Jeanne Schroell and the railwaymen – come too late?

Letter to Georgette, 26 March

Nous sommes terriblement inquiets et bouleversés . . . We are dreadfully anxious and disturbed by current news. Are you still confident about the final outcome.[9]

Newspapers told Madame Rischard that thousands of British soldiers had been killed, thousands taken prisoner. An official French bulletin in the *Landwirt* of 28 March reported fierce fighting south of Amiens; Germany had doubled the assault on the whole stretch of front between Noyon and Chaulnes.[10] On 29 March Madame Rischard wrote again. She had heard nothing since Georgette's letter of the 9th.[11] In the hope that Bruce was still in Paris, she included a train-watching report:

Letter to Georgette, 29 March

Thionville–Arlon March 27th–29th
3 trains artillery

---

* *'Die Engländer verbrennen auf ihrem Rückzug französische Ortschaften und Städte. Mit weittragenden Beschützen wurde die Festung Paris beschossen.' Der Landwirt,* 25 March 1918.

6 trains cavalry
2 trains various.[12]

Eleven trains – and another five went through on those two days:

Der Landwirt, 2 April

Thionville–Arlon March 27th, 29th

4 trains artillery
6 trains infantry
4 trains cavalry
2 trains various.[13]

And sixteen more:

Der Landwirt, 4 April

Thionville–Arlon March 30th–31st

16 trains constituted units:
2 artillery
4 infantry
6 cavalry
4 various.[14]

According to Bram, these thirty-two had come from Italy. This was so. The traffic was part of the 200th Division, moving up to Cambrai from Lorraine, where it had paused en route from the Italian Front.[15] How were the Allies to stand against such an accumulation of men and weapons?

Madame Rischard felt as if she were casting messages into the void. The last letter she had received from Bruce, that of 9 March, had acknowledged her report in the *Landwirt* of 4 March, told her to pay over the 11,000 francs and noted her remarks about Garnier, Baedeker and Lieber. That was all. Since 20 March, the date on which Bruce's letter had arrived at Boulevard Royal, she had heard nothing. She had no idea whether subsequent reports had been received, decoded, understood. The last thirty-two trains, for example: had the footnote about Italy been useful? Bram had asked whether he should supply more precise information, about the exact destination of ammunition trains, for instance, and regimental numbers of accompanying troops.[16] Assuming that such identifications would be helpful, she had urged Bram to give as much detail as he could. But no encouraging words, no praise, came from her masters.

Bruce had explained to Madame Rischard that his letters would be infrequent. Except in emergencies, she should expect to hear from the Garlands no more than once a fortnight. The Paris Office managed many agents and, although he did not discourage Madame Rischard by saying so, her needs would not always have priority. The sympathy his officers felt toward her must not be allowed to obscure the fact that the principal reason for correspondence between Boulevard Royal and Rue St Roch was not to provide re-assurance but to get secret information out of Luxembourg and instructions into it. Security and efficiency came first. Even if she had understood why he did not write, it would not have been much comfort. For Madame Rischard, two weeks was fourteen days too long to be cut off.

She was not alone in thinking that these days might be the begin-ning of the end. As long-range shelling continued, Parisians became more terrified. Stations already packed with refugees from the *zone des armées* could not accommodate those who sought to flee the city. On the morning of 27 March 2,000 queued before the *guichets* at the Gare d'Orsay, and at the Gare Montparnasse the sale of third-class tickets was suspended. Nine hospitals were hit and on Good Friday, 29 March, the church of Saint-Gervais; of the 91 killed in this last outrage, most were women and children. Through a Swiss intermediary, the French government asked for a twenty-four-hour cessation to bury the dead. Germany agreed. Firing resumed on the 31st.

Even hardened soldiers were apprehensive. On 3 April the French and British Prime Ministers – Clemenceau and Lloyd George – met at French GHQ at Beauvais. Sir Henry Wilson, CIGS, accompan-ied Lloyd George, and General Bliss was present as United States Military Representative at Versailles. Haig, Foch, Pétain and Pershing were in attendance. Discussions were frosty. Haig resented Lloyd George's allegations that Gough had instructed the Fifth Army to run away from the enemy. Foch and Pétain were determined not to be pushed by Haig into a counter-offensive they thought premature. When Pershing assured the meeting that nearly half a million infantry were on the way to France, Haig, Foch and Pétain remembered that they had not yet seen Americans in action. At last, it was agreed to reinforce the arrangements decided at Doullens, nine days earlier. Foch's authority was extended to embrace strategic direction of military operations in the field; he now had full powers to allocate British and French reserves as he believed necessary.[17] To balance this, the British, French and American Commanders-in-Chief – Haig, Pétain and Pershing – retained control of the tactical action of their respective armies and each was given the right to appeal to his own government if he believed that his army was likely to be endangered by any order issued by General Foch. This outcome did not increase mutual confidence.

As they left Beauvais in Haig's car, the Commander-in-Chief emphasized to Lloyd George that Gough had pulled back the remnants of the Fifth Army for sound tactical reasons.* The Prime Minister was not in a mood to listen. On the following day Haig received, via the Secretary of State for War, a direct order to send his commander home. In London, Gough was shunned in the clubs by men who did not know the wider circumstances. It was true that immediately after the first German attack the Fifth Army had collapsed, but Gough's decision to withdraw had been based on his conviction that the enemy must not be allowed to break the front.

By the end of March the troops that had been in such disarray had been reinforced and revived. The German advance was slowed. It could not be arrested. On 4 April, the day of Gough's dismissal, the enemy stood five miles from Amiens. Shells flew into the market gardens that supplied Paris with melons and lettuce; the station roof was holed. Sandbags surrounded the cathedral; Madame Joséphine, who ran an eating-house much patronized by officers, had left with her cooking gear in a cart. Improvised units defended the town, railwaymen and engineers among them. The Australian Corps surprised

* 'He had few reserves, a very big front entirely without defensive works, recently taken over from the French, and the weight of the enemy's attack fell on him.' Haig, Diaries, 3 April 1918.

the Germans and the line held. Amiens was saved – for the time being.

In Flanders a mere sixty miles of ground lay between the Germans and the sea. If the Belgian army and the British Second and First Armies could be sent packing, the enemy would be able to secure the whole of the Channel coast, Brittany and Normandy. Moving south, they might then take Amiens from the rear, bearing down on to the French army from three sides. French GHQ would be swept away. Through forests, across rivers, German soldiers would come to claim the squares and avenues, bridges and spires of Paris.

Reinforcements required for Ludendorff's second thrust were already arriving in Flanders, brought by the constituted units Bram and his colleagues had observed as the trains passed through Luxembourg between the middle and the end of March.* As the convoys proceeded north into Belgium, through Namur and up to Mons, I(b)'s watchers had monitored their progress. Piecing together scraps of information – a glinting badge, the flash of a cockade, a number painted on a gun – the Intelligence Staff traced the origins of battalions, regiments, brigades, divisions, constantly revising their estimates as they sought to draw up the German Order of Battle. One assumption was unarguable: confrontation must come soon. From what Cox told him, Haig was certain that a concentrated German offensive was likely at any time. On the 8th Cox reported that the enemy had 196 divisions at the front, 88 battle-ready.

The Germans attacked on 9 April. The pattern was the same: relentless pounding with gas and shells, artillery fire, an onrush of men and horses toward the wire. Forward defences were firmly built – week after week, for years, the occupants of these trenches had appraised walls and parapets – but it was impossible to repel such an assault. Eight German divisions were thought to have been thrown into the attack; 'thick mist', Haig said, 'made observation impossible'.[18] At Neuve-Chapelle the Portuguese tried to make a stand but, unable to hold the position, dissolved into the surrounding country, taking their guns.

Each spring for three years the two sides had fought over this

---

* Ludendorff gave this second offensive the code-name 'Georgette'.

ground, each summer, each autumn, in a nightmare minuet, gaining and losing yards. No small acquisitions now. On the first day the Germans advanced six miles, forcing the British back towards the River Lys. By nightfall on the second day, 10 April, Haig estimated that 160,000 of his troops had been gassed, shot, blasted by shells, drowned in mud. The French, with only a small presence in this section, lost between 20,000 and 25,000 officers and men.

In conference that night, Foch agreed with Haig that it was Ludendorff's intention to destroy the British army. The focus of the German effort, Foch believed, would be in the middle of the front, between Arras, south of the past two days' fighting, and the Somme, further south, just above Amiens. Rather than sending French soldiers north to help the British in Flanders, Foch proposed to concentrate his reserves in this southern section, ready for the battle he was sure would take place at Arras. In Flanders the British would have to draw on their own reserves, such as remained, supported only by the Belgian army, emerging from its enclave to take over part of the British line, and by the Royal Flying Corps.

The troops were staunch, the odds overwhelming. Two days into battle, five more enemy divisions joined the fighting. More than a dozen waited in reserve. On 11 April Haig's Order of the Day concluded with these words:

There is no other course open to us but to fight it out! Every position must be held to the last man. There must be no retirement. With our backs to the wall and believing in the justice of our cause, each one of us must fight on to the end. The safety of our homes and the freedom of mankind alike depend on the conduct of each one of us at this critical moment.[19]

There was no wall, only scarred ground and, beyond, dunes and the open sea.

Civilians who had never been to this part of France knew its geography by heart: Ypres, Passchendaele and the Somme, the lines of the La Bassée Canal and the meandering Lys, coalfields at Bruay, roads to Armentières and Hazebrouck, Béthune and Arras. Although domestic atlases were out of date and newspapers censored, noncombatants could follow the broad sweep of operations. At the Rischards' breakfast table the *Landwirt* was gloomy reading. Half of every issue was taken up with statements from Berlin, Paris and London, extracts from speeches by heads of state, prime ministers and generals, news from Warsaw, Berne, Tokyo and Vienna. According to official reports, German forces were moving west, north and south; in days, it was implied, a German government would be installed in Paris. The Rischards knew that the office in Rue St Roch had continued to function up to 20 March. A letter posted on that day had reached Boulevard Royal on 6 April, assuring Madame Rischard that all correspondence had so far been received, all *Lokal-Neuigkeiten* understood. Bruce had assured her that future letters from the Garlands would be sent at shorter intervals, although all parties understood that, in such fast-changing and precarious circumstances, news from Paris was bound to have been superseded by the time it arrived.

The Germans had nearly taken Paris in September 1914. The city had been spared. Three and a half years later its occupants again prepared for the worst, building sham targets, to decoy the enemy guns, in empty country on the outskirts: artillery made of wood, fake watchtowers, false streets lined with lamps, a model Gare de l'Est and Gare du Nord. To hold up an enemy advance, smoke machines were placed at key points along the rivers. Banks sent their strong-boxes to the provinces. A secret group of deputies discussed arrangements for mass evacuation.

'Fear nothing. We are completely confident,' said Nicole's next letter.[20] Written on 28 March, it reached Madame Rischard in the same post as one from Georgette dispatched two days later. Bruce's principal concern was that the *Landwirt* should not run short of newsprint. Had the 11,000 francs been paid? The question was disguised as an account of the discovery in an antique dealer's shop of eleven engravings after Huet, so valuable a find that Georgette had bought them without negotiating a price.* These two compositions arrived at Boulevard Royal on 10 April.

* Bruce to Madame Rischard, 30 March 1918, received 10 April 1918. The reference was apposite, although Bruce knew little about French painting. Either aesthetes in the Paris Office had made the drafting suggestion or the allusion was a coincidence. Like Madame Rischard, Paul Huet (1803–69) had a secret life. A landscape painter of the Romantic School, at seventeen he had joined the *Carbonari*, followers of the agitator François-Joseph Charbon. In 1830 he fought on the barricades beside Alexandre Dumas, in protest against the restoration of the House of Orléans.

The next *Landwirt*, delivered the day after Haig's 'backs to the wall' exhortation, had bad news from the Grand Duchy. At one o'clock on the afternoon of 5 April an RAF squadron had dropped some twenty bombs on the central station, hitting houses, badly injuring three people and killing four, among them a railway employee.[21] Had the Luxembourg operation been eliminated just as it had begun to produce results?

Over the following days there were more raids, always in early afternoon. People became used to the howl of sirens and then stillness, broken by the sound of splintering glass. Although this was the first time Madame Rischard had experienced an air raid, let alone one conducted by her own side, she reacted neither wildly nor angrily. She simply raised her eyebrows, remarking, in a letter to Nicole, that this 'bizarre' development had made life 'singularly complicated'.[22] It was not until 10 April that she mentioned the raids in a report. Her message was cool:

Uselessness of air attacks on Luxembourg station to be seen from the long [news] paper articles. The aviators should either stay away or, since up to the present nothing has been done for defence, come so low as to be sure of hitting their target. Why not tear to pieces in several places the Moselle line from Trèves to Thionville?[23]

The Air Staff thought otherwise. Repeated bombardment of large yards was expected to paralyse local traffic, as panicking railway employees downed tools. According to this doctrine, bombs need not be heavy, numerous or particularly well directed: 'It is the frequency of the attack, not its violence or its effectiveness, which should be relied upon to produce the moral effect required.'[24] On 10 April the bombers came again. Luxembourg station remained operational but neighbouring streets had to be evacuated.

Bonnevoie was badly hit; among those who lost their houses was superintendent foreman Bram. Fear of further attacks at first depressed rents in streets near the railway yard but speculators moved in, buying property while it was cheap and driving prices up again. If Bram cursed the bombers, Madame Rischard did not say so. But he had to find somewhere to live. Bram had refused payment for his services but Madame Rischard now insisted that he accept a subsidy,

Bruce's file copy of a letter from 'Georgette' to 'Tante Lise'. The inclusion of '1918' shows that the letter contains a message in code. The 'spelling' technique allowed Madame Rischard to extract from the first page, ostensibly about Michel's recent illness, the instruction to take great care when mentioning subjects and facts which the censors would be able to verify: plus grande prudence *[line 10]* . . . qu'il éprouve *[line 11]* . . . qui ne peuvent être vérifiés *[line 12]*. Material should not be repeated: ne pas répéter *[page 2, line 18]*. Reports in the Landwirt *had been excellent and were quicker than letters:* la cousine Marie *[line 21]* . . . est préférable . . . aller plus vite *[line 22]* . . . sont excellents *[line 25]*.

125 francs a month, to cover the cost of renting a house close to the station. Hansen had been paid 510 francs for his articles of February and March and for future work had agreed to a monthly fee of 375 francs.[25] As soon as newsprint was delivered to Diekirch, the 11,000 francs would be debited, as arranged with Charles Denis. This list of payments, with the coded identifier for Hansen (34), was worked into a letter as commentary on Georgette's purchase of the Huets, figures given as references to numbered engravings.

It was fortunate that bombs and sirens did not disturb Madame Rischard's concentration. The texts that passed between Rue St Roch and Boulevard Royal were increasingly intricate. Imaginary characters mixed themselves up with real people, made-up stories ran alongside actual events. When Tante Lise spoke of seeing a baby nephew, the child existed; when she talked of buying outdoor furniture, new chairs, solid in space and time, appeared under the trees in her garden. This three-dimensionality was imperative: Bruce had warned Madame Rischard that, as censors might choose to follow up factual statements in letters, all must be verifiable.

To extract meaning from the correspondence, truth had to be separated from falsehood, reality from invention. This was not the only challenge. Language and style mattered as well. Messages were communicated in one or more of three ways. Some statements were *en clair*: that a letter had or had not been received, for instance, or that paper had been ordered. Some matters were reported in code, using 'spelling' and key word methods based on agreed sentences in Garnier, Baedeker and Lieber. Specific information, about troop movements, for example, was so conveyed. Other subjects were dealt with by allusion and metaphor. 'The cousins who had gone to live in the country' meant Bram and his family; anything concerning 'Marie' referred to Jeanne Schroell and the *Landwirt*. Characters and themes recurred, new ideas being introduced only when necessary. Familiarity was essential not only to avoid misunderstanding but also to make the narrative uninteresting to outside readers.

In letters Madame Rischard said nothing about the bombs. There was not much to say. Work in the marshalling yard had not been suspended nor the station closed. Although sudden bangs made

20

June 19th 1918.

My dear Aunt Lise,

Mademoiselle says that I must write to you to-day, but she insists that I write to you again in English, so I will try. Unfortunately I have been very lazy lately! Maman came back on Wednesday and I do not think she is very satisfied about Aunt's condition, which is not very favorable, but it is certain now that no operation will be necessary; we are still waiting to hear when Uncle Jean is coming; and I fear that we shall have to remain here until he arrives! Maman received your letter of the 1st June and we were all very upset at the terrible accident of which you wrote. Every time I think of this dreadful accident I feel really quite ill! When I went to meet the train at eleven o'clock this morning there was a man who was walking on the track quite close to a train which was arriving; I was very nervous but I suppose that these people become accustomed to it!

I see Marie very frequently and I go to see her uncle several times a week; I went to luncheon there yesterday but I could not remain with her afterwards as Maman wanted me at home; Mademoiselle is going away next week but she has not yet decided where she will spend her holiday, and she does not think that she will see her parents at all; I wish that she would not leave us and she knows very well that we want her to come with us! We have tried frequently to persuade her to change her plans but she has quite made up her mind that it would be preferable to take her holiday alone!

Robert was not very well on Sunday, and I think that he caught a cold

File copy of coded letter from 'Nicole' to 'Tante Lise'. Bruce and Baschwitz are at Verdun, hoping for a change in the wind: condition . . . not . . . favourable *[line 4]* . . . still waiting . . . *[lines 5–6]*.

people jump and in the early afternoon eyes turned skywards, booking clerks and inspectors continued to turn up for duty, shunters and signalmen reported as normal. On 11 April there was another raid, after that no more. Traffic was not interrupted: between 8 and 15 April an entire German division passed through Luxembourg on its way to Mons.[26] The *Landwirt* gave every train: two artillery and two infantry movements between 8 and 9 April; three artillery, three infantry and one cavalry movement between the 9th and 10th; four infantry between the 10th and 12th; two artillery and two infantry between the 13th and 15th; six artillery on the 15th.[27]

German transports were precisely programmed, arrivals and departures planned to the minute, times given when troops and horses were to be fed and watered. Instructions were exact: kit was to be kept together, men were not to go wandering about. In practice, travel meant liberation. Troops were tempted out of trains by the scent of frying sausage and rumours of poached eggs. The homesick tried to post letters, loners went to have a smoke in private. Pretty girls made soldiers late. The distracted mislaid knapsacks and caps. Bladders and bowels behaved erratically. Ropes frayed, tarpaulins loosened, heavy equipment shifted out of place, small items went missing. Freight meant for one destination fetched up in another.[28] Delays and mishaps made people talk; there was always something to be overheard, if, like Bram, you happened to be passing. Even at night information could be got. Jolted out of sleep, men cursed in strange dialects and, looking out to see where they were, forgot to cover their badges. As trains slid in and out of the sidings, watchers counted the darkened wagons.

On 14 April Cox's briefing reported the presence of 203 German divisions at the front, of which 24 were in reserve; on the 19th, 206, of which 187 were fit for battle.[29] Slivers of intelligence brought GHQ closer to an accurate forecast of the German Order of Battle. The *Landwirt* of 13 April, for instance, had stated that infantry units going through on the 10th had come from Bohemia. This, coupled with other train-watchers' reports and statements taken from prisoners, gave a complete picture of the route. Bruce received a report on one of Speyer's brown slips:

... the 216th Div. entrained at Faurei in Roumania on the 3rd April and travelled via Buzeu–Crăiova–Orsova–Temesvar–Prague–Dresden–Frankfurt a/M–Saarbrücken–Diedenhofen–Luxemburg–Arlon–Namur . . .[30]

From Luxembourg, so distant from the front, Madame Rischard's messages gave early warning. They also provided a check against which to assess observations by watchers further up the line in Belgium and occupied France. Madame Rischard had reported, for example, that four of six artillery trains going through Luxembourg on the 15th carried field guns and that accompanying troops wore shoulder straps with a yellow crown.[31] Building on this information, Speyer traced men and weapons to the point where they left the wagons:

The artillery units are probably part of 9 batteries of F. A. R. 276 from COURLAND, which detrained in the CINEY art. practice area. Other reports (2) give respectively 6 and 5 art. units for the period 15th–16th April.[32]

Ciney was south of Namur. Guns that were being brought up might be en route to Flanders. The British were now so hard-pressed in that part of the front that the Belgians had taken over defence as far south as Ypres. Or the guns might be destined for the area between Arras and the Somme, where Foch expected a major attack; a third possibility was that they were going further south, for pointing at the Aisne, at the Marne, at Paris. Regiment on regiment, division on division: no one had ever known such a concentration of force. Haig's instructions prepared his commanders for the end. Guns must be fought to the last; 'then, if they cannot be got away, they must be blown up'.[33]

The pressure was unceasing. In a tank battle on 24 April the Germans took the high ground at Villers-Bretonneux, within sight of Amiens. British and Australian forces recaptured the ridge on the 25th but within a week a Jäger Division – a *corps d'élite* – was sent into the line in the same sector, with four other good German divisions, 'of much better quality', Haig observed, 'than the Divisions relieved'. Further north the enemy made a final effort to cross the Lys and drive the British from high country south of Ypres, which, once taken, would enable them to pitch the Allies into the sea. In fierce fighting, with constant use of poison gas, Germany regained ground painfully won by the Allies in 1917. More than 20,000 allied troops were killed, 80,000 wounded. Having failed to capture two decisive positions, the Germans stopped the advance on the 29th. Ypres and the Yser salient were saved. For how long? Haig believed that the enemy's strategy was to fight on in the north, to draw French reserves to that part of the front. 'When he thinks he has succeeded sufficiently he will probably attack astride the Somme and try to take Amiens, and push on to the Coast so as to separate the French and ourselves.'[34] Ludendorff's next offensive might be the last.

Experience showed that, in the two or three weeks before a major attack, railway traffic patterns changed. Rather than bringing new divisions up to the rear of the line, commanders concentrated on preparing those recently delivered. Troops had to be rehearsed, gas and munitions distributed, artillery tested for range and effectiveness. Reports from Luxembourg indicated that this ominous moment had now arrived. Apart from three trains of infantry and one of artillery, going through between 26 April and 2 May, no reinforcements were moved over the Thionville–Arlon line between mid-April and the end of May.

Although there was little to report, the Luxembourg network adhered to its routine. Bram and Schmit played cards together at the Casino in Rue Notre-Dame, the teachers of literature and mathematics continued to call at Boulevard Royal, the Hansens to drink *tisanes* with Madame Schroell. No one must be allowed to connect the card-playing, the lessons and the tea-drinking with the passage of constituted units through the marshalling yard. Not wishing to disappoint the benefactor who was contributing to his rent, Bram hunted for other intelligence. In *Landwirt*s of 27 and 29 April Madame Rischard was able to give the location of three principal ammunition depots, on 1 May the disposition of a trench-mortar battalion and a gun battery.[35] From Paris Chocqueel assured her that she should not be shy about sending negative results. Nil returns were as valuable as sightings of constituted units and she should insert reports in the *Landwirt* as usual.[36] Chocqueel did not make the point that her coded reports in the *Landwirt* were their only means of knowing that she and her team had not been arrested.

For plausibility, *Lokal-Neuigkeiten* lived up to its name. Over the course of a week readers could find news, from a few lines to several paragraphs, relating to Ettelbrück, Esch, Gilsdorf, Bettendorf, Grosbous, Mersch, Asselborn, Rippweiler, Walferdingen, Weimerskirch, Vianden, as well as Luxembourg and, of course, Diekirch. To save time at the Paris end, it had been agreed, at Madame Rischard's suggestion, that any coded material inserted in *Lokal Neuigkeiten* would be dated at least two days earlier than the issue in which it was printed. The report concerning bombing raids, for example, was embedded in a paragraph headed 'Luxemburg. 7. April', printed in the *Landwirt* of 10 April. The report about artillery trains, in a paragraph headed 'Luxemburg. 16. April', appeared in the *Landwirt* of 18 April.[37]

Three and four times a week Hansen delivered his copy to Jeanne Schroell at the house in the Esplanade. Mathias Finck set the type; Jeanne checked his work herself. When Finck asked why a clever man like Sepp Hansen should be interested in the price of horseflesh and the transport of potatoes, she advised 'Metty' not to ask unnecessary questions. He held his tongue. Once started, chatter about Hansen would have been difficult to stop. The intimacy between the Hansens and Madame Schroell was not unobserved. Opposite the Schroells' house on the Esplanade was a café, owned by Pierre Hannesse, who liked to walk about at night. His establishment attracted many locals. Mathias Schmit sometimes met Hansen there, two schoolmasters talking about their day. Everyone knew the Hansens drank their evening *infusions* with Jeanne Schroell, who was working so hard to keep the papers going while her husband was away, but few were aware that the schoolmaster was *Lokal-Neuigkeiten*'s main contributor. No one at the works talked outside about the authorship of the articles, nor about the care with which Madame Schroell supervised their setting. There was no gossip about the subscription list and, if anyone marvelled at the loyalty of that faithful reader, Father Cambron, now resident in Switzerland, nothing was said to the Germans.

Metty Finck's instinct was right. Hansen found the work tedious and Madame Rischard's reports too long. She thought he might require a higher fee.[38] Through Chocqueel, Bruce suggested an increase from 375 francs a month to 1,000.[39] Madame Rischard said this was too much. People would notice that the schoolmaster was in funds. She advised 500 francs a month each for Hansen and Bram. This she paid on 14 May, with the 11,000 francs for the newsprint, now at the works.[40]

Hitherto, all but one of the constituted units had been switched through the marshalling yard on to the line leading north, through Arlon, up towards Namur, Charleroi and Mons. The exception had been a movement on 20 March in which four infantry trains, believed to be Austrian, had left the marshalling yard on the line going south, through Longwy, toward Longuyon and Mézières.[41] From there troops and guns could be moved north-west toward Arras, west toward Amiens or south-west to the Marne. The Longwy–Longuyon–Mézières line interested Bruce for a number of reasons. It was a vital artery for bringing reinforcements from southern Germany, Italy and Alsace; it served the steel town of Longwy; and it was one of the few sections of line where, in the RAF's view, bombing might be more than temporarily effective.

As a rule the French and British Air Staffs considered it pointless to try to destroy railway lines more than fifty miles from the front. So many branch lines were available that within hours the enemy was able to set up other routes; track repair was neither difficult nor time-consuming. Destroying engine depots and workshops was effective – twenty to thirty skilled men took a year to build a loco-motive – and bombing railheads, roundhouses and marshalling yards was thought to slow down work. Few long-range aircraft could be spared for such missions, however, and as in the case of the Luxembourg yard even repeated bombing appeared to be ineffective. Once alerted, the Germans sent guns and fighters to guard import-ant rail links. Luxembourg station was one of the sites that, having been targeted, was now protected by anti-aircraft weapons.

In five places, however, and those five only, breaking track would sever a key railway connection between Germany and the occupied parts of Belgium and France. So the British and French Air Staffs believed: 'if persistent bombing of points so far distant can be carried out . . . the transport of all material and of reinforcements from Germany would for the time being be interrupted.'* Of the five sections, three were on lines carrying a large percentage of traffic. The Longuyon to Mézières line was one, specifically the section of track between Carignan and Sedan. These places had figured in Bruce's plans from the earliest days of the Luxembourg scheme. Madame Rischard had their coded identifiers by heart: 44/45 for the Longuyon section; 48/49 Mézières; 76/77 Carignan.

At the end of the first week of April Bruce asked Madame Rischard about traffic on this line. He knew it would be difficult to station observers in the relevant sections, Longwy and Longuyon being across the border in occupied France. Perhaps this was something for Conrad, once he got to Luxembourg?[42] Madame Rischard agreed; she was confident that observers could be placed on this section.[43] Meanwhile, Camille had talked to the assistant station masters. Trains en route from Trier to Longuyon now bypassed Luxembourg and Longwy on a new line through Thionville. In mid-May Madame Rischard sent crucial information about activity on that part of the railway. Ten thousand crack stormtroops from the German Sixth Army, commanded by Prince Rupprecht of Bavaria, were leaving Longwy and Longuyon. It sounded as if the next attack was about to begin – but where? One army corps was also moving through Thionville in the same direction.[44] Madame Rischard had allotted identifiers to the Longwy section – 72/73 – and Arlon to Flanders – 74/75 – as a basis for future reports. Until Conrad arrived, intelligence from this line would be sketchy. The network was becoming too elaborate for her to manage. Could Bruce tell her when she might expect him?

The reply:

He awaits only a favourable wind.

The letter, sent on 29 May, came from Chocqueel.[45] By that time Baschwitz and Bruce were behind the line at Verdun, caught in Ludendorff's third offensive.

* The other sections were Gemmenich–Vise Junction, on the new German line Aix–Tongres; Angleur station, on the outskirts of Liège; and, less heavily used, Marloie–Ciney, on the Arlon–Namur line; and Houyet–Dinant, on the lines from Libramont or Bertrix to Namur.

21

If the Worst Comes to the Worst

Baschwitz had spent the early spring in London, training at Pollock's Free Balloon School on the Hurlingham polo ground. His new associates knew him as 'Meau'; they continued to think that he was French, on loan to GHQ from French Intelligence. If Joseph Ide, Wallinger's man, recognized a fellow-Belgian, he kept quiet.

On 7 March Campbell came over from Paris to discuss how, wind permitting, agent and balloon were to be insinuated into the Grand Duchy. Detailed maps were one requirement. Before the war, material relating to Luxembourg had not been much asked for in British bookshops and since the German invasion nothing recent had been published. Jubert had lent Bruce a pre-1914 map, last used in bicycling days, and the Admiralty War Staff Intelligence Department was known to have another, marked up by observers in the Royal Naval Air Service. On 8 March Campbell took Jubert's map to Dr H. N. Dickson, who ran the Admiralty's secret cartography section: Hertford House, Manchester Square, 'back entrance'. Having briefed Dickson, Campbell next went to No. 4 Dean Stanley Street, in Westminster, headquarters of the Heavier Than Air Supply Department. Here he called on Lieutenant-Commander Williams, who had promised to provide luminous statoscopes and luminous aneroids, four of each. They had been ordered, Campbell reported, and were expected daily.* Other necessaries – balloon, basket, ballast, bags, hooks, and so forth – were being 'arranged' by Williams, in consultation with Pollock.

'The only other instruments required by MEAU', Bruce advised

---

* To measure, respectively, verticality and air pressure.

Campbell, would be a good watch and a luminous compass, 'the latter for use more particularly after landing'.[1] While airborne, it would be difficult to establish the direction in which the balloon was travelling. To do so, Meau would have to identify a landmark, whose exact position he knew, against which to measure progress. If he found that he was going off-course, he would be unable to change direction. By throwing off ballast, he could take the balloon up, by expelling gas, bring it down, but that was all. His route would be chosen by the wind.

Campbell experienced this for himself when he went down to Hurlingham to meet the Commander. Having shaken the visitor's hand, Pollock put him in a balloon and sent him off, in Meau's charge, on a brisk south-easter. The expedition demonstrated both Meau's increasing competence and the perils of the forthcoming enterprise. Above Campbell's head a huge globe of inflammable gas filled the sky; beneath him, thousands of feet down, was the round O of the tower at Windsor Castle, waiting for them to fall into it. As the sun set, Meau and Campbell floated down toward the Thames. A lorry from Hurlingham had tracked their flight. The crew hauled at the ropes and the great sphere subsided into the water-meadows. When Meau landed in Luxembourg, no friends would be present to give assistance.

This point was now being addressed. Once the balloon touched down, the simplest way to hide it would be to send it up again. Indeed, this would happen naturally. When Meau found a convenient place to descend, he would lower the balloon by releasing gas. As the basket touched the ground, he would jump out, reducing the weight. The balloon would immediately shoot skywards. If it could catch a current in the upper air, it would ride the wind out of Luxembourg and into Germany, falling to earth only when shot down or when all its gas had leaked away. If the enemy got hold of the empty skin, as was probable, meteorological records would allow them to work out the route the balloon had taken. The capacity of the skin would tell them about lift and range; as to load, they would assume that the basket must have held someone or something. The country over which the balloon had passed would be scoured for strangers who might have disembarked, or fallen out.

The further the balloon travelled onward after depositing Meau, the less likely the Germans were to realize that it might have come down in the Grand Duchy. The longer it stayed up, the more time he would have to conceal himself. Was there a means of keeping the balloon in the air? Boosting the amount of gas in the skin would give it extra buoyancy. The 'tin pot stunt' suggested how this might be done. In that venture, small, collapsed balloons had been dropped into enemy territory, with simple kits for inflating them: a packet of chemicals for dilution, to produce hydrogen, and a canister, fitted with two spouts, one for introducing water, the other to feed gas into the balloon. A contrivance of this sort, on a bigger scale, would enable Meau to top up the gas in his balloon. The flaws were obvious. Once on the ground, Meau would want to leave the disembarkation point as quickly as possible. Lingering beside a huge tethered sphere to engage in scientific experiment was out of the question. If he were caught with chemicals, his captors might suspect him of intended sabotage. Suppose he had enough time to recharge the balloon. How was he to dispose of the dual-spouted canister? The apparatus could be sent onward with the balloon but, when it was eventually found, technicians would ask questions about its purpose. Calculations would be made and the hunt would begin.

Pumping in more gas was not the only way to keep the balloon in the air. Buoyancy could also be maintained by jettisoning ballast. Meau having left the balloon, this would have to be done by some automatic device. There was a precedent, the mechanism Pollock's people had developed for the 'pigeon stunt'. Alarum clocks had been built in, to time the flight and prompt the release of the cross-piece. As ballast, a water-filled canvas bag was attached to each pigeon-balloon. Before take-off a hole was punched into the bag to let water trickle out, its rate of escape compensating exactly for the gradual seeping out of gas, keeping the whole at constant altitude until all water was expelled. Something on these lines might be of use to Meau.

This work was now put in hand. Pollock produced measurements relating to pressure of gas at varying altitudes, to leakage and lift. Distances were worked out, meteorological records examined. Equipment and instruments were weighed, as was Meau, wearing various outfits. An officer from the RNAS, one Plant, set up an experiment, using stopwatch and slide-rule, bags of water, stopcocks and valves. New maps were prepared, with refinements. Meanwhile, Meau took Campbell for a second outing. The air was cold as they sailed over the Chilterns and, by nine, when they came down in the dark into High Wycombe, faces and hands were chilled. Warm clothes would be needed for the night flight to Luxembourg. Not the pink combinations of English wool favoured by Pollock; if Meau were intercepted or shot down, there must be nothing to suggest a British connection. Before the next weighing, he must be fitted out with garments of appropriate origin, taste and style. But appropriate to what? As he did not speak Luxembourgeois, let alone local dialect, he would have to be French. It was time to think about cover.

Meau had been rehearsing what he would say if his voyage were interrupted. In his small, precise hand, he set out the possibilities. At the top, he put his watchword:

'Never Confess'

Devise: 'N'avouer jamais'

and below, in English, the heading:

If the worst comes to the worst

His analysis ran as follows:

First Hypothesis:
I am intercepted, following some accident or other, over the German lines, having obviously come across from the French lines.

Explanation:
My name is X and I am a French meteorologist, from the meteorological station at X. Instructed to make certain observations on this particular night, I find that my retaining cable has snapped, I know not how, and by the time I become aware of it, it is too late to try to descend into the French lines.

Precautions:
Be ready to dispose of Luxembourg ration cards and any victuals. Carefully hide German currency. Ensure that a piece of frayed rope is attached to the

basket. Carry various instruments for meteorological observation and have plausible notes on the right kind of pad. All this will also serve to deflect suspicion as to my ultimate destination, as it will be supposed that this was only an observation balloon, that began to climb only when it became detached.

To support this story, he had to be sure of certain facts:

Points for consideration:
Name, position, precise duties: attached as a *civilian* to the Ministry of War? (Remember that they can find all this out via their own agents.) Name of the meteorological station. Is it likely that a little hydrog. balloon would be used for met. observation? How would such a balloon have been attached: to a special vehicle? Rehearse various plausible details as to the supposed observations, in case I find myself among professional experts. Balloon, statoscope, barometer being of English manufacture, find out whether there are any joint meteorol. stations. Can French documents of official appearance be obtained, stating that I am M. X, attached to meteorol. station X? Such papers to be destroyed on arrival in Lux. Arrange, in case I am taken prisoner at this point or subsequently, a name and address in Paris to which I may send correspondence. This name and address to be supposed to be those of my father or brother (hence with the same name as myself).

What if he managed to complete the ballooning part of his journey but was seized as he set foot on Luxembourg soil?

Second Hypothesis:
I am arrested at the moment of landing in Luxembourg or the immediate neighbourhood.

Explanation:
I am a German engineer or balloonist engaged in an experimental flight for the army. Depending on the circumstances, we were either two in the balloon and I had just disembarked, leaving my colleague to continue the experiment alone, or I am on my own and it was part of the experiment to let the balloon go. If the balloon is entangled or held down, I will so position myself as to cause it to break free at a given moment. I will then inquire exactly as to where I am and which road or train I should take to reach a town in the opposite direction to that of the capital. If asked for precise

details as to name, rank etc., I will call myself, say, Heinrich Rengert, engineer or civilian balloonist, temporarily attached to the Xth army to make secret experiments (which explains the travel by night). My documents: I will discover that I have unfortunately left them in the balloon. The place from which I have come: to be considered. To which I am going: Thionville? If, at the end of this tale, my explanation is not persuasive and if there is only a single man to be dealt with, I will dispose of him. If they are several and I am taken away and absolutely obliged to confess, I will ultimately find it necessary to admit that I am French, a meteorologist etc. See First Hypothesis. I will say that I did not dare to come down earlier for fear of falling into the German lines and that by remaining in the balloon I hoped to be drawn further to their rear.

Precautions:

As in the first case. False German papers would be dangerous, because, if I have to fall back on the story about being a French meteorol. whose balloon has gone adrift, it will be obvious that the flight has been premeditated.

Points for consideration:

Exact rank: Engineer or *Luftschiffer*. Belonging to the '*Kommandierenden Generals der Luftstreitkräfte*' or the '*Chef des Feldflugwesens*' and attached to which army? '*Armée-Flug-Park*' from which I have come? In the event, claim that I am attached to the '*Landesaufnahme*', of which some personnel are actually civilian.*

What was to be done if, having landed unobserved, he were to be apprehended on his way to the town?

Third Hypothesis:

No one sees me land and I proceed towards Luxembourg. I am arrested en route.

Explanation:

If this happens at night, at an unusual time to be wandering about the countryside, I will say that I am a doctor, called out as a matter of urgency. I will

---

* Engineer or balloonist. Belonging to the 'Air Detachment, General Command' or the 'Head of Air Operations in the Field' and attached to which army, military airfield, from which I have come? . . . I am attached to the 'Topographical Survey' . . .

call myself, say, Dr Wagner. My papers: forgotten in my haste to rush to my patient. If there is no time to give this explanation, I will start asking questions before they do so themselves. I will begin by inquiring where I am, pretending that I have lost my way in the dark. If I am stopped in daylight, any story will do, depending on the circumstances. If there is a mine nearby, for instance, I could be a '*Bergwerckdirektor*';* otherwise, perhaps preferably, M. X, Swiss consul in Luxembourg, etc. As to papers, I will continue to claim that I have forgotten them – after vainly searching my person – and will offer to go with them to Luxembourg. I will declare, furthermore, that I am accustomed to walking about the place and that until now no one has ever asked me for my papers. If despite my best efforts there is no means of getting away from them and things become dangerous, I will tell them after some hours who I am: a French private or NCO, taken prisoner in Flanders or Picardy, at such and such a place, on such and such a date; that I managed to escape in transit, in the neighbourhood of X, got into Belgium and eventually reached Brussels, then Namur, where I have friends who gave me money to buy clothes and to continue my journey, as they dared not hide me themselves. I will say that these people advised me that the electric fence would prevent my getting into Holland, something I had already been warned about in Brussels, and that they had therefore sent me to Arlon, where they had a reliable friend who got me into Luxembourg. I had been hoping to find a family friend in Luxembourg but had unfortunately learnt (or, depending on the circumstances, do not yet know but will let the Boches find out for themselves) that this friend has left the country. I will perhaps refuse to name him, until, threatened with the firing squad, I may at last decide to do so. I will say that I also chose to come to Luxembourg as I thought it was a neutral country where I would not be arrested. If they wish to force me to name the people in Belgium who helped me, I will refuse, and also make the point that if any of the Germans present found themselves in my situation they would certainly not be so base and dishonourable as to denounce their friends (??? = the honour of the Boches).** I will say that I regret having been so cowardly as to name the man in Luxembourg, but that I did so knowing that this person cannot be punished, having given me no assistance, and indeed that it is impossible to know whether, had he been able to help me, he would have done so.

* Spelt thus in original. '*Bergwerkdirektor*', manager of a mine.
** The parenthesis was meant to be ironical.

Precautions:

Not to claim to be an officer, to avoid being sent – if that should arise – to an officers' prison camp where I might have spent time already or where I might be recognized and from which it would be more difficult to escape. Know as precisely as possible the exact conditions under which I was taken prisoner and, lest I be confronted by French soldiers of the regiment to which I am claiming to belong, identify a regiment from which a great many men have been captured, but select a company of that regiment from which, so far, no soldier has been taken prisoner. Also know about another regiment, from which no one has been taken prisoner, which I might have left fairly recently to be attached to my new regiment.

Admit to being an escaper only under the most extreme pressure and then hold on to that explanation whatever might follow.

Points for consideration:

Name and address of the Swiss consul in Luxembourg and of other important people.

Advantages arising from being a private or an NCO.

Place, date, details, circumstances, etc., in which I was captured.

Name of regiment (division, etc.), name of colonel, commandant, captain and other officers.

Route followed by prisoners and rough whereabouts of place where I made my escape.

Itinerary followed from there to Namur.

Name of a Luxemburger who has recently left the country.

My name: if necessary, I must be able to ask the French government to certify that a man by the name of X, of Regiment X, disappeared during the battle of X. I think, moreover, that [another Baschwitz joke] given the medieval mentality of the Boche, it would be useful for me to sport some aristocratic title and to claim to be connected to the French nobility. I know from experience that the Boche swells with pride when he can say '*Herr Graf*' and that he will think twice before shooting a '*Herr Graf*'.

Look up a suitable name.

Examine the advantages of my claiming to be a married man, with wedding ring; also of my being the father of a family.

All straightforward, although the references to extreme pressure and firing squads were sobering. Best, however, to prepare for every contingency.

Fourth Hypothesis:
In the course of time I am arrested, carrying papers in the name of Conrad Bartels or some other.

Explanation:
First possibility: That they have no absolute proof against me:
I am simply suspected. They will try to establish that my papers are false and will ask for witnesses to certify that I am indeed C. B. It will clearly be impossible to produce such people but I will maintain to the end that this is my name and that I am a citizen of Luxembourg, who left the country as a young man, etc. All this depends to some extent on the sort of papers I have on me.

Second possibility: That they have no absolute proof against me, but my papers are shown to be false and I cannot deny that they are:
I will decide to admit that I am a French prisoner of war, who has escaped, etc. (See Third Hypothesis.) I will then have to explain the origin of the false papers, an explanation which will depend on how we obtain them in the first place. If I can have the name of a Luxembourg man, who has left the country and has no intention of coming back until the war is over, and whose interests will not be compromised, the simplest explanation will be to pretend that he has given me the papers, either out of friendship or for a large sum.

Third possibility: That they know the facts, either because I have been betrayed or for some other reason, and the proof is absolute:
Whatever happens, I will deny everything deniable, but I cannot foresee the point at which it will be impossible for me to continue to deny, all the more because I know perfectly well that admissions – even if true (and I believe it futile to declare that I will always be able to keep the truth from them) – that admissions will do nothing at all to change my situation. I may nevertheless be able to play one last round with them, to deflect suspicion and put off interrogation of other people. I would wait until they are able to prove that I have a method of transmitting information and then, at the very last moment, reveal some secret ink or code that I had apparently used.

I would offer to transmit false information to you by this means. There is clearly little likelihood that this ruse would work but, if by chance it did, the arrival of a message that was not in our own code would alert you to the fact that this was false information and that it was an SOS. From your end, you would reply to me in similar fashion, giving, if appropriate, false information which would perhaps interest the Boches and encourage them to continue this little game, at least for a time. Meanwhile, depending on circumstances, I might be able to escape. All this is unlikely but at any rate it would give me a small extra chance. We need only decide on an indicator for SOS messages.

Fourth possibility: That, for some special reason, the preceding case is aggravated by the fact that they catch me in the middle of transmitting a message and that various clues are revealed which allow them to discover the nature of our code:

They will not be able to reconstitute the code itself but, in order to follow the scheme outlined above, we need to agree on some code or other, incomplete and with a vague but sufficient resemblance to the indices (letters and numbers) of our own code to justify their further use. In this case, obviously, there would be no question of revealing secret inks.

Fifth possibility: That, in one or the other of the four preceding cases, they prove that I have dealings with Madame and it becomes obvious that it would be more dangerous for Mme if I deny that I know her, if only in some perfectly ordinary way:

I can quite simply say that I made her acquaintance while being treated by Dr R. and that I know these people in the same way as I know others. But if – because we must think of everything in advance – they find out that I am in some way assisted by these people and it seems puerile to try to make them believe that I am just a normal patient of Dr R's, whom Fate has thrown in my way, I can say:

i. if my papers are thought to be genuine and I am thought to be C. B., that the R and B families are related, or some similar story, arranged with Mme, to justify their helping me out of friendship;

ii. if I am French and an escaped prisoner, that I am a friend of their son or of the former husband, or a relation of the same, and that she could not do otherwise than help me when I got to Luxembourg.

To be clear, should I find myself in either the third or the fourth of the cases above, M. et Mme R should know absolutely nothing about my collecting and transmitting reports.

Other aspects of this are examined below:

Sixth possibility: That I find myself in one or the other of the above situations and by some extraordinary reason they discover my real identity:
After my escape from Germany, it may be that the Boches took no further interest in me and have no idea that I returned to the Belgian army. If so, I will tell them that, having escaped, I went straight to Belgium, then to Luxembourg, etc. If they do know that I rejoined the Belgian army, I will tell them that I transferred myself to the Foreign Legion and was captured again, etc. The same story as that of the French soldier, with one difference, perhaps. I would have to say that I was an officer in the Foreign Legion, as it would seem odd to them that, having been an officer in the Belgian army, I would have gone back to serve as an NCO or a private.

Points for consideration:
Name of a man in Luxembourg (for the Second Case). Sympathetic ink or code to give away to the Boches. Agreed sign for SOS messages (colour of writing paper, heading or other practice that could be explained to the Boches as indicating that the letter contains a message). Nature of false information that you would be able to send the Boches.
Information about the son and first husband of Mme R. Information about the regiment from the Foreign Legion (similar to that required for the Third Hypoth).

Fifth Hypothesis:
In one or the other of the above circumstances, I am made a prisoner.
In case I am allowed to write, we should agree on three names and addresses in Paris: first, for the First and Second Hypotheses; second, for the Third and Fourth Hypotheses; third, for the Sixth Case under the Fourth Hypothesis.
For such letters, I would definitely write in code.

There was one other variation.

Sixth Hypothesis:

'They' shoot me dead. The service will continue without me, because 'they' will have been told nothing.

For this variation, Meau offered only a characteristic *adieu*:

> *Ni fleurs, ni couronnes!*
> No flowers, no wreaths!

As Meau said, everything should be considered in advance. At 41 Rue St Roch the officers went through his summary. Points about the French army, the Foreign Legion and the French meteorological service were referred to Wallner's people. Jubert was asked about matters relating to the Grand Duchy. Bruce and Chocqueel tried out code-words for SOS messages, to be refined by Campbell when he returned to Paris. Every precaution was being taken. But the six hypotheses were unpleasant reading, made worse by Meau's gallant flourish at the end.

22

Aloft

Like Bar, Lefebvre and others who had gone before, Meau was to make his journey in a hydrogen balloon. Practice would be useful but Campbell and Pollock feared that the extra gas and use of a pumping team might be too expensive for the Admiralty. Bruce agreed:

. . . we don't want to make things too difficult by pressing for things which are not absolutely essential. However, you are on the spot, and must judge what is best to be done . . . Try to make things as easy as possible for Pollock. My personal view is that no dress rehearsal is of any value, unless you are prepared to wait for it as long as we are prepared to wait for the real day, and this is not practical politics.[1]

They need not have been so cautious. Hydrogen balloons were allocated by the Heavier Than Air Supply Department, headed by Wallinger's friend, Captain Maitland, Assistant Director of Naval Services. There would be no difficulty about hydrogen, Maitland told Campbell. Meau could have whatever was wanted for as many practice flights as necessary. Others were equally accommodating. Pollock had suggested that filling appliances could be borrowed from Hazeldine's establishment at Bruay. When Campbell asked Wallinger about this, 'he was a bit vague as to what Hazeldine actually had and strongly suggested that a complete outfit of everything should be sent'.[2] Williams agreed, Maitland approved. Pollock was authorized to draw on Admiralty stores at Wormwood Scrubs and to send everything down to the Military Control Officer at Southampton, for forwarding to Priestley, I(b)'s man at Havre. A receipt was required from the officer in charge, to confirm that Admiralty property had been transferred to the War Office for the use of GHQ. This was normally given before equipment left England but, to save Bruce a journey, the signature was again 'arranged' by Williams. All who were approached offered assistance, including MI 1(c). Before he left London, Campbell went to Dansey and from him to Cumming. Support would be available if required. The excitement was catching.

At Drake's suggestion Bruce had applied to Major Gold, of the Meteorological Section of Royal Engineers, for advice about wind direction and speed.* What awaited Meau in the upper atmosphere? Were winds at high altitudes predictable? Did they vary with the seasons, like the tides? A balloon, Bruce explained, was to be sent over from France to Luxembourg in May or early June. Three starting-points were being investigated, chosen to minimize the length of flight: Châlons-sur-Marne, Souilly and Nancy, the first two being south-west of Luxembourg, the last due south. The shortest path would be on a south-west line from Souilly, with no veering. Having heard the essentials, Gold introduced Bruce to Captain Brunt, meteorological officer in an RFC squadron in that part of Picardy. Brunt had access to French meteorological observations and was also in touch with his counterparts at American GHQ. The RFC's consent would be required before I(b) could use Brunt but, once Drake had seen to that, Gold would instruct him to do everything necessary. For day-to-day liaison with the Paris Office, Gold recommended Second Lieutenant Hay, who was attached to the Service Géographique at the French Ministry of War in Rue de Grenelle. Hay would be able to arrange a meeting with Colonel Delcambre, head of the Meteorological Section of the French army, *Météo*, who was at present in Paris.[3]

Speed and discretion were vital. Bruce's supporters – Dickson, Williams, Maitland, Gold – operated at a level where they either had, or assumed they had, authority to sidestep committees. Each

---

* Although soldiers complained that no attention was paid to forecasts, scorching sun being always on their backs or rain pouring down their necks, information provided by 'Meteor', as the service was known, was included in every briefing. Haig began each diary entry with a reference to the weather, for troops and equipment could not be landed in storms, men, horses and tanks struggled in torrential rain, aeroplanes were useless in fog and, when gas was used, death came on the wind.

knew the people – Plant, Hay, Brunt – whose expertise and connections could help the ballooning scheme. There was no time for argument about protocol and resources. On 28 April, Bruce told Drake that Meau was now fully qualified. He had gone up fifteen times by day and night, often solo, and had so perfected his descents to a given objective in the dark that Pollock believed he had an excellent chance of reaching Luxembourg and landing in the right place. Meau had memorized all he needed to know about the German army and had the code by heart. Practice in train-watching and in 'general matters' – espionage technique – had gone well. As he would not carry a pistol, he had prepared himself with a course in ju-jitsu, making such progress that he had put his instructor's elbow out. Information was still being collected to establish suitable cover; meanwhile, Meau was receiving advanced instruction in make-up and disguise.[4] His black curls and moustache had been helpful for the manufacture of the dummy face left on the bolster at Magdeburg but in Boulevard Royal and the railway stations of the Grand Duchy these distinctions would be a liability.

Bruce had found another map of the Grand Duchy, more detailed than the one Jubert had used for bicycling: fifteen sheets on a scale of 1 to 50,000.[5] Close inspection suggested that they should launch the balloon from somewhere near Verdun. Pollock's advice was to wait for a steady south-west wind of about 20 miles per hour at 4,000 feet, sinking to a very light breeze on the surface, weather that could be expected at this time of year. He would have liked to be present for the launch but, thinking the Admiralty would not spare him, had proposed that Hazeldine should superintend the sending-off. If I(b) agreed, Pollock suggested that Hazeldine should first spend a few days at Hurlingham 'to rub up his knowledge'.[6] Bruce had asked for lorries to carry the hydrogen cylinders and balloon gear and for a motor-car to ferry himself and his party between the base and Meau's point of departure. The vehicles were to be provided by GHQ, balloon handlers by the Admiralty, local drivers by the Air Force. Brunt was investigating the neighbourhood and would advise on the best place for Bruce, Meau and their entourage to camp while they waited until conditions were right for take-off.

Bruce meanwhile called on General Newall, commander of the

8th Brigade of the RAF (as the RFC had recently become). Their discussions took place at Froville, close to Bayon, on the Moselle, where the brigade was stationed. Having explained the scheme to Newall, his Brigade-Major, Captain Prout, and Intelligence Officer, Major Paul, Bruce asked the question which had brought him to Froville. How much aerial reconnaissance might be feasible? A course in observation was essential, Newall thought, and Meau should also be flown over the prospective route. The best people to advise were summoned: Major Grey, of the 55th Squadron, based at Tantonville, fifty miles west, and Lieutenant-Colonel Baldwin, of the 41st Wing, flying from Châlons-sur-Marne. Grey's was a day bombing squadron – it was to this that Brunt was attached – and Baldwin a night bombing commander. The officers knew the flight paths over the Grand Duchy and into Germany: the Luxembourg marshalling yard had been attacked by bombers from Châlons.

The two experts set out the objections to a trial run: that a machine might be lost; that the observer – Meau – might be lost; and, mindful of Ministry accountants, that extra work and expense might be thrown on to the RAF. As to the first point, Grey and Baldwin believed the risk of losing a machine to be 'almost nil'. Second, even if the pilot were forced down, Meau might survive. His journey accomplished, there would be no need for the balloon: 'provided he is equipped with maps etc., he would have an odds on chance of reaching his objective'. Third, additional work would be minimal. It was not far to Luxembourg and machines were available, either a two-seater F. E. (Fighting Experimental) or an H. P. (Handley Page). The latter had room for four and, as the proposed route was almost exactly on the line of approach used for raids, a reconnaissance flight might be 'worked in' with a bombing mission, avoiding extra cost.*

Grey and Baldwin knew that, even if routes could be plotted beforehand, nocturnal navigation was difficult, especially on starless nights. Pilots used 'dead reckoning': charting the course according

---

* In the F. E. 2 two-seater, the engine was behind the pilot and the gunner in front of him. Designed as a daylight bomber, it was later, as the FE2b, used for night-bombing raids. The 0/400 was a more powerful version, used for strategic bombing. It carried a 1,650-pound bomb, the largest in general use.

to the time required to reach the objective (distance divided by speed), with compensation for the angle and velocity of any deflecting wind. To check direction of flight, navigators took compass readings against static landmarks seen against the horizon, the earth's rim being discernible on all but the darkest nights. Local features, known from maps and confirmed by 'observation', gave further guidance. Even at 4,000 feet the keen-eyed could make out chalky roads, see the glint of rivers and railway lines, trace the passage of trains by bursts of sparks. Industrial areas like Longwy were recognizable by the glow of flares and furnaces; searchlights, installed to chase away raiders, identified important towns, depots and junctions. With practice, 'at any rate on moonlit nights', it was thought that pilots should be able to find their routes with nearly as much certainty as by day.[7] Nightfliers, notoriously daring, knew that 'nearly as much' was not always enough. Prolonged focusing on emptiness tricked the eyes and fooled the brain and, lacking the nocturnal vision of the owl and the echo-locating ability of the bat, men who flew by night relied on instinct, refined by experience, to sense the position and angle of their machines and their distance from the ground.* 'The night fighter pilot', it was said, 'should be . . . so fond of flying that he seizes every opportunity to get in the air – day and night.'[8] Meau's ascents and descents over the Berkshire Downs had been no more than a beginning.

Intrepid themselves, Grey and Baldwin thought the proposed mission extraordinarily audacious. Bruce's agent intended to set off alone over unfamiliar territory, in the dark, suspended from a balloon, with no mechanical means of propulsion. His information would be minimal: a meteorological briefing on what winds to expect at a

---

* See the account of a sortie in December 1916 by Tryggve Gran, a Norwegian pilot seconded for anti-Zeppelin duty with the RFC's No. 39 Squadron: 'Everything turned into a chaos of fog and darkness in which only my instruments could be seen . . . Suddenly I discovered under the brim of my upper plane some flaming flares – I was flying upside down and with a terrible speed.' Quoted in Ken Delve, *Nightfighter*, London: Cassell & Co., 1995. Nightfighting units often chose the bat as their emblem. Their machines were agile, but, unlike their mascot, had no 'radar' to indicate the proximity of obstacles. Landing was especially dangerous. Thinking they were at least fifty feet up, pilots would suddenly find the ground hitting them before they had time to 'flatten out'.

range of heights and, once airborne, altitude readings from an aneroid barometer. On that basis – the 'time-flying' Meau had practised under Pollock's supervision – he should be able to estimate how long it would take to reach his goal. But unlike a pilot in a conventional aeroplane, he would have no means of adjusting his course to allow for the effect of wind. He might not be aware of any veering. His one means of measuring progress would be against 'observation', navigation by reference to known landmarks. Otherwise, his sole connection to his fellow-mortals would be the ticking of his watch. That is, until the enemy spotted him. Unlike the pilot of a night-fighter, he would be unable to dart and dive. He could only hang, directionless in space, waiting to be shot at.

Grey and Baldwin made the best of it. Though few, night land-marks on the suggested route were not so numerous as to be confusing. Those that were to be seen would stand out clearly. Searchlights at Metz and Thionville were clearly visible to several thousand feet. A single flight should impress them on the observer's mind. Luxembourg being very small, the balloonist would have to keep a sharp lookout in case he was carried into Belgium or Germany but this smallness meant that it should not be difficult to memorize the relative position of the Grand Duchy's component parts. Once over Esch-sur-Alzette, Meau should be able to locate the city of Luxembourg and other significant centres of population. As to descent, a reconnaissance flight would show whether the proposed landing-place was guarded by anti-aircraft guns or other defences. In sum, having been trained in 'time-flying' and with 'observation' as a check, Bruce's man would be as well supported as a balloonist could hope to be. His confidence that he would be able to reach his objective should, they thought, 'be doubled'.[9] Whether they them-selves shared that confidence, doubled or not, they did not say.

The discussion at Froville left Bruce in no doubt as to the hazards of the voyage to which Meau was now committed. Grey and Baldwin had assured him that his agent would have no difficulty in finding the searchlights; there was no need to make the point that, if Meau were to be carried off course, he could also expect the searchlights to find him. Assuming that he survived his traverse across the German lines and into Luxembourg, careful timing should bring him over his objective at first light. Sailing in on a summer dawn, he would be able to see enough from 4,000 feet to enable him to select a landing-place. Equally, early risers would not fail to notice the balloon, floating down into the morning, its skin shining silver, its gilded basket and its captain increasingly distinct.

So advised and – partly – reassured, Bruce went back to Paris. Further information had come in from Meteor: in an average May, the desired conditions were likely to occur on perhaps no more than two nights. They were not expected for at least ten days, that is, until 10 or 11 May at the earliest. In the meantime, Brunt said, he had arranged to move from Tantonville to Froville. His new office had direct telephone lines to Brigade HQ and to the nearest French meteorological station at Bayon, this latter being connected by telephone to associated establishments at Dijon and Belfort in the south, Souilly and Châlons to the west and a chain of four further observatories to the east and north. From these, Brunt would be able to receive minute-by-minute weather reports and forecasts.

Bruce had given Brunt Jubert's map, on which Dickson and Pollock had identified possible take-off points in France and landing-places in Luxembourg. He had also acquired another, in colour, from the French army's cartographical service. Drawn to a scale of 1:80,000, it showed every hamlet along Meau's proposed route. Using the French map, Bruce identified a landing-place in a secluded spot south of the city of Luxembourg, near a local railway line. Brunt charged his fine-nibbed pen with the purple ink favoured for the writing of equations and set himself to measuring. On 1 May he submitted his first assessment. The area Bruce had identified was roughly rectangular, some seven miles from north to south, twenty from west to east. The balloon was to be launched from a location just inside French lines, about forty miles from the objective. Brunt suggested that they aim for Reckange, south-west of the capital. The balloon would have to travel on a wind blowing from 225 degrees between south-west by south and south-west by west, with less than five degrees deviation. The correct wind was essential; a five-degree variance over forty miles would mean that Baschwitz would miss his goal by some six miles.

Brunt's report was guarded.

These are rather narrow limits and you may find at the last moment that it will be necessary to be content with reaching a point to the SE of Luxembourg. I think this ought to be borne in mind if your man does a reconnaissance.

I am confident that the thing can be done, though it will certainly demand some patience.[10]

Wherever and whenever such a wind manifested itself, the ballooning party would have to be ready to catch it. Pollock and Bruce had identified a suitable launch-place in a forest clearing at Souilly, south of Verdun, an area accessible by lorry but out of sight of German observers in fixed balloons. But it might be weeks before the wind blew from Souilly in precisely the right direction. Was there any other launch-place, at a similar distance from the objective? The angle of approach would be different, the result the same. On the French map Bruce drew a section of circle on a fifty-mile radius, the city of Luxembourg at the centre, and looked at points along the circumference. There was nothing suitable on either side of Souilly. The difficulty was military: the windings of the front at this point – German lines ran close to Verdun to the north and east – meant that at forty miles Souilly was the only possible starting-point.

Might it be advisable to try to find a launch-place further from the front? Pollock thought the balloon might go seventy miles at least without great leakage of gas. Bruce tried another section of circle, on a radius seventy miles from Luxembourg. From here a steady wind, 'say due South . . . might possibly offer an opportunity . . .'[11] Brunt got to work again with the fine-nibbed pen. At this more generous distance there were certainly places from which a south or south-west wind regularly blew. All had disadvantages. The ground between Toul and Nancy was afforested, that between Nancy and Pont-à-Mousson had unexpected clefts. From points between Commercy and Toul a south wind would take the balloon over Metz and Thionville, towns illuminated by searchlights and thought to be guarded by 'nets', ranks of small balloons and kites from which fine wires were suspended to trap intruders. Anywhere east of Nancy was too close to the German front. Furthermore, enemy observers monitored all these places from the sky. Brunt suggested a launch-place further back, as far, even, as ninety miles. East of Commercy might do, on a south-south-west wind. It was too exposed to German eyes to keep the lorries there for long but, if the wind promised to last, there might be time to bring them over from Souilly. They would have to move quickly but ten miles an hour on rough country roads was just feasible.[12]

Whatever the starting-point, a meteorologist must be present to make last-minute calculations. Brunt was keen but, in case he had to be elsewhere on the appointed day, he advised Bruce to ask for Hay, Meteor's man in Paris. Bruce lost no time in arranging Hay's secondment to the ballooning project – and in making use of Hay's connections. On 15 May Hay took Bruce to see Delcambre in Rue de Grenelle. Having heard Bruce's proposal, Delcambre offered to provide Hay with an *Ordre de Service*, making him in effect a temporary member of Delcambre's own staff, authorized to ask for any French meteorological data, however sensitive, without giving reasons. The order required the signature of Delcambre's senior officer, a general; he need not know its purpose, Delcambre assured Bruce, just that it was to do with 'experiments for the aviation'.[13]

Hay was not the only member of the ballooning party for whom clearance was required. The area in which Bruce hoped to prepare the launch – bordered to the north by the Aisne, to the south and west by the Marne, and to the east by the curve of the front – was largely a French army zone. Since Nivelle's disastrous push toward the Aisne in the previous spring, this sector had been comparatively quiet; soldiers called it 'the sanatorium'. German attacks had been concentrated further up the line at Cambrai, Arras and Amiens and east of Ypres on the Lys. Haig believed that Ludendorff intended to continue the assault in the north, drawing the French away from the middle section of the front, and that the enemy would then strike at Amiens, pushing on toward the coast, where the Somme debouched into the sea. In this way, French and British would be divided. Whether or not Foch concurred with this view – he gave no definite opinion – on 1 May he and Haig decided that tired British divisions should be sent south to rest in the French zone. In their place fresh French divisions were to be brought up to the battle area. Haig remained sure that the front at Ypres was, as he put it, 'the *decisive* point'.[14]

When these movements were ordered, Bruce had been in the south, discussing reconnaissance flights and meteorology with Newall, Grey and Baldwin. On the following day, 2 May, the French and British prime ministers, their political advisers and military commanders conferred at Abbeville. They agreed on two strategic imperatives: that the French and British armies should be kept close together and the Channel ports protected. If it looked as if the two armies were being separated, the Commander-in-Chief, that is, Foch, would retire south towards the Somme. Foch indicated that he thought this would not be necessary; he was, Haig observed, 'most confident, but asked for more labour to dig lines of defence'.[15]

The southern zone had been chosen as the starting-point for Meau's journey because of its proximity to Luxembourg and relative calm. Here, it was thought, there was no immediate prospect of shell-fire, aerial bombardment or poison gas. Any difficulty, at least with the first stage of the ballooning expedition, would come from the Allies' own side. French Intelligence knew through Wallner that Bruce's party would be circulating in the district but the project was too sensitive to mention to local commands. In a war zone, however, local troops would be on the lookout for unusual movements and the convoy from Havre was bound to be noticed. If the lorries were impounded and their crews taken away for questioning, the chance of catching a wind might be lost altogether. As a precaution Wallner had alerted an intelligence officer, Captain St Martin of the *Quatrième Bureau*, who was attached to Berthier's army in the south. St Martin's telephone number was to be given to the NCO in charge of the lorries and any French officer who refused to let the convoy through was to be told to ring it up. If the telephone line were working and the caller were to find St Martin at his desk, there might be only minimal delay. Other obstacles – arguments with disdainful officers, disbelieving subordinates, suspicious villagers and townspeople – could be dealt with only as they arose.

There was another complication. Since February 1918, when he first applied to Pollock, Bruce had worked on the aviation aspects of his scheme with officers of the Royal Naval Air Service and the Royal Flying Corps. At the beginning of April these services had been brought together to form the Royal Air Force, under General

Trenchard, commander of the RFC in France since August 1915. At first Bruce's plans were not affected; relations remained the same with the RNAS team who dealt with the ballooning side – Pollock, Maitland, Williams – and with the RFC people – Newall, Baldwin, Grey, Brunt – who advised on flight paths, reconnaissance and weather. In correspondence, Bruce had only to remember to write RAF, rather than RFC. At the end of April, however, there had been further rearrangement. Some months earlier the War Cabinet had created a new government department for military aviation, to which Trenchard was now required to report. The general, who disliked political interference, believed it a mistake to remove responsibility for air warfare from the War Office just as the RFC was at last beginning to see itself, and to be seen, as a crucial adjunct to the army. Trenchard declined to take up the RAF post, asking instead to continue in an operational role at the front. In early May he was given command of a special service, the Independent Air Force, consisting of the four long-range strategic bombing squadrons of the 8th Brigade.

These developments followed close on Bruce's visit to that same brigade – he was with Newall from 29 April to 1 May – and the implications were worrying. The status of the Independent Air Force was unique and undefined.[16] It was not recognized by the French government; it took orders neither from Foch nor from Haig. For all practical arrangements, including provision of aerodromes and transport of fuel, Trenchard's staff and commanders depended entirely on the support of the French, specifically of General de Castelnau, Commander of the Group of Armies of the East, who had his headquarters nearby. Fortunately for the Independent Air Force, de Castelnau was a strong believer in the offensive deployment of air power.*

Although Bruce was not directly involved, the peculiar status of the Independent Air Force brought new concerns. The few who knew about the ballooning venture were in GHQ, the RAF, the French army and French Intelligence. Trenchard's organization was still

---

* De Castelnau had proposed that mechanical and agricultural equipment arriving from America should be used for levelling airfields and constructing hangars.

formulating its procedures for communicating with these other organizations and, meanwhile, his long-range squadrons were eager for action. Without effective liaison Meau might find himself caught up in a strategic bombing raid launched by his own side. Drake did what he could to keep the 8th Brigade up to date and, to make doubly sure, Bruce turned to Hay. The meteorologist was about to leave for the weather station at Froville, Delcambre's *Ordre de Service* in his pocket. He set off from Paris on 17 May, carrying a personal letter from Bruce to Major Paul, Newall's intelligence officer. 'In about a week,' Bruce wrote, he hoped to be in the Major's neighbourhood, 'all ready to start'.[17] The letter included news of operational significance: that anti-aircraft guns had been installed at the Luxembourg railway station. Although Bruce did not say so, this intelligence had been received directly from the Grand Duchy, together with Madame Rischard's report of the movement of troops of Prince Rupprecht's army into Flanders.[18] This message had appeared in the *Landwirt* of 11 May, the last issue Bruce saw before he left for London to collect Meau.

Bruce had warned Madame Rischard that he would be away. The Garlands were thinking of an excursion to the mountains; Nicole, though a novice, wanted to climb the Jungfrau.[19] The reference needed no elaboration. When they read Bruce's letter, the Rischards understood that it was 'Conrad's' *ascension* of which he spoke. In reply, Madame Rischard had alerted Bruce to a new hazard. On 3 May Commandant Tessmar had announced that conscription was to be extended to all males aged between sixteen and forty-nine, a move that revealed the enemy's desperate need for manpower.[20] Workers in the iron and steel industries were exempt. The ruling applied to German nationals living in Luxembourg; those claiming to be French were advised that their documents would be rigorously examined. Meau was thirty-two and obviously fit; when 'Conrad Bartels' appeared in the Grand Duchy, people might ask him why he was not at the front. His cover would have to provide him with French nationality and a French home address. As Meau would have no identity or ration cards in his new name, it might be wise for him to hide himself until he had acquired a convincing set of papers. Would Pierre Huss be able to receive him? Madame Rischard would not hear of it. Conrad was their guest and he should come straight to Boulevard Royal.

Meau was to take to the air, broken cord affixed to the basket, as Charles de Belvaux of the French Aeronautical Service, on attachment to the headquarters of the Second Army. Wallner had acquired a pass, authorizing the bearer to circulate throughout the Second Army's zone in order to perform experiments with water ballast (First and Second Hypotheses). Once safely down in Luxembourg, de Belvaux would disappear, along with pass, balloon, and the scraps of paper on which he had ostensibly been making notes about the atmosphere. Assured by Madame Rischard that passengers were not usually asked to show their documents, Bruce had obtained the 1918 timetable for services to Luxembourg from various country halts and the Secretariat had typed out extracts for Meau to memorize.[21] 'NB', Bruce added in pencil, 'Deuxième Classe'. If Meau got into trouble on his way into town, he might have to fall back on the story that he was a French prisoner of war who had escaped from his German escort as they went through Flanders (Third Hypothesis); not being an officer, he would hardly be travelling first class.

His onward repertoire of aliases had been drastically pruned. 'Engineer Rengert' and the mine manager had gone, along with the Swiss consul, Jubert having pointed out that Switzerland now had no representative in Luxembourg. 'Dr Wagner' had also been dropped. Not for want of experience – put to the test, Meau would have been able to deliver a baby or bluff his way through an appendectomy – but because military people masquerading as civilians were generally shot. Though de Belvaux was no more, Meau intended to present himself as a serving soldier, dressed for his entry to Luxembourg in some semblance of French uniform. 'If the worst came to the worst', though not the very worst, he would tell his story about being an escaped prisoner of war.

Wallner's office had supplied character and history. A battle had been identified that fitted requirements, an attack on the evening of 28 June 1917, east of Verdun, before the Bois Canard on the left bank of the Meuse. In that affair the left section of the 18th company of the 367th French Infantry Regiment had been captured, with eighty men from another section. This latter group included the fictional soldier who was to be Conrad's other self: Jacques Rubaud from Aix-les-Bains, Savoie. Rubaud would be able to give names (provided by Wallner) of senior officers. If he were asked to describe his companions in the line, he would say there had been no time for him to get to know them, as battle had been joined shortly after he had arrived from divisional headquarters. He would explain that he had been dug in to the Delhomme Trench but that before he could familiarize himself with his surroundings his section of the line had been overwhelmed. If pressed, he would be able to draw a rough map of the ground (Bruce had made a sketch) but would maintain that he remembered nothing of the fighting and little of his march as a captive into Flanders.

If absolutely required to say what he was doing in the Grand Duchy, Rubaud would confess that while on the run in Belgium he had been advised to look for help to a man, known to be anti-German, who lived in Luxembourg. Asked to supply a name, Jubert had lighted on a Monsieur Brezol, a former commercial traveller in his sixties who had connections in Belgium. This was a safe choice, the real Brezol having died in 1917. His widow was elderly and retiring and, if she were questioned, Jubert was sure no harm would come to her or her family. (The Brezols' only child, a son, had left the Grand Duchy to fight in France.) Usefully, although Brezol had lived in Luxembourg, he had no obvious link with the Rischards. Jubert also provided names of prominent people in public life in the Grand Duchy, so that Meau could be '*au courant* with affairs generally'.

If Rubaud were caught, he would demand to be treated as a soldier and to be allowed to inform his family.[22] He would direct his letters to Paris, either to 109 Avenue Mozart – Chocqueel's address – or to the office of an obliging uncle of one of Wallner's men. It would not matter what name Meau put on the envelope: he would address letters to Famille Bartels, Famille Rubaud, depending on the circumstances. He would use the code, with slight but significant modifications now being devised by Campbell. If his captors managed to make Rubaud confess that he was an agent, he would tell them that he had arranged to send coded reports from Luxembourg to a relation in Paris, who had agreed to forward his letters to someone else.

Unknown to the relation, that someone worked for French Intelligence. He would explain the nature of the code, up to a point, and induce his new masters to make him send false reports to Paris. 'Here are the coded phrases,' Rubaud would say, 'in which I am letting my French controllers know I have been captured and that I have agreed to serve the enemy. When this is read in Paris, they will think I am only pretending to have been turned and that I am still acting for them, whereas I shall in fact be working for you.' In those same letters, however, Meau would secrete messages in the true version of the code, describing his present situation. To support Rubaud's story, the Paris Office would reply in the amended version of the code. This would allow them to communicate with Meau while he played his 'one last round'. (Fourth Hypothesis, third, fourth and fifth possibilities.)

The mechanics of this double-double-crossing operation had been carefully worked out. By what route would it be convincing and feasible for Rubaud to show that he was receiving replies from France? The conventional way would be via personal advertisements in a newspaper that was on sale in Luxembourg. On 7 May Chocqueel wrote to Madame Rischard for advice on this point.[23] Which French or French-Swiss newspapers could be bought in the Grand Duchy? None, she replied. It was forbidden to import publications in the French language.[24] They would have to concoct some other story. The solution? A Swiss postbox, set up by Campbell in the name of Brasseur at the Hôtel Verenahof in Baden. Although the Germans would read any communications received by the prisoner, their understanding of the contents would be incomplete. Rubaud would have given them a code but not the code within the code.

These refinements were in place by late May. In the third week of that month the ballooning force set off in the direction of Verdun, the heavy vehicles being first to leave. On the 23rd three lorries carrying the equipment for the launch rumbled out of RAF Advanced Depot No. 2 at Rang du Fliers, south of Etaples. The vehicles were driven by three aircraftsmen, supervised by an NCO, Corporal Freeman. Corporal Israeli and Aircraftsman Cheeseman, balloon-handling experts, accompanied them. The Air Force had been generous: a divisional commander would have thought himself fortunate to have so many motor lorries at his disposal. Each drew a trailer loaded with thirty cylinders of compressed hydrogen; trundling carefully along bad roads, they managed fifty to sixty miles a day. Bruce, Hazeldine and Meau left Paris on 26 May in a GHQ car with driver, Private Lansley. Campbell, Chocqueel and Tangye remained in Rue St Roch as liaison with GHQ and London. Pollock had taken leave from Hurlingham for a week and was coming with Hay on the train by the Paris–Nancy line. All were to assemble at Châlons on 27 May. Drake would join them as soon as he could get away from GHQ. Agents' reports suggested that a German assault was imminent but, if he could be spared, Drake wanted to be present for the launch.

In the event, he did not leave Montreuil. On 26 May Cox warned Haig that an attack might come next day. Enemy preparations indicated that they intended to break the line in the middle section of the front, north of Amiens. South of the Oise no serious activity was expected. The weather had been hot in the west of France; all waited for another blazing summer day. In the southern sector men roused themselves for stand-to, flexing stiffened limbs. The temperature dropped at night and at three in the morning a chill rose from marsh and river. In this part of the line, quiet for weeks, influenza was a worse killer than the guns. As the sentries watched for dawn the ridge beyond Soissons was suddenly illumined. Air became hot smoke. Then all light was extinguished and the sky rained earth and stones and steel.

The German First and Seventh Armies had struck along a twenty-five-mile line from Laon to Reims. Haig and Foch believed the attack was meant to draw allied troops away from other parts of the line, exposing the front between Albert and Arras. If this was Ludendorff's tactic, it did not work. The assault was so overwhelming, the German advance so fast, that by the time French and British commanders had recovered their breath the enemy had reached the Aisne. Moving even one division south would have taken the Allies at least two days; it was already too late. As an offensive, 'Blücher'/'Yorck' was an easy triumph.* In places, the enemy found nothing between

---

* The code-names for the two-pronged offensive.

themselves and the river. Local people recoiled, 'as if struck by a thunderclap', and fled, driving their animals before them.[25]

On that first morning of battle the various components of the ballooning expedition were travelling towards Châlons. In places the route took them within ten miles of the front. Information was fragmentary and at this stage based largely on rumour but it appeared that the Germans were sweeping in from the north bank of the Aisne. If the enemy could not be repulsed, Châlons would be engulfed from the north and cut off to the west. There being no means of communication between Bruce's car, Pollock's train and the convoy of lorries, none of the parties knew the whereabouts of the others. Leaving Château-Thierry behind, Lansley pressed on towards Epernay. All morning he and his passengers heard the noise of guns; two million shells were fired by Bruchmüller's artillery* in the space of four and a half hours. The road followed the bends of the Marne and driving was difficult. Dispatch riders on motorcycles appeared out of nowhere; staff cars raced past, throwing up dust. Lansley looked for an alternative route but carts had rutted the lanes and tracks petered out into fields. Like all military drivers, he had been trained to seek a path among shadows cast by walls, trees and buildings but in midday sun there was little shade. A bomb from above would eliminate them all. The railway line was equally exposed. Whenever the train stopped, Pollock and Hay heard the pounding of artillery and the delayed thud of exploding shells. Nor was there much cover for Freeman, Israeli, Cheeseman and the men, grinding along at six miles an hour. Fifteen yards was the prescribed gap between one lorry and another, on gradients forty, but the naval party took care to keep a much greater distance. If the brakes failed on a lorry pulling a trailer loaded with gas cylinders, the momentum would be unstoppable. As the airmen knew, so well spaced a convoy would catch the eye of an aerial observer. The threat was not only from the sky: a burst tyre or a broken axle might send lorries and trailers off the road. They might be stuck for hours.

In the late afternoon the car and its occupants reached Châlons. A local intelligence officer, Captain Lainey, had arranged a billet.

---

* Colonel Georg von Bruchmüller, Ludendorff's artillery expert.

Train-weary, Pollock and Hay were delivered from the station at Bar-le-Duc. There was no sign of the lorries. Freeman's instructions were to wire from each stop but no recent message had been received. Information from posts along the line was not reassuring. The enemy had swept into the area known as the Chemin des Dames, driving everything and everyone aside. What defences there were had been overwhelmed. General Duchêne of the French Sixth Army, who had been given warning of the attack, had instructed his commanders to concentrate troops at certain vulnerable points but to delay their fire until enemy gunners revealed their position. The General's tactic was mistaken. The German bombardment tore into the ground protected by closely packed troops, killing thousands. Much artillery and other valuable material was lost. The enemy was moving rapidly towards the Aisne; at this pace they would be across by nightfall. The German advance had been so swift that by the time Bruce heard these grim reports they were out of date.

The French Second Army's GHQ was situated near Châlons. When Bruce went round to report the arrival of his party, the mood was sombre. On such a day his presence might have been regarded as superfluous, his project an irrelevance. A telephone call to Captain Dugenet, on attachment from the *Deuxième Bureau*, made everything smooth. Bruce and his colleagues were expected. Vouched for by Wallner, they were to be officially accredited to the Second Army, with authority to circulate unimpeded on whatever business had brought them to this zone.

The lorries did not arrive that night or in the morning. Freeman was an experienced map-reader. Surely he had not misread his instructions? While Bruce took Meau to the 8th Brigade to meet General Newall – a three-hour journey, Lansley at the wheel – Pollock and Hazeldine trawled the lanes. Had the convoy been shelled? It would be difficult to persuade GHQ to replace so much specialized kit. And the men? Had they been caught? If so, what had happened to the lorries and their load? Had there been time to destroy balloon and fittings, tip the cylinders into a river? Heartbreaking, especially to Pollock, but destruction would be better than giving the enemy an idea of what was being planned. At last the searchers saw through the dusk three vehicles, discreetly parked under the trees. The aircraftsmen were apologetic and very hungry. It seemed that a French officer had sent them astray. There was no time to make inquiries. Only a day and a half remained before Pollock had to start for London and he was anxious to unpack the lorries and rehearse the procedure for dealing with the hydrogen.

That evening, 28 May, Bruce and his companions heard that the German advance had reached the outskirts of Reims. Estimates of the previous day's losses had been confirmed. In the first assault the enemy had taken 15,000 French prisoners and over the last twenty-four hours thousands more. Some infantry regiments had lost all their senior officers. General des Vallières, commander of 151st Division, had declared that he would command two such officer-less regiments himself;* on his way to join them, his car, flag flying, had been caught in machine-gun fire. General Duchêne had hoped to hold the bridges over the Aisne; if they had to be blown up, he said, he would give the order himself. When he did so, it was received too late. The Germans were already crossing the Aisne, crossing the Vesle, making for the Marne.

Next morning Bruce and Meau went over to 41st Wing to arrange the reconnaissance flight with Baldwin. Pollock, Hazeldine and Hay drove to Souilly with the lorries. With the blessing of Commandant Renaud, Head of the French Aeronautical Service, space for gear had been provided by the French army at Souilly Castle.** There was a great deal to unpack. The RAF had supplied not one but two balloons, their ship-like names, 'Vedette' and 'Vow', evoking the RFC's origins in the navy. Other hampers contained the balloon basket, net, hoop and fittings. A 200-foot trail rope had been provided, woven of 1-inch Italian hemp; there were 75 sandbags, with hoops, and a great many fillers and valves, the latter with leather covers. Twenty spare nipple elbow adaptors and 60 washers had been sent, plus 25 pilot lights for the balloons, a 10-inch hydrogen hose 124 feet long, and three different weights of balloon cord. For this special voyage the balloons were not the usual spheres of rubberized fabric. Like the miniature balloons used in the tin pot stunt,

---

* The 403rd and the 410th.
** Pétain's headquarters in 1916.

they were made of very thin, pliable vellum. Innumerable lambs had made their contribution; each balloon had a capacity of 11,500 cubic feet, requiring many hundreds of square feet of gold-beater skin.* Six extra square feet had been included in the consignment, for repairs, with glue pot, one pound of glue, a pint of glycerine and a pair of scissors. Three electric torches were provided, with 36 spare batteries, and a 20-foot square groundcloth on which everything could be laid out. All this and the 90 cylinders of gas Corporal Israeli had signed for, on Bruce's behalf.

While Pollock supervised the unwrapping and counting, Hay busied himself with meteorological reports from Souilly and connected stations. The desired conditions for the launch, a wind between south-west by south and south-west by west at 3,000 feet, blowing at some twenty miles an hour, required a depression centred over the British Isles and comparatively high pressure south of Verdun. Every two hours Hay made new calculations. The outlook was not promising. Souilly had been selected in the hope of finding a favourable wind but, as Pollock pointed out, other factors had also to be considered. There must be no moon, no rain and no wind on the ground immediately over the launch-place. Hay had a field almanac with a moon-light diagram; at the end of May the moon was almost at its brightest. The nights of 4–10 June would be safer, if they could wait that long.

The following day, 30 May, was spent exploring flat ground east of the Forêt de Souilly, along the valley of the Meuse, suggested by Renaud as a suitable site for the launch. The Commandant had made many local ascents by balloon. He entered fully into the present venture, offering more lorries, more hydrogen, any number of telephones, whatever his colleague from Hurlingham might require. Alas, Pollock had no time for aeronautical reminiscence, his stay in France being almost up. The delayed arrival of the lorries and the unsuitability of the weather meant that he would miss the launch and all the preliminaries: checking aneroids and statoscopes, inflating the balloon, shaking Meau's hand before take-off, saluting as the basket disappeared from view. But the Commander could not postpone his

---

* Approximately 2,463 square feet, for a balloon 28 feet in diameter. Retrospective calculation is difficult, given the elasticity of the vellum.

departure. On 30 May, armed with messages for Campbell and Drake, he left on the late-night train for Paris.

One of his last duties had been to check the arrangements for keeping the balloon in the air after Meau had disembarked. Pollock had calculated that on its onward flight the balloon would leak gas at the rate of about twelve pounds per hour. To compensate for loss of buoyancy, ballast was to be jettisoned. As in the pigeon stunt, water trickling out at a predetermined rate was to be used for this. Ballast loaded at the outset of Meau's journey must not be so heavy as to impede the progress of the balloon; Pollock had indicated that, given the weight of the instruments and of Meau, some sixty additional pounds could be carried in the basket without loss of efficiency. In the pigeon stunt the water had been put into bags, punctured just before take-off; for the present purpose, Pollock had suggested lightweight tanks.

Plant, the RNAS expert, had examined the variables. To achieve a controlled rate of drip, size of aperture was obviously important. So was the volume of the tank. The fuller the vessel, the greater the pressure on the outlet and the faster the rate of flow. Two cylindrical tanks had been constructed, each fitted with a narrow jet, opened and closed by a tap. With fine-tuning, Plant had achieved a rate of trickle pretty near that required by Pollock: one tank lost seventeen pounds of water over three hours, the other fourteen pounds. The jets, of aluminium, were protected by thin copper tubes; manipulation of the casing at the base would alter their shape, increasing or diminishing outflow. Two aluminium brackets had been made, to be bolted into opposite corners of the inside of the balloon basket. The tanks, also of aluminium, were to be strapped to these, their funnels, from which the jets protruded, being wedged into holes in the base of the basket. The device itself added little extra weight to the balloon; empty, each tank weighed only three pounds, each bracket thirteen ounces.

The apparatus, sent by Campbell from Paris, arrived at Souilly on 29 May. Careful handling was required:

PLANT suggests that you test them both yourself before using and is emphatic on the point that absolutely clean filtered water must be used,

otherwise the jets will get obstructed . . . PLANT suggests that . . . should
a bump be expected, a piece of felt or rubber be put on the brackets . . .
The tanks are not strong and if they have rough treatment, especially when
full of water, will get easily bent . . .[26]

Plant's calculations were appended and diagrams showed how to
adjust the jets. To clean them, Campbell was trying to find a set of
prickers, like those used to unblock the jets of Primus stoves.

Bruce had left Meau in the care of 41st Wing. There was a good
moon on 30 May, bright enough to fly by and for the apprentice
observer to acquire an understanding of the terrain. That night they
took him up. Leaving the allied lines and German trenches, the
nightfighter made for the Luxembourg border. Above bigger towns
searchlights invited the machine toward the guns. The pilot turned
and in seconds they were away. On his next mission Meau would
have no means of steering his balloon, no engine to power his escape.
His odyssey would end as the wind decided. Next morning he went
over the maps with Baldwin. *Jastas* patrolled here, anti-aircraft
batteries were situated there. This river, these roads, that railway
line, would tell him whether he was over Luxembourg, Belgium or
Germany. By the time he got through, if – unspoken – he did get
through, it would be light enough to look for a landing-place.
Baldwin wished him well.

Bruce had been engaged in his own reconnaissance. On 31 May
Hazeldine took him along the upper Meuse valley to the proposed
launch-place, just south of Ancemont on the left bank of the river.
It was perilously close to the front. The German lines were less than
five miles away and, if there were fighting between Verdun and St
Mihiel, the roads would be so crowded with troops and vehicles that
the three lorries would take hours to get through. Hay's calculations
settled the matter. This narrow band of ground was the most likely
place to find the wind needed to deliver the balloon to the objective.
The decision made, Freeman, Israeli and Cheeseman were instructed
to familiarize themselves with the route.

On 1 June Bruce sent a report to Drake, summarizing activity since
the 28th, communication with GHQ having been interrupted by the
battle: 'The present position is that we are now absolutely ready and

only require suitable weather to complete the job.'[27] Pollock's train had failed to arrive in Paris – the enemy had cut the main line – but otherwise all was well. Although he promised to wire as soon as prospects were favourable, Bruce thought it would be difficult to give Drake enough notice to allow him to reach the Meuse in time for the launch. Telephoning was hopeless. The line was poor and it was impossible to get through until after dinner. A car from Paris would take at least ten hours – 'Distances are very big down here' – and timings were unpredictable. As it was, Bruce expected that in present circumstances Drake would be fully stretched at GHQ.

The offensive was now in its sixth day. East of Château-Thierry the Germans were at the Marne. To the west they were poised to sweep up through the woods to the key allied position at Villers-Cotterêts and attack Soissons from the rear. On 30 May Pétain had braced himself to order the withdrawal of French troops from Verdun, Nancy, Lorraine and the Vosges. Among these was the Second Army, to which Bruce and his party were attached. Pétain was not the only one who believed that sacrifices must be made. On 31 May General Franchet d'Esperey, commanding the Fifth Army Group, ordered his subordinate, General Micheler, to evacuate Reims. Micheler refused to execute the order and, although shells set streets and markets on fire, the town withstood the bombardment and the enemy was kept out. The cathedral was saved, houses, shops and cellars were not plundered. This was an important setback for the Germans, whose lines of supply had been stretched to breaking-point by the rapidity of the advance.

All commanders were aware of the risk of moving tired troops forward too far, too fast. Foch expected the enemy to halt, recoup and reprovision. He was sure that German strategy had not changed and that, having drawn the opposition to Picardy, Ludendorff's next move would be to order an offensive in the north. When Pétain begged Foch for reinforcements to be sent to the Marne, he was refused. Foch did not know that after the astonishing success of 27 and 28 May the German High Command had resolved to build on Ludendorff's diversionary manoeuvre. Reims was to be forced to yield. Verdun would follow. Down the Marne from Reims and Soissons, down the Oise from Noyon, lay the roads to Paris.

Soissons and Château-Thierry were taken from the north on 1 June. The French still held Villers-Cotterêts but their situation was precarious. Fifty thousand men had been captured and no reinforcements sent to replace them. Fighting was moving back and forth in woods to the east along a twenty-five-mile front and reports from agents and the field warned the Allies that they faced a force so huge that Ludendorff would be able to attack in Flanders without diluting the effort on the Marne. Foch knew that fresh and rested German troops could be marched into the line between Arras and Albert at less than twenty-four hours' notice. He was determined not to move French divisions positioned there, despite the deteriorating situation in the south. Instead Foch proposed that American divisions be deployed to relieve Pétain's hard-pressed forces. Haig disagreed. Although the American First Division had been blooded at Cantigny on 28 May, the British Commander-in-Chief believed that Pershing's troops were not yet ready to resist a concentrated attack.

On 1 June Lloyd George and Clemenceau conferred at Versailles, each supported by ministers, generals and advisers, 'wrangling and wasting time'.[28] The complaint was Haig's. As he saw it, British divisions that had been sent to rest in the southern sector were seeing the worst of the fighting. Impatient with politicians, angry with Foch, doubting the Americans, nothing pleased him. The war could not be won by arguments in an airless palace: 'the large waiting-room downstairs was crammed to overflowing with Secretaries, Interpreters and others. Not a single window was open. The place was stifling.'[29] While the leaders debated, shells from German guns were bursting over the Seine. 'William's guns', the Parisians called them, as if the Kaiser were a naughty child, but the enemy was less than fifty miles from Paris. The Madeleine was hit; what would be next? Notre-Dame, the Panthéon, the Louvre? On the night of 1 June the city was attacked by eleven German bombers. The government got out the plans that had been made in September 1914 and prepared to evacuate to Bordeaux. Panicking members of parliament led an outcry against Foch, newspapers demanded his resignation.

But Foch's sangfroid was legendary; he spoke when he had something to say, moved his pieces, like a chessmaster, only when he understood his opponent's strategy. He knew from his Intelligence

Staff, as Haig knew from his, that German divisions were massing in the middle sector of the front. By 3 June Prince Rupprecht's army group had thirty-seven divisions in the line, thirty-two in reserve, waiting, it was thought, for the order to advance across the Somme and into Amiens. When Foch asked for a reserve of three British divisions to be sent up to the Somme, Haig complied only under protest. Since 27 May he had lost more than 24,000 men. The War Office had told him that the British could now maintain only twenty-eight divisions, a figure queried by Foch, who thought it pessimistic. Hearing this, Lloyd George told Clemenceau to send an expert to examine the figures. And still the German forces grew: by 4 June Rupprecht had forty-one divisions in the line, forty-nine in reserve. Foch turned to the Americans. Pershing agreed to give him four divisions and on 4 June they began to move toward the Somme.

In the southern sector the attack was flagging. Ten days of marching and fighting had exhausted the German infantry and supply lines were stretched too thin. They paused and, seeing this, their opponents were invigorated. Two American divisions prevented the enemy from crossing the Marne at Château-Thierry and together the Allies held the line. On 4 June Ludendorff suspended 'Blücher'/'Yorck'. But Paris was too tempting a prize for the German High Command to leave matters as they were. Foch knew from intelligence reports that another major attack was being prepared and on 5 June he sent the Tenth Army to reinforce the French position between Villers-Cotterêts and Compiègne. Four days later, on 9 June, the Germans began a new offensive, 'Gneisenau', north of the Oise along the front between Montdidier and Noyon.

The ballooning party had been at Souilly for an eternity, waiting for the wind. Since the beginning of the month the weather had been stable but observations on the early evening of 8 June indicated that change was on the way. Readings at one a.m. on the 9th confirmed Hay's forecast: 'Accordingly . . . I advised Captain Bruce to prepare to operate that night . . .'[30] The lorries started for the launch-place, Meau, Bruce and Hazeldine preceding them in the car. Hay had asked for pilots to assess the force and direction of the wind in the upper air. Flights at six a.m. indicated that 4,000 feet above Souilly and Verdun a variable wind was blowing west-north-west. By eight p.m.

it had backed to south-west. By ten p.m., when it would be dark, there was a hope of a wind in exactly the right quarter. The ballooning party waited for sunset. There was a new moon, no more than a sliver. At nine p.m. Bruce, using a field telephone, heard from Hay that above Châlons and Verdun the wind had begun to veer to the west. Judging by reports from Ireland, where the barometer was rising rapidly, this change was likely to persist. There was no hope of delivering the balloon to the objective. Hay's recommendation: 'I advised to "wash out".'[31]

The party returned to Souilly. Day after day, night after night, they watched the sky. At this season the sun rose early and set late. During the few hours of darkness the waxing moon shone with ever more startling brilliance. By midsummer eve there would be hardly any night. To give Meau the best chance, they must get him off by 16 June. But the wind continued to blow from the wrong direction.

The German offensive ended on 13 June. It had been only a partial success. North of the Oise the enemy had reached Montdidier but at Compiègne a determined Franco-American effort had checked the advance. German reinforcements were still being brought up to the front. The Nineteenth Army was known to be at St Avold, entraining for Metz, en route either to Flanders in the north or Verdun in the east.[32] Hospitals were being emptied and German wounded sent home to make room for a new wave of casualties.[33] To conserve his forces for the next round, Foch ordered the Tenth Army to protect Compiègne, without attempting to push back the German line.

In war there is much waiting. This did not comfort the ballooning party, guests of the French Second Army, with little to do. At six p.m. on 16 June reports showed that the wind was moving to the south-west. Hay immediately requested that pilots be sent up to monitor wind direction above Souilly and Luxembourg. For an estimate of what was coming he rang Gold in Paris to ask for special observations from GHQ. If the right wind was on the way, it would arrive just in time. Hay thought the readings promising. The lorries were mobilized, and Bruce, Meau and Hazeldine readied themselves for the dash to the launch-place. As the cylinders were being loaded, Hay telephoned to say that the backing was only temporary and local: 'I again advised to "wash out".'[34]

In his first discussions with Bruce, Brunt had explained that in this part of France a steady wind in the desired quarter might be expected on one or two nights in an average May. Chances in June were less good and during the past three weeks had been particularly poor. An anti-cyclone had settled over the British Isles and France, producing a regular and persistent north-easterly. Even if there were a change in the weather, in two or three days' time there would be too much moon. By 23 June it would be at its fullest, waning to half full by the month's end. If they could not send Meau now, they would have to put off the mission until the beginning of July.

Late afternoon weather reports came in at six p.m. On 17 June, as on the 9th, they showed a depression approaching from the west of Ireland. Meteor's next bulletin was expected at one o'clock next morning. Outside the ballooning party's lodging the grass was white in the moonlight. Was Bruce imagining it or was there a change in the air? At one a.m. on the 18th reports confirmed the rapid approach of a depression, with the likelihood of south-west winds by evening. Pilots were requested. Conditions appeared favourable.

Once more the lorries sloped through the dusk, followed by Meau, Bruce, Hazeldine and Commandant Renaud in the car. At the launch place Israeli directed the unloading of the cylinders. Basket, trail rope and balloon were assembled, the hose attached. Thirty-pound bags of sand held down the balloon as it swelled. Bruce spoke to Hay by field telephone: conditions favourable. Smoking was forbidden so near to so much hydrogen, but a thermos was produced and coffee dispensed, under the ominous moon.

More telephoning: still favourable. Bruce looked again at the moonlight diagram. That night, 18/19 June, moonset was at 1.21 a.m. summer time. Sunrise was at 4.48 a.m. and it was expected that it would begin to get light an hour earlier, that is, at about 3.50 a.m. Two hours and twenty-nine minutes were available for Meau's journey. In order to assess the ground on which he proposed to land, he would have to come down in the light. Forty miles to Reckange: on a thirty-m.p.h. wind he would need just under an hour and a half. Launch should be at 2.20 a.m., an hour after moonset.

The aircraftsmen gently fixed Plant's water tanks into the basket.

Each was filled with thirty pounds of water. When the balloon was completely inflated, Israeli and Renaud took off all but eight of the sandbags and tried the lift. Too sluggish. Two more were removed. Too eager. Israeli put back half a bagful, draping the sack over the edge of the basket for ejection immediately after lift-off. Meau, in civilian clothes, put on his workman's overalls and over them a 'rather heavy Burberry overcoat'.* His colleagues tried the torches. It was midnight. An hour and twenty-one minutes to moonset. Another telephone call from Hay. He had spoken to Brunt. They were sorry. At 4,000 feet the wind was blowing too far to the south. He must advise them 'to "wash out"'.[35]

The balloon tugged at the trail rope. Meau and Bruce conferred. If a wind from this angle would not take the balloon to Reckange, they could aim for a different objective. They might wait for ever for the perfect night. Bruce was doubtful. Pressed by Meau, he put the matter to Hay. This new path would take the balloon toward Arlon, a good way west of the original objective. To avoid landing in Belgium, Meau would have to travel at least thirty miles further. If he were to take off, say, thirty minutes after moonset, at what height would he find a steady wind? Hay gave an estimate based on the pilots' readings: 3,500 feet. What would be the wind's likely direction and velocity? Twenty-eight m.p.h. at 210°, 'with a tendency if anything for the velocity to increase . . . and the direction to back but not more than 5°'.[36]

On the reverse side of Meteor's moonlight diagram Bruce wrote out the distances: 36 kilometres from Verdun to Longuyon, 48 from Verdun to Longwy, 66 from Verdun to Arlon. Three bits of figuring: translated into miles, this was 22, 30 and 41. At 28 m.p.h. the balloon would reach Longuyon in just over three quarters of an hour, Longwy in a further fifteen minutes, Arlon about half an hour after that. If Meau were to leave at two a.m., he should reach Arlon by 3.30, just as it was getting light enough to see. Swift mental arithmetic – French geographers use a 400° circle, the British a 360° – gave the new course. This was much riskier. Bruce had hoped to

---

* As described by Bruce, 'Conditions of Start', 29 June 1918. This may have been the 'unregulated' belted mackintosh favoured by British army officers.

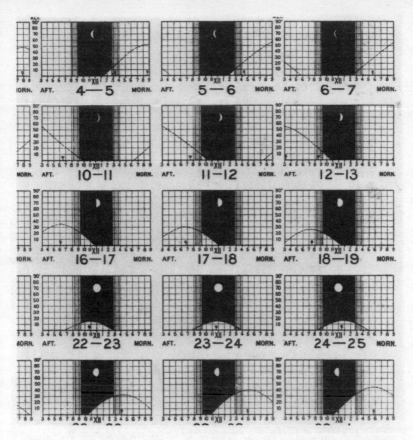

Meteor's moonlight diagram. By 17–18 June the moon becomes noticeably fuller and brighter.

send the balloon well inside the Grand Duchy, on the route rehearsed with 41st Wing. On that path Meau would have looked out for Esch-sur-Alzette and, once over it, started his descent, disembarking at a spot between five and ten miles south of the city of Luxembourg. This new course would take him further west, along the edge of the Grand Duchy, above the Belgian/Luxembourg frontier. To know where he was, he would have to find Arlon, on the Belgian side. The town should come into view after an hour and a half's flight and as soon as he saw it he would have to begin his descent, landing either among scattered hamlets in the Grand Duchy or just inside Belgium. The country here was wooded and if he disembarked on the wrong side of the border he should be able to slip across unseen. If after an hour and three quarters he had not yet identified Arlon – whether because of cloud, unfamiliarity with the layout of the place or because the wind had veered – he would have to come down without knowing his position. At 3.45 there would at least be sufficient light to enable him to find a landing-place. If the direction of the wind had been reasonably constant, he would either have hit Belgium or the Grand Duchy. On no account should he stay in the air. A fast wind and another quarter of an hour would take the balloon into Germany.

Meau studied the map, memorizing the geography of roads and rivers, location of settlements, arrangement of railways. He put away his watch and luminous compass. In his pocket he had 415 German marks in notes, none larger than 100, and a German map of the Grand Duchy and surrounding country, tied up in a package small enough to be stuffed down a rabbit hole. His washing things, in a leather travelling-case, had been put into the basket with a thermos of coffee and in another pocket was a slab of chocolate and the observer's pass in the name of de Belvaux. The manner in which he checked these preparations left no doubt that he intended to go.

It was agreed.

They waited, torches extinguished. Lights were dangerous so close to the front. They spoke in whispers. At this hour every sound was magnified: an owl's cry, the scream of a stoat's prey. One o'clock. The balloon swayed, bumping the basket against the grass. Reminded of the hydrogen, smokers in the party fought against the longing for cigarettes. One-fifteen. The moon had almost left the sky. Meau took off the Burberry. On top of overalls it was constricting and he needed his arms free for managing the balloon. The upper air would be cold but he had a civilian overcoat, slung over the basket.

Final instructions, solemn handshakings and salutes. At 1.50, not liking this at all, Bruce gave the order. The cords fell away and, as the basket left the ground, Baschwitz jettisoned the half sandbag. In seconds he was gone.

The balloon shot upwards, 500 feet a minute. Six thousand feet,

7,000, 8,000. Having celebrated its release, it descended, abruptly at first and then more gracefully, to the altitude at which its buoyancy exactly balanced its load. As Pollock had predicted, equilibrium was attained at 3,500 feet. There the balloon found a current and for the first half hour it moved steadily north-north-east, carrying Meau over the German lines.

Shortly after take-off he saw searchlights streaking out from Metz. The balloon seemed to be entirely motionless – after so much practice, he was used to the sensation – but as the lights receded he knew he was making progress. Hay had forecast that at 3,500 feet the wind would be blowing at about twenty-eight m.p.h.; Meau could only assume that this was the case. By 2.25 the Thionville searchlights appeared, more or less where he expected them to be. He was not aware that the wind had swung to 205°, putting extra miles between himself and Thionville's anti-aircraft batteries. Assessing distance was impossible. Looking out into an immensity of dark, he might as well have tried to measure the spaces between stars.

Below and to the west was a dim confluence of rivers and railway lines. Longuyon, twenty-two miles from Verdun, was not supposed to appear until 2.35. Was the wind blowing more briskly or had the balloon veered further to the north? The answer, unknown to Meau, was both. The current at 3,500 feet had increased to thirty-one m.p.h. and, having moved from 210° to 205°, the wind had now swung another five degrees, to 200°. The balloon was travelling not northeast but north-north-east, ten degrees off the path on which it had started out.

Suspended in nothingness, Meau perceived no alteration in the angle of flight. At 2.45 an orange emanation suggested that Longwy was in the offing. Drawing near, he saw that the glow of these unsleeping hearths was not to his left, as he had expected, but to his right. The furnaces gave him a bearing: the balloon was being carried either north-north-east to Arlon or north-west, deeper into occupied France, toward the German depots at Carignan and Sedan. If the latter, he would have a long walk back to the Luxembourg border.

Three a.m. The space in which he hung seemed less intensely black. He had the map by heart: from Athus, north of Longwy, the railway ran west to Virton, where it met another line, coming in to

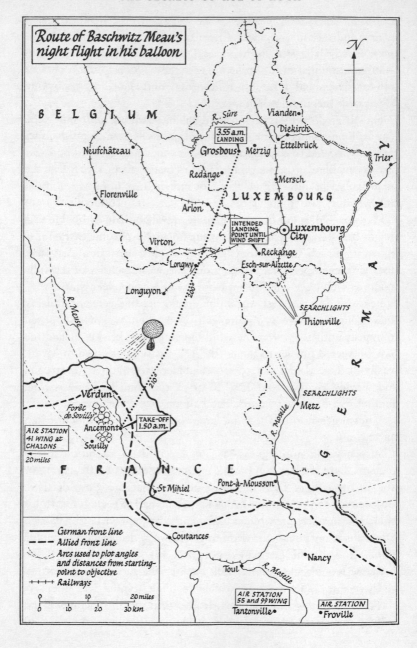

Route of Baschwitz Meau's
night flight in his balloon

BELGIUM

LUXEMBOURG

GERMANY

FRANCE

N

Vianden
R. Sûre
3.55 a.m.
LANDING
Diekirch
Ettelbrück
Grosbous   Merzig
Neufchâteau
Trier
Redange
Mersch
Florenville
LUXEMBOURG
Arlon
Luxembourg
City
INTENDED
LANDING
POINT UNTIL
WIND SHIFT
Virton
Reckange
Esch-sur-Alzette
Longwy
SEARCHLIGHTS
Thionville
Longuyon
R. Meuse
R. Moselle
Verdun
SEARCHLIGHTS
Metz
Forêt
de Sovilly
Ancemont
TAKE-OFF
1.50 a.m.
AIR STATION
41 WING at
CHALONS
Souilly
20 miles
St Mihiel
Pont-à-Mousson
Coutances
Nancy
German front line
Allied front line
Arcs used to plot angles
and distances from starting-
point to objective
Railways
Toul
R. Moselle
0   10   20 miles
0 10 20 30 km
AIR STATION
55 and 99 WING
Tantonville
AIR STATION
Froville

288

the town from Neufchâteau to the north. From the other side of Virton lines went west to Montmédy, north to Florenville. All four lines had been laid along the banks of rivers. In minutes some of this should be visible. If he were to see the shining V-shapes of the two sets of lines, he would know that the balloon was travelling westward into Belgium. The sky was the black-green of the end of night. It would not be easy to find ground suitable for landing, the country here being either inhabited or covered with trees, but if the balloon had drifted so far off course he would have to bring it down. He must do so before daybreak. Transit camps here were full of soldiers, any one of whom might, on waking, look up to assess the weather.

Ten past three. Behind and to the right, the horizon threw off pale light. That being east, the balloon was evidently going north-east or north-north-east, toward the frontier between Belgium and Luxembourg The ground was blue-black, massy. An intermittent shine drew the eye: two railway lines, snailing in parallel curves, linked by a third. The geography was familiar: the line on the left ran north–south between Arlon and Messancy, that on the right between Steinfort and Clémency. The Arlon–Messancy line was on the Belgian side of the border, the Steinfort–Clémency line on the Luxembourg side. South of Arlon was a junction where an east–west line came in, bringing traffic from the Grand Duchy to Belgium, military traffic, en route from the Luxembourg marshalling yard.

Three-twenty-one. Meau had not expected first light until 3.48 but already thin colour washed upwards in the east. Ahead and to his left he could see Arlon. The pace at which he came up to the Messancy–Arlon railway suggested that the balloon was moving fast. As it crossed the frontier the night watch might still be on duty, too sleepy to look at anything but the clock. Bruce had instructed Meau to begin his descent as soon as he could see Arlon. It would take fifteen minutes to come down from 3,000 feet. If he did so now, the angle at which the balloon was entering the Grand Duchy would bring it down among market towns and farming villages. He would do better to wait for Grosbous.

Half past three. In the eastern sky, delicate blue dissolved into rose. Below the balloon, slightly to the west, houses and a church clustered round a *place* that was not quite square. Redange. As soon as he cleared it, he could start the descent.

Three-forty. Meau heaved on the valve cord. He had already put his things together – thermos, washing kit, overcoat – and checked the water tanks. As the balloon lost height he appraised the ground: smooth, surrounded by woods. There was no wind to disturb the balloon's serenity as it floated down through the new summer morning. Baschwitz let go the valve cord, opened the taps on the water tanks and, as the basket brushed the meadow, jumped out. Relieved of its passenger, the balloon leapt upwards, found equilibrium and sailed away toward Germany. It was five minutes to four.

Having disposed of de Belvaux's papers, Conrad Bartels made his way across the grass to a secluded corner where he could look at his map. Although the sun had not yet risen, it was almost light enough to read without a torch. Grosbous seemed small, Merzig, its neighbour, little bigger. People here would notice a stranger. The nearest place of any size was Mersch, about twelve miles away. The highway was exposed but he could get into the town by scrambling through woods. Mersch was about halfway along the Diekirch–Ettelbrück–Luxembourg railway line. Dodging through the country would require a good four hours. From Ettelbrück a train left for the city of Luxembourg at 7.55, stopping at Mersch at 8.25. That was manageable. The journey from Mersch to Luxembourg would take half an hour; he could be at Boulevard Royal for a late breakfast, a pleasant prospect after a night in a balloon basket.

He considered the risks. The Ettelbrück–Luxembourg service originated at Diekirch, fifteen minutes up the line. If he were to get into trouble at the station or on the train, other passengers might be drawn in. The Diekirch schoolmaster was presumably a regular traveller on this section of the railway. It would be awkward for Meau and Hansen, who had never met, if either one were to suspect the other of shadowing him as far as Madame Rischard's doorstep. Worse: if the authorities were already following the schoolmaster, they might both be caught at once. But this being a weekday morning, the schoolmaster was more likely to be attending to his pupils than catching an early train. Meanwhile, the balloon might have been noticed, a search might be underway. Bruce was anxious for news, the Rischards for his arrival. The sooner he got himself to Boulevard Royal the better.

He had not breathed such air for weeks, nor heard so many birds. A golden sunrise promised a bright day, tramping unstiffened his legs. It was as if he were escaping again, with better clothes and better boots. He took his time, listening for saws and axes being worked among the trees, carts coming through the lanes. Smoke rose from cottage chimneys as kitchens awoke. Fine weather for walking – and for pegging out washing, chasing hens, scything grass. He slipped past gardens, skirted orchards, strode into Mersch and presented himself at the railway ticket office.

Luxembourg terminus. The station was busy. On its outside wall the stone-carved head of a Minister of Public Building and Works, an earlier Rischard, presided over the Place de la Gare. Overalls rolled in a bundle, overcoat on his arm, Meau made his way to Boulevard Royal. No. 20 was as Madame Rischard had described it: five doors opening on to three streets, one of which ran along the side. In the garden flowery bushes flourished with summer life. He slipped into green shadows. The curtains had been drawn back, windows opened to the morning air. The sounds from within were friendly, domestic, the shapes moving behind the glass unmilitary. For long minutes Meau watched the house. Satisfied that he was not propelling himself into a trap, he approached.

Madame Rischard was not at home. She had gone early to the market. He would wait. The maid took his things and gave him a chair.

When Madame Rischard returned, the maid hurried forward, full of misgiving. A strange man in strange uniform had said he was expected. He was waiting in the morning room.

'Madame Rischard?'

'I am Madame Rischard.'

'Conrad Bartels.'

He had come from Mersch, he said, and had concealed himself in her garden.

Was it Conrad Bartels or a German substitute? How was she to tell? In Paris, to protect the network, they had been kept apart.

'I know no one of that name.'

He was not like Rose or Réséda, lanky British officers with bony faces. This Bartels was little taller than herself. He was as poised and springy as a cat.

'Were you not expecting me?'

From his accent one would have supposed him to be French. For security, Bruce had not told her what Conrad looked like nor how he might be disguised. He was their friend, Bruce had told her. They had as much confidence in him as in themselves.[37] His name was Conrad Bartels and he would be sent in to Luxembourg when the wind was favourable. That was all she knew. Messages in the *Landwirt* had referred to him by his code-number: 66. It had been thought too risky to discuss a password.

'No Monsieur Bartels is expected here. Are you sure you have come to the right house?'

His reply was more an observation than a question.

'Do you remember the destination board for the No. 8 bus on the staircase in Rue Soufflot?'

This was no impostor.

23

Mademoiselle Testu's Surprise

In these days a new enemy crept through the lines, infiltrated camps, sidled into offices, an influenza that the Germans called 'Flanders fever', the French *'grippe espagnole'*.* It had first appeared in February 1916, recurring in the hard winter of early 1917. The symptoms then were relatively benign, forty-eight hours of shivering, sweating and high temperature, followed by four or five days' weakness. When the pneumococcus – as it was thought to be – returned in 1918 it seemed more ferocious than before; previous exposure appeared to give no immunity. In April an outbreak north of Compiègne spread quickly through the trenches. Hearing that Cox had collapsed – an understudy, Colonel Butler, delivered the intelligence briefing – Haig asked for a report on the health of the army.[1] Soldiers were inoculated, to no purpose. By the end of June disease had taken hold. Commanders soaked wet feet in mustard baths, sent away subordinates who were looking flushed, had windows closed or, if Scots, opened. Haig rode furiously along the sands at Le Touquet, breathing sea air; Foch trusted to a careful diet (for lunch one sardine and a hard-boiled egg). The German army was worse afflicted. Exhausted, ill-fed troops had little resistance and, by the time 'Gneisenau' was brought to an end in mid-June, sickness was neutralizing whole divisions.

The front was not inactive. On 4 June American marines, 'so new and smart with their long leggings',[2] launched a counter-attack against German troops entrenched beside the Marne west-north-west of Château-Thierry. The Americans lost 5,000 men, including half

* After the influenza that had killed 200,000 in Spain in 1889.

their officers, but took Bellau Wood on 25 June. Along the line between Soissons and Reims, allied guns kept up the barrage: 'tons and tons of high explosives . . . Never ending. Always ready to engage any bit of German territory at any moment . . .'[3] On 4 July at Le Hamel, north-east of Villers-Bretonneux on the Somme, the Australian Corps attacked German batteries in an innovative action that used tanks to clear the ground for infantry. Along the whole length of the line raiding parties went out every night to reconnoitre, looking for dead and wounded, listening for the whispers of scouts from the other side.

North of Verdun the front went east for twenty miles, then turned sharply south to St Mihiel. Through spring and early summer the Allies had expected an attack from German divisions assembled at Mézières, Sedan, Longwy. It was from this vulnerable piece of country, exposed to the enemy on both the northern and eastern sides, that Meau had been sent into Luxembourg. Bruce made haste to remove the evidence. The spare balloon was gathered up and packed with the remaining gear into a basket, empty cylinders were loaded into the lorries and, as dawn broke on 19 June, the party returned to Souilly. At six o'clock next morning Freeman and the men left for Fleury, where a French army quartermaster had ready provisions and 1,500 litres of petrol for the five-day journey back to Rang de Fliers. Eight days' extra rations had been allotted in case they met trouble on the road. As before, Freeman was instructed to send a wire from each stop, advising Bruce that the designated section of the route had been completed. Lansley drove Bruce, Hazeldine and Hay to Paris.

On 21 June Bruce returned to his desk at Place Anglaise. During his absence two letters had come in from Madame Rischard, asking about the implications of the German advance. She had paid for newsprint and arranged the increase for Hansen and Bram. Redecoration had at last begun at 20 Boulevard Royal. Furniture had been shifted, rooms were being repapered at triple the pre-war price. It was pleasing to know that Conrad was to be received in a freshly painted house.[4]

Meau should have made himself known to his hosts by now. At this moment Madame Rischard might be writing to say so, might already have written. Letters could take a fortnight to reach Rue St Roch; if Meau had arrived safely, it was likely that the first news would come via the *Landwirt*. So far, five days was the fastest time for a *Landwirt* to get from Diekirch to Paris. The balloon had been launched on Wednesday 19 June; if Meau had found Boulevard Royal without mishap, Jeanne Schroell would have put a report in the edition of Thursday 20 June. Yesterday's issue. At the earliest, that paper would arrive in Rue St Roch on 24 June. Monday. Three days to wait.

Urgent business done, Bruce asked for the files relating to the ballooning expedition. It was difficult to think of anything else. He dictated a letter to Major Neame of the RAF, telling him how well Freeman and the men had done and that the lorries were on their way back to the depot. He wrote to GHQ, thanking the transport people for the loan of the motor-car and the services of Private Lansley. The morning was going very slowly. He calculated how much pay had been advanced to Lansley, Israeli and Cheeseman during their attachment to GHQ and informed the RAF accordingly. He made out postal orders to a total of £3 13s 6d for forwarding on Israeli's behalf to someone in London. He clipped the counterfoils to a copy of the covering letter and gave the whole to Miss Done for filing. There was nothing more to do. Perhaps he should let Pollock know how they had got on. He wrote a line for Israeli to carry to Hurlingham, outlining the conditions in which Meau had taken off. Although the wind was not ideal, it had been too good a chance to lose. 'I have every confidence that he arrived successfully,' he told Pollock, 'and I will of course let you know as soon as we get definite news.'[5] But as Bruce worked at his letters, he could not forget the veering of the wind.

Midsummer, the longest day. In Place Anglaise it seemed as if time had stopped. He thought of the launch as he went back to his rooms, as he dined, prepared for bed. Above the roofs of Paris the moon was full. When he woke, he remembered. Had he sent Baschwitz straight into the arms of the enemy? So many scarce resources had been diverted to this project: hydrogen, lorries and drivers, special pilots . . . had all this been wasted? On Saturday 22 June he drafted an account of the circumstances of the launch:

Meau's dress; equipment, alibis; final decisions as to ballast; arrangements, in case of arrest, for letting them know. In a separate memorandum, marked SECRET, he described the weather. 'The only contingency which seems to give cause for anxiety,' he concluded, 'would be that, fearing the light, that he would have tried to come down in Belgium, and, miscalculating the force of the wind owing to its increase, that he would have come down on the Belgian frontier.'[6] The 'thats' were like a firing squad.

Sunday was interminable. He had hoped to have information about recent wind patterns but nothing had been sent over from the *Service Géographique*. Hay was preparing a report for Gold, explaining the two postponements on the nights of 9 and 16 June and the thinking that had led to the launch on the night of the 18/19 June, and Bruce had asked for a copy for the file. Although he, and he alone, had made the decision to proceed, it would be a comfort to be able to assure himself that his judgement had been well-founded. But where was Hay's report?

On Monday it was on his desk. Rather than waiting to have it typed, Hay sent a hand-written duplicate. His account matched Bruce's recollection; according to pilots' observations, the wind at 3,500 feet had been steady. Hay was about to leave Paris to join the Third Army in the field. 'I should like if you would drop me a note when you hear.'[7] Monday 24 June: they waited all day but no *Landwirt* was delivered.

Tuesday 25 June. One *Landwirt* was brought in, that of Wednesday 19 June. Hansen's column had a message about trains between Arlon and Thionville. German wounded, evacuated from hospitals in Soissons, were being brought home through Luxembourg. It was foolish to hope for mention of Meau's arrival: this edition would have gone to press on 18 June, just before the balloon took off. As the *Landwirt*'s regulars looked at the headlines over breakfast – '*Amtliche deutsche Kriegsmeldungen*', '*Flieger über Paris*', '*Demission des bulgarischen Kabinetts*', '*Milner's Hoffnung aus Amerika*'* – Meau should have been stepping out for Boulevard Royal.

* 'Official German War Bulletins', 'Aircraft Movements over Paris', 'Bulgarian Cabinet Resigns', 'Milner's American Hopes', *Der Landwirt*, 19 June 1918, received 25 June 1918.

Wednesday 26 June. No *Landwirt*. It was a week since Meau had left them. While they shuffled paper – GHQ had been inquiring about Lansley's meal allowance – Baschwitz might be lying for his life. When Bruce thought about it, he felt sick.

Thursday 27 June. At last.

Lokal-Neuigkeiten. Date of relevant item, two days earlier than that on the masthead. *Luxemburg, 18. Juni*.

They counted off the words: . . . *'angekommen'* . . . *'wohl'* . . . *'heute'* . . . *'Mittwoch'*: 'arrived' . . . 'safe' . . . 'today' . . . 'Wednesday'.[8] Thank God.

But where had he come down? Next day they knew:

Lokal-Neuigkeiten.
Ettelbrück. 20. Juni.

A passage about the transport of potatoes:

. . . *'heruntergekommen'* . . . *'Umgegend'* . . . *'Grosbous'* . . . *'ohne'* . . . *'grosse'* . . . *'Schwierigkeit'* . . . *'in'* . . . *'früher'* . . . *'Morgenstunde'* . . . *'bei'* . . . *'hellem'* . . . *'Tag'*.

. . . 'descended' . . . 'neighbourhood' . . . 'Grosbous' . . . 'without' . . . 'great' . . . 'difficulty' . . . 'in' . . . 'early' . . . 'morning' . . . 'in' . . . 'clear' . . . 'daylight'.[9]

From Bruce's desk word went out to all who had been involved. Reaction was triumphant. Captain Dugenet: 'infinitely happy . . . a huge relief . . .'; Commandant Renaud: *'Bravo, Bravo! . . .'*[10] Wallinger sent an enthusiastic scrawl: 'Your telegram arrived whilst Buckley was actually in the office . . .' Drake said little. Hazeldine described his approving grunt: 'RJD had nothing to say, except that he was glad to hear the show had gone off . . .'[11] High-ranking and low expressed delight at 'the success of the stunt' (the phrase was Israeli's).[12] Although Bruce reminded his correspondents about security – 'I would ask you very kindly to burn this letter . . .'[13] – he was too elated to follow his own advice. The balloon scheme had been given unstinting support, at a time when men and materials were not readily available. Those who backed it – people even more senior than Drake – had high expectations. As Pollock observed: 'It now remains to be seen . . . what "results" are forthcoming.'[14]

aus
ank.
Ge-
Nik.

lan-
ab-

:ber-
ffen!
dbin,
cken
Ju-
Ein-

- ich
- —
ollys
, die

eine
inze.
lsein

urch
Mer-
lein,

...tete. Seinem Heimatdorf hat er als Präsident des Lokalvereins wertvolle Dienste geleistet. Sein Andenken wird bei seinen Freunden in Ehren bleiben.

Luxemburg, 18. Juni. Die Zeit ist also wieder angekommen, wo die gottgesegneten Luxemburger zum Abgewöhnen oder wohl auch weil heute sonst keine Sorgen uns quälen, wieder in den politischen Kampf sich stürzen, und die verschiedenen Parteien — die hiesigen Sozialisten haben auf Mittwoch Abend bereits eine vorbereitende Versammlung einberufen — rüsten sich zu dem von den Klerikalen dem Lande aufgezwungenen Kampf. Allerdings werden die meisten mit Widermut in das Gemenge sich stürzen; denn betrübender, beschämender und kindischer als dieses erbärmliche Gezänke mitten in dem blutigsten Weltkriege wird unsere Geschichte nichts, hinsichtlich unseres Solidaritätsgefühls, den zukünftigen Geschlechtern erzählen.

Luxemburg, 20. Juni. In Anbetracht der unhaltbaren Lage, in welcher sich das Personal der Sekundär- und Kantonalbahnverwaltung infolge der Gewährung unzureichender Gehalts- bezw. Teuerungszulagen seitens der betreffenden Verwaltungen befindet, hat der „Landesverband Luxemburger Eisenbahner" zur Besserung der Lage der Kleinbahnkollegen bei der großherzog-

gele
6 U
9
gele
und
E

—

M

neb
1
biti-

2

A coded report was always dated two days before the edition of the newspaper in which it appeared. The paragraph headed Luxemburg 18 June – note the pencil mark in the margin at the beginning – gave an ironic account of local political developments: 'The time has once more arrived [angekommen] when, either because we feel secure [wohl] or because we have no other worries to plague us today [heute], the blessed Luxemburgers are once more hurling themselves into the political fray and the various parties – our home-grown Socialists have already convened a preparatory meeting for Wednesday [Mittwoch] night – are buckling on their armour for the battle the Clericals have forced on the country.'

So it was that Bruce spelt out the message that Baschwitz's balloon had landed without mishap.

They were soon apparent. Madame Rischard's operation was straightaway put on a more professional footing. In the four months since Bruce had last seen her in Lausanne, the only means of instructing her had been by letter. Meau could now explain complicated points about tidying up the code. Baedeker and Lieber and other sources of key words were dropped, punctuation and spelling methods improved and changes made to ensure that runs of letters did not occur too frequently. Complex descriptive sequences were amended, like the system for identifying uniforms, which Madame Rischard had found cumbersome: 'Could Conrad bring a neater formula?'[15] The alterations made coding and decoding easier and faster. They were also a precaution. An outsider who might have begun to catch *Lokal-Neuigkeiten*'s inner secrets would have to start again.

Sensitive issues could now be dealt with face to face. The Garlands' letters had been artful but certain matters were too delicate to explore on paper. One concerned the expansion of the network. At the French end three people only understood the code: Bruce, Campbell and Chocqueel. If Paris fell, there would be a burning of papers in Place Anglaise and Rue St Roch. The office would be emptied, its staff dispersed. Chocqueel might be able to work under cover but Bruce and Campbell would be obliged to withdraw. Communications with Luxembourg would have to go through other channels. How was the operation to be enlarged without prejudicing security? Through Meau, Bruce asked the Rischards what they thought of two possible recruits: Paul Schroell and Mademoiselle Vanvers. Schroell might be no more than a stopgap; if the Germans took Paris, the editor of *Le Luxembourg Libre* would have to move on. Could I(b) rely on Madeleine Vanvers for long-term support?

Madame Rischard consulted Hansen about Schroell, keeping in mind the fact that the schoolmaster did not know that it was the British, rather than the French, Secret Service that read his articles in the *Landwirt*. Schroell could be made *au courant*, Hansen replied, but he did not believe he would be much good at decoding.[16] Madame Rischard thought Mademoiselle Vanvers would be eager to help. She would need careful schooling but, if an auxiliary were needed, she would serve.

In suggesting these two names, Bruce had in mind the intimacy of the Luxembourg operation. Madame Rischard's network was tightly bound: her chief of staff was her husband, her intermediary in Switzerland, Madame Fresez-Settegast, her aunt by marriage. Meau's tactful questions encouraged Madame Rischard to reflect on these relationships. On whom could she rely if the Germans tightened their grip? If Conrad were captured, if she and Camille were arrested, who would send word? And who could take over from 'Tante Marie' if, at sixty-one, she found the work a strain? In answer to this last question, Madame Rischard suggested Madame Fresez-Settegast's daughter, Madame Ruymaeckers. Tante Marie was going with her daughter and grandchildren to the Waldhotel Bellary in July; as usual, letters between Paris and Luxembourg would be forwarded from there. If Tante Marie were to tell her daughter why she was receiving such a voluminous post while they were in Grindelwald, Margot Ruymaeckers would not talk. As for her own position, Madame Rischard had identified an assistant – if need be, a successor – in Annette Bergh, wife of Paul Rischard, youngest of Camille's brothers. Annette had an eighteen-month-old son, Charles-Edouard, but might nonetheless have time to engage in a coded correspondence with Madame Fresez-Settegast. She, Madame Rischard, would warn Tante Marie that letters signed 'Annette' were 'for us' and should be handled in the customary way.[17]

So Conrad settled in. The Rischards did not advertise their guest. Whatever the servants had been told, they said nothing. Monsieur Bartels seemed to be part of the family. He came and went; where and how he spent his time was a mystery to most of the household. Not to the Rischards. Briefed by Camille, Meau was exploring the railway network and talking to the men. He had in his sights a key German staging-post: Longuyon, in Lorraine. From this crossing-point, fed by roads, rivers and railway lines, trains went north to Flanders, west to Amiens and Paris. Longuyon was the nearest town to Verdun and the closest to the Longwy steelworks. Bruce had long wanted a post there. Longuyon, '44', was inaccessible to the Allies from south, west or east but an agent or agents might now be managed from the north, that is, from the Grand Duchy. Meau hoped to find at least one sympathizer among the railwaymen working the

Luxembourg–Longuyon line on the Lorraine side of the border. His first objective was to make himself known. In the Casino in Rue Notre-Dame and the cafés round about the marshalling yard he shared a smoke with signalmen, shunters and plate-layers, listening to their views on the conduct of the war. He made a glass of wine last a long time, this Bartels; otherwise he was like themselves, from his habits of speech to the oil-stains on his overalls. His associates began to confide in him. Would the Germans get to Paris? Would the Americans get to Luxembourg? 'Good hopes of succeeding at 44,' Meau reported on 27 June, 'but impossible to say for certain.'[18] It would take time, Madame Rischard warned Bruce, and they would have to be patient: 'Hoping to find a friend at 44, awaiting reply. Until then, pointless and too risky for 66 to go there.'*

Bartels brought a trained eye to the assessment of posts. New recruits came forward; when he recommended that an insufficiently '*sérieux*' train-watcher be dropped, there was no difficulty in finding another to take his place.[19] So many reports came in that Madame Rischard was coding until two in the morning. In the Paris Office the Secretariat charted the decodes on long sheets of squared paper: Arlon–Thionville; Thionville–Arlon; Thionville–Audun; Virton–Luxemburg–Thionville; Thionville–Luxemburg–Virton; Thionville–Luxemburg–Longwy; Trèves (Trier)–Virton; Trèves–Thionville; Artillery; Infantry; Cavalry; Various; Empties; Actual Identifications Received; Units Identified; Remarks. If the office had to be evacuated, these papers would be among the first to be removed.

German bombs were smashing windows in Paris; in days, the enemy might be marching down the Champs Elysées. How did Ludendorff propose to take the long-sought prize? Five German army groups were now in place from Flanders to Lorraine, ready to push forward to Ypres, Amiens, Reims, Verdun, St Mihiel. Allied generals remembered the diversionary tactic of late May, when Ludendorff had surprised them – when, indeed, he had surprised himself. They faced an impossible choice. If they moved reserves north to support the defence of Arras, Albert and Amiens, they would expose the

* '44', Longuyon, '66', Bartels. Madame Rischard to Bruce, 12 July 1918, received 24 July 1918.

Soissons–Reims section of the line. Ludendorff might then order an attack in the south, which, if successful, would open the way along the Marne and the Oise to Paris. That supposition might be incorrect. Ludendorff might repeat his earlier tactic but this time carry the deception through. A swift jab in the south, a rain of blows in the middle sector and the enemy would be across the Somme.

Foch had to rely on luck and instinct. If by good fortune he sent his reserves to the sector Ludendorff had chosen, if allied preparations could be concealed from German Intelligence, allied troops, though outnumbered, might be able to hold out until the winter. Rain, mud and exhaustion would end the offensive. By spring Pershing would have eighty divisions in France, with vast amounts of weapons and equipment. During the winter American recruits could train alongside the next wave of French and British conscripts, boys learning to be men. Tired troops would have time to revive.

Foch conferred with Haig, Pershing with Foch, Haig with Pershing. Haig believed that Ludendorff intended to focus on the north. Since 'Gneisenau' had been suspended in mid-June, Haig pointed out, the enemy had been bringing heavy batteries up from Liège. Prisoners and deserters spoke of an imminent attack on the Lys, observers reported that, along the front from La Bassée Canal, north of Arras, to the Somme, preparations were being made for the arrival of troops in large numbers. Pershing, who now had nineteen divisions in France – fourteen with the French, five with the British – continued to insist that American troops should be deployed together in a concentrated assault; where this was to be was not yet clear. Foch, suspecting an attack on the Marne, asked for British reserves to be sent there to support Pétain. Foch's request, in truth an order, was not well received by Haig. As for Ludendorff, he was still making up his mind.

Cox returned to duty on 1 July. His illness had been severe. The influenza had become an epidemic – in Munich, it was said, there had been 1,500 cases – but it was still thought that within a month the sickness would have run its course. That would be mid-July. By then, surely, Ludendorff would have decided in which order the five German armies were to move.

He had already done so. On 7 July, a week after Cox's return, a coded telephone message from Bruce told GHQ that German troops were going south. According to reports from Luxembourg, on 28 June two trains had been moved from Arlon to Thionville, on 29 June two more.[20] Subsequent reports indicated that the trains of 28 June were carrying cavalry and infantry, those of 29 June men of the Machine Gun Marksman Company.[21] Futhermore, between 23 and 26 June 15,000–20,000 men who had been resting at Arlon had left for Longwy. Between 23 and 24 June alone, Bruce told Speyer, nine trains had been sent from Arlon through Longwy to Longuyon. Although Bruce's signal did not say so, these reports were derived from information Baschwitz had acquired from a workman at Arlon station, confirmed by a document obtained from an employee at the Luxembourg marshalling yard.

If these troops had been returning to Germany, they would not have been going south-west to Longwy and Longuyon but north-east to Trier. Baschwitz and the Rischards were not only confident that the trains had turned south but also that no military traffic had gone north from Thionville to Arlon. As *Lokal-Neuigkeiten* assured those who could read the code: 'No movement . . . in these two sectors could go unnoticed because they are always announced beforehand by telegraph.'[22] The Luxembourg network chiefs were very well informed.

Perhaps too well informed. Reports in Parisian newspapers at the beginning of July stated that a number of arrests had taken place in the Grand Duchy. Eight or ten railwaymen were said to have been among those seized. Had the reports Bruce was receiving been planted by the Germans? No warnings, either in original or altered code, had been sent to Rue St Roch from Meau or Madame Rischard and neither Madame Schroell nor Pierre Huss had tried to alert Paul Schroell. Inquiries suggested that Bruce's team was intact but it sounded as if more than one network was operating in the Grand Duchy. On 4 July Bruce wrote a private letter to Dansey:

obviously anything of the kind must increase the difficulties, especially as the circle of possible recruits there is limited and very much interconnected.

If Cumming had agents in Luxembourg, they must have been installed by Tinsley's Dutch service.

For this reason I am wondering whether you would consider it possible and advisable to let T. know that our service is giving satisfactory results at the present time, just in case the arrests in question may have been due to efforts on his part to extend into that country, than which nothing could be more natural.

Bruce was diplomatic:

For physical reasons our transmission, 5–8 days, is necessarily quicker than anything which could possibly be established by courrier [sic] to Holland, and, in these circumstances, it would perhaps be reasonable to ask T. to refrain from any further efforts, should he contemplate such.[23]

Dansey took the point. A 'certain incident', he said, had occurred in March, 'where the Boche got hold of a telegram', resulting in arrests 'very wide of the mark'.

It may comfort you to know this, and that T. does not appear to have a contact in the Grand Duchy; nor do I know of him trying one; in fact it was discouraged.[24]

A further report from Dansey was more unsettling:

I have made enquiries and found out that in August 1917 T. did have a service or the elements of one amongst the railway men of the Grand Duchy. It always seems to have been rather a precarious and uncertain one, and in last March he attempted to clear up the situation only to find that those concerned had 'all disappeared'.[25]

However careful, Bruce's agents were vulnerable to other people's misfortunes and mistakes.[26] There had been narrow squeaks. Offenheim, for instance, was interrupted by a German officer who asked him what he was doing among the files. Seizing a broom and then throwing it down, the principal assistant station master told the German he could clean up his own mess if he preferred. The man apologized and Offenheim went on tidying up. When he called at Boulevard Royal to tell Dr Rischard the story, Offenheim fainted at the memory.

GHQ was admiring. The troops the railwaymen had identified were the 20th Division, some of Germany's finest.[27] Intelligence from

Luxembourg was supported by aerial reconnaissance and information extracted from troops captured by the French on 14 July. From these prisoners General Gouraud, commander of the French Fourth Army, east of Reims, learnt that enemy artillery had been ordered to open fire at 12.10 a.m. on 15 July. At four a.m. stormtroops were to go forward with machine-guns and grenades. Further east, near Epernay, a prisoner told one of General Berthelot's officers that on 15 July France would receive the *coup de grâce*. Foch's instinct had been right. The German offensive would begin in the southern part of the front.

Gouraud anticipated the German attack by forty minutes. At 11.30 p.m. on 14 July artillery of the Fourth Army released a barrage of such violence that Parisians were woken from sleep. It was customary to celebrate the anniversary of the storming of the Bastille but these bangs were overdoing it. Ten minutes after twelve, as ordered, German guns replied. By nightfall on 15 July it was evident that in this section of the line the enemy's plan had failed. Gouraud had lost 5,000 men, the Germans more than 40,000. Further west along the Marne, between Epernay and Château-Thierry, the enemy made better progress. By early afternoon infantrymen from Boehn's Seventh Army had crossed the river in small boats. Bridges were being constructed for the force that was to follow. The two British divisions sent to assist Pétain were still a day's march away. Wishing to prevent the enemy from advancing further, Pétain called up the French Tenth Army, commanded by General Mangin, *'le Marteau'*.* Within minutes, Pétain's summons was countermanded by Foch. The Tenth Army would be wasted if it were used as an anvil. Mangin was a hammer for striking blows. Supported instead by Italian Senegalese and two American infantry divisions, Berthelot's Fifth and Degoutte's Sixth Armies held the line.

On 17 July Ludendorff brought *'Friedensturm'*, his 'Tempest of Liberation', to an end. The Second Battle of the Marne, as it came to be called, now turned into a Franco-American counter-offensive. Four French armies – Mangin's Tenth, Degoutte's Sixth, and Berthelot's Fifth, with de Mitry's Ninth in reserve – pressed forward

* 'The Hammer'.

as one. At five o'clock on the afternoon of 18 July the German line was broken. Mangin ordered the cavalry through the gap, one of the last such charges in European warfare. On 19 July Boehn abandoned the south bank of the Marne, on 21 July the enemy evacuated Château-Thierry. Cut off from the main road that ran between that town and Soissons and from the railway line linking the Aisne and the Marne, German troops in the 'Aisne pocket' had difficulty in obtaining supplies and ammunition. They stood their ground, hoping for reinforcements from north of the Vesle and the Aisne, where a reserve 70,000 strong awaited the order to march. These divisions formed part of the Crown Prince of Bavaria's Army Group, augmented by troops from Prince Rupprecht's GHQ in the north.

Parisians rejoiced, flocking to stations to cheer school-leavers who were off to find glory at the front. Women threw flowers at the *char à bancs*, hung with banners, bringing conscripts to the registry in each *arrondissement*. There were other reasons for happiness. 'Bertha', silent since mid-June, had bombarded the city on 15 and 16 July and then stopped. Had French aviators destroyed the *supercanon*? Although newspapers reported an increase of influenza in the provinces, Paris seemed to have been spared. Nastier symptoms were mentioned – swelling, blue skin, delirium, asphyxia – but laboratories from France to North America were known to be working on a vaccine. Rain in the second week of July had watered crops after worryingly dry days and now the sun shone on gardens, allotments and pots of herbs on sills. Bare-kneed small boys perched on the exhibits in the Place de la Concorde and the Tuileries: remnants of German guns, tank parts, the ruins of a Zeppelin. On Sunday afternoons in the Jardin du Luxembourg Jamin conducted his musicians in patriotic airs. Were Captain Bruce and Miss Done among the audience, sitting on curly green metal chairs, under the trees?

Was it a dream? The Germans had been chased away in 1914 in the other Battle of the Marne. Ludendorff might produce new weapons, his generals new tactics. And German divisions were still being brought to France. Madame Rischard had sent word of exceptionally heavy traffic through Conflans-en-Jarnisy, including much foot and field artillery, and Meau's sources had told him that there were movements near Verdun: 'Watch this neighourhood and to the south of this place.'[28] Trenchard's pilots had a look, flying great distances, 250 miles out and back by day, 280 by night. These were narrow margins: machines with five and a quarter hours' supply of fuel just managed to get home. A miscalculation of five minutes meant disaster. The German response was largely defensive. Searchlights and anti-aircraft guns swept the sky above railheads, factories and camps. '*Flak Zug* anti-aircraft troops', Madame Rischard reported. 'Black cap band, red shoulder flash, insignia howitzer with yellow fins and number of platoon. Accompanying searchlight operators same insignia but letter S instead of number.'[29]

Further warning came from Baschwitz:

Important movement of Austrian troops is reported for several days prior to July 21st through Thionville towards Audun.

Between 21st July and 24th July twelve such trains passed through Thionville of which three were diverted through Luxemburg to Arlon where the troops detrained.[30]

'Particulars perhaps tomorrow,' the message said, and there they were, in an article about farming politics:

Thionville–Arlon

21 July: 4 unidentified

22 July: 1 artillery
          2 unidentified

23 July: 1 artillery
          1 unidentified.[31]

Austrian *Landsturm*, Baschwitz thought. This was so: the 35th Austro-Hungarian Division moving to Conflans en route to Verdun.

By 28 July the French had advanced twelve miles north of the Marne. What remained of Soissons was retaken on 2 August. The Germans had been driven back to the Vesle but Ludendorff had long since turned away. On the night of 17 July he had left his observation post in Champagne and gone north to Prince Rupprecht's headquarters at Tournai. From there he proposed to launch a lightning offensive on the Flanders front while the Allies were occupied on the

Marne. German troops were to be brought straightaway from Reims to launch an attack long considered and long in the making.

But the next great battle did not take place in Flanders, nor in Verdun, and its timing was not of the Germans' choosing. Knowing that Rupprecht's reserves had been depleted by the dispatch of reinforcements to the south, Foch believed the time had come to unleash his armies. On 24 July he explained his strategy to allied Commanders-in-Chief, assembled at his headquarters at Bombon, a 'plain, simple, substantial' château – Haig's description – between Melun and Nangis, twenty-five miles south-east of Paris. Foch's plan was as uncomplicated as his house. The task, he said, was to secure railway lines and roads leading north of Paris up to Amiens, Albert and Arras. These arteries, taking traffic to and from Flanders and the Channel, ran alongside – in places, through – Santerre, an expanse of flat country, cut by ditches, canals and, winding across its middle, the Somme. Péronne was situated in the centre, Bapaume in the north, Montdidier and Noyon in the south; over the last four years all had been invaded, liberated by the Allies, and, in the spring of 1918, recaptured by the Germans. If road and rail links could be retaken, a series of attacks might drive the enemy back beyond Cambrai and St Quentin, producing an allied front line to join up with that now being established between Soissons and Reims. The tactics proposed were based on General Rawlinson's successful action at Le Hamel in early July. There was to be no preliminary bombardment by long-range guns, betraying their position. Instead, massed tanks would launch a surprise attack, supported by aircraft. Infantry would follow, covered by a creeping artillery barrage. The operation would have to be completed by mid-September, when the low-lying fields of Santerre turned to mud.

General Debeney had been protecting the west bank of the Avre, the river that ran south from Amiens. On 28 July his First Army and General Rawlinson's Fourth Army were placed under Haig's orders. After ten days and nights of stealthy preparation, tanks, artillery and French, British, Canadian and Australian troops moved forward after dark on 7 August. At 4.20 a.m. on 8 August the attack began in a blaze of fire, a racket of tanks, grenades and shells. On that 'black day of the German army', as Ludendorff described it,

27,000 of his compatriots were killed or wounded. The Allies advanced eight miles. Montdidier was encircled, then taken, on 10 August. When the battle of Amiens ended on 13 August, Ludendorff had lost 32,000 prisoners, more than 650 heavy guns, thousands of machine-guns. The following day he told the Supreme Command at headquarters at Spa, south-east of Liège, that military victory was now out of the question.

Bruce wrote at once to Madame Rischard. His letter, sprinkled with exclamation marks and explosives – '*utopie*', '*banalités*', '*anicroches*' – was ecstatic. Mademoiselle Testu had offered her resignation, he said, and left the house.[32] The governess had been driven out. So was Bertha. After a last effort on 5, 6, 7 and 8 August, she was dismantled and sent back to Essen.

Mademoiselle Testu's expulsion was not the only cause for celebration. Dansey had sent an extract from the *Bremen Bürgerzeitung*, reporting the landing near Rotenburg of an English captive balloon. 'The occupants were missing and it is presumed that they jumped out and escaped.'[33] Based on weather reports, Hay had estimated that Meau's balloon might manage to get as far as northern Holland before gas and water tanks were exhausted. Rotenburg, between Bremen and Hamburg, was further east but in the right latitude. 'It looks', Bruce told Drake, '. . . as if this must be our balloon.'[34]

Madame Rischard's news was disappointing. After six weeks of negotiation, the prospective agent at Longuyon had failed them. They would have to start again.[35] There was no falling-off at other posts. German Mechanical Transport columns camped at Charleroi were reported to be leaving for the south. A steady stream of trains, carrying Austrians, was moving up from Thionville to Audun; they had been en route since mid-July. German troops were being sent in the opposite direction, to Saarbrücken and beyond. According to Meau's acquaintances among the German troops, Austrian divisions were relieving part of the German Fifth Army, which was leaving for Russia.[36] Was the enemy in chaos or re-grouping? Haig thought the latter: 'Colonel Butler (Intelligence), reports that the 30th Austrian Division has arrived at Arlon in Luxemburg.* This seems to indicate

* 'From Luxemburg' must have been meant, Arlon being in Belgium.

that the Germans are very short of men. It is possible that the enemy is distributing his reserves *on the defensive*.'[37]

That assumption was supported by other reports. Constituted units were no longer coming from Germany. The Secretariat filled in the charts:

Art.: Nil; Inf.: Nil; Cav.: Nil; Var.: Nil.

A nil return was as significant as an identification. With no insignia or weapons to describe, messages recording an absence of trains were easier to encode but in other respects the work of reporting was just as demanding. Hansen was finding it increasingly difficult to find new ways of making points about crops and prices and in mid-August Madame Rischard recommended that they raise his fee. Bruce had also asked her to advance to Conrad whatever sums he needed.[38] So far, the operation had cost 15,010 French francs, of which 11,000 francs had been for newsprint.*

Four times a week Metty Finck set up the type, four times a week the censor read the *Landwirt* and sent it on to Father Cambron. The paper had retained its bounce. When 'The Enchanted Princess' reached its fifty-second and final episode, it was succeeded by 'The Moth Flees the Light'.[39] That was on 13 July in the middle of the second battle of the Marne. For all the *Landwirt* knew, the occupier might bind Luxembourg still tighter but, halfway down every front page, the title of the new serial was a recurring subversive murmur.

The moth was fragile. In mid-July the civilian bread ration in Berlin had fallen from a pound to half a pound; eggs, two a day in May and June, were rationed to one every four days. The daily quarter-litre of milk, with 'a little cream', had gone. People had to supply themselves if and when they could. The official line was that cuts were due to 'the pause before the harvest' but people knew the distribution system was failing.[40] There were strikes and demonstrations in Berlin in May 1918, mass protests in Munich in August. At Ingolstadt police used tear-gas when rioters set fire to the city hall. If the *Landwirt* heard stories of unrest, it could not print them.

---

* *Der Landwirt*, 21 August 1918, received 27 August 1918. These sums amount to roughly £45,030 and £33,000 in today's money.

They would have been only partial comfort. The collapse of the German economy would crush the Grand Duchy and Alsace-Lorraine. Occupied, Luxemburgers lived in fear and misery. Change might be worse. If the Reich won the war, the Grand Duchy would be annexed and squeezed dry. If the Allies prevailed, retreating armies would not abandon occupied territory without a fight. They would destroy everything they could not take.

In the meantime, where there were hands to scythe, bind, stack and thresh, the harvest was good. Stubble lay gold under a haze of heat. Haig had taken a small bungalow at Le Touquet, close to the links, although he had little opportunity for golf. The sand was smooth and easy for riding, the waves tempting. On 26 August Cox, enfeebled by 'flu, was pulled under and drowned. Butler looked after the daily briefing until General Clive took over as Head of Intelligence on 18 September. A second, more virulent wave of influenza had appeared: Bruce had been caught in late July but recovered quickly. Research had failed to produce a vaccine; instead, Parisians covered their faces with scarves soaked in eucalyptus oil, balsam or turpentine. 'Gas masks', said the joke, 'had given way to gauze masks.' Although allied armies, like the German, were weakened by sickness, Foch and Haig were determined to thrust forward in the Santerre. 'We are engaged in a "wearing out battle",' Haig told Churchill, Minister of Munitions, when he visited the front. 'If we allow the enemy a period of quiet, he will recover, and the "wearing out" process must be recommenced.'[41]

There was no tranquillity. On the morning of 21 August, in heavy mist, Byng's Third Army moved toward Bapaume. Tanks went first. Troops suffered much in the hot sun but that day they took Courcelle-le-Comte, Achiet-le-Petit, Beaucourt-sur-Ancre, once villages, now only antique names. At dawn on 22 August Rawlinson's Fourth Army seized Bray and Chuignes. New methods and new weapons assisted the offensive. Enemy guns were located using acoustic monitoring devices, rather than trial fire. Formality was sacrificed for speed and agility. Covered by tanks – a 29-ton Mark V could move at 4 m.p.h., a 14-ton 'Whippet' at 8.3 m.p.h. – allied infantry ran toward an enemy already beaten down by storms of mortars and fire from rapid-action Lewis guns. Risks that a month ago would have been criminal, Haig told his commanders, 'ought now to be incurred as a duty'.*

Yard by yard the Third Army moved nearer to Bapaume. General Debeney's French troops meanwhile made ready to take on enemy reserves waiting in the curve of the Somme between Péronne and Chaulnes, the upper section of a semicircle of German-held ground extending south through Roye and Noyon. To buy time, Ludendorff intended to take his forces back to the Hindenburg Line, a barrier of trenches, barbed wire, steep-sided canals and machine-gun posts running for sixty miles from its northernmost point, five miles west of Cambrai, to its southernmost curve, between the Aisne and the Marne, twelve miles north of Soissons. Here Ludendorff hoped to wait out the winter. As he ordered the retreat, Debeney moved. Roye was taken by the French early on 28 August, Bapaume by the New Zealanders on the 29th. Noyon was freed on 30 August, Péronne on 2 September. By the first week of September the Santerre had been entirely liberated, the enemy driven back to the Hindenburg Line.

They were still formidable. On the same day on which Haig issued his order to act opportunistically, General Sixt von Arnim, Commander of the Infantry, addressed the German army. Unfavourable ground would be yielded 'here and there', as planned, and resistance concentrated. Every man in the army should defend to the last, 'on the spot where he is put into the battle, the ground entrusted to him'. Reserves behind would be ready to counter-attack.[42]

During the whole of August two divisional motor transport columns had been the only military traffic through the Luxembourg

---

* 'It is no longer necessary to advance in regular lines step by step. On the contrary, each division should be given a distant objective which must be reached independently of one's neighbour, and even if one's flank is exposed for the time being. Reinforcements must be directed on the points where our troops are gaining ground, not where they are checked. A vigorous offensive against the sectors where the enemy is weak will cause hostile strong points to fall, and in due course our whole army will be able to continue its advance. This procedure will result in speedily breaking up the hostile forces and will cost us much less than if we attempted to deal with the present situation in a half-hearted manner.' Haig, Operations Special Priority, O. A. D. 911, 22 August 1918.

marshalling yard. On 25 August it was attacked by Baldwin's long-range bombers, a raid that was a surprise not only to Baschwitz but also to Trenchard. On inquiry, it appeared that Baldwin had received no order to avoid the Luxembourg main station.[43] No train-watchers had been injured, Meau reported, all but one of the bombs had missed the lines and that hit had been trivial. Might he suggest a better target? Locomotives, now scarce, were kept in the engine rotundas north and south of the station. Knocking those out would be much more useful.

Two days after Meau sent this message, his observers reported fresh activity in the station and along the lines. Between 4 and 8 September fifteen trains moved north through Arlon toward a point south of Namur. This time they were empty. When they returned, some twelve hours later, they carried foot and field artillery. Were these being positioned to reinforce the bulge of ground at St Mihiel? 'As we are informed too late,' Meau reported, 'details next time.'[44] The intelligence was important. Foch had decided to expel the Germans from St Mihiel, which they had held since 1914. This task he assigned to Pershing. It was hoped that if the Americans were to triumph on their own stretch of front their confidence would be increased in the field and at home, making it difficult for Pershing to sustain his argument that American troops, unused to taking orders from French and British generals, required a separate and independent command.

Meau now discovered that more trainloads of reserves had moved down through Arlon than had originally been reported. The usual arrangements for the timing and routing of trains had fallen away and paperwork passing through the station office had told only half the story. Meau believed that some constituted units had gone through at night. Their passage had not been recorded, the most reliable agent – Superintendent Foreman Bram? – having been occupied elsewhere. Another observer had reported that eighteen foot and three field artillery trains had gone south during the first week of September but this informant worked a day shift and had no night observations. Furthermore, being untrained, he had been unable to give details. Meau had also heard, however, that enemy plans had changed. These constituted units were destined not for Verdun but for Colmar, down the line from Strassburg in the south-east of Alsace.[45] Acknowledgement from O.B. Ciphers indicated that, according to Belgian train-watchers, they had started from Ciney, the German artillery practice area south of Namur.

The artillery was not delivered to St Mihiel. When, on 12 September, the American army, now almost twenty divisions strong, attacked the St Mihiel pocket, only eight German divisions were positioned there. By 15 September Pershing's troops had unlocked this triangle of ground. Seven thousand Americans had been killed or wounded in their first significant victory of the war. A key section of front had been smoothed out and the Paris–Verdun and Paris–Nancy railway lines – the latter was that on which Pollock had been stranded – were vulnerable only from the air.

The Americans' next thrust was to be a joint operation with the French, an assault in the Argonne region, between the Aisne and the Meuse. The object: to recapture and secure the section of railway running up to Cambrai and, particularly, to take the Charleville–Mézières junction. The front was fed by trains coming on this line from Saarbrücken and Metz, via Thionville, and from Flanders, via Arlon, units that were restocked and reconstituted as they waited in the Luxembourg marshalling yard.

Action began on 26 September. It was stiff going. The ground, partly forested and cut by rivers and streams, was difficult for tanks and, since March, when the Germans had taken the area, defences had been dug and traps prepared. Twenty-two French divisions fought alongside the Americans. Troops moved to the Argonne after the conclusion of the St Mihiel operation brought the number of American divisions up to fifteen; for efficient command, Pershing divided his forces into a First and Second Army. The Allies faced an enemy used to hard fighting. These German divisions had been brought from Flanders in a series of train movements that had started in mid-month: from 12–28 September 150 empty trains had gone north on the Thionville–Arlon line, each returning some two days later. Meau's identifications showed that these, plus another 14 trains, carried mainly Austrian foot and field artillery. He further indicated that 24 trains on the Thionville–Luxembourg–Longwy section had delivered units of the 52nd Division on 27, 28 and 29 September.

The departure of enemy troops from Flanders eased the Allies' difficulties in the north of the front, where since mid-September King Albert of the Belgians had been commanding at Foch's request a joint force of twelve Belgian, one French and six British divisions, installed between Dixmude and Ypres on the Flemish plain. Dysentery and influenza had weakened them and, despite the reduction in the German presence, they were confronted by seventy-two batteries of enemy artillery. Bad weather in late September churned the ground to mud and in streaming rain the Allies struggled in the dark to bring forward guns and ammunition. The allied attack started on 27 September. In twenty-four hours the joint force advanced five miles; by 30 September, with many dead and 10,000 wounded, they had retaken Dixmude, the German stronghold on the Yser, expelled the enemy from a large strip of country in the southern sector of line and captured 6,000 prisoners and 250 guns. The King ordered a halt for troops to rest while heavy artillery was brought up. During this respite, the Germans put in six fresh divisions.

Tracking activity in the yards and on the railways was now prodigious work. From Waldhotel Bellary Madame Fresez-Settegast posted on the Garlands' letters and cards to Luxembourg and, when she finished her holiday, from Lausanne, but Madame Rischard had little time to reply. There was no need for auxiliaries, she told Bruce, and the Verenahof arrangement could now be suppressed.

Prefer to do without Brasseur and everyone else. Address letters if absolutely necessary in German or French to Mme. Heldenstein, Rue Guillaume, Luxembourg.*

Outgoing post from Luxembourg was now very slow. Madame Rischard concentrated on coding. Her messages were not only about trains. On 11 September Meau sent intelligence regarding the arrival in Alsace of troops from Russia and large stores of poison gas, on 14 September he described a new sort of egg-shaped anti-tank mine, which 'a trustworthy source' had told him was being manufactured

* Madame Rischard to Chocqueel, 30 September 1918, received in Paris 18 October 1918. Madame Hélène Heldenstein-Settegast was Madame Marie Fresez-Settegast's younger sister. 'Rue Guillaume' should properly have been translated as 'Avenue Guillaume'.

MESSAGE IN N° 140 of 14th SEPTEMBRE.

RECEIVED 20th SEPTEMBER.

1.-   THIONVILLE - ARLON   9th - 12th   Nil.

        September 13th   ARLON - THIONVILLE

            5 Trains Austrian Foot Artillery

            3 trains German Minenwerfer Companies.
            Marks on vehicles M.W.B.B.

        Ess ist nicht 54 aber wohl Buchstaben B.B.

        (This is not 54, but really the letters B.B.)

2.-   Zur Bekämpfung der Tanks wie wir zuverlässig erfahren
        lassen die deutsch jetst unzählige Bomben in Form von
        Eiern verfertigen welche auf dem Boden umhergestreut
        unter der schweren Last platsen ünd die in allernächster
        Zeit in Anwendung kommen sollen.

            Translation:-

            To resist the Tanks as we hear from a trustworthy
        source the Germans are now manufacturing immmense quantities
        of bombs in the forme of eggs which are scattered about
        on the ground and blow up under the great weight. They
        are to be employed shortly.

*A report from Baschwitz Meau, decoded at 41 Rue St Roch and typed out
by the Secretariat.*

in immense quantity and was to be deployed shortly.[46] He gave warning of a so-called Luxemburger, a German spy with stolen papers, and confirmed rumours that certain newspapers and certain people were more pro-German than they claimed. Trains, however, were his principal work. Meau's train-watchers were efficiently organized, their reports increasingly accurate. The improved code worked well. Between 29 September and 11 October he gave identifications for eighty-four trains passing through Thionville to Arlon and the northern section of the front.

Early in October Meau reported that the Germans had transferred their Military Railway Directorate No. 2 from Sedan, a few miles east along the line from Charleville–Mézières, to Metz, either for more effective handling of traffic or in fear of an allied incursion.[47] Perhaps both. In Sedan, people felt that something momentous was under way. '*La ville est assez agitée*,' a child wrote in his diary: 'the town is agitated . . . everyone making ready . . . there is a fall in the price of vegetables . . .'[48]

Bruce congratulated the Luxembourg team – and asked for more intelligence. What was happening in Lorraine? He could send in a young Belgian, who spoke German like a native and had friends to receive him.[49] Back came Meau's answer. Managing an agent at that distance would be tricky.[50] More from Bruce. If 44 (Longuyon) remained difficult, could they get more information about traffic through 76? This was Audun-le-Roman in Lorraine, a small place but 'hugely important', for it sat on a branch line connecting Longuyon, the steelworks at Hayange, and the Thionville junction.[51]

The Luxembourg network now encompassed posts throughout the country: north-east toward Trier, north-west to Arlon, south-east toward Audun, south through Thionville and on to Metz, south-west toward Saarbrücken, west to Longwy. Astonishingly, Meau had made his way across the frontier to this latter place, travelling in disguise. Bruce had given him the name of a local *contrebandier* and, having found the man and assured himself that he was genuine, Meau engaged him to smuggle intelligence back along the railway line.[52]

On 11 October Butler sent Drake a congratulatory wire. The drafting was wooden:

recent reports received from Capt. Bruce have been most useful, the numerous identifications supplementing the train movements being most valuable . . . The heavy train movements through Luxemburg during the past month have given this service an opportunity of showing that it is very efficient.

Nevertheless, it was reassuring to the Paris Office to know that its contribution was not only appreciated but was being used. An instance:

In particular, his [that is, Bruce's] wire No. 80 of the 8th Oct. Reporting the move of the Guard Ersatz Division to Flanders was a very good example of an excellent agent's report.[53]

This latter item had been part of a report describing constituted units passing through the marshalling yard on 29 September. Inserted into the *Landwirt* of 30 September, received in Paris on 8 October, it had been decoded by Bruce's team and telephoned to O. B. Ciphers at four o'clock that same afternoon. Like many of Meau's reports at this time, it was long and complex, a string of 164 coded groups. Hansen, expert at this trick, had concealed it in an article about the persecution of minorities among populations desperate for food, a text interesting enough to be realistic but not so controversial as to upset the authorities. One stroke of the censor's pen would wipe out hours of coding, ordering and spacing.

Meau's information concerning the Guards Ersatz Division was followed over the next ten days by observations relating to movements of foot and field artillery of the 243rd Division, the 41st Division and the 44th Reserve Division:

. . . also troops with:
Black sh. strap & No. 29
Grey sh. strap & No. 828
Grey sh. strap & No. 7T
Violet sh. strap & No. 8
Grey sh. strap & No. 44
Black hat bands.[54]

These reports were confirmed by O. B. Ciphers by subsequent evidence from train-watchers further up the line in France and Belgium. The

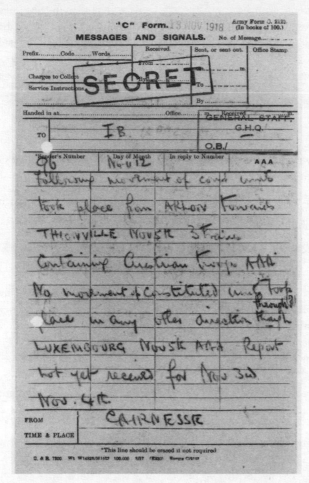

"C" Form. 18 NOV 1918   Army Form C. 2121.
(In books of 100.)

MESSAGES AND SIGNALS.   No. of Message

Prefix.........Code.......Words......... | Received. | Sent, or sent out. | Office Stamp

SECRET

TO   I.B.   GENERAL STAFF. G.H.Q.

O.B./

Sender's Number   Day of Month   In reply to Number   AAA

86   Nov 12

Following movement of enemy units took place from ARLON towards THIONVILLE Novsk 3 trains containing Austrian troops AAA No movement of constituted units took place in any other direction through LUXEMBOURG Novsk AAA Report not yet received for Nov 3rd Nov 4th.

FROM   CAIRNESSE

TIME & PLACE

*This line should be erased if not required

One of the pink slips sent to O.B. Ciphers at GHQ, containing an intelligence report from Bruce, 'Cairnesse', at the Paris Office.

information was timely. In the north and central sections of the front the British were making for the Hindenburg Line. It was to this part of the battlefield that enemy reinforcements were being delivered.

The Line was a colossal obstacle. The allied attack began on 27 September with an unrelenting storm of shells, almost a million fired over twenty-four hours. Although German heavy guns were silenced, trenches and barbed-wire entanglements caught American and Australian infantry at the north end of the line. The inner sides of the St Quentin Canal sloped fifty feet down into three further feet of sludge and wet. Tanks could not ford it. Commanders had hoped that access might be made through a tunnel at the end of the canal but their armoured vehicles were trapped in pits, excavated in ground already softened by autumn rain. In places a new type of trench mortar – Meau's 'egg-shaped devices' – had been sown. Unprotected by covering fire, hundreds of allied soldiers fell; 377 were killed and 658 wounded in the 107th US Infantry Regiment alone. Better progress was made at the south end of the Line, where on 29 September, after an extensive artillery barrage, the 46th North Midland Division crossed the canal and broke through. By 5 October the Line had been breached from end to end. On that day the Allies took Cambrai and on 12 October, after a five-day battle, Le Cateau was recaptured.

By the end of the first week of October it had become evident that the enemy was in disarray. On 29 September, when the Hindenburg Line was broken, the German High Command had informed the Kaiser, the Chancellor, von Hertling, and the Foreign Secretary, von Hintze, that an armistice was inevitable. The sick and starving Central Powers could no longer resist. From Vienna the Austro-Hungarian Emperor, Charles I, had already appealed to President Wilson for terms; fearing the deliquescence of his realm, on 16 September the Emperor declared the Hapsburg empire a federal state. As for the Kaiser, knowing that the Allies would not conclude an armistice with the existing German regime, on 3 October he dismissed von Hertling, replacing him with Prince Max von Baden, an unfanatical pragmatist. Months earlier, on 8 January 1918, President Wilson of the United States had set out to the American Congress his 'Fourteen Points' for the restoration of peace. The Kaiser now ordered his new Chancellor to approach the President to discuss an armistice. On 4 October von Baden did so.

In Rue St Roch they hardly dared to hope. Unpleasantness might yet lie in store. On 9 October, however, Bruce allowed himself to astonish Madame Rischard:

I have amazing news: I know how interested you are in our former governess, Mademoiselle Testu! Can you guess what has happened? . . . Mademoiselle Testu is getting married![55]

It was too soon to celebrate. Fierce fighting continued in Flanders. North and east of Le Cateau, the British battled with Boehn's divisions for control of the reedy country beside the River Selle. Meanwhile, the joint force commanded by Albert of the Belgians had resumed the push towards the River Lys, the Lys Canal and the River Scheldt. His divisions did not move east unimpeded, the vigour of German resistance being sufficiently worrying for Foch to decide to send reinforcements. Roulers, a key town, was surrounded by Belgian and French forces on 15 October; on the 18th the British crossed the Lys and entered Courtrai. Although Belgian infantry reached Ostend, reclaiming the harbour and that section of coast, the enemy did not give up. Reports from Luxembourg between 22 and 24 October indicated that units of 28th Reserve Division, including foot artillery, infantry reserve and troops from the Ersatz Pioneer Battalion, were being brought up from Conflans-en-Jarnisy, their destination Ghent. At the south end of the front the French–American force inched up toward the Kriemheld Line, a key enemy position. German troops were still arriving. At Virton, Meau reported, ten trains had been received between 8 and 11 October, six of these being aviation units, and on 12 October he sent word of three trains, part of a constituted unit carrying men of the 1st Landwehr Division, coming down from Trier.

Bruce's letter to Madame Rischard predicted better times. Could this astounding news be true? By return of post, she asked for details:

Quick! Tell me the name of this phenomenon who has fixed on the virginal creature who, for so many reasons it would take too long to explain, I've always considered as a permanent old maid.[56]

The style was perfect: one long-married woman writing to another in a fever of fascinated condescension.

An engagement was not a wedding. Ludendorff was retreating but he was not yet beaten. The Allies might have to fight on to the Rhine. There must be no relaxation. The railwaymen saw there was confusion – orders in one telegram countermanding those in another, wagons accumulating in sidings, urgent shuntings and switchings – but, steadied by Meau, they continued to count, note and describe. Trains were mixed, making it hard to distinguish what they contained: cavalry, infantry, artillery, 'various'. A batch of thirty reported as moving south to Audun between 19 and 25 October carried foot and field artillery, a trench howitzer company, a telephone detachment and a veterinary hospital, all from the 241st Division. Chains of 'empties' were suddenly interrupted by late consignments of men and weapons, infantry of the 91st Division, for instance, en route north to Arlon with a howitzer company. Meau, Hansen, the Rischards and their observers did not flag, although others felt the strain. 'Herewith corrected copy of 89,' O. B. Ciphers wrote to 'Cairnesse', Paris, on 31 October. 'Error regretted, result due I fear to extreme pressure of work.'[57]

Haig's divisions were over the Selle by 25 October; on 1 November they began to move towards the Sambre. King Albert re-entered Bruges on 25 October; on the 31st he started to advance toward the long canal that ran between Bruges and Ghent, against valiant defence by German marines. Oudenaarde, a key position on the Scheldt, was taken by the Americans on 1 November. In Italy Austria was routed on 24 and 25 October; an armistice beween those powers was signed on 4 November. Bulgaria and Turkey capitulated on 30 October.

On 19 October the War Cabinet met at 10 Downing Street to discuss British conditions for an armistice. The CIGS, Sir Henry Wilson, had told Haig that in his opinion, shared by Foch, Germany should be ordered to lay down her arms and retire to the east of the Rhine. An armistice, Haig knew, was only a first step, agreement on terms for ending war as a prelude to making peace. He believed that Germany was not ready for unconditional surrender. The German army was still capable of retiring to and holding its own frontier. If there were an attempt 'to touch the honour' of the German people, they would fight with the courage of despair. Demanding conditions the enemy would not stomach could prolong the war, give Germany time to repair roads and railways as her troops fell back, and allow her army to recover over the approaching winter. Haig's recommendation to the War Cabinet was threefold:

Immediate evacuation of Belgium and occupied French territory;

Metz and Strasbourg to be at once occupied by allied armies, and Alsace-Lorraine to be vacated by the enemy;

Belgian and French rolling-stock to be returned, and inhabitants restored.

A further meeting of the War Cabinet considered naval proposals. If the German High Seas Fleet gave battle, the British Grand Fleet could defeat it entirely but at the loss of six or seven ships. An armistice should therefore require that all modern German ships be handed over to the British.

Six days later, on 25 October, Foch summoned a meeting of allied Commanders-in-Chief at his GHQ in Senlis, to discuss the framework for an armistice. Haig repeated the observations he had made in London. Pétain supported Foch's view that the enemy must surrender all ground up to the left bank of the Rhine, with bridge-heads, conditions also favoured by Pershing. Indeed, Pétain described a future in which French troops would occupy territory up to the Rhine until Germany paid an indemnity, a sum so great that payment might never be completed. Haig thought such demands a dangerous gamble.* His Intelligence Staff had empha-sized that too little was known to predict the reaction to harsh terms. Who was in charge in Germany and Austria-Hungary? Hohenzollerns and Hapsburgs? Their field-marshals and generals? Government ministers? If military commanders and civilian politi-cians supported a continuation of the war, if the German Kaiser and the Austro-Hungarian Emperor refused to accept allied condi-tions, would their subjects follow them? Hungry, destitute, robbed of fathers, sons and brothers, people still had their hills and fields,

---

* 'The enemy might not accept the terms which Foch proposed because of military necessity only – and it would be very costly and take a long time (perhaps two years) to enforce them, *unless the internal state of Germany compels* the enemy to accept them . . .', Haig, Diaries, 25 October 1918.

rivers, woods and mountains, their languages, flags and hymns. Would they hold fast to the cause for which so many had died? Or would there be revolution?

In Austria-Hungary the unravelling had begun. Despite Charles I's concessions, his empire was disintegrating. On 6 October Serbs, Croats and Slovenes declared a provisional government in 'Yugoslavia'; on the following day Poland proclaimed its freedom and independence. A Czech-Slovak government announced itself in Prague on 28 October; two days later a constituent assembly, representing the Hapsburg Emperor's German subjects, claimed the right to determine foreign policy for a new Austro-German state. On 1 November Hungary reminded the world that it was constitutionally an independent kingdom.

And Germany? 'Defend to the last' had been the order. On the battlefields of Flanders and the Meuse the rearguard action was courageous. Emboldened, Ludendorff refused to accept the terms proposed by the American President. Prince Max von Baden thereupon invited the Kaiser to choose between Ludendorff and himself. The Kaiser chose to back his Chancellor and on 26 October Ludendorff was ordered to resign. Hindenburg gave the Kaiser his resignation; the offer was declined. Three days later the Kaiser turned his back on the politicians in Berlin and joined his army at Supreme Headquarters in Spa.

He did not understand that it was the end. On 29 October news came that crews had refused to take out their ships in a 'Death Ride' to save the honour of the German navy. On 4 November the admiral at Kiel, Prince Henry of Prussia, the Kaiser's brother, fled the port in disguise. Soldiers mutinied and seized crossings over the Rhine. At Spa some talked about sending the army home to restore order but in Berlin imperial certainties were sliding away. Prince Max led the realists. He had ensured that Ludendorff's successor was not a soldier of the old school: General Groener, former sergeant in a railway transport corps, had no 'von' to his name. Having secured this appointment, Prince Max then insisted that the delegation formed to negotiate the armistice should include soldiers as well as civilians, to bind the military into whatever terms were agreed.

On 7 November a revolutionary government manifested itself in Bavaria and demanded a 'Bolshevik Free State'. In Berlin crowds swelled to the summons of Bolshevik orators, demanding a general strike. Friedrich Ebert, leader of the Majority Socialists, warned the Chancellor that if the Kaiser did not abdicate there would be revolution. Prince Max telephoned to Spa. He spoke, he said, not simply as Chancellor but as a member of the family. Abdication had, alas, become necessary to save Germany from civil war. He indicated that he himself was preparing to resign. The Kaiser was too proud – too patriotic, as he saw it – to receive his brother-in-law's advice. Abdication was out of the question. They must both do their duty. As Chancellor, Prince Max had offered an armistice; it was up to him to accept its conditions.

The German delegation already knew what was required. At Rethondes, in the forest of Compiègne, Foch had presented the Allies' terms. They were humiliating: evacuation of all occupied territory, including Alsace-Lorraine; repudiation of treaties under which Germany occupied territories she had conquered in the east; surrender of military equipment, supplies and rolling-stock; internment in allied hands of all submarines and capital ships of the High Seas Fleet; payment of reparations for war damage; military evacuation of the western bank of the Rhine and of three bridgeheads – Mainz, Koblenz and Cologne – on the eastern side; continuation of the allied blockade.

Nothing could be signed until German delegates were so instructed. But to whom were they to look for orders? The army was in such a state of indiscipline that, as he tried to carry the terms from Compiègne to Spa, Captain von Helldorf was first fired on by German troops marching on the road and then halted when they broke down the bridges on his route. Anticipating the inevitable, on 9 November Prince Max announced in Berlin that the Emperor had abdicated and the Crown Prince waived his right to the succession. Having invited Ebert to become Chancellor, Prince Max resigned. In Spa the Kaiser talked furiously of treason. Still believing he had the loyalty of the army, he summoned his chief and deputy chief of staff. Hindenburg said nothing. Across the immense distance between emperor and sergeant's son, Groener spoke. Fortified by the opinion of fifty regimental commanders, he told the Kaiser that the army wanted an armistice at the earliest possible moment. The soldier's oath of obedience, the *Fahneneid*, sworn on the regimental colours? Groener was obliged to tell the Kaiser that, today, the *Fahneneid* had become merely a form of words.

Spa was no longer a sanctuary, nor Belgium a refuge. In Brussels a procession of several thousand, preceded by a lorry filled with rifles, marched from the station to the Palais de Justice, waving red flags. In one square speakers proclaimed a republic, in another the German flag was trampled on, in a third, at the request of a German marine, the Belgian flag was hoisted over a café. Near the Stock Exchange German officers were hauled from their motors and their epaulettes torn off. In the park there were bonfires of papers and files. German soldiers sang the *Brabançonne* and the *Marseillaise*. A German captain made a speech from the balcony of the Palais de la Nation, announcing the arrest of General von Falkenhayn, governor of Belgium, as a red flag waved above. German officials begged the Spanish ambassador to help them reach the coast. At Ghent, all motor-cars having been requisitioned, they were compelled to take a cab. The ex-Kaiser was more fortunate. At five o'clock on the morning of 10 November he left Spa for Holland, with the ex-Kaiserin, the Crown Prince, Hindenburg, an entourage of forty-seven, and the archives, in the still so-called royal train and a convoy of motors.

The Allies' requirements had been telegraphed from Compiègne. At Spa Hindenburg had protested that it was physically impossible for the army to relinquish so many weapons, vehicles and supplies so quickly. From Berlin Ebert's ministers warned Foch that under such conditions Germans east of the Rhine would starve. He refused to soften the terms. Foch's attitude to the German delegates, he told Haig afterwards, was 'correct but desiccated'.[58] At 5.15 a.m. on 11 November, in Foch's railway carriage at Compiègne, the armistice was signed. It was over.

That afternoon the *Landwirt* published a late, single-page edition. Metty Finck had got out his largest type:

Deutschland eine Republik!

Annahme de Waffenstillstandsbedingungen.

Germany a Republic! Peace Terms Accepted.[59]

On the reverse side of the sheet *Letze Nachrichten* – Latest News – gave a single paragraph in modest print. A wireless message had been received at Metz from the Workers' and Soldiers' Council in Berlin. At eleven a.m., French time, on the orders of Marshal Foch, hostilities had ceased.

24

Appointment at Huîtres Prunier

Church bells rang in the Grand Duchy, sparkling wine was liberated from secret cellars. For those who knew their men would not come home it was a hollow celebration. Some 5,000 Luxembourgers had fought alongside the Allies; every parish had families who grieved or who were bracing themselves for bad news.

On 12 November the Luxembourg parliament met to consider the future. Dissociating themselves from Germany – a choice *légionnaires* and resisters had made long ago – ministers and deputies proposed, variously, independence, union with Belgium, joining up with France, a referendum. There was mention of the Grand Duchess and the Court. One speaker alluded to events in France in 1789. Outside the chamber students marched. A huge gathering of a newly formed Workers' and Peasants' Party assembled in the Place Guillaume, demanding a republican constitution. 'Hotspurs', the *Landwirt* called them, but its main article on 13 November, 'VOX POPULI VOX DEI', suggested that the paper was inclined to agree. Next day's editorial echoed the cry:

A New Dawn
Luxembourg's hour in world politics has sounded!

'Away!' the *Landwirt* proclaimed. 'Away with compromise and half measures! . . . (To be continued).'[1]

Fever in the streets, fever within. In October thousands died from influenza; the first week of November saw 771 deaths in Paris alone. Stuffy rooms, warmed by stoves, encouraged disease. Parents dared not let children leave the house and when they went out themselves, noses and mouths covered, they hurried about their business. Crowds

were breeding grounds for Bolshevism and disease. Weak governments trembled, ill-nourished bodies shivered and burned. Troop
movements accelerated infection. Hundreds of French prisoners of
war arrived at the Luxembourg station on their way home. They
were greeted with cheers, '*Moi aussi Français!*', and when the
barracks were full people took men into their homes for the night.
Algerians straggled along the road toward Sedan, relieved to have
left the misery of German camps. German conscripts, winding back
from Flanders, slept on the floor of Diekirch school. Convoys came
through night and day, lorries flying the red flag, wagons with slogans
painted on the sides: 'Home we Go!'; 'Here's the Password!';
'Reservists, Rest in Peace!' German columns marched out of the
Grand Duchy toward the frontier, drums beating, trumpets sounding,
in a brave display. Seen close, the soldiers were battered and worn.
'You're lovelier to me when you come like this!' locals jeered.[2] But
speech had been knocked out of the defeated. Only the same song,
as they went into the distance:

> . . . *Nach der Heimat, nach der Heimat,*
> *Da gibt's ein Wiedersehen* . . .

> . . . Homeward, homeward,
> There we'll meet again . . .

Alice and Gaby Schroell, now thirteen and eleven, had seen the
German troops arrive; now they watched them go. The family newspaper reverted to its ordinary role. *Lokal-Neuigkeiten* continued –
readers liked it – but the edition of 14 November carried the last
of Meau's reports. There was no further reason for Rockenbrod and
Offenheim to inspect the telegrams that went into and out of the
station master's office, no need for Diderich, Kneip and Kraus to
record what went into the sidings. Bram and friends no longer noted
signs on carriages and wagons, the uniforms of those who travelled,
numbers and letters on the guns. Madame Rischard finished her
course in French literature and Hansen went home. Dr Rischard
told Schmit that he had no time for advanced mathematics. The
Landwirt's agricultural reports being less intricate, Jeanne Schroell
no longer checked the copy every night. 'The Moth Flees the Light'

had stopped, mid-chapter, on 11 November, the joke having been superseded.

Madame Rischard received two more letters from Georgette, before the Garland family disappeared for ever. The first answered Tante Lise's questions about the governess's engagement. The happy man, Georgette replied, was a banker, known to Jacques, altogether a fortunate catch. Mademoiselle Testu's replacement, Mademoiselle Duval, charmed them all. She had sent one of Nicole's essays to an educational magazine; Tante Lise would be pleased to know that the child had been specially complimented. Mademoiselle Duval was Drake, the congratulations those he now conveyed from GHQ to the Luxembourg team. 'All 68 received up to and including 153,' Bruce's letter read:

Meilleurs compliments à tout le monde pour travail superbe . . .
Best compliments to all on splendid work, the object of special recognition by GHQ.*

The special recognition related to the reports of mid-autumn, in the anxious weeks when the Allies were pressing forward on all sections of the front. That early intelligence had been a key plank in building up GHQ's picture of Ludendorff's Order of Battle, the strength and capability of his army and his likely response. This achievement alone justified the effort they had expended.

By the time Madame Garland's final letter arrived at Boulevard Royal, the world had changed. Ludendorff had gone, the Kaiser was in Spa, allied Commanders-in-Chief were discussing terms for an armistice. Georgette's last letter was brief. She talked again of marriage, this time the wooing of Marcelle, Jacques' niece, by a young lawyer, not yet qualified. The Garlands, she said, were well, although everyone round them had the flu and Jacques was worked off his feet. By the time this message arrived, the war was over. Decoded, it gave Madame Rischard the news she most longed to hear. Her son Marcel had left the front, he was attached to the French army's legal staff, was in good health and no longer in danger.[3]

Georgette Garland was no more. It was George Bruce who next

---

* Bruce to Madame Rischard, 18 October 1918. '68' was the code-number for *Der Landwirt*; '153' the number of the edition of 9 October 1918.

wrote, not from the Garlands' imaginary home in Switzerland but from GHQ at Montreuil. The letter, *en clair* this time, was not entrusted to Madame Fresez-Settegast in Lausanne but to Charles Jubert, who was going back to his post in Luxembourg. Jubert's return gave Bruce the opportunity to send a line of greeting, congratulation and thanks:

Les renseignements que nous avons eus grâce à votre dévouement ont été d'une valeur incalculable . . . The reports we have received, thanks to your devotion, have been of incalculable value. They have contributed significantly to the triumphant outcome of our efforts, as we hoped for so long and during such difficult days.

At last he could tell her that her reports had been used not only by the British but also by French High Command.

Il vous fera, je le sais, un plaisir spécial de savoir que le haut commandement français . . . It will be a special pleasure to you, I know, to know that the French High Command, to which we sent your identifications as urgently and as promptly as they came to us, joins with us in expressing their satisfaction; the regularity of the reports has been as admirable as their exactitude.

This paragraph was the nearest that French and British Intelligence could give to a citation. Honours might come but of these nothing could be said. For non-British civilians they took months to obtain, if they were given at all.

'Cold and unfeeling' she had once called him. Since that time, chief and agent had travelled far:

A vous, Madame, à l'ami Conrad . . . To you, Madame, to our friend Conrad . . . *et à tous vos collaborateurs* . . . and all who have worked with you . . . *je dis de tout mon coeur, merci* . . . I say thank you from my heart . . .[4]

With this was another letter, in English, to be given to Conrad. Soldier to soldier, friend to friend:

My dear Baschwitz, Bravo! . . . I cannot say how much I am looking forward to seeing you and hearing all about it . . . I expect the best thing will be for you to come and see me quietly as soon as I get anywhere near you and you will be able to tell me how it will be best for me to see Madame and other friends on the spot.

It was difficult to anticipate how this was to be done. Bruce was at present with GHQ, working on arrangements for the occupation of the west bank of the Rhine. Campbell had gone home to recover from an attack of flu that had nearly killed him. Jubert could send messages out of Luxembourg in the diplomatic bag. Buckley, in charge of the office in Rue St Roch, would forward them. Meanwhile, it would be best for Meau to stay where he was.

We must remember that it is still only armistice and that there is a possibility of our work being not yet finished. It is amazing and very pleasant to be writing to you like this and under this heading. We did not foresee, those burning days in June at Souilly, that things would take this turn![5]

Bruce and Baschwitz had already discussed the unfinished business to which he alluded. Once an Armistice was signed, Meau would go into Germany. Intelligence from Berlin was wanted as background to negotiations over the terms of the peace and, looking further, there was Bolshevism. If Germany went the way of Russia, might France and Britain be next? One of Haig's generals reported that soldiers in hospitals at home and in France had been heard asking: '"Why should we have a King?", "It's very costly, etc. etc."'[6] With his fluent German, quick mind and ability to mix with every sort of person, Baschwitz was the ideal agent. He was ready – but how was he to be got to Berlin?

The success of the Luxembourg operation had brought Bruce promotion to major, six shillings extra pay per day and the ear of the head of the Intelligence Staff, General Clive. In the last week of October Bruce had asked Clive whether the Independent Air Force could drop Meau into Germany. 'I have had a long talk with Bruce,' Trenchard wrote to Clive,

who is, of course, enthusiastic, and I have gone through all the points I have gone through for the last four years again . . . Broadly speaking, if you want the man landed from an aeroplane at night, there is an 80% chance of his being injured or captured, but if he lands by a parachute from an aeroplane, there is only a 40% chance against it.

Trenchard's resources were stretched but he could not bring himself to say no. Bruce's zest and Baschwitz's courage had drawn the RAF into the ballooning scheme, reconnaissance flights, special pilots and all. Here was another glorious experiment:

I am enquiring:

a) Whether I can get an aeroplane and parachute in time.
b) Whether I can get a machine fitted with a parachute.
c) Whether I can get a machine capable of flying at night, and landing on unknown ground, as I have none.
d) If I have a pilot capable of doing it.[7]

The next moon, Trenchard advised, was the time, and before that the agent 'ought to see people dropped by an aeroplane by parachute, which I believe can only be done in England'.[8]

A second exchange of letters and Trenchard was hooked. He was pressing for both b) and c), he told Clive, 'so that we shall have two strings to our bow'.[9]

Weather and events overtook them. Storms made it impossible to fly, the collapse of the Central Powers pitched the Intelligence Staff into an even more urgent agenda. It was not easy for Bruce and Baschwitz to communicate. Madame Rischard did not wish Jubert to know that Conrad had stayed at Boulevard Royal, in case the secret escaped and made trouble in the future. German sympathizers were still about. Having sent his one letter to Baschwitz via that to Madame Rischard, Bruce dared not risk doing so again.

In the third week of November, however, American troops moved into the Grand Duchy. The Schroell girls cheered them as their trains came into Diekirch on the Ettelbrück line; Tante Lily told them they must shout Hip! Hip! Hurrä! with an umlaut. An American intelligence officer, Lieutenant Mayer, arranged for letters to be carried from Bruce and, having traced Conrad through his friends at the Casino, an American soldier delivered them. Baschwitz, meanwhile, had sent his own letter to Paris via Bontemps, the French Commandant who had taken temporary charge in Luxembourg. What did Bruce wish to be done? They were waiting *'with great impatience'* for his coming. Madame and the Doctor insisted on seeing him there and refused to let their guest go until Bruce arrived. In any case, having no identity papers, Meau was unable to travel: 'So I'll wait for you.'[10]

This letter reached Paris on 1 December. Buckley read the contents to Bruce over the telephone and a reply went off from GHQ that morning. Bruce had now to go to Spa, where an International Committee was discussing detailed plans for civil and military administration in the occupied part of Germany. As soon as he was released, he said, he would come to Luxembourg as fast as he could. Buckley also sent a line to his 'dear old Meau'. The escaping expert had lost none of his verve: 'It was simply top hole to see your writing again . . . I am putting aside half a case of fizz to celebrate our meeting . . .'[11] Everyone was fit and Campbell had written to say that he was now strong enough to walk three and a half miles a day.

So complicated were Bruce's travels at this time that going to Luxembourg was out of the question. After Spa he returned to Abbeville. Not wishing to keep Baschwitz waiting in the Grand Duchy – 'You must be longing to get back to Brussels to see your people' – he spoke to Drake. There was no difficulty; General Clive himself wished to meet the hero.[12] Buckley saw to Meau's attire. Leche, the intelligence officer in Rouen, kept a stock of British army insignia and in two days a captain's badges and buttons were on Buckley's desk (total cost, frs. 38.50).[13]* Through Mayer, Baschwitz was brought back to Paris. To his astonishment he was put into British uniform, congratulated and informed that for his outstanding work behind the lines he had been invested with the DSO. That was on 11 December. On 17 December Baschwitz left Paris on the 9.30 a.m. train. Six months, less one day, after they had parted at Souilly, he and Bruce were reunited.

In days they were in Cologne, on orders from Drake, making ready for the installation of the army of occupation. Travel was restricted, vehicles and petrol being hard to find, even for those working on the staff of the military governor. By the end of January, however, Baschwitz and Bruce had made a number of useful friends. The information they acquired went straight to GHQ, evidence, Drake wrote afterwards, which suggested that the old German intelligence apparatus, still intact, was busily at work, its principal object 'the promotion of Bolshevism

* £36.30.

and Separation'. This was not a surprise. The special contribution of Bruce and Baschwitz was to supply names and whereabouts of agents. Having been tracked and watched, these 'suspects and undesirables', as Drake put it, were taken into custody.[14]

The arresting was done by Tangye, who came to Cologne at the end of February. Bruce moved back to GHQ, taking Menzies' place on the Intelligence Staff; Baschwitz returned to Brussels. On 15 March the Permit Office was closed. After three years of hard use, the type-writer keys were erratic; in jumpy type Staff Sergeant Quick, who had replaced the Secretariat, made out the petty cash account. Debits: 3 francs outstanding for gas, the gas company having credited 10 francs as a refund of the original deposit; 6 francs, 75 centimes for electric light. Credits: 3 francs from the sale of old stamp handles, the stamps themselves having been removed. The balance remaining, 93 francs, 25 centimes, was transmitted to Colonel Drake. Monsieur Baud took back his building and, having inspected it, put in a claim via the Paris Area Rent Office for 953 francs, 22 centimes for dilapidations.[15]

To conclude, a small luncheon party was arranged at Prunier's Oyster House in Rue Duphot, the street that leads up from Rue St Honoré to the Madeleine.* Jubert brought Madame Rischard to Paris by train. It was a fine feast:

Les Huîtres

Oeufs brouillés aux Truffes

Poulet Rôti
Pommes Chipped
Petits Pois à la Française
Salade

Mousse Chocolat
Petits Fours

Vins:
Savenières 1911
Ch. Lafite 07

* Although this restaurant still exists, its archives have been destroyed. The exact date of the luncheon party is therefore, alas, unknown.

The celebratory luncheon

They were thirteen. All signed the menu: Georgette, Nicole, L. G. Campbell, R. J. Drake, A. Dorgebray, R. S. Barnes [a code-name?], Charles [Jubert], Francis R. Verdon, H. H. MacColl, P. Wallner, L. Rischard, V. D. Done, A. B. Meau.

The menu is illustrated with the portrait of the oyster-carrier, depicted on tiles inside the entrance to the restaurant.

25

What Became of Them All?

The War Office Secret Service was officially dissolved in April 1919. Wallinger, now head of the British Military Intelligence Commission in Brussels, closed the accounts and tidied up the papers. For the record, Drake summarized the history of I(b)'s field operations from January 1917, when he took over from Kirke, to the end. The total number of agents employed by the GHQ Service in the war was, he said, roughly 6,000. The fate of some was still in doubt, shortage of transport having delayed the work of tracing them. Of the 6,000, 91 were known to have been caught and executed, 4 to have died in prison before execution, 2 to have been shot and 1 electrocuted while crossing the frontier. Six hundred had been imprisoned, 19 of whom had been sentenced for life, 25 for an indeterminate period, 10 deported. They had worked either for nothing or for remuneration that, in Drake's view, was in most cases 'absurdly small'.[1]

The Luxembourg service was fortunate. No one was arrested, no agent lost. The only casualty was Bram's house. The scheme had been meticulously planned, the participants scrupulously careful. All were lucky, even with the wind. Drake described the operation as one of the most successful pieces of intelligence work known to him, 'from an S.S. point of view':

Thanks to the spade work performed by Madame Rischard and to certain improvements in the code which past experience in communicating with her had suggested, Lieutenant Meau was able to set up the best train watching service, as far as the reporting of results goes, which had up to that time been established . . .[2]

For all Cameron's anxieties, the cost of the Luxembourg operation hardly dented the Secret Service budget. The largest sum paid out by Madame Rischard was 11,000 francs for newsprint. Hansen's fee and Bram's expenses brought the total to 19,085 francs. Balloon training and equipment, lorries and hydrogen were not charged directly to the Paris Office, nor were Meteor's services. Reconnaissance flights and special pilots must have been expensive; again, these costs were not taken from Bruce's budget. When the accounts were finally closed in May 1919, Bruce sent Wallinger a cash balance of 6,002 francs, five centimes, plus a nominal amount of 131 Belgian francs, written off as valueless, being German issue.[3]

Wallinger also asked for a sample of the office records:

Attached are:
1. Short statement of the work of the Paris GHQ office.
2. Account of Luxemburg service with 2 maps.
3. History of the Paris office codes with the following enclosures:
   a) Code A.
   b) Graphs.
   c) 3 copies of the *Landwirt* with sample messages decoded.[4]

Having weeded the files, Bruce kept the remaining documents, maps, letters and *Landwirts*. This was contrary to rules.

After much correspondence and difficult negotiation, the following honours were awarded:

Madame Rischard:	CBE
Dr Rischard:	OBE
Hansen, Offenheim and Rockenbrod:	MBE
Diderich, Kraus, Kneip, Bram and Schmit:	Medal of the British Empire Order
Miss Done and Mademoiselle Dorgebray:	MBE
Chocqueel, Dugenet and Renaud:	Military Cross

Father Cambron accepted no worldly honours. He came to London, was received by Menzies and had a jovial evening with MacColl.

Chocqueel returned to Bergues to practise law. He was elected

Mayor and, as a result of his efforts, his town, reconstructed, looked as pleasing as before.

Mademoiselle Dorgebray, wooed by at least one British officer, decided to remain in France.

Woolrych founded an Association, with the aim of reuniting secret service colleagues at an annual dinner. The Wallinger brothers were among its most faithful members.

Campbell came back to London, bringing Bruce's gramophone; its music, mislaid en route, turned up in the Lost Property Office at Victoria Station. He also rescued Chocqueel's mandolin, found in a packing case in 41 Rue St Roch. Campbell's present to himself was a new rifle, taken on to the boat in a bag of golf clubs, confiscated by the police and retrieved by his colleagues in 'I'. His intention, he told Bruce, was to celebrate the end of the war with fishing, shooting and other country pursuits.

Buckley returned to The Queen's College at the University of Oxford, where his studies and sports had been interrupted in 1914. He played with 'the best College Rugger XV' and got a pass degree.

Fuller returned from Evian to practise at the Bar.

Tangye was promoted to Major, General Staff Officer 2, 'the odds against', he told Bruce delightedly, having at one time seemed overwhelming.

In 1924 Cameron, the balance of his mind disturbed, shot himself in his rooms at army headquarters.

Drake remained in intelligence. His official report on the work of I(b) was eventually released by the Public Record Office and published on the internet.[5] This would have surprised him.

Kirke survived the war and afterwards, as 'Mervyn Lamb', published a romantic thriller, *On Hazardous Service*.[6] He was recalled to the army in 1933.

Jubert returned to the Grand Duchy and the International Federation of Bicyclists.

Wallner took advantage of a new law, obliging French police officers to retire at fifty-six, and set up a detective agency with Béliard. Delicate representations from Bruce ensured that, before Wallner left the Ministry of War, it was agreed that young Huss could be sent home to his father.

Hansen was at last able to concentrate on schoolmastering and his writing. He was stunned to find that he had been working for the British, rather than the French, but shock soon turned to pride.

Schroell came back to Luxembourg in December 1918. Surprised at how independent his wife and daughters had become, he eventually moved into a separate house. In 1920, at Mollard's urging, Jeanne Schroell was presented with a silver medal of honour by the French Foreign Ministry. The *Landwirt* and the Diekirch press were sold in 1925 to Emile Schumacher, who amalgamated the newspaper with a liberal daily, the *Luxemburger Nationalzeitung*.

In March 1919 Madame Rischard and Baschwitz Meau were introduced as *Chevaliers* into the *Légion d'Honneur* on the recommendation of Marshal Foch. Three months later, the Rischards, Hansen, Offenheim, Rockenbrod, Diderich and Bram were presented to General Weygand, Deputy French Commander-in-Chief, on a hot day – Madame Rischard held her parasol erect – in Place Guillaume in Luxembourg. A guard of honour stood alongside. All received British decorations and French medals, in Madame Rischard's case the *Croix de Guerre*, with Palm.

These excitements over, the Rischards resumed their quiet life at 20 Boulevard Royal, their chief delight being excursions to the cinema, with the dog. (It liked jumping on the flap-up seat.) When Camille died in 1939, Madame Rischard moved to an apartment in Rue de Longwy. In early 1940, fearing a German invasion, she destroyed her records of the Luxembourg operation. Conscious of her increasing frailty, she confided her story to her nephew, Charles-Edouard, a young doctor, who later worked with the Luxembourg resistance. Lise Rischard died in February. The German authorities had noticed the awards made to Madame Rischard and her colleagues in 1919. On 10 May 1940 German troops came to find her and her files. They were too late.

They also looked for former Assistant Station Master Rockenbrod. As he had left Luxembourg in May 1940, they arrested his son, telling him that Germany had lost the last war as a result of what his father had done. Hearing that his son had been taken to the Grund prison in Luxembourg, the elder Rockenbrod came home and gave himself up. The two were released after a week, on condition that they paid regular visits to Gestapo headquarters.

Madame Schroell was another who received a visit from the Germans. They were looking for Paul, but he had died at the end of 1939. Jeanne had given refuge to a Jewish family and in 1942 she, Alice and Gaby were taken away and interned in a series of camps, eight in all. Throughout their exile she carried, secreted in a small packet, the letter in which Mollard had told her that the French government wished to honour her. When she and her daughters came back to Luxembourg in 1944, gaunt and ragged, they found that Aunts Maisy and Lily, sixty-five and sixty-seven years of age, had been harbouring a Canadian aviator in the attic, despite the presence of a German officer who had taken over the ground and first floors of the house.

In March 1919 Madame Garland's preoccupation with affiancings and romance was seen in a new light, when the engagement was announced between Major Bruce and Miss Dorothy Done. 'Of course I guessed,' said Bruce's sister Jean, who had read between the lines of his letters. Buckley had suspected it for months: 'I suppose Campbell, the sly old dog, was in the know all the time.'[7] Chocqueel wrote a charming letter of congratulation, depicting, '*dans le royaume hypothétique*', a wedding procession to Eglise St Roch, Mademoiselle Testu keeping everyone in order.[8] The marriage took place in June 1919, with Campbell as best man.

Baschwitz Meau returned to Africa to manage an import/export business in Dar es Salaam. In 1936 he was told that he did not qualify for a Belgian war pension as his service at the front had lasted only eighteen days. He explained that for the remainder of the war he had been in prison, on the run, at Wulveringhem, and attached to British Intelligence. The Belgian authorities denied this last claim. He had been on unpaid leave, they said, having resigned his officer's commission. Bruce wrote letters, Major Neefs, Meau's friend at Wulveringhem, testified to the discussion that had led to Meau's conversation with Athlone. The record of Meau's service was produced; Foch and Haig were cited in support. The pension was paid.

When the affair was concluded, Baschwitz came to London. The Balfours of Burleigh (as George and Dorothy now were) and their six children lived at that time at No. 31 Bedford Gardens and also at 29 and 33, acquired as the family expanded, the whole establishment being connected by voice-pipe. Robert, eleven, had eyes only for Baschwitz Meau, the man who had escaped five times from German prisoner-of-war camps, had been sent, alone, into enemy territory in a balloon, and was now entering the sitting room in No. 31.

Baschwitz Meau, the boy thought, was surprisingly small. He was thin and lithe, like a cat. His eyes were bright, he had black curly hair and a stylish moustache. In the excitement no one noticed that the visitor had chosen a chair with a missing castor. Gracefully, Baschwitz sat down. The chair tipped slightly. Baschwitz made a small adjustment, rebalanced. Back straight, no change of expression, he gave no hint that anything was amiss. Robert watched, fascinated. The chair remained steady, Baschwitz unruffled. He conversed, drank tea, inclined his head, laughed, all the while balancing on three legs, until with an elegant manoeuvre he rose to go.

'So typical of Baschwitz,' said the former Miss Done.

They did not see him again. When it seemed that another war was likely, Balfour wrote to ask Baschwitz whether he could help him with a new mission. The Belgian longed to work with his old chief but could not leave his job in Africa. After 1939 he vanishes.

There was always something magical about Baschwitz Meau.

Epilogue

In later life Major Bruce alluded only rarely to his time in the Paris Office. When Baschwitz Meau came to tea at Bedford Gardens in 1937, the children were aware that the visitor, a secret agent, who had been sent in a balloon across German lines, had been a colleague of their parents in the last war. They knew, too, about the saucer of milk into which their father had stepped when he first came to the office in Paris where their mother was working. About the work itself, they had little idea, except that it had been something to do with spying on enemy trains in the Luxembourg marshalling yard.

Another glimpse came in 1947, at the railway station in Lausanne. To celebrate the end of the more recent war and release from confinement at home, the Balfours of Burleigh, as George and Dorothy Bruce had by then become, arranged to take the four younger children for a winter sporting holiday in Switzerland. They reached Geneva in time for the afternoon train to Sierre and the mountains. It was strange to be chugging along the lakeside, in a carriage unlike the ones at home, full of ruddy-cheeked people with stout boots, stranger still to hear announcements in German and French. But the most remarkable declaration was the one their father made as the train drew into Lausanne: it was here, he said, on this very platform, that he had got out; *here* he repeated, standing with his children outside the station, looking over the concourse, while Dorothy, who prudently remained in the compartment, watched the station clock, that he had realized that he was being followed.

'How did you know you were being followed?'

'You know when you are being followed. Someone behind you

stops and starts when you do. Up that alley, that's where I went to throw him off . . .'

'How did you throw him off?'

'Dodged through the streets, over that side of the square, sometimes doubling back, till I was sure.'

'How did you know you'd thrown him off?'

They saw their father's tall, lean figure. Had he worn the grey 'plus twos' he had brought for skiing?

Mother: 'PLEASE get into the train.'

What had he been doing in Lausanne? Why had he been followed? Further questions were deflected. Discussion would disturb their mother, who had fallen asleep. The last five years had taught the young people not to talk carelessly in railway carriages and in any case the early start, the burst of cold air on the platform, the warm compartment, had made them all too sleepy for conversation.

The story was locked away. More precisely, it had been locked in a narrow Victorian cabinet, five feet high, its ten drawers secured by a hinged wooden flap with a Bramah spring-loaded lock. The cabinet stood in 'B of B's' bedroom in his house in Scotland. Once, in the mid-1960s, he showed his son Robert its contents: yellowing files, bundles of letters, photographs, maps.

'The espionage mission,' he said. 'Meau insisted on taking off, although the wind kept changing. No word for days. It was one of the worst weeks of my life. The balloon was picked up in the sea.' In the cabinet was a complete run of copies of the *Landwirt*, the newspaper, Bruce said, in which coded messages had been inserted. One file contained a description of the code. It looked, Robert thought, a Girl Guide sort of effort – A=1, B=2, etc. – but these were perhaps only the *Principes Généraux*, as it said at the top of the page.

An hour with the documents and they had to go. The files were replaced, the flap closed, the cabinet locked.

Robert's father died in 1967. Papers were sorted but the key to the cabinet had been lost so no one bothered with that. Now and again, as the years passed, historians wrote to ask whether Robert had any documents relating to the First World War. One persistent inquirer told him to force the lock with a jemmy. 'If he has no respect for furniture,' Robert observed, 'how can I trust him with papers?'

He did nothing until, in 1991, his eldest sister Lætitia drew his attention to an advertisement, placed by Mr George Olifent, locksmith, in the *Law Society Gazette*. Mr Olifent hoped to hear from solicitors, entrusted by long-dead clients with keys to deed boxes and safes. He wanted keys of any shape or size, to augment his stock of spares. Robert wrote post-haste. He had quantities of keys of varying antiquity, and might be able to help. Furthermore, Mr Olifent might be able to help him. Could the cabinet be opened without damage to the wood? 'It is full of papers on a subject about which there is no urgency, but which we would like to get at.'

From his office, 'The Keyhole', Mr Olifent answered by return. This type of cabinet was called a Wellington Chest. 'Try all your keys again . . . Once the strength of the spring has been ascertained, try turning the keys with minimum force at varying depths in the lock . . .' If no good, 'carefully wedge or hold the locking flap . . . Protecting the woodwork with thin card or similar, take a piece of hacksaw blade and saw through the link-plate. Remove lock and link-plate and send them to us for repair and a key . . .'

'Dear Mr Olifent,' Robert replied. 'Brilliant! . . . I entirely understand, having had some early training at filing and fitting;* I shall carry out your instructions at once.'

But there were many keys to try and, if they failed, it would be a shame to take a hacksaw to the brass. There was no urgency. Linkplate and lock were not removed.

On a fine Easter morning in 1995 a shaft of sun suddenly struck the Wellington Chest. From the attic Robert brought a box of keys, two hundred or so, many of them rusty. Some had metal tags: 'Metropolitan Water Supply' (from 31 Bedford Gardens); 'Kit Bag' (which war?). Some had cloth labels: 'Key of Safe in Library at Kennet' (demolished long ago); 'D. H. Garage Yellow Key. Doesn't Work'.**

---

* Holidays among the sawdust in the joiner's workshop at home and later an apprenticeship at the English Electric Company.

** 'D. H.' was 'Dark Horse', a Ford Consul, given by the staff of Lloyd's Bank – maximum subscription one shilling each – when the former Major Bruce, now Lord Balfour of Burleigh, retired as chairman. It was named after the employees' magazine.

Robert and I selected the Bramah keys that might fit. The first was too large, the second too small. This would take hours. The third had a circular brass tag: 'No. 94'. Too stiff. But no. Surely not? Robert coaxed the lock, as Mr Olifent had advised. The spring yielded, the key turned. What if the drawers were empty? But if empty, why locked?

The flap moved back on its hinge and we opened the drawers. There it all was: envelopes, files, the *Landwirt*, and, on the top, a photograph of Baschwitz Meau.

That autumn, having listed names and places that appeared in the documents, we went to Luxembourg. People were helpful – at 20 Boulevard Royal, now an hotel, at the Rockenbrod estate agency, at the station – but the most important discovery began with the telephone directory. Various Rischards were listed, one a doctor. We rang, mentioned Captain Bruce. 'I think you would like to see my husband. Can you come at two?'

Waiting outside the house was an elderly man, looking eagerly along the street. We got out of the car, he came forward, put his hand on Robert's arm, said – who could forget it? – '*Êtes-vous le fils de Rose ou de Réséda?*'

'*Je suis le fils de Rose.*'

Without another word, Dr Rischard took us inside. On a table were glasses and a bottle of champagne. He had waited fifty-five years to tell us his aunt's story.

There were to be other meetings with other descendants of those who took part in the Luxembourg scheme: Schroells, Hansens, Chocqueels. Let us finish with these last.

A damp afternoon in a little château at West Cappel, near Bergues. In the churchyard next door, the graves of men of the Welsh Guards, who died defending the château in 1940, during the retreat to Dunkerque. Inside, unwarmed by a fire that disappeared up a huge chimney, Jean Chocqueel's grandson, Abbé Delplanque, Jean's great-niece, Maud, and her niece, Béatrice. In the cellar of this château, while the Welsh Guards fought outside, Jean Chocqueel had distracted his grandchildren by telling them the story of his adventures in the Great War. 'You must write it out for us,' they said. Chocqueel's records were destroyed as the Germans came through Bergues in 1940 but after the war he had done as his grandchildren had asked. *Evasion 1915*, Chocqueel's account of his adventures during and after the siege of Lille, was finished in 1954. There was no supporting evidence, he warned his readers. But he gave them his word that the story of the escape from Lille was not a myth, nor the Luxembourg scheme a fiction.

He did not know that Captain Bruce had kept the files. Evidence existed, just enough.

Appendix

A Private Language

Those interested in codes may like to look more closely at the scheme designed for the Luxembourg operation.

First, the concepts. Bruce and Campbell drew up a list of twenty key subjects in which they were interested: 'Section of line and two dates', for example, or 'Description of Uniforms'. Taking their twenty numbers, from 1 to 19, plus 0, they assigned a number to each of the twenty subjects. Thus: 'Section of line and two dates' was Subject 3 ('*Sujet* 3'), and 'Description of Uniforms' was Subject 10 ('*Sujet* 10').

Each number was matched to a letter of the alphabet, in order: A = 1, B = 2, and so on.

'Subject 3', that is, 'Section of line and two dates', was thus represented by 'Statement C' ('*Enoncé* C').

'Subject 10', that is, 'Description of Uniforms', was represented by 'Statement L' ('*Enoncé* L').

These twenty main subjects and their corresponding letters were the first steps in building the vocabulary of the code.

Next, the first rule of grammar. The sender of the message could write a text on any topic that seemed appropriate, the weather, for instance, or fashions in hats. The first letter of the first word of the first line would indicate the subject of the hidden message, using the basic vocabulary.

Thus:

'<u>C</u>old winds this week',[†] or '<u>C</u>*hapeaux ronds sont à la mode*',[†] would indicate that the subject of the hidden message was C, 'Section of line and two dates'.

[†] These and subsequent examples marked with a dagger have been constructed by the author.

'Low cloud tonight',[†] or '*Luxe partout*',[†] would indicate that subject was **L**, that is, 'Description of Uniforms'.

Under each of the twenty main subject headings, the sender of the message would give items of subsidiary information.

A message concerning 'Section of line and two dates', for example, would be expected to include the names of the stations at each end of the section of line; the date on which the sender made the observation; the date on which the message was sent.

Bruce and Campbell listed, for each of the twenty main subjects, all relevant subsidiary information, broken down into separate statements. Each statement was given a number, each number matched to its corresponding letter.

Take railway stations and places where observers might be posted: Arlon was 1, that is, **A**; Libramont was 6, that is, **F**.

A line of text beginning with **A** indicated Arlon; one beginning with **F** indicated Libramont.

A grammatical rule dealt with the order in which places were given, indicating, for instance, the direction in which trains were seen to be travelling:

A, then **F** = from Arlon to Libramont.

Dates needed special treatment, as the numbering system went only from 1 to 19. How were dates between 20 and 31 to be accommodated?

Bruce set out the solution in a handwritten annotation: '*Au lieu de la vraie date il est par conséquent convenu qu'on donne le nombre obtenu par la soustraction faite entre la date du mouvement et celle du jour où on écrit le rapport.*' ('In place of the actual date, the number given is that obtained by subtracting the date of the [observed] movement [of the train] and the date on which the report is written.')

If the report were dated the **25th**, for example, and trains had been seen to leave Arlon on the **22nd**, subtraction would give the date of departure from Arlon as **3**, that is, **C**. This would be the first letter of the first word of the relevant line of text.

But with only twenty numbers (1 to 19, plus 0), and twenty-five matching letters (**A** to **Z**, excluding **W**), how was the sender of the hidden message to deploy them, so that a main subject would not be confused with a subsidiary subject or one subsidiary subject with another?

For instance, C represented 'Section of lines and two dates' (main subject) but also 'Bettembourg', a station on the line (subsidiary subject).

And under the main subject heading 'Description of Uniforms', indicated by L, came grey (subsidiary subject), third in the list of possible colours, that is, 3, also expressed as C.

This was why rules of grammar were essential. A limited number of letters could be used to represent a very large number of main subjects and subsidiary subjects, as long as the users of the code – senders and recipients of messages – kept strictly to an agreed order.*

For each main subject, therefore, subsidiary information was to be given in an order firmly set out in the rules. Having announced, as the first letter of the first word of the first line of text, the subject C, for instance, 'Section of line and two dates', the second line would *always* deal with the first station or observation post, the third with the second station or post, the fourth with the date of departure of a train, the fifth with its date of arrival.

Madame Rischard's exercises give examples:

PREMIER EXEMPLE:

L'information à transmettre porte sur:

Le secteur LIBRAMONT–CARIGNAN.
La date du mouvement observé dans ce secteur est celle du 12.
Le rapport est daté du 13.

---

* There is a parallel in the conventions relating to campaign ribbons. Information about campaigns in which a soldier has fought is given not just through the *colours* of the ribbon stitched on to his uniform but also through the *arrangement* of colours in stripes of varying widths. An onlooker may read the information represented by a succession of coloured stripes; for the reading to be correct, wearer and onlooker must each apply the same set of rules. If Captain Bruce had seen a ribbon striped red, green, red, for instance, he would have known that the wearer had served with the British and Indian armies in the 1878–80 Afghan Campaign; blue, white, blue, white, blue would have told him that the wearer had seen service in the 1882–9 Egyptian Campaign.

Enoncé	B	la 1ère ligne commencera par	B
LIBRAMONT	6	la 2me ligne commencera par	F
CARIGNAN	4	la 3me ligne commencera par	D
Date du mouvement	1	la 4me ligne commencera par	A

Madame Rischard wished to send a simple message about 'Section of line and a date'. The first line of text indicates that everything that follows in the next three lines will be about statement **B**. The first letters of the first words of the second and third lines therefore indicate the stations at which observations were made, Libramont, **F**, and Carignan, **D**, showing also the direction in which the train was going. The date of the observed movement being the 12th and of the report the 13th, subtraction according to Bruce's system gives 1, expressed as **A**, employed as the first letter of the first word of the fourth line.

The simple message that a train was observed moving from Libramont to Carignan on the 12th could then be hidden in a letter about something quite different. Like this:

Beer is unavailable. Alas, it goes so well with
Food. However, we must make do with Father
Daudet's cider. This is delicious, as for some reason
Apples ripened early but did not fall off the trees.[†]

It is unlikely that an unschooled reader would see that there is a hidden announcement here. Only those who have the key may read it.

Next, there might be a more complex message, concerning not just the movement but also the components of a constituted unit. The Paris Office wished to know the exact composition of the long serpent of trains that made up each constituted unit: how many trains there were and what each one carried. Relevant information was listed and, again, set out in an agreed order.

Five lines of text were reserved for this. Having stated the subject, 'Movement of constituted units', signified by **D**, the second line *always* gave the 'Number of trains carrying artillery batteries', the third *always* the 'Number of trains carrying cavalry squadrons', the fourth *always* the 'Number of trains carrying infantry battalions', and the fifth and last *always* 'Various'.

Where there were no trains in a particular category, this was *always* declared using o, so that all five reserved lines of text were utilized. Zero was represented by one of the six letters of the alphabet less frequently used in French, so the absence of trains in any category would be shown by beginning the first word of the relevant line with **H, K, V, X, Y** or **Z**.

A more difficult exercise for Madame Rischard thus went like this:

EXEMPLE:

L'information à transmettre porte sur le passage de:
8 trains transportant des batteries.
o trains transportant des escadrons.
15 trains transportant des bataillons.
6 trains transportant divers.

Enoncé	D	la 1ère ligne commencera par	D
Batteries	8	la 2me ligne commencera par	I
Escadrons	o	la 3me ligne commencera par une des lettres égales à o	(H, K, V, X, Y, Z)
Bataillons	15	la 4me ligne commencera par	Q
Divers	6	la 5me ligne commencera par	F

Embedded in an innocent text about, say, a plague of cockchafers, the above message would appear like this:

D̲rame au village.
I̲nvasion des insectes, les
H̲annetons énormes.
Q̲uels cris d'horreur des
F̲emmes terrifiées.†

The procedure for encoding was thus quite simple. Once the subject of the message had been identified, relevant items of information listed in the agreed order and each item assigned its correct letter, the sender of the message need do no more than concoct a text in which the first word of each successive line began with the appropriate letter.

To decode the text, the recipient simply identified the subject, by means of the first letter of the first word of the first line of text, and then, taking the first letter of the first word, line by line, read off places, dates, numbers, types of train, and so on.

ANOTHER USE FOR PUNCTUATION

As it was likely that one message would cover a number of subjects, each main subject and the relevant subsidiary information had to be separated from the next in a way that was obvious to the recipient of the message.

Each main subject, plus its subsidiary information, was described by Bruce and Campbell as a 'phrase' and its beginning and end were indicated by using various punctuation marks: a stop, a semi-colon, an exclamation mark, a question mark or a new paragraph. Other punctuation marks – a comma, a colon or a dash – had no hidden meaning.

Take messages about the composition of constituted units:

Trains and their contents were categorized in one of three ways:
'Usual', Subject F.
'Less Usual', Subject G.
'Unusual', Subject I.

Under all three of these main subjects, subsidiary subjects were listed, numbered as always from 1 to 19 plus 0.

In each category the first six subsidiary subjects were the same:

Bavarian,	1.
Landwehr,	2.
Reserves,	3.
Having a single-digit identifying number,	4.
Having a double-digit identifying number,	5.
Having a three-digit identifying number,	6.

Under main subject F, 'Usual', came further subsidiary subjects:

Regiment, for instance, was 11.
Field Artillery, 13.
Foot Artillery, 14.

Cavalry, 15.
Landsturm, 18.
Saxon, 19.

Under main subject **G**, 'Less Usual', were, for example:

Fusiliers, 7.
Light Horse, 13.
Uhlans, 0. (These were the regiments with the deaths' head cockades.)

Main subject **I**, 'Unusual', included:

Veterinary Hospital, 10.
Motor Transport Column, 17.
Telephone Detachment, 19.

More difficult exercises could thus be performed by Madame Rischard:

PREMIER EXEMPLE:

L'information à transmettre porte sur:
Le passage du 13ème Régiment bavarois d'artillerie de campagne.

Enoncé	*F*	*la 1ère ligne commencera par*	F
Bavarois	*1*	*la 2me ligne commencera par*	A
Artillerie de campagne	*13*	*la 3me ligne commencera par*	O
Régiment	*11*	*la 4me ligne commencera par*	M
Numéro composé de deux			
chiffres	*5*	*la 5me ligne commencera par*	E
Le chiffre 13	*13*	*la 6me ligne commencera par*	O

DEUXIÈME EXEMPLE:

L'information à transmettre porte sur:
Le passage de l'hôpital vétérinaire Numéro 1.

Enoncé	*I*	*la 1ère ligne commencera par*	I
Hôpital vétérinaire	*10*	*la 2me ligne commencera par*	L
Numéro de 2 chiffres	*5*	*la 3me ligne commencera par*	E
Le chiffre 10	*10*	*la 4me ligne commencera par*	L

Punctuation was added.

Ending an introductory sentence with a dash indicated that it was not part of the coded message.

The next passage, ending with a full stop, contained the first, six-line, message.

Then came another sentence, ending with a semi-colon, to indicate another sentence with no coded message.

The four lines ended with an exclamation mark, showing that this hid another coded message.

The two messages encoded above, about the Bavarian Field Artillery and the Veterinary Hospital, might thus be concealed in news about the younger generation.

They do grow up so quickly –
Frederick at seventeen is
Already six foot three and
On Monday starts work at a
Motor repair shop although he's not much of an
Engineer and his mother is wondering how to get
Oil off blue overalls.
Luckily your uncle's car is looked after somewhere else;
I'm surprised that with so
Little training Frederick can get a job in an
Establishment where he might be let
Loose on these expensive cars![†]

The main subject list included a quick method of indicating that a section of text contained no hidden message. Subject **M** was employed here. When a phrase began with **M**, the reader could disregard all text as far as the next full stop.

The above examples look odd but, conveniently, Madame Rischard's reports were transmitted in German, in which nouns are capitalized.

FULL OR EMPTY TRAINS, MOVING OR STANDING STILL?

Separation of text into 'phrases' allowed further sophistication. Twenty main subjects were really too few to cover all the topics in which Bruce was interested.

For instance, Madame Rischard might wish to report movement of a constituted unit, the number of trains and their composition, Subject 4, Statement D. Or she might wish to report movement of a constituted unit made up of empty trains, Subject 5, Statement E. How would she label a constituted unit that was standing still? Or a constituted unit of empty trains that was standing still?

Bruce and Campbell had to be able to expand the list of main subjects. As the numbers available ran only from 1 to 19, plus 0, sub-sets, 1a, 1b, 1c, and so on, were required. These were introduced in the following way:

As explained above, each main subject was assigned a predetermined number of lines. Five, for example, were set aside for a report on movement and composition of a constituted unit, subject 4, statement D.

Where the first letter of the first word of the first line was D, therefore, followed by *four* lines of information, the recipient of the message would know that the subject was the movement and composition of a constituted unit. This was now referred to as 4a.

If, however, the first word of the first line of a 'phrase' began with D, but the phrase continued with a number of lines *other* than four, the recipient would know that the subject was *not* 4a. In this example, according to the expanded table a number of lines other than four, following D, would indicate that the subject was 4b, representing a constituted train that was standing still.

The table of main subjects could thus be expanded, as long as the sender kept conscientiously to the agreed number of lines required to cover subsidiary items of information covered by each main subject. Careful separation of each phrase, using appropriate punctuation, was therefore vital.

EPAULETTES, ESCUTCHEONS AND GRENADES

Some 'phrases' could be very long. For example, the number of lines of text assigned to 'Description of Uniforms', L, required a minimum of eleven lines, fifteen if there was a three-digit regimental number.

Madame Rischard's instructions set out an extensive list of identifying features, *always* to be reported in the prescribed order.

Description of Uniforms   L
Colour of cap band
Nationality of cockade
Does the neckband bear an escutcheon?
Colour of epaulette
Piping of epaulette
Does the epaulette bear a crown?
Does the epaulette bear a single grenade, two grenades, or none?*
Does the epaulette bear a monogram?
Colour of insignia on the epaulette
Number on the epaulette

The last item, the regimental number on the epaulette, could take several lines of text: one line to indicate that the observer had seen, say, a three-digit regimental number; three subsequent lines to give each of the three digits, in order.

The list of colours had also to be memorized, in order. White, for instance, was 1; Grey, 4; Red, 7; Green, 8. Other features were similarly listed: '*Badois*' (from Baden), 9; Bavarian, 10; Prussian, 11; Saxon, 12; '*Wurtembourgeois*', 13. This was complicated by the fact that, under other main subject headings, F, for example, applying to trains of a 'Usual' nature, Bavarian was 1, Saxon was 19, and '*Wurtembourgeois*' 0.

Madame Rischard was expected to learn each '*Enoncé*' and then, by rote, the list of subsidiary subjects applying to it. Hard work for someone whose schooldays had ended thirty years before.

* From Bruce's and Campbell's instructions, typed by Mademoiselle Dorgebray in French. '*Grenade*' is here translated as 'grenade', rather than its identical twin, 'pomegranate'.

Another of Madame Rischard's practice messages concerned a soldier wearing the cockade of a Prussian regiment, with blue epaulettes, bearing the number 270, with white piping, no escutcheon on the neckband, and no other features observed. Characteristics not seen are *always* given a line, '*non vue*'.

EXEMPLE:

L'information à transmettre porte sur:
Un uniforme de cocarde prussienne
Ayant la patte d'épaules: bleue
Le numéro 270
Le liséré de la patte d'épaules: blanc
Aucun écusson au col
Aucun autre point à signaler

Enoncé	**L**	*la 1ère ligne commencera par*	**L**
Couleur de la bande de bonnet			
	non vue	*la 2me ligne . . .*	**H, K, W, X, Y, Z**
Nationalité de la cocarde			
	prussienne 11	*la 3me ligne . . .*	**M**
Couleur de la patte d'épaules			
	bleue 2	*la 4me ligne . . .*	**B**
Liséré de la patte d'épaules			
	blanc 1	*la 5me ligne . . .*	**A**
Couronne	**non vue**	*la 6me ligne . . .*	**H, K, W, X, Y, Z**
Grenade de la patte d'épaules			
	non vue	*la 7me ligne . . .*	**idem** [the same]
Monogramme de la patte			
d'épaules	**non vue**	*la 8me ligne . . .*	**idem**
Couleur des insignes	**non vue**	*la 9me ligne . . .*	**idem**
Numéro du régiment			
(trois chiffres, 270)	**18**	*la 10me ligne . . .*	**T**
Numéro du régiment chiffre 2	**2**	*la 11me ligne . . .*	**B**
Numéro du régiment chiffre 7	**7**	*la 12me ligne . . .*	**G**
Numéro du régiment chiffre 0	**0**	*la 13me ligne . . .*	**V**
Autres observations	**aucune**	*la 14me ligne . . .*	**H, K, W, X, Y, Z**

Readers will have noticed that, against *non vue*, **W** appears rather than **V**. Moreover, in drafting the exercise, Bruce has left out the line describing the escutcheon on the neckband, the third item in the 'Description of Uniform' subsidiary list. This omission, of course, alters the numbering of subsequent lines of text, so that 'Colour of Epaulettes' moves to line 5, 'Piping' to line 6, and so on. On the relevant sheet in the file, Mademoiselle Dorgebray made a note of the necessary amendments in shorthand, adding another layer of code to the draft text.

Such a description would require a long message, an account, say, of an attempt on the life of a South American parrot:

Le perroquet de notre ami
Henri Robluchon est
Merveilleux, avec ses plumes
Bleues/vertes. C'est un perroquet d'
Amérique du Sud. Il a la tête
Verte/rouge.
Henri m'a dit qu'on la trouve à
Valparaiso. (Son frère
Hubert y était en '92.)
Tante Jeanne en avait un qui
Bavardait toute la journée.
Georges, son neveu,
Voulait l'étrangler. Ce perroquet était
Vraiment insupportable.[†]

Inserting the line about the escutcheon on the neckband – assuming one was seen, that is, **vue = R** – allows further rhapsodies about feathers:

. . . Merveilleux, avec ses plumes
Resplendissantes, couleur
Bleue/verte. C'est un perroquet d'
Amérique du Sud . . .[†]

O FOR THE WINGS OF A DOVE

Confronting Madame Rischard with a seventeen-column table was evidently thought too daunting. Instead, it was broken up into six tables, of between two and six columns each, typed out by Mademoiselle Dorgebray. Bruce and Campbell assured their pupil that memorizing these would not be as difficult as she might at first think: '*Les tableaux suivants, qui sont loin d'être aussi compliqués qu'ils n'en ont l'air, sont à retenir par coeur.*'*

This section of the code addressed a problem that will already be apparent: without a method of abbreviation, messages covering several subjects, with detailed descriptions of each, would be too long.

To shorten the coded message, some words could obviously be written *en clair*. Why, in describing a uniform, encode the word 'blue', for instance, when a text about the sky, or someone's eyes, could include 'blue', without being suspect? The code dealt with this in the following way: the original list of twenty main subjects reserved six numbers 13, 14, 15, 16, 17 and 18, matched by the corresponding six letters, O, P, Q, R, S and T, for each of the six tables.

The first table, Subject 13, represented by the letter O, showed how the sender of a report could indicate that a word *en clair* was also a word in the hidden message. Punctuation announced that in the next paragraph the sender would begin a new phrase. If the first letter of the first word of the first line of the phrase began with O, therefore, the reader would be ready to look for a word *en clair*.

If the second line of the phrase began with A, the reader would know that the *first* word of the preceding line was the word to pick out. If the line began with B, the reader should select the *second* word of the preceding line, and so on. J and K were for some reason omitted from the list. L directed the reader to the *tenth* word of the preceding line.

---

* 'The following tables, which are much less complicated than they appear, should be learnt by heart.'

Thus, seeing:

O for the **wings** of a
Dove[†]

directs the reader to 'wings' (D = 4).

Nine letters remained. M indicated that both the *first and second* words of the preceding line should be selected, and so on up to V, for the *ninth and tenth* words.

Thus:

Organ music will be played next **Thursday evening**.
Try to come, won't you?[†]

The second table, Table 14, with its matching letter P, continued the pattern. P told the reader to look in the remainder of the phrase for sequences of words *en clair*; the first letter of the next line drew the reader's attention to the relevant words. A led the reader to the *first, second and third* words of the preceding line, up to I, for the *ninth, tenth and eleventh* words.

Please do **ask for help** if you can't
Carry all that firewood.[†]

L directed the reader to the *first, second, third and fourth* words in the preceding line, up to V, for the *tenth, eleventh, twelfth and thirteenth* words.

Papa fumes about the molehills. Three came on Wednesday, **six more on Thursday.**[†]
Violent banging does no good, so we resort to cyanide. Rather horrible.[†]

A final line beginning with W (= 0) indicated that this particular phrase was finished.

We do not tell the neighbours that there is cyanide in the garden shed.[†]

THE DANGERS OF SPELLING

Ingenious though this system was as a way of reducing the number of lines of text required for reports, it had one major disadvantage. Campbell's system was designed to hide key words, so that anyone who might intercept Madame Rischard's messages would not realize that they were in code. *Groups* of key words, however, might arouse suspicion. If as a result the messages were passed on to enemy experts, this section of the code, based on simple word identification, using the alphabet, might easily be broken. A sequence of four words was the most Campbell dared use; even that was risky.

The remaining four tables, Q, R, S and T, therefore directed the reader to single letters, enabling the sender to spell out whole words which would be too conspicuous if written entire.

A phrase beginning with the letter Q alerted the reader.

Then, if the second line began with A, the reader took the *first* letter of the preceding line; if B, the *second* letter, and so on, as far as V, for the *nineteenth* letter.

A phrase beginning with the letter R indicated that pairs of letters were significant.

If the second line began with A, the reader looked at the *first and second* letters of the preceding line, as far as V, for the *nineteenth and twentieth* letters.

Table S indicated that groups of three letters should be chosen.

A at the beginning of the second line pointed to the *first, second and third* letters of the preceding line, as far as V, pointing to the *nineteenth, twentieth and twenty-first* letters.

Table T covered groups of four letters.

If the second line began with A, the reader selected the *first, second, third and fourth* letters of the preceding line, and so on, as far as V, which picked out the *nineteenth, twentieth, twenty-first and twenty-second* letters.

For these four tables, too, a final line beginning with W (= o) indicated that the phrase was finished.

A sequence of four letters was very nearly a word. It might well be suspect, especially to a censor fond of crossword puzzles or of games relying on breaking words into syllables (like the acting game known in Britain and France as 'Charades'). Madame Rischard was accordingly instructed to use the letter-spelling tables, and indeed the word-spelling tables, only for general subjects, the state of the weather, say, or the fact that illness had prevented an observer from making a report. The tables were, as Bruce and Campbell promised, '*loin d'être aussi compliqués qu'ils n'en ont l'air*'; once they were noticed, messages written with the letter-spelling system could be quickly unravelled by anyone with the smallest knowledge of standard codes.

When Madame Rischard complained that the spelling system was too time-consuming, the code was modified. Three texts – Garnier's *Dictionary*, a volume of Baedeker, and Lieber's *Code* – were instead used as sources of key words. Letters and numbers directed the reader to the passage of text from which key words and sequences of key words had been taken.

A spelling system of some sort, though dangerous, was neces-sary to allow Madame Rischard to refer to matters not covered by Bruce and Campbell's original list of main subjects, names of people and places, for example. The extent of Madame Rischard's network was not known in advance and, if Bruce and Campbell had supplied an exhaustive list of proper names (**Ab, Ac, . . . Abb, Acc . . .** etc., **A** being the '*Enoncé*' for name of a place or a person), it would have been too ambitious to expect Madame Rischard to memorize all of it.

The last main subject heading, **19**, matched by **U**, was therefore employed for names that had not been included in the original list.

Using Table **Q, R, S** or **T**, the name of the person or place was spelt out and the phrase ended. To indicate that this was what the sender was doing, the first line of the next phrase would begin with **U**. The second line of this second phrase would begin with the letter, and thus the matching number, which the sender would henceforth assign to the person or place whose name had been spelt out in the preceding phrase.

Here is a final example, a message indicating that the name of a person or place would henceforth be represented by **17**, that is, **S**.

The letter U is an awkward one with which to start a phrase, but a remedy for nettlerash will serve as a theme.

Urticaire – le remède recommandé par
Sébastien est une application de camomille.[†]

O for the wings of a dove, indeed.

Sources and Acknowledgements

When the Wellington Chest was opened, it was found to contain papers relating to the Luxembourg espionage scheme: exchanges of minutes and signals; letters, including those between Madame Rischard, Captain Bruce, Interpreter Chocqueel and Captain Campbell; a file marked 'Code'; correspondence between Bruce and Baschwitz Meau; a complete run of *Der Landwirt* from 21 February to 14 November 1918; registers of reports received from Luxembourg and communications between Luxembourg and Paris; full sets of decoded reports as sent on to GHQ, with GHQ's acknowledgements; meteorological summaries, a moonlight diagram and a map, four feet square, showing paths on which a balloon might be sent into the Grand Duchy.

This collection is one of few relating to British military intelligence during those years. In 1919 officers in the Intelligence Corps were instructed by the War Office to burn nearly all files; papers that survived the weeding were mostly destroyed in the Blitz. Significantly, for he was meticulous about security, Major Bruce retained much material from the Paris Office. Although he said little about that story, he knew it was important and instructive. Based on this archive, the historian can reconstruct a full and detailed account of a First World War espionage operation, from its origins in a daring idea to its successful execution. I am fortunate to have been that historian. First thanks must go to Major Bruce's son, Robert, and not only because he is my husband. He and I have done this work together.

From the turning of the third key to the deciphering of the last message, we have had great luck. The late Dr Charles-Edouard

Rischard, the nephew to whom Lise Rischard told her story, read every draft of this book. I am immensely grateful to him and to his wife, Huguette, for their permission to quote from Lise Rischard's correspondence and to reproduce the photographs for plates 5 and 6a. Without the support of Dr and Madame Rischard, this history would be neither thorough nor complete.

In Luxembourg we also found the Hansen family, Monsieur Rockenbrodt, Madame Francine Rockenbrod-Schmit and Monsieur André Schroell. The latter used to visit his aunts, Paul and Jeanne's daughters, in their old age. Quiet and devout, their greatest excitement, as he thought, had been to translate the Psalms into the Luxembourg language. Papers they had deposited in the Luxembourg National Archives told otherwise. I would like to thank the archivists there and all who helped to put us on the trail of those who managed the espionage operation in the Grand Duchy. Special thanks are due to Judge David Edward and his wife Elizabeth, who gave much advice, help and hospitality in Luxembourg and Scotland.

We were as fortunate in Flanders. With help from French colleagues, we traced Jean Chocqueel's descendants, Madame Maud Chocqueel, her niece Béatrice Guilbert and her cousin Abbé Delplanque, who gave us a copy of Jean Chocqueel's unpublished memoir, 'Evasion 1915'. It has been indispensable to the telling of this story and I am grateful to his family for allowing me to draw on it.

Baschwitz Meau was more elusive. We wrote to dozens of that name in Europe and America – I would particularly like to thank Robert Baschwitz, Joachim Baschwitz, Madame Maria-Antonia Bertrand-Baschwitz, Frau Renate Baschwitz and Frau Ursula Wirth for their replies – but found no direct descendants. Madame Micheline Gutmann-Marcus, of the *Association de Généalogie Juive Internationale*, instituted a special search, as did the Jewish Genealogical Society in London and, prompted by the director of the British Council in Belgium and Luxembourg, the *Association des Vétérans Coloniaux*. Izabella Olivant, Pam Mills and Geoff Rollason inspected the address in Surbiton where Baschwitz Meau's cousin was said to have lived. Although we discovered little and much of it irrelevant, I am grateful for the efforts of all these supporters.

At the office of the Brussels Municipality, however, we found Baschwitz Meau's birth and marriage certificates (and were also invited to have a TB inoculation) and, after various false leads including misdirection to the King's private library, a hospital ward and the Justice Ministry, discovered Baschwitz's service file in the Military Archives in Brussels. I wish to thank those archivists, and also Dr Richard Boijen, Head of the Documentation Centre at the *Koninklijk Museum van het Leger en de Krigsgeschiedenis*, and Vice-Admiral Herteleer, Chief at Forces GHQ, Belgian Army, for supplying records. Judge Melchior Wathelet, of the European Court of Justice, was instrumental here and has my thanks.

Despite war and time, some of the buildings mentioned in this book still stand. I wish to thank Monsieur Alain Rix for showing us the interior of 20 Boulevard Royal, now Hôtel Rix-Pavillon Royal; Madame Chantal Voisin and Madame Nicole Raoult for taking us into 41 Rue St Roch; Madame Marguerite Aviez for describing the layout of 38 Rue de Moscou when her mother-in-law was its concierge; and the families Schild and Najakima for looking out the registers for 1916, 1917 and 1918 at the Waldhotel Bellary in Grindelwald.

Piecing this account together has been exacting. I am especially grateful to Mark Seaman, then Historian at the Imperial War Museum, for telling me I should do it. The archivists at that Museum have been unfailingly helpful. I wish to thank them and their colleagues elsewhere: the *Archives Militaires* at Château de Vincennes; the *Archives Nationales* in Paris; the *BundesArchiv*; the *Croix Rouge Française*; the *Historial* at Péronne; the Defence Intelligence Security Centre at Chicksands; the Liddell-Hart Archive at King's College, London; the Lloyds Bank TSB Archive; the London Library; the National Library of Scotland; the Porthcurno Trust; Oxford University Archives; the National Archives at Kew and the staff of the Photographic Section of the Royal Commission on the Ancient and Historical Monuments of Scotland, who prepared the photographs that illustrate this book. I would also like to thank Professor Cameron Hazlehurst and Roger Faligot for directing my attention to out-of-the-way sources. Mrs Hilda Morgan noticed that the code-names by which Bruce and Campbell introduced themselves to Madame Rischard were echoed in Louis Aragon's Resistance poem, *La Rose et le Réséda*, a mystery I am still exploring.

Many others have given information, supplied intelligence, shared knowledge, sometimes all three. I especially thank: Mrs Christine Beith; Steve Blake; Charles Bland; Dr Alan Borg; Dr James Bradburne; Simon Brett; Donald Cameron of Cameron's Balloons; Lord Cameron of Loch Broom; George Carmany; Mary Godwin; General Sir Michael Gow; Colonel Frédéric Guelton; Trevor Harding; Albrecht Hassman; David Heal; Stephen and Liesl Hearst; Madame Hélène Heldenstein; Reavis Hilz-Ward; Brigadier Christopher Holtom; Major-General Alastair Irwin; Sir Colin McColl; Eileen Mackay; Madame Elisabeth Marchal; Simon Marriott; Professor Marie-Madeleine Martinet; Christopher Morgan; Edmund Morgan; Oliver Morgan; Madame Marie-Louise Navarro; the late Professor Richard Neustadt; Mademoiselle Anne-Gaël Noussan; Carol O'Brien; Mrs Jennifer Ogilvie; Mr George Olifent; Karen Otterbeck; Graham Paul; Jean Bruce Poole; Guillaume Rischard; Sir Lewis Robertson; Trevor Royle; Madame St Loubert-Bié; Karen Sampson; Rudolf and Juliana Schwage; Adrian Seville; Frank Siebrecht; Robert and Mihaela Smith; Antoine de Tarlé; Professor Hugh Torrens; Ralph Torrens; Shirley Torrens; Susan Watt; Nigel Wenban-Smith; Wilfried and Marianne Winkler. My compliments, too, to the waiters at Restaurant Théâtre Sarah-Bernhardt, still in its original home, and to Monsieur François Barber of Huîtres Prunier, which flourishes as Goumard-Prunier at 9 Rue Duphot.

I would also like to thank those who prepared this book for publication: my literary agent, Jenny Brown; the editor, Stuart Proffitt, and his assistant, Liz Friend-Smith; Richard Duguid and Ruth Pinkney; the copy-editor, Janet Tyrrell; Reg Piggott, the cartographer; Chris Shamwana at Ghost Design, who designed the cover; and Douglas Matthews, the enthusiastic indexer. They could not have been more tactful and encouraging.

Last, one admission. Nearly everything in this book is based on evidence: reference to Madame Rischard's distress at the state of her stair carpet, for example, derives from her subsequent letter to Georgette. There is one exception. I do not know that, feeling peckish, travellers from Zürich to Offenburg thought about a bite, nor that gentlemen looked at pocket-watches as the train crossed the frontier into Germany. But after many journeys on Swiss and German railways in connection with writing this book, I think it likely.

Janet Morgan
August 2003

Notes

1 The Office in Rue St Roch

1. Kirke, Lecture on Prevention of Leakage of Information, December 1915, Intelligence Corps Museum. His suspicion is supported by the experience of one of Robert Graves's relations, a von Ranke, who, according to Graves, lost seniority in the German consular service because he refused to use the London consulate as a clearing-house for secret service reports. Graves, *Goodbye to All That*, London: Cape, 1929.

2. Commandant Ladoux, *Mes Souvenirs*, Paris: Editions de France, 1937.

3. Letter from Lieutenant-Colonel S. H. C. Woolrych, 5 July 1969, Intelligence Corps Museum, Chicksands, Bedfordshire.

4. See the account by its chief, Colonel M. Nicolai, *The German Secret Service*, published in translation by Stanley Paul & Co., London, 1924.

5. Woolrych Papers, Intelligence Corps Museum.

6. A member of I(b), Captain W. L. MacEwen, explained the method to Kirke in May 1916. A sketch may be found in Major Kirke's Diaries, Imperial War Museum, London.

7. Diaries, 6 January 1916.

8. Woolrych Papers, Intelligence Corps Museum.

9. Kirke, Diaries, 6 January 1917.

10. *Mr Standfast*, the novel written immediately after the war by Bruce's friend John Buchan, begins with a similar interview (Edinburgh: Thomas Nelson & Sons, 1919).

11. Report of the Clyde Munition Workers, December 1915, Cd. 8136. So called because it was based on evidence given by the workforce, the owners having at first declined to do so. When these latter changed their minds, the chairman told them that they had missed their opportunity.

12. Haig, Diaries, 7 January 1917, National Library of Scotland, Edinburgh.

2 Peculiar Arrangements

1. The assumption that the SSB worked only for the War Office has been corrected by Alan Judd. See *The Quest for 'C'*, London: HarperCollins, 1999.

2. Kirke, Letters, 7 and 14 July 1913, quoted in Christopher Andrew, *Secret Service*, London: Heinemann, 1985.

3. Fuller descriptions may be found in Andrew, op. cit., and Michael Occleshaw, *Armour against Fate*, London: Columbus Books, 1989. The papers on which this present book is based have enabled some gaps to be filled and some contradictions to be resolved.

4. The opening – but only the opening – of one of John Buchan's novels, *A Prince of the Captivity*, Edinburgh: Thomas Nelson & Sons, 1933, mirrors this story.

3 Qualifications

1. As he did. *Caroline* opened in London in February 1916. Maugham's mission provided him with material for his collection of stories about the Secret Service agent Ashenden. Some chapters read as if they are incomplete, perhaps because Winston Churchill, as Secretary of State for War during the period covered by the stories, recommended that Maugham's early drafts should be burnt, on the grounds that they contravened the Official Secrets Act. Ashenden's chief, 'R', shared many characteristics with Maugham's immediate superior, Captain John Wallinger (brother of Kirke's man in London), including the belief that secret intelligence was best got from foreign waiters. See *Ashenden*, London: Heinemann, 1928.

2. Uniform and kit can be seen in the Musée de l'Armée in the Invalides in Paris.

3. Jean Chocqueel, 'Evasion 1915', an unpublished memoir, written for his grandchildren, completed in October 1954.

4. See Kirke, Diaries, 13 March 1916: 'Monsieur Chocqueel . . . sends long list of agents.'

5. See Margaret Darrow's *Frenchwomen and the First World War*, Oxford: Berg, 2000.

6. Evans's book, *The Escaping Club*, London: The Bodley Head, 1921, was one of several histories of escaping adventures published after the war by John Lane.

7. Kirke, Diaries, 28 July 1915.

4 Tangled Webs

1. Compare Madame Defarge's knitted register in Charles Dickens's *A Tale of Two Cities*, London: All the Year Round, 1859. 'What do you make, madame?' 'Many things.' 'For instance . . . ?' 'For instance . . . shrouds.' See also Ovid's *Metamorphoses*, in which Philomela weaves a record of her rape and mutilation. Compare, too, the archives of the Inca, preserved in complex sequences of knotted string, and the maps, woven with weed and sea-shells, used for navigation by the Marshall Islanders.

2. Woolrych Papers, Intelligence Corps Museum.

3. The expression used by Captain Ivone Kirkpatrick, who worked for I(b) from January 1916. Kirkpatrick Papers, Vol. 1, 79/50/1, Imperial War Museum, London.

4. Major Reginald Drake, *History of Intelligence (B), British Expeditionary Force, France, from January 1917 to April 1919*, PRO/WO 106/45.

5. Drake to Best, 29 July 1947. Papers of Captain Sigismund Payne Best, Imperial War Museum, cited in Michael Occleshaw, *Armour against Fate*, London: Columbus Books, 1989.

6. In today's money, £188 for curtains, £516 for gas-fires, £212 per month lease, £14 six months' typewriter hire, £433 for furniture. Maison B. Maurice made a £35 loss on repurchase, as the French franc/pound sterling rate fell in 1919.

7. In the words of Gilbert Trausch, whose book, *Le Luxembourg, Emergence d'un Etat et d'une Nation*, Belgium: Fonds Mercato, 1989, gives a full history of the Grand Duchy.

5 Miraculous Arrival of Father Cambron

1. See Helen McPhail, *The Long Silence: Civilian Life under the German Occupation of Northern France, 1914–18*, London: I. B. Tauris, 1999.

7 Stiff Tests for Madame Rischard

1. Drake to Bruce, 31 March 1917.

2. Memorandum from French Army Intelligence, translated for file at Rue St Roch, 24 April 1917.

3. Bruce to Drake, 4 April 1917.

4. Drake to Bruce, 6 April 1917.

5. Before they brought the coffin back from St Helena. See the lithograph, '*Ouverture du cercueil de Napoléon devant le Prince de Joinville, le général Bertrand, l'aumônier Coquereau, Saint-Hélène, 15 octobre 1840*', in

G. Lacour-Gayet, *Napoléon, sa Vie, son Oeuvre, son Temps*, Paris: Hachette, 1921.

6. Madame Rischard to Bruce, 20 April 1917.

7. A display of these German helmets and cockades, in a case several feet long, may be seen in the Military Museum in Brussels.

8. Madame Rischard to Bruce, 22 May 1917.

9. Ibid.

10. Bruce to Madame Rischard, 25 May 1917.

11. Chocqueel, 'Evasion 1915', unpublished memoir, 1954.

12. Ibid.

13. Cameron to Bruce, 18 May 1917.

8 Appearances and Disappearances of Baschwitz Meau

1. Memorandum, Bruce, 4 June 1917.

2. Bruce to Leche, 4 June 1917.

3. Leche to Bruce, 7 June 1917.

4. Bruce to Baschwitz Meau, 20 June 1917.

9 Doubt and Delay

1. Her name and that of her daughter's family are in the hotel registers for 1916, 1917 and 1918. Hermann Hesse, who stayed there for some months in 1902, mentions the fine oaks of the Villa Bellary in *Innen und Aussen, Gesammelte Erzählungen*, Frankfurt: Suhrkamp Verlag, 1977.

2. Cameron to Bruce, 18 May 1917.

3. Bruce to Cameron, 31 May 1917.

4. Madame Rischard to Bruce, 2 June 1917.

5. Bruce to Cameron, 8 June 1917. The sum was the equivalent of £9,427 today.

6. Cameron to Bruce, 12 June 1917. £2,828 today.

7. Bruce to Cameron, 13 June 1917. The amount suggested, 500 francs, was about £471.

8. Madame Rischard to Bruce, 10 June 1917.

9. Bruce to Madame Rischard, 12 June 1917.

10. Madame Rischard to Bruce, 14 June 1917.

10 The Escapers' University

1. J. L. Hardy, *I Escape,* London: The Bodley Head, 1927. The title was

selected by the publisher against the wishes of the author, who thought it boastful.

2. Ibid.
3. Ibid.
4. Ibid.
5. Ibid.
6. Ibid.
7. A. J. Evans, *The Escaping Club*, London: The Bodley Head, 1921.
8. Ibid.

11 Letters from Lise

1. Kirke, Diaries, Imperial War Museum, London.
2. Major Reginald Drake, *History of Intelligence (B), British Expeditionary Force, France, from January 1917 to April 1919*, PRO/WO 106/45, paras 26–28.
3. Campbell to Bruce, 10 May 1917.
4. '. . . heard from Wallinger that ANTONIO had started for Zurich', Kirke, Diaries, 5 February 1915.
5. Campbell to Bruce, undated but attached to the memorandum of 10 May 1917.
6. Campbell to Bruce, 18 June 1917.
7. Madame Rischard to Bruce, 29 June 1917.
8. Madame Rischard to Campbell, 1 and 2 July 1917.
9. Madame Rischard to Campbell, 4 July 1917.
10. Campbell to Madame Rischard, 7 July 1917.
11. Madame Rischard to Campbell, 8 July 1917.
12. Campbell's report to Bruce, 9 July 1917.

12 *Der Landwirt*

1. Memoir written in the 1950s by Alice and Gabrielle Schroell. Fonds Schroell, Archives Nationales de Luxembourg.
2. '*Le service des renseignements . . . appellation sous laquelle se dissimule le service français de contre-espionage*', Ch. Lucieto (a nom de plume), *La Guerre des Cerveaux: Le Diable Noir*, Paris: Berger-Levrault, 1928.

13 Not Singly . . .

1. Bruce to Madame Rischard, 11 August 1917.

2. Bruce to Drake, 15 August 1917.

3. Major B. E. M. Neefs, 'Déclaration Rélative aux Services de Guerre de Sous-Lieutenant BASCHWITZ', a statement made in May 1936, supporting a claim by Baschwitz for a military pension. Baschwitz Meau, personal file, Archives of the Military Museum, Brussels.

4. Bruce to Drake, 15 August 1917.

5. Bruce to Drake, 4 September 1917.

6. Drake to Bruce, 7 September 1917.

14 . . . But in Multitudes

1. Madame Rischard to Bruce, 14 June 1917, 9 August 1917.

2. Madame Rischard to Bruce, 31 July 1917; Madame Rischard to Chocqueel, 2 August 1917.

3. Chocqueel to Madame Rischard, 28 July 1917.

4. Madame Rischard to Bruce, 18 August 1917.

5. Chocqueel to Madame Rischard, 31 August 1917.

6. Madame Rischard to Bruce, 15 August 1917.

7. Campbell to Bruce, report of visit on 8 September 1917, written on 12 September 1917.

8. Bruce to Campbell, 8 September 1917. Hansen's proposed monthly fee was the equivalent of £353 today.

15 Strafes

1. Undated memorandum. That is, in today's money, £14, £2.83 and £5.65.

2. Handwritten copy, Bruce to Cameron, 1 September 1917.

3. Cameron to Bruce, 5 September 1917.

4. Bruce to Cameron, 6 September 1917.

5. Cameron to Bruce, 8 September 1917.

6. Drake, *History of Intelligence (B), British Expeditionary Force, France*, PRO/WO 106/45, paras 24 and 25.

7. Bruce to Drake, 17 and 25 September 1917. Was Logiest an agent who had got into trouble? The lawyer's fee was the equivalent of £188 today.

8. £1,828 at today's values.

9. Bruce to Drake, 17 September 1917.

10. Bruce to Cameron, 17 September 1917.

11. Drake to Bruce, 13 September 1917.

12. Bruce to Drake, 29 September 1917.

13. The expedition to Madrid cost £473 at today's values.

14. Cameron to Bruce, 19 September 1917.
15. Cameron to Drake, 25 September 1917.

16 Snakes and Ladders

1. Madame Rischard to Campbell, 29 September 1917.
2. Bruce to Madame Rischard, 24 October 1917.
3. Haig, Diaries, 15 October 1917, National Library of Scotland, Edinburgh.
4. Brigadier-General Sir John Charteris, *At GHQ*, London: Cassell, 1931, 21 April 1917.
5. Madame Rischard to Bruce, 28 October 1917.
6. Drake to Bruce, 30 September 1917.
7. Bruce to Drake, 4 October 1917.
8. Drake to Bruce, 7 October 1917.
9. Bruce to Baschwitz, 5 October 1917.
10. Bruce to Drake, 19 October 1917.
11. Charteris, op. cit., 9 October, 10 October 1917.
12. Drake, *History of Intelligence (B)*, PRO/WO 106/45, para. 51.
13. Undated memorandum.
14. Madame Rischard to Bruce, 21 November 1917.
15. File I(b) 4124, 15 August 1917, Imperial War Museum.
16. Madame Rischard to Bruce, 25 November 1917.
17. '*C'est toi personnellement que je désire voir* . . .' Madame Rischard to Bruce, 11 November 1917.
18. Madame Rischard to Bruce, 9 December 1917.
19. Chocqueel to Madame Rischard, 8 December 1917.
20. Madame Rischard to Campbell, 11 December 1917.
21. Madame Rischard to Campbell, 12 December 1917.
22. Madame Rischard to Campbell, 15 December 1917.
23. Ibid.

17 Bifurcation

1. Sir John Charteris, *At GHQ*, London: Cassell, 1931, 5 July 1917.
2. Ibid.
3. Drake, *History of Intelligence (B)*, PRO/WO 106/45, para. 29.
4. Chocqueel to Madame Rischard, 19 December 1917.
5. Madame Rischard to Bruce, 22 December 1917.
6. '. . . *la grandeur des buts que nous avions en commun*', Bruce to Madame Rischard, 26 December 1917.

7. Madame Rischard to Bruce, 28 December 1917.

8. Ibid.

9. Bruce to Madame Rischard, 1 January 1918.

10. Madame Rischard to Chocqueel, 7 January 1918.

11. Chocqueel to Madame Rischard, 12 January 1918.

12. Madame Rischard to Bruce, 14 January 1918.

13. Baedeker's guidebooks: the series published from the 1840s at Leipzig by Karl Baedeker and his successors. They were all arranged in a similar way: places of interest, categorized by geographical location, were listed in a logical progression. By referring to the combination of letters and numbers identifying each attraction, an agent could direct the recipients of a coded letter toward a particular sentence in a volume of Baedeker. That sentence provided the key to unlock the cipher. 'Lieber's *Code*': Dr Francis Lieber's set of 'Instructions for the Government of Armies of the United States in the Field', drafted during the American Civil War and approved by President Lincoln as No. 100 of the General Orders of the War Department. The code's terms were later used as the basis for the Hague Conventions of 1899 and 1907. 'Lieber's *Code*', as it became known, was published in April 1863. It was laid out in 157 articles, grouped into ten sections; an agent sending a coded letter had only to refer to a pair of numbers and initiates would know where to look for the key. Bruce and his colleagues were not the only ones to employ Lieber's *Code* in this way. A volume, at the great price of two guineas, was one of Cumming's first purchases when he set up MI 1(c).

14. Campbell's report to Bruce, 24 January 1918.

15. Ibid.

16. Ibid.

17. '. . . *si par hasard la clef ne tournait pas bien dans la serrure et tu avais des problèmes durs à résoudre!*', Bruce to Madame Rischard, 6 February 1918.

18. Bruce to Madame Rischard, 6 February 1918.

18 Pigeons and Balloons

1. Haig, Diaries, 27 September 1917, National Library of Scotland, Edinburgh.

2. Priestley to de Ceuninck, 18 December 1917.

3. Baschwitz to Bruce, 6 January 1918.

4. Bruce to Athlone, 8 January 1918.

5. Haig, Diaries, 21 January 1918.

6. Ibid., 25 January 1918.

7. Ibid., 20 December 1918.

8. Boccard to Bruce, 9 February 1918.

9. Boccard to Bruce, 20 February 1918. The quotation is from Edmund Blunden, *Undertones of War*, London: Cobden Sanderson, 1928.

10. Alan Judd, *The Quest for 'C'*, London: HarperCollins, 1999.

11. Kirke, Diaries, 16 October 1914, Imperial War Museum, London.

12. Ibid., 1 November 1914.

13. Ibid., 3 December 1914. The French declared the bomb to be at least 150 years old; 'actually', Kirke noted next day, 'latest German model!'

14. Kirkpatrick attributed it to Best, Drake to Wallinger. Ivone Kirkpatrick, Papers, Vol. 1, 79/50/1, Imperial War Museum, London.

15. Ibid.

16. See G. A. Braithwaite, *Fine Feathers and Fish*, privately published, Edinburgh: T. & A. Constable Ltd, 1971.

17. Document issued by Captain G. S. Schlieffen, 77th Reserve Division, 1a 223, 31 May 1918, cited by Kirkpatrick, op. cit.

18. Kirkpatrick, op. cit.

19. Kirkpatrick, op. cit. and his memoir, *The Inner Circle*, London: Macmillan, 1959.

20. Drake, *History of Intelligence (B)*, PRO/WO 106/45, paras 72 and 73.

21. Jock Haswell, *British Military Intelligence*, London: Weidenfeld & Nicolson, 1973.

22. Wallinger to Bruce, 20 February 1918. 'My Belgian' was probably 'Emile', that is, Joseph Ide.

19 Madame Rischard's Other Occupation

1. See a song noted in the town of Jülich in January 1917:

> '*Morgenrot, Morgenrot, England hat noch keine Not,*
> *Frankreich backt noch frische Brötchen,*
> *Rußland hat noch Schweinepfötchen,*
> *Deutschland nichts als Marmelade,*
> *Und dazu noch Erdkohlrabien.*'
> 'At sunrise, at sunrise, England still lacks nothing,
> France still bakes fresh rolls,
> Russia goes on eating pigs' trotters,
> In Germany we've only got jam and kohlrabi.'

Quoted in Ute Daniel, *The War from Within*, Göttingen: Vandenhoeck & Rupprecht, 1997, in which much detail may be found.

2. Madame Rischard to Bruce, 18 February 1918.

3. Bruce to Drake, 26 February 1918. 'B. P.' stood for *Bureau Paris*.

4. Chocqueel to Madame Rischard, 27 February 1918.

5. Madame Rischard to Bruce, 19 February, delivered in Paris 28 February.

6. *Der Landwirt*, 23 February 1918, received in Paris 28 February 1918.

7. *Der Landwirt*, 25 February 1918, received in Paris 2 March 1918.

8. Madame Rischard to Bruce, 22 February 1918. Eleven thousand francs was the equivalent of £10,370 today.

9. Madame Rischard to Bruce, 22 February 1918.

10. Chocqueel to Madame Rischard, 28 February 1918.

11. '*Tâche de t'en tenir au 68 autant que possible, c'est épatant et plus vite.*' Ibid.

12. *Der Landwirt*, 27 February 1918, received in Paris 5 March 1918.

13. *Der Landwirt*, 28 February 1918, received in Paris 6 March 1918.

14. *Der Landwirt*, 2 March 1918, received in Paris 8 March 1918.

15. *Der Landwirt*, 4 March 1918.

16. *Der Landwirt*, 13 March 1918, received in Paris 20 March 1918, and *Der Landwirt*, 14 March 1918, also received 20 March 1918.

17. Letters from Madame Rischard to Chocqueel, 13 and 15 March 1918.

18. '. . . *un peu bohème, mais excessivement intelligent* . . .', Madame Rischard to Chocqueel, 13 March 1918.

19. Madame Rischard to Chocqueel, 13 March 1918.

20. *Der Landwirt*, 18 March 1918, received 24 March 1918; 21 March 1918, received 26 March 1918; 23 March 1918, received 28 March 1918.

21. Madame Rischard to Chocqueel, 15 March 1918.

22. Note by Madame Fresez-Settegast sent with letters from Madame Rischard to Bruce, dated 26 and 28 March 1918, received in Paris 5 April 1918.

23. Madame Rischard to Bruce, 20 March 1918.

20 Sowing and Reaping

1. Brigadier-General Sir John Charteris, *At GHQ*, London: Cassell, 1931, 7 December 1917.

2. Haig, Diaries, 7 January 1918, National Library of Scotland, Edinburgh.

3. Ibid., 11 March 1918.

4. Ibid., 19 March 1918.

5. Ibid., 25 March 1918.

6. Ibid., 26 March 1918.

7. Ibid.

8. Madame Rischard to Bruce, 25 March 1918, received 3 April 1918. LIR: *Landwehr* Infantry Regiment?

9. Madame Rischard to Bruce, 26 March 1918, received 5 April 1918. Interrogative omitted in the original, as question marks were used as signifiers in the code.

10. *Der Landwirt*, 28 March 1918.

11. Madame Rischard to Chocqueel, 28 March 1918, received 5 April 1918.

12. Madame Rischard to Bruce, 29 March 1918, received 7 April 1918. Details of uniforms and insignia were also given.

13. *Der Landwirt*, 2 April 1918, received 7 April 1918. Other details were given.

14. *Der Landwirt*, 4 April 1918, received 11 April 1918.

15. A. W. Speyer, O. B. Codes at GHQ, to Bruce, 28 April 1918.

16. *Der Landwirt*, 6 April 1918, received in Paris 12 April 1918.

17. Haig, Diaries, 3 April 1918.

18. Ibid., 9 April 1918.

19. Commander-in-Chief's Order of the Day, 11 April 1918.

20. Chocqueel to Madame Rischard, 28 March 1918, received 10 April 1918.

21. Reported in *Der Landwirt*, 6 April 1918, received 12 April 1918. The Royal Flying Corps and the Royal Naval Air Service had been merged on 1 April 1918 to form the Royal Air Force.

22. Madame Rischard to Chocqueel, 6 April 1918, received 16 April 1918.

23. *Der Landwirt*, 10 April 1918, received 17 April 1918.

24. Enclosure A to (I) – G. T. – 5529. 'Principle Affecting the Selection of Points of Attack on the Enemy's Railway Communications. Attached to Minute from British Military Representative, Supreme War Council to Secretary, War Cabinet', 24 July 1918. 'G. T.' may have been General Trenchard, commander of the RFC in France since August 1915, and first RAF chief of staff until his resignation in the spring of 1918, when he returned to France to command the Independent Air Force, nine squadrons of long-range bombers.

25. The proposed subsidy for Bram was, at today's values, £117 a month; Hansen's fee for his articles was £480 and his monthly retainer £353.

26. Speyer to Bruce, 24 April 1918.

27. *Der Landwirt*, 11 April 1918, received 17 April 1918; *Der Landwirt*, 13 April 1918, received 19 April 1918; *Der Landwirt*, 15 April 1918, received 21 April 1918; *Der Landwirt*, 17 April 1918, received 24 April 1918.

28. See *Tagebücher von Paul Klee 1898–1918*, Cologne: Verlag M. DuMont Schauberg, 1957, for a description of travel on the railway as a private in the German army in the spring of 1918.

29. Haig, Diaries, 14 April 1918 and 19 April 1918.

30. Intelligence Summary No. 530, 14 June 1918.
31. *Der Landwirt,* 18 April 1918, received 25 April 1918.
32. Speyer to Bruce, 28 April 1918. F. A. R.: field artillery regiment.
33. Haig, Diaries, 18 April 1918.
34. Ibid., 1 May 1918.
35. At Réhon, Micheville and Moulaine, *Der Landwirt,* 27 April 1918, received 4 May 1918, and 29 April 1918, received 5 May 1918; the Staff of the Minenwerfer Battalion No. 13 at Paillencourt and Landwehr Field Artillery Regiment No. 255, Battery No. 5 at Nieuport, *Der Landwirt,* 1 May 1918, received 13 May 1918.
36. Chocqueel to Madame Rischard, 5 May 1918, received 14 May 1918.
37. 'Only news antedated at least two days is of interest.' *Der Landwirt,* 11 April 1918, received in Paris 17 April 1918.
38. Madame Rischard to Bruce, 19 April 1918, received 27 April 1918.
39. Chocqueel to Madame Rischard, 2 May 1918, received 11 May 1918. The proposed increase, at today's values, was from £353 to £942.
40. Madame Rischard to Bruce, 27 May 1918, received 6 June 1918. The monthly fee advised by Madame Rischard for Hansen was the equivalent, at today's values, of £471, an increase of £118, and her proposed subsidy for Bram the same amount, £471.
41. *Der Landwirt,* 23 March 1918, received 28 March 1918.
42. Bruce to Madame Rischard, 7 April 1918, received 16 April 1918.
43. Madame Rischard to Bruce, 18 April 1918, received 25 April 1918, and *Der Landwirt,* 20 April 1918, received 26 April 1918.
44. *Der Landwirt,* 11 May 1918, received 17 May 1918.
45. Chocqueel to Madame Rischard, 29 May 1918, received 16 June 1918.

21 If the Worst Comes to the Worst

1. Bruce to Campbell, 10 March 1918.

22 Aloft

1. Bruce to Campbell, 13 March 1918.
2. Campbell to Bruce, 27 March 1918.
3. Memorandum, entitled 'Meteor', on meteorological aspects of the operation, written by Bruce, 10 March 1918.
4. Memorandum 179/652 to I(b) GHQ, 28 April 1918.
5. Bruce to Campbell, 13 March 1918.
6. Memorandum 179/652.

7. This was the opinion of Major C. A. Longcroft, Officer Commanding No. 1 Squadron, Home Defence, in 1914, cited in Ken Delve, *Nightfighter*, London: Cassell & Co., 1995.

8. RAF *Manual of Employment*, cited in Delve, op. cit.

9. Bruce, 'Memorandum of Visit to 8th Brigade, RAF, April 29th–1st May', 1 May 1918.

10. Brunt to Bruce, 1 May 1918.

11. Bruce to Brunt, 4 May 1918.

12. Brunt to Bruce, 6 May 1918.

13. Bruce to Drake, 15 May 1918.

14. Haig, Diaries, 1 May 1918, National Library of Scotland, Edinburgh.

15. Ibid., 2 May 1918.

16. The description is that of Maurice Baring, Trenchard's Private Secretary, in his *Flying Corps Headquarters 1914–1918*, London: G. Bell & Sons, 1920.

17. Bruce to Paul, 17 May 1918.

18. *Der Landwirt*, 11 May 1918, received in Paris 17 May 1918.

19. Bruce to Madame Rischard, 1 May 1918. It would be a difficult ascent for a beginner.

20. The previous limits had been eighteen and forty-four. Proclamation issued by Tessmar, Général-Major et Commandant des Troupes au Luxembourg, 3 May 1918, printed in *Der Landwirt*, 15 May 1918, received in Paris 21 May 1918.

21. *Der Landwirt*, 13 May 1918, received in Paris 19 May 1918, and 23 May 1918, received in Paris 30 May 1918.

22. Campbell to Bruce, 30 May 1918.

23. Chocqueel to Madame Rischard, 7 May 1918.

24. *Der Landwirt*, 18 May 1918, received in Paris 24 May 1918.

25. Official communiqué from Jean de Pierrefeu to General Pétain at French GHQ, Provins, quoted in de Pierrefeu, *Au GQG, secteur un*, Paris: Editions Françaises Illustrées, 1920.

26. Campbell to Bruce, 29 May 1918.

27. Bruce to Drake, 1 June 1918.

28. Haig, Diaries, 1 June 1918.

29. Ibid.

30. Memorandum written for Bruce by Hay, 23 June 1918.

31. Ibid.

32. *Der Landwirt*, 12 June 1918, received in Paris 18 June 1918.

33. *Der Landwirt*, 19 June 1918, received in Paris 25 June 1918.

34. Hay, op. cit.

35. Ibid.

36. Ibid.
37. Chocqueel to Madame Rischard, 29 May 1918.

23 Mademoiselle Testu's Surprise

1. Haig, Diaries, 19, 20 and 21 June 1918, National Library of Scotland, Edinburgh.
2. Paul Maze, *A Frenchman in Khaki*, London: William Heinemann, 1934.
3. Letter from Major Cyril Ormerod to his parents, 29 June 1918, Imperial War Museum.
4. Madame Rischard to Bruce, 27 May 1918, received 6 June 1918; Madame Rischard to Bruce, 1 June 1918, received 10 June 1918.
5. Bruce to Pollock, 21 June 1918.
6. Bruce, memorandum, 22 June 1918.
7. Hay to Bruce, 23 June 1918.
8. *Der Landwirt*, 20 June 1918, received in Paris 27 June 1918.
9. *Der Landwirt*, 22 June 1918, received in Paris 28 June 1918.
10. Dugenet to Bruce, 30 June 1918; Renaud to Bruce, 1 July 1918.
11. Wallinger to Bruce, 27 June 1918; Hazeldine to Bruce, 1 July 1918.
12. Israeli to Bruce, 6 July 1918.
13. Bruce to Pollock, 28 June 1918.
14. Pollock to Bruce, 4 July 1918.
15. *Der Landwirt*, 20 April 1918, received in Paris 26 April 1918.
16. Madame Rischard to Bruce, 28 June 1918, received in Paris 10 July; Bruce to Madame Rischard, dated 18 June 1918, sent 16 June 1918.
17. I.e. for the Paris Office. Madame Rischard to Bruce, 28 June 1918, received in Paris 10 July 1918.
18. *Der Landwirt*, 27 June 1918, received 3 July 1918.
19. Madame Rischard to Bruce, 12 July 1918, received 24 July 1918.
20. *Der Landwirt*, 1 July 1918, received 7 July 1918.
21. Madame Rischard to Bruce, 3 July 1918, received 13 July.
22. *Der Landwirt*, 13 July 1918, received 24 July 1918.
23. Bruce to Dansey, 4 July 1918.
24. Dansey to Bruce, 8 July 1918.
25. Dansey to Bruce, 11 July 1918.
26. The contents of Dansey's second letter throw light on a puzzling reference in the memoirs of Henry Landau, who ran the Belgian service known as '*La Dame Blanche*' (*All's Fair*, New York: Putnam's, 1934). Landau talks of meeting, after the Armistice, a Major Steffen, who had parachuted into the Grand Duchy with a basket of pigeons. It must be said that Landau is not always accurate.

27. Bruce to Madame Rischard, 18 July 1918.

28. *Der Landwirt*, 15 July 1918, received 25 July 1918.

29. Madame Rischard to Bruce, 19 July 1918, received 29 July 1918.

30. *Der Landwirt*, 24 July 1918, received 5 August 1918.

31. *Der Landwirt*, 25 July 1918, received 5 August 1918.

32. Bruce to Madame Rischard, 13 August 1918.

33. *Bremen Bürgerzeitung*, 25 June 1918.

34. Bruce to Drake, 2 August 1918.

35. '*Fiasco après six semaines de pourparlers agent espéré pour 44 ayant peur et refusant. Tout est à recommencer.*' Madame Rischard to Bruce, 6 August 1918, received 14 August 1918.

36. *Der Landwirt*, 14 August 1918, received 20 August 1918.

37. Haig, Diaries, 4 August 1918.

38. Bruce to Madame Rischard, 2 July 1918.

39. '*Eine Motte flog zum Licht.*'

40. '*Die Pause vor der Ernte*', headline in *Der Landwirt*, 13 July 1918.

41. Haig, Diaries, 21 August 1918.

42. Captured order, issued by General Sixt von Arnim, for Rupprecht, Army Group Commander, 22 August 1918.

43. Noted by his private secretary, on Trenchard's visit to 55th Squadron the following day. Maurice Baring, *Flying Corps Headquarters 1914–1918*, London: G. Bell & Sons, 1920.

44. *Der Landwirt*, 7 September 1918, received 13 September 1918.

45. *Der Landwirt*, 9 September 1918, received 14 September.

46. *Der Landwirt*, 11 September 1918, received 16 September 1918, and 14 September 1918, received 20 September 1918.

47. *Der Landwirt*, 2 October 1918, received 8 October 1918.

48. Yves Congar (then aged fourteen), *Journal de la Guerre 1914–18*, Paris: Editions Cerf, 1997.

49. Bruce to Madame Rischard, 19 September 1918.

50. Madame Rischard to Bruce, 8 October 1918, received 19 October 1918.

51. Bruce to Madame Rischard, 5 October 1918.

52. Bruce to Madame Rischard, 9 October 1918; Madame Rischard to Bruce, 14 October 1918, received 25 October 1918.

53. Butler, I(a), to Drake, I(b), 11 October 1918.

54. *Der Landwirt*, 12 October 1918, received 18 October 1918.

55. Bruce to Madame Rischard, 9 October 1918.

56. Madame Rischard to Bruce, 14 October 1918, received in Paris 25 October 1918.

57. O. B. Ciphers (signature illegible) to Bruce, 31 October 1918.

58. Haig, Diaries, 12 November 1918.
59. *Der Landwirt*, 11 November 1918.

24 Appointment at Huîtres Prunier

1. *Der Landwirt*, 14 November 1918.
2. In Diekirch dialect, *'T'ass net mé sô schén, wé se era si kom'*. *Der Landwirt*, 13 November 1918.
3. Bruce to Madame Rischard, 7 November 1918.
4. Bruce to Madame Rischard, 14 November 1918.
5. Bruce to Baschwitz, 14 November 1918.
6. Haig, Diaries, 16 November 1918, National Library of Scotland, Edinburgh.
7. Trenchard to Clive, 27 October 1918.
8. Ibid.
9. Ibid., 3 November 1918.
10. *'Donc, je vous attends.'* Baschwitz to Bruce, 27 November 1918.
11. Buckley to Baschwitz, 2 December 1918.
12. Bruce to Baschwitz, 1 December 1918.
13. £36.30.
14. Drake, *History of Intelligence (B)*, PRO/WO 106/45, para. 45.
15. £73 the balance, at today's values; £756 the claim for dilapidations, the 1919 exchange rate being less favourable to the French franc.

25 What Became of Them All?

1. Drake, *History of Intelligence (B)*, PRO/WO 106/45.
2. Ibid.
3. Bruce to Wallinger, 12 May 1919. The total cost of the operation was £17,992 in today's money. £4,761, at the 1919 exchange rate, was returned to Wallinger.
4. Ibid.
5. *History of Intelligence (B), British Expeditionary Force, France, from January 1917 to April 1919*, PRO/WO 106/45.
6. *Blackwood's Magazine*, Part I: vol. CCVIII (1920); Part II: vol. CCIX and Part III: vol. CCX (1921).
7. Jean Bruce to George Bruce, 7 April 1919; Buckley to Bruce, 30 March 1919.
8. Chocqueel to Bruce, 18 April 1919.

Index

Note: Ranks and titles are generally the highest mentioned in the text.